ADVANCE PRAISE FOR Navigating Borders

"Ricardo Castro-Salazar and Carl Bagley navigate the borders of history and humanity with persuasive clarity. Their book is both forceful and compelling, its voice singular and convincing."

—Tom Miller, Author of *On the Border: Portraits of America's Southwestern Frontier*

"*Navigating Borders* considers one of the most compelling and heart-rending issues in the agonizing immigration policy impasse that has stymied forward movement in the U.S. Congress in recent years—the fate of undocumented young people who face a cruel and uncertain future because of their immigration status. With scholarly skill, passion for the subject, and extensive experience as educators, Ricardo Castro-Salazar and Carl Bagley utilize Critical Race Theory to explain the great dilemma faced by 'DREAMers' (undocumented students) in Arizona, the state that has enacted and served as a model for the most extreme anti-immigrant legislation in the nation. This is a timely book that deserves a wide readership."

—Oscar J. Martinez, Regents' Professor of History, University of Arizona; Author of *Troublesome Border*

"*Navigating Borders* is at once a challenge to dominant historical narratives and current political platforms of exclusion as well as a scholarly call to critically re-think American identity. With the use of real life testimonies, it is a timely contribution to the debates on the condition of undocumented (young) Americans, and their personal counter-histories prove to be a powerful political tool for democratic empowerment."

—Antonio Carmona Baez, Department of Political Science, University of Amsterdam; Former Director of the International Institute for Research and Education, The Netherlands

"*Navigating Borders* is an impressive and timely effort to debunk myths surrounding the anti-immigration rhetoric that has shaped much of the public discourse in the United States in recent years. Ricardo Castro-Salazar and Carl Bagley have taken a bold step to establish a counter-narrative grounded in the empirical reality drawn from history, politics, and economy. Written with defiant clarity, this path-breaking book will undoubtedly enable ordinary citizens, lawmakers, and civil society associations to make important choices in tackling the rise of xenophobia in a country that promotes democracy and freedom in much of the world."

—Fahim Quadir, Director, Graduate Program in Development Studies, York University, Canada

"No hay barrera que la determinación no pueda trascender, pero debemos 'navegar fronteras' para lograrlo. Las historias en este libro así lo demuestran."

—Miguel Méndez. Author, *Peregrinos de Aztlán* (*Pilgrims in Aztlán*)

May 30th, 2012

Navigating Borders

Dear Greg:

It is been an honor meeting you and learning from you.

¡ Muchas gracias!

History is a weapon

Ricardo

Studies in the
Postmodern Theory of Education

Shirley R. Steinberg
General Editor

Vol. 415

The Counterpoints series is part of the Peter Lang Education list.
Every volume is peer reviewed and meets
the highest quality standards for content and production.

PETER LANG
New York • Washington, D.C./Baltimore • Bern
Frankfurt • Berlin • Brussels • Vienna • Oxford

Ricardo Castro-Salazar and Carl Bagley

Navigating Borders

Critical Race Theory Research
and Counter History
of Undocumented Americans

PETER LANG
New York • Washington, D.C./Baltimore • Bern
Frankfurt • Berlin • Brussels • Vienna • Oxford

Library of Congress Cataloging-in-Publication Data

Castro-Salazar, Ricardo.
Navigating borders: critical race theory research and counter history
of undocumented Americans / Ricardo Castro-Salazar, Carl Bagley.
p. cm. — (Counterpoints: studies in the postmodern theory of education; v. 415)
Includes bibliographical references.
1. Mexican Americans—Social conditions.
2. Citizenship—Social aspects—United States.
3. Dual nationality—United States.
4. Illegal aliens—United States. I. Bagley, Carl. II. Title.
E184.M5C374   973'.046872—dc23   2011030849
ISBN 978-1-4331-1262-1 (hardcover)
ISBN 978-1-4331-1261-4 (paperback)
ISBN 978-1-4539-0183-0 (e-book)
ISSN 1058-1634

Bibliographic information published by **Die Deutsche Nationalbibliothek.**
Die Deutsche Nationalbibliothek lists this publication in the "Deutsche
Nationalbibliografie"; detailed bibliographic data is available
on the Internet at http://dnb.d-nb.de/.

Cover photographic design: Alejandro González
Cover image: Sculpture "La Frontera Está en Todas Partes" (The Border is Everywhere)
by Ricardo Castro-Salazar

The paper in this book meets the guidelines for permanence and durability
of the Committee on Production Guidelines for Book Longevity
of the Council of Library Resources.

© 2012 Peter Lang Publishing, Inc., New York
29 Broadway, 18th floor, New York, NY 10006
www.peterlang.com

Printed in the United States of America

A mis co-navegantes Kelley y Ana
—RCS

. . . *nunca la vida es nuestra, es de los otros* (life is never ours, it belongs to the others),
la vida no es de nadie, todos somos la vida (life is no one's, we all are life)
–pan de sol para los otros (bread of the sun for the others),
los otros todos que nosotros somos (the others that we all are)–,
soy otro cuando soy, los actos míos (when I am I am another, my acts)
son más míos si son también de todos (are more mine if they are also the acts of all),
para que pueda ser he de ser otro (in order to be I must be another),
salir de mí, buscarme entre los otros (leave myself, search for myself in the others),
los otros que no son si yo no existo (the others that don't exist if I don't exist),
los que me dan plena existencia (the others that give me total existence),
no soy, no hay yo, siempre somos nosotros (I am not, there is no I, we are always us) . . .
—Octavio Paz (1990: 28–30). *Piedra de Sol.*

What we believe depends on what we learn.
—Ludwig Wittgenstein (1969: 37e). *On Certainty.*

There are no truths . . . Only stories.
—Thomas King (1993: 432). *Green Grass, Running Water.*

Contents

Part One: Counter-History

Part Two: Making History

Counter-History

Navigating Conceptual Borders: Demarcating Coordinates and Boundaries

History cannot "speak" except through human ventriloquism
—Donald Kelley (2006: 240)

One can be impartial, and fair, and factual, and be untrue
—Chris Hedges (2010)

History is not what occurred in the past, but merely a story of what people thought and experienced at the time an event occurred. Inevitably, the belief system and context of the narrator (the historian or individual recalling the past) influence any interpretation, modern or otherwise. Thus, historical narratives are continually retold and elucidated, undergoing vast transformation as they are reinterpreted at different points in time. As famously expressed in 1936 by G.M. Young, "the real central theme of history is not what happened, but what people felt about it when it was happening" (quoted by Brading, 1991). Since then, historical narratives of remote and current events have evolved dramatically, be they about crucial transformations like the French Revolution and the arrival of Europeans en masse to the Americas, or about the interpretation of historical texts like the Maya Codices and the Bible. Without changing a single word, successive reinterpretations of the U.S. Constitution have transformed into new paradigms providing for desegregation, gender equality, labor rights, political dissent, the expansion of civil rights, and the evolution of the political process. In order to make the new political reality continuous with the past, history had to be reexamined and revised in each of these cases. Such reinterpretations indicate an understanding by U.S. politicians and historians of the importance of historical narrative and its effect on national mindset. This makes damaging omissions and marginalizations of historical narratives even more damning, particularly when one considers the reputation the U.S. has earned of possessing a far-reaching amnesia. Scholars have repeatedly pointed out that U.S. people and their leaders tend to be "chronic ignorers of history" (Molineu, 1990: 6).

This amnesia becomes damaging when it forms the boundaries of inclusiveness in modern narratives of U.S. identity and citizenship. The quotidian narratives of history and current events in the United States overlook that "America" encompasses two continents and includes Argentineans, Brazilians, Canadians, Colombians, Cubans, Dominicans, Guatemalans, Haitians, Jamaicans, Mexicans, Salvadorians, Venezuelans, and many other nations traveled by European explorers in the 1500s. In a proclivity for simplification and abbreviation, many U.S. people, *United Statesians* (we consider this term further later in the chapter), have forgotten that the United States is *of* America and not the other way around. The United States is located in North America but has shaped the realities of Central and South American nations. Those less conspicuous "Americas," also referred to as Latin America, are home to well over half a billion people who live in some of the most inegalitarian countries on Earth, whose economic and social disparities resemble a caricature of their northern, much richer neighbor. Those Americans, like peoples from underdeveloped nations around the globe, emigrate to industrialized countries in search for survival and opportunity. For historical, financial, geographical, and social reasons, most Latin Americans who emigrate seeking economic survival and opportunity move to the United States.

Like Americans from the United States, Americans from Latin America express many different identities, ethnic origins, and histories. This book tells the story of Americans who have been deprived of full Americanness both in the United States and in Latin America. It is about United Statesians who were born in Mexico and brought as minors, sometimes infants, to the United States. Many of these involuntary immigrants do not remember the land of their parents. They could have been born anywhere in the world, but their ethos still would be United Statesian. They are involuntary immigrants not only because they were brought to the U.S. involuntarily, but also because the U.S. legal system has labeled and discursively positioned them as "illegal immigrants." For them, however, being "American," having a United Statesian identity—like any other national identity—means having a sense of place, values, language, behaviors and attitudes that define one's sense of belonging to a particular society. Therefore, although they are not officially "U.S. citizens," they are historical, economic, cultural, linguistic, social, emotional, and even spiritual members of the U.S. and are indistinguishable from other United Statesians. They lack a U.S. birth certificate but possess all the intrinsic attributes of U.S. born citizens, have been educated in the U.S. system, and have grown up pledging allegiance to the U.S. flag. They are undocumented Americans.

History forms a particularly important emphasis in the case of Mexican-origin Americans because of their unique foundation in the United States. Undocumented Americans of Mexican origin represent the modern echo of U.S. history, but their memories and stories are not predominant in the accepted historical "facts" of the majority. Their history, vis-à-vis the dominant version of American history, evokes Donald Kelley's assertion that

> There are no "facts." There were facts, no doubt; but all we have is their recollection, records, or remains; and again such evidence will be viewed differently by different historians. This is not a deeply epistemological argument, for if we can often establish that a particular event did occur, its historical presence remains a product of human imputation. In the forest the tree does not "fall" without an observer; the fact is meaningless, indeed nonexistent, without human apprehension (2006: 239–40).

Ironically, undocumented Americans of Mexican origin have a double American identity (United Statesian and Mexican) and possess a stronger historical connection with the American continent than the majority population in the U.S. People of Mexican origin, meaning those with a blend of indigenous and European heritage, lived in the lands that are now the Southwestern United States centuries before U.S. expansionism dispossessed Mexico of half of its territory. Those who perceive Mexican-origin Americans as a threat to American "Anglo-Protestant identity" do not overlook this; they fear that "No other immigrant group in U.S. history has asserted or could assert a historical claim to U.S. territory. Mexican and Mexican-Americans can and do make that claim" (Huntington, 2004a: 35). This book is not an apology for such a claim, nor does it support the Mexican takeover of the southwestern U.S. that some extremists accuse Mexicans of plotting. Such a naive pretension would be like demanding the return of all Native American lands to their original owners.

It has been expressed that Native Americans, or Amerindians, are the "true Americans" or "the only Americans who are not immigrants." Nonetheless, in contrast to the minuscule proportion of Amerindians who have survived European colonization in the United States, 30% of the Mexican people are predominantly Native American and 60% are *Mestizo*, meaning a mixture of Amerindians with Spanish and other Europeans (CIA, 2010). Statistically, this means that 90 percent of Mexicans have more Native American DNA in them than 99% of United Statesians who are not of Latin American origin. Furthermore, since Mexican-Americans have so much more indigenous ancestry than Anglo-Americans and, since the Amerindian legacy was stronger among the poor in Mexico (the majority of Mexican immigrants to the U.S.), it has been argued that Mexican-Americans are the largest Native American group in the United States (Forbes, 1964). Hence, although Mexican-origin United Statesians have not been subject to the "blood quantum" laws used in the U.S. to determine Native Americanness, they also have a powerful reason to feel American in the most extensive sense.

This book has been written in the midst of growing anti-immigrant and anti-Mexican sentiment in the United States. Since the beginning of the century, xenophobia, nativism, ethnic hate, and racism have expanded like apocalyptic curses due to economic conditions, socio-political events, and demographic transformations. By October 2010, 61% of all Latinos in the U.S. felt that discrimination against Hispanics was a "major problem" across the nation (Lopez et al., 2010). FBI hate crime statistics support this perception: The previous year, a staggering 62.3% of all crimes committed due to the victims' ethnicity or national origin were perpetuated against Hispanics, the highest proportion in recorded history (Federal Bureau of Investigation [FBI], 2010). Furthermore, according to FBI figures, out of 6,604 hate crimes perpetuated in the United States in 2009, 3,816 "were racially motivated" (*Ibid.*: 3).

Immigrants from Latin America are increasingly seen as a threat and, irrespective of their status, they are conflated with "illegals." Similarly, dark-skin Latino Americans, irrespective of their national origin, are commonly conflated with "Mexicans." Contrary to these negative trends, we argue that undocumented Americans, who are fully integrated to their communities, speak English, and are part of United Statesian socioeconomic structures, constitute an asset to the country. Furthermore, while their struggles, values, courage, and aspirations have been disparaged by anti-immigrant narratives, they have stories that are more complex than what is covered in the media. Their values are consistent with the principles on which the United States of America was founded. Their undocumented stories reveal honor, respect, hard work, liberty, and entrepreneurship that benefit the U.S. Many have faced racism, discrimination, and ostracism, and some have overcome great obstacles despite the odds. This book explores their stories and their history.

Although the research focuses on the stories of undocumented Americans of Mexican origin, their narratives echo the stories of innumerable other undocumented individuals in the United States. The stories in this book not only intersect with the lives of involuntary immigrants who came to this country as minors, but they are microcosms of the millions of human beings who live in the darkness of "illegality" as economic refugees. They have no official voice and are victims of human rights abuses, labor law infringements, and discrimination; thus they share similar untold stories of pain, human resilience, and hope. Although our stories occurred in the state of Arizona, they resemble the undocumented stories of countless Americans across the nation who silently suffer similar uncertainties and fears. In this context, the narratives in this book become an act of "counter-storytelling": giving voice to those whose voices have been marginalized by the dominant discourse (Solorzano and Yosso, 2000/2001/2002). Similarly, we create "counter-history" as we explore an alternative version of history that challenges the majoritarian memory. Placing the stories of undocumented Americans in the interpretive light of a colonizer-colonized relationship challenges the stories and dominant ideology of those in power. Their counter-narratives, counter-majoritarian stories situated in a counter-historical dimension, contest the colonizers' constructed histories and oppose the exclusionary notion of who "belongs" in the United States.

Research shows that, irrespective of origin, immigrants in general tend to be entrepreneurial, creative, and hard-working. Yet it would be worthless to deny that immigrant populations of all historical eras have included individuals good and bad, bright and unintelligent, inspiring and dull. This book focuses on hard-working, perseverant young people who do not fit into a neat category of "immigrant" because their cultural and social upbringing makes them a developmental product of the United States. They have been raised, nurtured, and educated in the United States and, after spending most of their lives there, have no significant connections with their birthplace. This is the story of youth who speak English, know the National Anthem, think of themselves as "American" and, for all practical purposes, are United Statesians. The undocumented Americans in our stories have proven their worth to the country by succeeding in school in spite of great obstacles like living in poor socioeconomic neighborhoods, experiencing the daily uncertainty of an undocumented family, and not having access to financial support for their studies. They express a great appreciation for the opportunities they have received, but they live in a judicial limbo through no fault of their own. They did not choose to be undocumented; they did not choose to be United Statesian or Mexican, but they now find themselves as young adults in an impossible in-between space. They are neither yet both United Statesian and Mexican. They experience tensions in both dimensions, but do not renounce their love for either one, just like children love equally nurturing parents. These are the children of history and hope, and they have lessons for us if we open our hearts and laws to receive them.

In summary, this book ennobles and dignifies the stories of Mexican-origin United Statesians and their larger historical context, which have been obscured by what Ronald Takaki (2008) has termed "the Master Narrative of

American History" (4). The Master Narrative acts like a powerful filter that tells us that the U.S. has been built by white European settlers and that the founding civilization of this country was Anglo-Protestant. Thus, non-English speakers, brown, black and yellow people are seen as strangers, aliens, and "others." Thus, these groups create counter-histories in order to incorporate their own experience into the national narrative. These counter-histories, however, do not claim to be the definite history. Definite stories do not exist; different accounts of events nurture our histories and identities (Perhaps that is why "history" and "story" are the same word in Spanish [*historia*]). This study is based on scholarly research and the work of historians and social scientists but emphasizes some aspects of history that have been overlooked or minimized in the dominant narrative. We believe there are as many "truths" as there are perspectives and this book does not pretend to be neutral (is there such a thing as a neutral book?). Consistent with Freirean pedagogy, we believe "education is never neutral." An educational system usually facilitates the assimilation of unquestioned values that support existing societal structures and hegemonic narratives, but education also has the potential to "liberate by encouraging critical reflection (ideological critique) of the dominant values and taking action to improve society toward a more just and equitable vision" (Taylor, 2007: 357–58). Therefore, education either challenges the status quo or it preserves it. In the same way, the counter-history and counter-stories of undocumented Americans of Mexican origin challenge the dominant accounts of who is "American" in a context where "citizenship" is "the architect of legitimate social inequality" (Marshall, 1998: 93).

A Compass for Disoriented Identities

It is common in Latin American countries to refer to the people of the U.S. as *estadounidenses*, literally meaning "United Statesians." In English this term may seem clumsy, but it is not new to the English language or as a referent to certain North American Citizens. Latin Americans do not object to referring to U.S. people as "Americans" but have historically disliked the exclusive appropriation of "America" and "Americanness" by the United States and its citizens. As pointed out by London et al. (1975), for Latin Americans, "a more proper name for this nation would be the 'United States of the Central Portion of North America'!" (238). Latin Americans are not the only ones who have expressed this displeasure. Many French- and Anglo-Canadians have historically made a distinction between American and United Statesian For example, in 1899, in the *Canadian Magazine of Politics, Science, Art and Litera-*

ture it was expressed that "Canadian literature is English literature, but it is not British; neither is it United Statesian" (Cooper, 1899: 179). French-Canadians also have historically referred to U.S. people as *étatsunien*, an equivalent of the Spanish *estadounidense*. In the United States, one of the characters of Pulitzer Prize-winning novelist B. Tarkington (1905) declares "the recent willingness of the English to take some interest in the United-Statesians to be a mistake; for they were noisy, without real confidence in themselves; they were restless and merely imitative instead of inventive" (37). Almost a century later, Gloria Anzaldúa, a leading theorist of Chicano studies, referred to the "United Statesian-culture-swallowing-up-the-rest-of-the-world kind of mouth" (in interview with Lunsford, 1999: 63). Our usage of the term United Statesian, which we understand might be troubling for some people, is a deliberate attempt to incite reflection. More importantly, the term represents an unambiguous way to establish the necessary distinctions in this book's argument.

We are not declaring war against the use of the adjective "American" as a native of the United States. That is not our battle and, as the old Spanish saying goes, *El uso hace la regla* (use makes the rule). We use "American" in its traditional U.S. connotation and United Statesian as a more accurate term defining a socio-cultural experience and the possession of national attributes. Hence, a person whose origin is the United States of America will remain an "American," but the essence of what and who is "American" will continue to evolve and create controversy as it has done for over two centuries. Being a 100% American or an "American-American" has never been a fixed category. It could be argued, for example, that the indigenous peoples of the Western Hemisphere, as well as African slaves, were forced to become "American." By 1854, the Anti-Catholic Press in the United States bitterly criticized Catholic Irish immigrants and demanded: "NONE BUT NATIVE AMERICANS FOR OFFICE!" At this point, the definition of "Native Americans" exclusively included non-Catholic whites (THE KNOW, 1854). Other Western European immigrants from Italy, Germany, and Sweden were considered un-American at different points in history. Asian Americans, Jews, and Eastern Europeans were systematically discriminated against. In the late 19th and early 20th centuries, over one million Polish immigrants came to the U.S. but, "Though they might carry the flag and even fight for it, Poles were not considered Americans, no matter how much they were 'Americanized'" (Bukowczyk, 2008: 31).

The undocumented Americans of Mexican origin who are the subjects of this book exist only in the United States and they are not just American, but unequivocally United Statesian. They are not *de jure* citizens, but culturally, linguistically, socio-economically, emotionally, and spiritually they are *de facto* United Statesians. Like other United Statesians, they are inextricably embedded in the socio-economic fabric of their communities and have similar life experiences that converge in the possession of a majoritarian language and similar values, behaviors and beliefs. United Statesians are raised, educated, socialized and nurtured within and by U.S. institutions. From this perspective, there are certainly other undocumented United Statesians who were brought to the U.S. as children from other continents and raised and socialized as "Americans." Conversely, there are official citizens and residents of the United States who are not fully United Statesians in all these dimensions (they lack language ability, do not fully understand the culture, they are not familiar with the institutions, values, etc.). In any case, the term "United Statesian" is "a more geo-culturally precise term" (DeGuzmán, 2007: 274), and it can challenge the ethnocentric designation of the United States as "America," but it implies much more than that. The tragedy of undocumented Americans of Mexican origin who want to pursue an education and be productive citizens is that they cannot officially claim a national space even if, in theory, they are accepted as Mexican citizens. They do not want to be separated from their families, their United Statesian culture, and the lives they have built in the U.S. More troublesome, they have not been educated in Spanish and the Mexican education system, and therefore do not feel they fully belong to that system. The young people in this study represent the type of studious and ambitious citizens that societies want to develop. Nonetheless, they are increasingly denied their human rights to education and *de jure* citizenship in the country they love and grew up understanding as home.

It is clear that these Americans have an intricate identity that has strong links with their non-United-Statesian ancestors. But what is the most appropriate term to define this complex identity? Chicano, Latino, Hispanic, Mexican-American, American-Mexican, with or without a hyphen, or simply American? In the reality they live, all of these terms are politically charged; they all have objections, apologies, and complexities. In this book, we refer to Mexican-Americans (with a hyphen)[1] and to undocumented Americans of Mexican origin with a profound conviction. Mexican-Americans and undocumented Americans of Mexican origin are also United Statesians. In a sense, referring to "Mexican-Americans" can be as redundant as referring to "French-Europeans," but these are critical designations defining a more concrete reality in the U.S. and Europe as multicultural entities. In truth, we have identities within identities because, as expressed by Nobel Laureate Jose Saramago (2001), "we are stories of stories telling stories." Our multiple stories create and recreate our multiple identities in history. Therefore the words we choose to name ourselves and to tell our own stories are important. Américo Paredes, one of the founding scholars of Chicano Studies, referred to the historic dilemma of self-reference among Mexican-origin Americans during the period between the two World Wars:

> Highly suspect were those ethnic groups that attempted to preserve their own cultures, or that banded together for political or social action under the rubric of their ethnicity. The Melting Potters thundered out against these "hyphenated Americans" (Irish-Americans, German-Americans, Greek-Americans, and, of course, Mexican-Americans). They called on them to be just plain Americans like everybody else or to "go back to where they came from." All this must have given our "Latins" and "Spaniards" a case of nerves; they did not want to be included in the general condemnation of "hyphenated Americans." So they took care to write always "Latin American" and "Spanish American." Never with a hyphen.
>
> Strangely enough, many Chicano activists today make it a point to write "Mexican American" without the hyphen, maintaining that they do not want to be identified as "hyphenated Americans"—and thus making common cause on this point with the advocates of the Melting Pot philosophy. This may be due to lack of historical perspective, since some young Chicanos believe that "Mexican-American" is a term invented by the Gringo to insult the Chicano (1995: 159).

From another perspective, José Vasconcelos, one of the most influential thinkers of contemporary Mexico, referred to the *Mestizo* nature of Mexican culture as a "hyphen of the meeting point" between the Spanish and the Indian worlds who could become "a bridge to the future" (quoted by Alonso, 2004: 465). For Mexican-Americans as well, the hyphen can denote a meeting point and a bridge, but it is also a metaphor. The hyphen expresses a deep intimacy between the two words and is a symbol of defiance, a re-affirmation of our presence, a counter-majoritarian insubordination in opposition to the colonizer's tidy categories. As expressed by Morales (2002), the hyphen symbolizes the traumatic struggle to make sense of ourselves:

> There is a trauma involved in trying to make sense of life on the border, on the hyphen. But the mistake many writers and observers have made is the demonization of the hyphen, the self-negation of being on the border. Neither white nor black, we are, poor Latinos, wallowing in a pool of nothingness. We will never be anything until we're somebody else's idea of what it means to be an American. But we are not defined by negation, we are the celebration of contradictions, the revelers in the thorniness of the human condition, the slayers of category (20).

In contemporary literature the hyphen has been commonly dropped. According to one view, "The emergence of transnational communities and the efforts of the state to include migrants in its sphere of influence" has contributed to "a crisis of the hyphen" (Pansters, 2005: 84). Furthermore, according to modern style manuals, "Mexican-American" should be hyphenated only as a compound proper adjective (Mexican-American student, French-Canadian cuisine), but not as a noun denoting dual heritage (*National Geographic*, 2010). Nevertheless, in this book we utilize the gentilic "Mexican-American" as a symbol of the lived experiences of undocumented Americans of Mexican origin and the Mexican-American experience in the United States. The hyphenation of "Mexican-American" gives equal weight to both heritages, symbolizing the intimacy between the two identities and their continuity. It denotes that a Mexican-American is both Mexican and American and cannot exist without one of the two attributes. Without the hyphen, "Mexican" could be understood as the adjective and "American" as a noun, denoting that "American"—United Statesian—is the main identity and "Mexican" a characteristic of this particular American. This is not wrong for any Mexican-origin person who feels proudly "American" but being recognized as United Statesian should not be at the expense of Mexican affiliation. Asking first generation Americans of Mexican origin to be only United Statesian, is asking them to reject the heritage of the parents who love and raise them. Ultimately, the hyphen reminds us that, in this quandary of definitions, not everyone fits neatly into predetermined categories. Undocumented Americans of Mexican origin do not feel at ease on either side of "Mexican-American" and, perhaps more than anybody else, find themselves trapped in the hyphen, as expressed in a poem written by Wendell Aycock in 1976 entitled *Hyphen-nation*:

> Sitting atop the hyphen provides a marvelous view, but no direction.
> Does one face forward or backward? Look behind or ahead?
> the hyphen is incomplete; there is no where to go.
> the force of the dash,
> the inclusiveness of the parenthesis,
> the finality of the period.
> The Hyphen only supports. It does not connect.
> Japanese-American, Mexican-American, Italian-American
> Lacking the two slight marks that gives the arrow its certainty,
> the hyphen is incomplete; there is no where to go.
> Existing between two cultures,
> it is an eternal bridge
> with barriers and guards at both ends (2).
>
> *Reproduced with permission from the author*

This poem was probably not written as an apology of the hyphen, but it resonates as a painfully familiar description of the space where undocumented Americans exist. Thus, if in the eyes of the majority they are invisible, we acknowledge their presence by the use of the hyphen. In a way, *they* have become the hyphen, caught in between two worlds but not formally belonging to either one. In the words of a formerly undocumented student interviewed in this study, they are "*ni de aquí ni* from there" (not from here not from there). Nevertheless, they dream to become the "bridge" that connects both sides of the same space, the intersection of the two worlds, but without the "barriers and the guards at both ends." The hyphen is a needle in a compass that points in two directions, both ways home.

Arizuma, These Days Known as Arizona: The Anti-Immigrant Laboratory

The stories that served as inspiration for this book are derived and unfold in Arizona in the midst of one of the nation's worst anti-immigrant climates; engendering legislation that the American Civil Liberties Union has termed "Arizona's racial profiling law" (2010). The state shares an extensive history, ethnic heritages, and unique ecosystems with Mexico, while its Amerindian population is the second largest in the United States. Almost one fourth of Arizona is made of Native American territory, "an area considerably larger than most eastern states" (Gawronski, 2010: 197). Furthermore, nearly half of the students in Arizona public schools are Hispanic and, by 2007, at least one in five residents spoke Spanish at home (U.S. Census, 2009). Thus, Native American, Mexican-American, Latino and immigrant groups encompass a significant portion of the state's population and have protested against the state's increasingly discriminatory laws. The apologists of this type of legislation claim that the tough approach is necessary and is only directed to the "illegal invasion" of Latino immigrants in response to federal government's inaction. Yet this extreme anti-immigrant position contains no historical insight and creates a climate that affects large sectors of the population, including United Statesians of Mexican, Amerindian, and Latino origin. Highlighting the experimental nature of these rulings that threaten the freedoms of a great number of U.S. citizens, the North American Congress on Latin America has referred to Arizona as "the anti-immigrant laboratory" (Miller, 2010).

Nobel Peace Prize laureate, Archbishop Desmond Tutu (2010), in reference to the anti-immigrant climate and legislation in Arizona expressed that,

> Abominations such as Apartheid do not start with an entire population suddenly becoming inhumane. They start here. They start with generalizing unwanted characteristics across an entire segment of a population. They start with trying to solve

a problem by asserting superior force over a population. They start with stripping people of rights and dignity.

Such abominations are also possible because of ignorance and a lack of historical perspective. The great majority of Mexican- and Latino-origin people in the United States are citizens or legal residents, but many other U.S. citizens believe the opposite. At a moment when Mexican immigrants are seen as illegal invaders, a re-acquaintance with history is pertinent. In the turbulent history between the U.S. and Mexico, the first "illegal invasion" took place over a century and a half ago in the opposite direction during the Mexican-American War. At that time Congressman Abraham Lincoln condemned the illegality of the invasion of Mexico by the United States (Lincoln, 1848). Later, in his memoirs, President Grant expressed shame for such action and thought that the Civil War was God's punishment for the U.S. aggression against Mexico (Grant [1885–1886], 1995). These two great presidents could not have imagined that, in the year 2010, there would be a staggering 695,000 American military veterans of Mexican origin who had served the United States armed forces (U.S. Census, 2010a).

The narratives of wars, conquests, and victories can be dark or brilliant. The telling of their stories from different viewpoints may be contradictory, but their consequences are inevitable. The Spanish story of the brutal Conquest of Mexico may differ from its Amerindian version, but the emergence of the contemporary Mexican identity as a result of the fusion of the Spanish and indigenous cultures cannot be denied. Similarly, some of the causes of inequality, poverty, and indigenous marginalization in Mexico could be traced back to the Colonial era. Some of the existing social conditions could also be linked to the devastation of Mexico after the U.S. invasion and subsequent dispossession of its territory in 1848. In fact, some of the remote causes of contemporary Mexican immigration can be found in the counter-history of these bellicose actions by the U.S. This might never become a popular perspective, but at the end, countries—like individuals—are inevitable products of their history. The state of Arizona is an important part of this *historia*.

In an address before the American Geographical and Statistical Society in 1859, Sylvester Mowry contended that the name Arizona was derived from *Arizuma*, a word of Mexica origin, better known as the Aztec civilization, who spoke the Nahuatl language. According to Mowry, the word was transformed by Spanish speakers into its current version and continued to be used after the U.S. invasion of Mexico. He did not find definite information about the meaning of *Arizuma* (Mowry, 1859). Most Arizonans today ignore the Native American/Spanish/Mexican origin of the word. Nevertheless, the Arizona flag itself remains as a testament of the first Spanish explorers who came to the region 80 years before the *Mayflower* arrived in Plymouth Harbor and over three centuries before it became part of the U.S. The colors red and yellow were embedded in the state flag in remembrance of the flag flown by the first expedition led by Francisco Vasquez de Coronado in 1540–1542 (Derzipilski, 2004). Hence, Spaniards became the first European colonizers in these lands, as well as in the rest of Latin America, in many cases cruelly subjugating the Native Americans. As brutal as the Spanish conquest was, however, it had one essential characteristic the Anglo-European conquest did not: Spaniards and Native Americans mixed with each other to a great extent, creating the rich *Mestizo* identity and culture of Mexico.

Research shows that, ever since the northern half of Mexico was annexed to the United States in 1848, Spanish-speakers and United Statesians of Mexican origin have not been served appropriately by the colonizers' government structures and educational system (Baker, 1996; García, 1999; Gonzalez, Macias, and Tinajero, 1998). Despite codified legal protections, Mexicans of full or partial Native American origin were deprived of citizenship as well as political and civil rights. In general, only white Mexicans who were able to read English were allowed to vote, while Arizona enacted highly racist laws that had the objective of preventing Mexicans from having any power in government (Menchaca, 1993). Spanish was converted into a "foreign language," regardless of the fact that it was spoken in the Southwestern U.S. centuries before English arrived. City, state and street names as far north as the Strait of Juan de Fuca in northwest Washington reveal their foundation by Spanish-language speakers (Armadillo, Las Cruces, Los Angeles, San Diego, San Francisco, San Juan, and uncountable others). Mexican-origin people were segregated, discriminated against and mistreated, but they resisted in different ways. In the 1880s, in response to police abuses, they founded El Centro Radical Mexicano (Mexican Radical Center) in the city of Tucson in order to fight for civilized treatment. Mexican-Americans from Tucson also created La Alianza Hispano Americana (Hispanic American Alliance) in 1894, which grew beyond the borders of Arizona in defense of civil rights (Stacy, 2003: 191).

Later, the predominantly Mexican population was seen as problematic in the process of granting statehood to Arizona. As expressed by a *New York Times* editorial in 1910: "Arizona . . . will come into the Union with only 200,000 inhabitants, 60 percent of whom are of Mexican blood and frequently ignorant of the English language" (quoted by Powers, 2008: 469). By the 1920s, there were more than 40 Americanization Centers in the state, most of them under the supervision of a local "Community Committee on Americanization." Many organizations were involved in the process of Americanization, including the Catholic Church, the Y.M.C.A., public universities, and others (Lucero, 2004). During the Great Depression years, racist ideas disseminated by the majoritarian narrative characterized Native American and Mexican-American children as "foreign," irrespective of the fact that many of their immediate ancestors were present in Arizona long before it became part of the United States (Sheridan, 1986; Gonzalez, 2001).

Around the same period, blatant abuses against Mexican-Americans, Mexican immigrants, and immigrants in general were common in Arizona (Sheridan, 1986, 1995). A dark episode in Arizona's history that illustrates such abuses is the Bisbee Deportation of 1917. Immediately following the U.S. entry into World War I, copper miners in Bisbee, Arizona walked out on strike. The strikers were labeled by the press as "terrorists," "German sympathizers," and "enemies of the country" (Arizona Chapter, 1917?). On July 12, 1917, vigilantes rounded up more than a thousand strikers, most of whom were European immigrants and United Statesians of Mexican descent,[2] shipped them out of the state by rail, and abandoned them out in the desert of New Mexico in cattle carts without food or water (Bonnand, 1997; Watson, 1977.).[3] According to Fred Watson (1977), the only deportee whose oral history was recorded, many deportees were not strikers or even miners. Later, charges were brought against the vigilantes because of their brutal actions, but no court action resulted (Byrkit, 1972).

This event was crucial in the struggle for labor rights in Arizona's history, which had repercussions on developments throughout the U.S. (Arizona Board, 2000). The Industrial Workers of the World (I.W.W.) intensified their presence in Arizona and successfully recruited miners from minority groups. The union was most successful recruiting Bisbee's workers of Mexican origin, who were systematically given lower paying jobs (Ibid.). Nevertheless, the exploitation of Mexican labor and ethnic conflict would continue (Sheridan, 1995) and the struggles of United Statesians of Mexican origin would expand to other dimensions, including the educational arena. In all cases, race and racism appear to be, overtly and covertly, omnipresent elements of such struggles (Ruiz, 2004).

For more than a hundred years after the U.S.-Mexico War, the official demographics and the presence of Mexican-origin peoples in the United States were defined by a colonizing approach where racial differentiation was a predominant ingredient. Mexican labor was essential in the development and prosperity of Arizona and the entire southwestern United States, but they were almost nonexistent in the dominant narrative of U.S. history, even when they were U.S. citizens and soldiers. United Statesians of Mexican origin and Mexican immigrants are certainly counted in contemporary censuses, but the cycles of the U.S. economy still determine the open-door/close-door fluctuations of immigration policy. Mexican labor continues to be lured by the U.S. booming economy and ousted during economic recessions. New racialized structures and forms of exploitation have painfully evolved as Mexican-origin people are conflated with foreigners and outsiders. Consequently, the participation of Mexican-Americans in crucial events of U.S. national development has been excluded from many historical accounts. Even in recent versions of history, Arizonans are unlikely to learn about the contributions of Mexican-Americans and other minorities in the building of the nation. For example, the WWII 158th Combat Team, an Arizona National Guard unit made mostly of Mexican-Americans and Amerindians, described by General Douglas MacArthur as "the greatest fighting combat team ever deployed for battle" (Office of the Deputy Assistant Secretary of Defense for Military Manpower and Personnel Policy, 1997: 31) is not part of the prevalent "American" memory.

Cartoon by Hector Curriel. Reproduced with permission from the artist.

Cartoonist Hector Curriel (2007) criticized The War, a 14-hour documentary on WWII sponsored by the Public Broadcasting System (PBS) in 2007. The film, by prominent documentarian Ken Burns, showed extensive interviews with soldiers and survivors but inexplicably included no people of Mexican origin or Hispanics among the 40 testimonies he recorded (the omission was later corrected following popular protest *and a corporate sponsor "inspired" PBS and Burns to add to the documentary). On the contrary, Professor Rivas-Rodriguez (2005) has argued that as many as 750,000 United Statesians of Mexican origin served in World War II, proportionally earning more medals and decorations than any other ethnic group. Rivas-Rodriguez developed the U.S. Latino and Latina World War II Oral History Project at the University of Texas at Austin, which has compiled more than 500 interviews (http://www.lib.utexas.edu/ww2latinos/).*

In addition Mexican workers became a vital source of labor during World War II and beyond. The legal importation of workers continued after the war ended and, between 1940 and 1960, over 4.6 million agricultural workers were imported from Mexico (Daniels, 2005: 143) contributing to the great post-war economic boom. Arizona's industries benefitted, leading to rapid growth in its agricultural, farming, and mining sectors, all of which employed immigrant labor. Many of the legally imported workers stayed in the U.S. and became U.S. citizens, later bringing their families. More recently, the economic boom of the 1990s and emergence of the so called "New Economy" was greatly fueled by authorized and unauthorized immigration (Sum, Fogg, and Harrington, 2002). And so the cycle continues:

> For more than a hundred years Mexican workers have been encouraged to come to the United States when their labor was desired; when times turned bad they were harassed, even victimized and sent back. Sometimes attitudes of encouragement and harassment existed side by side. The evidence indicates that immigrant labor has always had, and continues to have, an overall long-term positive impact on the U.S. economy; nevertheless, periods of depression have invariably brought forward a "deport the Mexican" solution (Meier and Ribera, 1993: 263).

In recent history, flows of unauthorized immigration from Mexico have further complicated Mexican-American reality and polarized sentiments in Arizona. In 1988, Arizona adopted a constitutional provision stating that all political subdivisions in the State must "act in English and in no other language" except in limited circumstances involving health and safety issues. In 1995, the Ninth Circuit Court rejected the provision, stating that the law violates the First Amendment of the United States Constitution.[4] By the end of the century, a new wave of anti-immigration sentiments re-emerged in the state and the English-only movement started to acquire new impetus. Arizona was experiencing a fast-growing undocumented population, most of them originating in Mexico and Latin America (Hoefer, Rytina and Baker, 2009). This immigration became significant in a state with a population of around six million, where a third of its inhabitants were already of Hispanic descent.

In February 2000, a federal court ruled that Arizona's funding of programs for English-language learners was deficient and violated the Equal Educational Opportunity Act of 1974. Although the law required school districts to help students overcome language barriers in educational programs, the state did not respond to the federal ordinance. Near the end of 2005, a new federal ruling gave the Arizona legislature until January 24, 2006 to adequately fund education programs for the state's 160,000 English-language learners or be faced with steep fines (Zehr, 2006b). The president of the state Senate expressed that "much of the reason Arizona has to educate so many English-language learners is that the federal government hasn't done its job securing borders" (*Ibid.*). On August 23, 2006, the U.S. Court of Appeals in Arizona ruled that the state would not have to pay the accrued fines for failing to adequately fund English-language learners (Zehr, 2006a). From an educational policy perspective, research has found that restrictionist language policies pervade school reform efforts in Arizona. Most of the accommodations for English-learners are being reversed, and restrictionist policies negatively impact these students (Wright, 2005). At the same time, demographic trends indicate that the number of English-learners in the state most likely will grow.

In 2004, the number of apprehensions of undocumented immigrants in Arizona reached the equivalent of 51% of the nation's total (Barlett, Steele, Karmatz, and Levinstein, 2004). This phenomenon triggered a renewed anti-immigrant, xenophobic movement throughout the state. Consequently, as research by Kay-Oliphant (2005) and Wright (2005) show, new institutional structures started to be developed in order to subordinate these minorities throughout the legal, economic, and educational systems. In November 2004, in reaction to the intense anti-immigrant propaganda disseminated throughout the state, Proposition 200 was approved by 56% of Arizona voters, including many Latinos. This new law demanded proof of U.S. citizenship from anyone requesting basic public services from the state. After the bill passed, anti-immigrant groups nationwide focused their attention on Arizona, where intense misinformation and media coverage have spread fear and intimidation. As a result, even authorized immigrants became afraid to access public programs and legal protections to which they are entitled (see Kittrie, 2006; Massey, 2005; Ramos Cardoso, 2007; Veranes and Navarro, 2005). The same year, a Scottsdale teacher claimed to be enforcing English immersion policies when she slapped students for speaking Spanish in class (Ryman and Madrid, 2004).

In addition to this adverse environment, the distinction between documented and undocumented immigrants is more blurry than people realize. (Michelson, 2001). Furthermore, the national and anti-terrorist hysteria has the potential to be transmuted into new immigration laws that will reinforce institutional racism (Bacon, 2004a; Kay-Oliphant, 2005). With the mantle of national security, law enforcement agencies unapologetically utilize racial profiling, stereotyping, and other forms of racial discrimination that widely disseminate fear (Aguirre, 2004; Coleman, 2007; Delgado, 2006; Ramos Cardoso, 2007). These actions equally intimidate, and sometimes harass, citizens, authorized residents, and undocumented immigrants simply because of the way they look. At the same time, a group of conspicuous congressmen, media commentators, and scholars demand the militarization of the Mexican border and severe restrictions on legal immigration, while warning of an ominous threat to the U.S. and "Western civilization" (Buchanan, 2002, 2006; Huntington, 2004a, 2004b). Research has found that police immigration raids in Arizona maintain and reinforce the subjugation and colonization of working-class Latino citizens and immigrants (Romero, 2006). In a case study that analyzed a five day immigration raid in Chandler, Arizona, it was found that law enforcement practices specifically repress and place individuals of Mexican origin at risk before the law, turning them into second-class people with inferior rights without regard to their status in the country (*Ibid.*).

Scapegoats and Dreamers

Arizona has a history of legalized and *de facto* racism (Menchaca, 1993). From its very inception as a state of the Union, "Racial inequality was not simply an unfortunate corollary to full statehood; it was built into the very identity of Arizona" (Meeks, 2007: 37). The state was the only one west of Texas that fought to preserve slavery and joined the Confederate forces during the Civil War. Arizona forbade interracial marriages even among people of mixed bloods (anti-miscegenation laws were not repealed until 1962) and stubbornly denied Native Americans the right to vote until 1948. During WWII anti-Asian racism and violence were intense in the state, where two Japanese internment camps were established with the greatest number of detainees in the county, most of them U.S. citizens. Later, Arizona would fight the institution of Martin Luther King Day, demonstrating that its racist policies, practices and legislation have targeted more than just people of Mexican origin.

Despite racist laws and policies, Arizona owes a debt to its immigrant and minority communities. Since Arizona became a U.S. territory, immigrants helped to build the state's prosperity in the mining, agricultural, and ranching industries. More recently the service and construction sectors also profited from cheap immigrant labor. The economic pull and push phenomenon was also experienced in the state but with an important distinction in recent decades. During the past twenty years, Arizona and Nevada were the two fastest-growing states in the nation. The economic growth was steady and immigrant labor, in spite of being officially despised, formed a necessary component of the state's economy. Then the U.S. experienced an economic slump and subsequent house foreclosure crisis, both of which hit Arizona particularly hard. By 2009, Arizona had become the second-poorest state in the nation with the worst financial crisis in its history. In this context, the state political leaders have created and exploited anti-immigrant sentiment by scapegoating immigrants and directing prejudice against Mexican-origin people.

Among innumerable anti-immigrant initiatives, the state legislature has implemented measures to criminalize unauthorized immigrants, ban their access to social services, make English Arizona's official language (the U.S. Constitution does not establish an official language), and proscribe ethnic-studies programs in public schools. State legislation even bans undocumented immigrants from receiving punitive damages in civil lawsuits (Archibold, 2006), which makes them even more vulnerable and opens the door for further employer abuses. In March 2011, additional measures were defeated in the state senate thanks to strong pressures from citizens and businesses. Nevertheless, the president of the senate declared that he would not give up and would try to pass the bills in the future. The defeated measures would have required hospitals to report undocumented patients and to deny citizenship to their U.S.-born children. They also would have required parents' proof of citizenship when enrolling their children in school and would have denied admission to undocumented students into state universities and colleges irrespective of their ability to pay out-of-state tuition.

Even before its financial crisis, the state did not have a particularly strong reputation in its support of education and the well-being of its children. In 2005–2006, Arizona had the lowest percentage (45%) of high school graduates who enrolled in college immediately after graduating from high school (Baum, Ma, and Payea, 2010). In the Education State Rankings 2006–2007 by Morgan Quitno, Arizona ranked 50th, based on 21 key elementary and secondary education indicators (Morgan Quitno, 2006). Similarly, the 2008 Survey of Local Government Finances by the U.S. Census ranked Arizona 49th in per-pupil spending. In 2011, The Commonwealth Fund, a bipartisan foundation for health care improvement, ranked the state 49th in children's healthcare.

Some critics have blamed undocumented immigrants for these low scores, even though other states with large undocumented populations rank much higher in terms of education and child well-being. Undocumented immigrants have been systematically blamed for nonexistent higher crime rates, for costing more in social services than they pay in taxes, and for taking jobs from Americans. In spite of overwhelming research from government and private organizations showing the opposite to be true (we go into greater detail in Chapter 2), the racist-nativist rhetoric has risen to the level of hysteria. State Governor Jan Brewer, when defending draconian immigration laws, declared that Arizona law enforcement agencies had found "bodies in the desert, either buried or just lying out there, that have been beheaded" (Collins, 2010). Coroners' offices and law enforcement officials along the border refuted the governor's claims and determined that not a single decapitated body had been found. Similarly outrageous statements have been uttered by other public officials and State Congress people who fuel fear and anti-immigrant sentiments for political gain. Meanwhile, FBI statistics show a consistent decline in crime rates in spite of population growth and the presence of undocumented people, who in fact are statistically the least likely to commit crimes (Immigration Policy Center, 2010). The state's former attorney general, Terry Goddard, challenged the governor, asserting that "violent crime is at the lowest level it's been since 1983 and crime along the border is at least at a 10-year-low" (Collins, 2010). In reality, the attacks on unauthorized immigrants hurt immigrants in general and United Statesians of Mexican-origin in particular, but the poisonous nativist narrative is implacable. Events occurring in Arizona over a period of less than one year illustrate its callous and divisive socio-political environment with undeniable racial overtones:

- In 2010 Arizona voters passed Proposition 107, deceivingly termed the "Civil Rights Initiative," that ended Affirmative Action in the state. The phrase "affirmative action" was not part of the ballot.
- Senate Bill 1070 was also passed, requiring law enforcement officers to demand immigration documents from anyone they have a "reasonable suspicion" of being in the country without authorization. The new law made it a crime to transport and to harbor an "illegal alien" in any building. Consequently, any school allowing undocumented children in its buildings or on its buses would be breaking state law. A district judge issued a preliminary injunction against the law noting that "there is a substantial likelihood that officers will wrongfully arrest legal resident aliens" and that it would impose a "distinct, unusual, and extraordinary burden" on authorized immigrants (Archibold, 2010). Later the law was defeated in the Ninth U.S. Circuit Court of Appeals, but its apologists immediately took it to the Supreme Court.
- The city councils of Tucson and Flagstaff, Arizona voted to sue the state over SB1070, rejecting enforcement costs and the negative consequences

on the tourism industry (the state receives over 24 million "legal" Mexican visitors every year). Many businesses also opposed the law because Mexico is, by far, the most important trading partner and international consumer of goods and services in Arizona. Thus, polarization occurred among city governments, organizations, businesses, and citizens, including divisions among Americans of Latino and Mexican origin.

- After the passage of SB1070, a drunk individual in Phoenix approached his Mexican-American neighbor, Juan Varela, as he was watering plants in his yard, ostensibly to talk about the new law. He was armed and yelled racial slurs at Varela before he killed him ("You fucking Mexican, go back to Mexico!" according to several reports). The victim and his family had lived in Arizona for generations (Kiefer and Ruelas, 2011).

- The state passed House Bill 2281 prohibiting schools from teaching courses that "advocate ethnic solidarity" or cater to specific ethnic groups. The bill was overtly directed to Mexican-American and Chicano Studies programs. In essence, it inculcates an inferior status by negating the right of minorities to explore their histories and cultures. Ethnocide, the destruction of cultural and ethnic identity, is again legal in Arizona (Amster, 2010).

- A group of artists who painted a public mural for a school in Prescott, Arizona were ordered to lighten the skin tones of children depicted in the painting after complaints about the children's ethnicity (Wagner, 2010).

- The Arizona Department of Education asked school districts to remove teachers who speak with accents from classes for the benefit of students still learning English (Jordan, 2010).

- In her apology for tougher anti-immigrant legislation, a state senator read a letter in the senate chamber from a substitute teacher criticizing Latino eighth graders. One of the statements in the letter read: "most of the Hispanic students do not want to be educated but rather be gang members and gangsters. They hate America and are determined to reclaim this area for Mexico" (Hill, 2011).

- These poisonous narratives inevitably have penetrated the lives of those people the Arizona laws are not supposed to affect. In May 2010, during a graduation speech for students in the University of Arizona College of Social and Behavioral Sciences, Associate Professor of Women's Studies Sandra Soto was booed and jeered as she criticized SB 1070 and HB 2281 and asked new graduates to use the critical thinking skills they learned in college. Later she received threatening emails (Arizona Graduation, 2010).

- Similarly, Celeste González de Bustamante, Assistant Professor of Journalism at the University of Arizona, has been told to "go back to Mexico" following her published articles about immigration and SB1070 (González de Bustamante, 2010). Dr. González is not of Mexican origin but a third generation American of Filipino descent.

Arizona's contentious politics and ideologically motivated policies blatantly disregard scientific research, even from conservative think-tanks like the CATO Institute, which has produced a number of economic analyses that contradict the purported benefits of its draconian legislation. In 2009, the CATO Institute published a study that measured the potential economic effects of immigration reform. "A major finding of the study is that a program of tighter border enforcement *strongly* reduces the welfare of U.S. households" (Dixon and Rimmer, 2009: 3). Therefore, Arizona's policies might, in fact, contribute to the financial troubles of the state. According to data from the Department of Homeland Security, in 2008 there were 560,000 undocumented residents in Arizona. By 2010 this population had shrunk to 470,000 (Hoefer, Rytina and Baker, 2010). Contrary to the misinformation about undocumented immigrants, they pay an average of $80,000 more in taxes during their working life than they receive in government services. In fact, without citizenship or residency documents, they are not eligible for most social services (See American Graduate School, 2003 and Mohanty et al., 2005). Furthermore, Arizona is one of the ten states receiving the highest tax revenues from undocumented residents (Immigration Policy Center, 2011). Unfortunately history shows that, as economic conditions worsen, a negative spiral of prejudice continues to blame the most vulnerable and voiceless, namely the dehumanized "illegals" and other "outsiders."

It is not our purpose to reduce the history of Mexican-Americans and Chicanos to a victimization process where they have been oppressed, discriminated against, and exploited (Gonzales, 2000). The abuses have been documented extensively by different historians, and they need to be part of a counter-history that challenges the hegemonic majoritarian memory. Nevertheless, it is also important to underscore that, as Mexican-origin people and undocumented Americans have become United Statesians, they have not simply been passive victims in the process. That is why this book highlights the educational successes of six undocumented Americans of Mexican origin and their enormous potential as productive citizens, if they are only given the chance to flourish. At the same time, we argue that a large number of undocumented Americans have been the innocent victims of a great injustice. As expressed by The Center for the Human Rights of Children of Loyola University Chicago, the case of undocumented American students

. . . is a case of lost potential and broken dreams, and the permanent underclass of youth it creates is detrimental to our economy. Moreover, and in some ways more importantly, it is a case of violations of the human rights of children. Passage of the DREAM Act could remedy this situation (Kaufka Walts, 2010).

Indeed, as these children grow up in the United States, the enjoyment of their human rights is increasingly impeded. In the case of deserving undocumented students, their struggle to normalize their immigration status has lasted an entire decade in Congress. The Development, Relief, and Education for Alien Minors (DREAM) Act was first proposed in 2001 as a way to provide residency to undocumented young people who arrived in the U.S. as minors and who attend college or serve in the military for at least two years. If enacted, the law would grant 2.1 million "DREAMers" formal authorization to be in the country without economic and legal barriers to pursue their education and hence give them the opportunity to become more productive members of society.

Meanwhile, being exposed as an "illegal" student in Arizona and other states can involve the punishment of exile, family fracturing, severe emotional distress and permanent harm, not to mention the inhumane facilities and processes of the immigrant detention centers.[5] This entails a much crueler penalty than that given to many criminal citizens who, in spite of their deliberately illegal acts against society, were never categorized as "illegals." The category is not used for arsonists, rapists, or drug dealers but reserved only for a unique type of "criminal," whether acting deliberately or not, driven by desperation or for family unification. Even the zealous defenders of English as the only valid language in the U.S. have ardently—illegally?—transformed the adjective "illegal" into a noun. Ironically, research has shown that 90% of undocumented students of Mexican origin have high levels of civic engagement and are a positive community influence (Perez et al., 2010).

Another irony is that due to its warm weather and relative low cost of living, Arizona is a state with a substantial population of retirees who could benefit from more generous immigration policies and better educated minorities. It has been argued that, "The retiring and mostly white baby boomers will also largely depend on the contributions of these mostly Mexican American youth and their low education will translate into lower earnings to support these senior citizens" (Telles and Ortiz, 2009: 291). It is in this context that the lives and stories of undocumented American students become important to the interests of the majority. Yet, despite the potential benefits recognized by many legislators, normalization of such "law breakers" is too politically problematic.

Paradoxically, American popular culture has historically glamorized different types of anti-heroes: "entrepreneurs" without scruples who have profited from the misery of others; gangsters who have built economic empires; and frontiersmen who massacred Native Americans in order to "win" the Southwest. Anti-American values are romanticized and promoted in literature, television, video games, and film (from innumerable classic westerns to *Bugsy*, *Dirty Harry*, *The Godfather*, *Pulp Fiction*, and *The Sopranos*). In contrast, we have real fighters who have graduated from the educational system through sheer determination, demonstrating how they value and practice hard work, dedication, and responsibility in spite of extraordinary obstacles. Although they live in a judicial purgatory through no fault of their own, they are asked with the most un-American sense of unfairness: "What part of illegal don't you understand?" (Downes, 2007). To this, they legitimately respond: "What part of *American* don't you understand?" (Perez, 2011).

The rationale behind punishing the children of undocumented immigrants, the hardliners argue, is simply about strict respect for the law. Nevertheless, the U.S. justice system and its laws have continuously evolved for over 200 years in pursuit of the essential sense of fairness and justice that this nation aspires to. Today, black people are not property any more, women can vote, and the U.S. Constitution has been reinterpreted several times in tandem with an evolving sense of social justice. This is why the DREAM Act has been endorsed by President Obama, educators, researchers, business people, religious leaders, and major organizations and institutions who believe it will make the U.S. a better country. Arizona's conservative political leaders opine the opposite, and, in the dawn of the twenty-first century, they have converted the state in the anti-immigrant laboratory of the nation, inspiring other states to do the same.[6] This is not the first time they are on the wrong side of history. We only hope Arizona is not "the laboratory of our future"[7] as a nation.

Critical Race Theory Research and Counter-History

This study examines the evolution and challenges of undocumented Americans of Mexican origin and other Mexican-origin people in the U.S. as an internally colonized community. Traditionally, internal colonialism has been understood as:

> a structured relationship of domination and subordination which are defined along ethnic and/or racial lines when the relationship is established or maintained to serve the interests of all or part of the dominant group (Barrera, 1979: 193).

According to Valenzuela (1999), colonization is a form of racism that is projected against a conquered people (the colonized) by a conquering group (the colonizers). The conquered group is dominated and controlled through various means, including violence and more subtle attacks on the subordinated group's culture, language, religion, and history. The phenomenon becomes more complex when the colonized internalize the colonialist mentality and become part of the colonizing majority. In a pluralist capitalist democracy, those who have internalized the oppressor's mentality can become part of the colonizing structure and support many of its actions, as some Latinos, Mexican-Americans, and Native Americans did when they supported racially prejudiced legislation in Arizona. In this context, those considered "non-citizens" and "outsiders" are the most vulnerable and subjugated in a colonized community as well as the most exposed to racism. More broadly, racism refers to

> practices which restrict the chances of success of individuals from a particular racial or ethnic group, and which are based on, or legitimized by, some form of belief that this racial or ethnic group is inherently morally, culturally, or intellectually inferior (Peter Foster quoted by Gillborn, 1998: 43).

In order to critically examine the data obtained from research and interviews with undocumented Americans of Mexican origin, we utilize Critical Race Theory (CRT) as a framework for analysis. CRT draws on critical theory, a theoretical approach established in the 1920s by the Frankfurt School of thought as "a project of human emancipation" (Tierney, 1993: 4). German social thinkers emphasized that all knowledge is historical and, therefore, biased and subjective. Their critical theory of society rejected any claim to objective knowledge and focused on uncovering the oppressive mechanisms of society. The purpose was to understand such mechanisms in order to develop the conditions that would allow the oppressed to free themselves (*Ibid.*). Parker and Stovall (2004) argue that,

> One of the main problems in critical theory is dealing with the centrality of racism in education and its strong philosophical roots and connections to the political economy (170).

CRT, like critical theory, emphasizes the importance of perspective and historical context in analyzing phenomena, while claiming that race is a central, not a marginal, element in understanding individual experiences of societal structures (the law, schooling, work environment) and identity (Gillborn, 2006; Solórzano and Yosso, 2000, 2001, 2002). Hence, it has been argued that old critical theorists should become critical race theorists "and should recognize in their work the historic and differential importance of race in the modern world in general, and in the United States in particular" (Mills, 2003: 174). We agree and utilize CRT as the conceptual and interpretive tool to examine the intersection of race and power relations, as well as historical racism, in the lived experiences of Mexican-origin people in general and academically successful undocumented Americans in particular. We emphasize that race differentiation exists in institutional policies, programs, and practices that interfere with Mexican-American students' rights and abilities— irrespective of their status in the country—to obtain the same educational opportunities available to the dominant society (Villalpando, 2004).

From this perspective, "race" is not a biological but a socio-historical concept that allows researchers to analyze the sources of ethnic and "racial" identity in society, the role of cultural differences, formal vs. substantive equality, and diverse forms of subordination (Ladson-Billings, 1998). Similarly, "Whiteness" is not a fact of nature; but an artifact of white supremacy (De Genova, 1998). Hence, the U.S. hegemonic nation-state manufactures a "national identity and citizenship, inherently racialized as white" (Ibid.: 91). Drawing from this, assumptions of institutional racism, class, discrimination, castification, and colonization are underlying notions in this research. These are some of the societal mechanisms of power and privilege deeply embedded in the institutions of a capitalistic market economy (Fendrich, 1983).

Racial domination has been "central to the making of the modern world" (Mills, 2003: 220). Today, race inequalities and racism are integral components of western societies and their educational systems (Gillborn, 2005). CRT's premise is that racism is "normal," not aberrant, in U.S. society; therefore it is seen as natural (Ladson-Billings, 1998, 1999), and hence often not seen at all. Furthermore,

> despite the scientific refutation of race as a legitimate biological concept and attempts to marginalize race in much of the public, political discourse, race continues to be a powerful social construct and signifier (Ladson-Billings, 1998: 8).

Although race is a socially constructed idea, it has real impacts on real people who do not always understand the extensive implications of their "otherness." Holleran (2003) illustrates such implications by pointing to numerous studies that show "significant differences in life chances by phenotype for Mexican Americans" (352). This means that individuals with "European features" tend to do better with respect to income, perceived discrimination, education, and other categories than people with darker complexions and "Indian features" (Idem). To complete the vicious circle, there is strong direct association between social class and educational achievement, where the higher a student's social class, the greater their average educational achievements (Gillborn and Mirza, 2000). All this translates into real disadvantages in the material conditions of minorities. The latest Census data show that the wealth of whites is 20 times that of blacks and 18 times that of Hispanics, the widest gap since the Census started tracking such data in 1984 (Taylor, Fry, and Kochhar, 2011).

In this context, an understanding of CRT and other forms of *conscientization*[8] are in themselves empowering because such concepts promote self-determination. Villenas and Deyhle (1999) argue that critical ethnographic studies have proven that communities, families, and individuals armed with this knowledge can effectively resist castification by reclaiming their language and cultural identities. Therefore, by working together, parents and students of Mexican origin are able to create "counter-hegemonic narratives of dignity and ethnic pride" (*Ibid.*: 437). In collectively creating such narrative and exploring their counter-history, immigrant children and adults are able to survive the violence[9] of a xenophobic, nativist society. CRT scholars also criticize U.S. liberalism and argue that, since schooling in the USA claims to prepare citizens, the interaction between citizenship and race should be investigated (Ladson-Billings, 1998).[10] The use of CRT acknowledges the multiple dimensions of academic achievement and underachievement of non-citizens. Especially, it emphasizes the need for a *transdisciplinary* perspective that places issues of racism, colonization, discrimination, castification, and other forms of oppression in contemporary and historical contexts (Solórzano and Yosso, 2002). As underscored by Villalpando (2003), examination of the social conditions of colonized minorities "must be framed within a context that includes their sociohistorical experiences" (634). Consequently, our narratives challenge ahistorical, out-of-context explanations of underachievement in people of Mexican origin in the United States.

From this critical position, this study gives a voice to the victims of unjust structures who are not the subjects of official history and provides the opportunity for their voices to be incorporated into the official critiques of the system. Their stories are intrinsically political and deeply embedded in relations of power. They "challenge the fetishness about the certainty and objectivity of knowledge and the quest for universal truths" (Dhunpath, 2000: 544), legitimize the voices of racial minorities; and support the critical analysis of the dominant social order (Nebeker, 1998). Finally, CRT serves as the unifying framework in this study because it places the narratives of the participants in the historical, ideological, and socioeconomic contexts in which racism has been declared virtually eliminated, while colonized minorities continue to be victimized (Parker and Lynn, 2002).

This framework is useful in explaining to families and students of Mexican origin how the negative perceptions and castification of their culture are interrelated with the power relations and social structure in the United States (Villenas and Deyhle, 1999). A counter-narrative that triggers critical awareness and *conscientization* will allow minority parents, students, and their communities to become politically aware and socially active. Consequently, as they gain political and economic power as a group, they can come together and begin to transform societal structures and the educational system.

Counter-history, an alternative understanding of the official version of history, is necessary for the construction of a more democratic society. Unjust social systems are the consequences of historical developments influenced by politico-economic pressures (Pearl, 2002) that create the structures and institutions that allow or disallow people to reach positions of power. "History establishes the basis for inclusion and exclusion in various societal institutions" (*Ibid.*: 336). This historical legacy of inclusion and exclusion is strongly maintained by the educational system. In fact, it has been argued that postsecondary institutions and academic structures are mechanisms that give privilege to some ideas and constituencies and silence others (Tierney, 1993). For example, one of the oldest counter-historical precedents that has emerged from a U.S. university was written by Mexican folklorist Jovita González in her master's thesis submitted in 1929, where she offered a defiant vision of the history of Texas. Although it has served as a source material on the Texas-Mexican border region for more than seventy years, her work was not published until 2006 by Texas A&M University (González, 2006). This in no way means that González's work will be used to narrate Texan history to majoritarian student populations. Nevertheless, as a tool for conscientization and decolonization, it is essential that counter-narratives and counter-history be known and incorporated to our collective memory.

Counter-history, like official history, is not about facts but about cultural and collective memory. Narratives and counter-narratives are always shaped by intricate contexts and by those who tell the story. Therefore, what a community believes its history to be can be more important than "facts" in relation to the lived experiences of that culture. In this sense, what matters about a particular narrative is the meaning it gives to the collective subjectivities and identities of a particular people at a particular time (Friedman, 1992). This holds true for either the majoritarian population in the U.S. or for the minority populations anywhere in the country. Americans of Mexican origin in the U.S. need to comprehend the far-reaching ramifications of their past in order to understand their educational underachievement and other adversities as the consequences of internal colonialism, oppression, and systematic exclusion (Pearl, 2002).

In consonance with CRT tenets, we advocate a counter-historical narrative that contests the negative representations of Mexican culture and peoples of Mexican origin. CRT situates their narratives "in a broader perspective that includes economics, history, context, group- and self-interest, and even feelings and the unconscious" (Delgado and Stefancic, 2001: 3). The counter-narratives, counter-memories, and counter-truths contained in this work represent a recovery of history, "a 'counter-rhetoric' against the dominant side of American history, which is centered on the advancement of some by the exploitation of many others" (García, 1995). Paraphrasing Ireland (2001), it is from here that the researcher and the counter-narratives revealed through his research "say no to the colonizer[s]" who seek to exclude them. Similarly, this research "stands in opposition to dominant discourses on immigration" (*Ibid.*: 78). Moreover, through a CRT perspective, it supports the tradition of Critical Theory that focuses on the objectives of challenging the status quo and building mechanisms that enhance empowerment and democracy (Tierney, 1993: 5).

Critical analyses of American democracy and race relations in the U.S. have important historical precedents. In 1835, a decade before the Mexican-American War, in his influential work *Democracy in America*, Tocqueville (2003) was amazed by the distinctiveness of U.S. racism, which was able

> . . . to exterminate the Indian race . . . with singular felicity, tranquility, legality, philanthropically, without shedding blood, and without violating a single great principle of morality in the eyes of the world. It is impossible to destroy men with more respect for the laws of humanity (355).

A century later, and many decades after the Emancipation Proclamation, racism against blacks and other minorities was rampant throughout the country, from *de jure* segregation and exclusion to gross infringement of human rights and racially motivated lynchings (Markovitz, 2004). In 1965, the U.S. Commission on Mental Health concluded that "racism" was the number one mental health problem in the nation (Lee, 1983). Today we see the multiplication of hate groups; anti-immigrant, anti-Mexican, and xenophobic political rhetoric; a proliferation of racist radio talk shows; increasing hate against Muslims; and growing racial incidents on college campuses (Redden, 2006).[11] In this environment, anti-immigrant and racist politicians easily mask their discourses with the language of national security, stability, equity, and meritorious individual achievement. The reality is that the United States continues to be "a race-based nation" (Barndt, 2007: 18).

Our premise is that, from the moment Mexican-origin people were incorporated into U.S. society by conquest, they have coexisted with mainstream United Statesians in a system of racial adversity. This has not always been evident for everyone, including those who are the victims of such a system, because "racism" (as defined above) has been embedded in socio-economic and legal structures and institutions. Simultaneously, by dehistoricizing race and racism, the dominant ideology has consistently attempted "to close down any space in which to question racism and the structures that produce and sustain it" (Macedo and Gounari, 2006: 3). After the election of the first African American president, we are told that we live in a post-racial society where opportunity and equality allow anyone to achieve the "American Dream." Thus, it is essential that we understand racial adversity in a historical framework that allows us to see beyond the official memory and, in this way, recognize the truths and social structures revealed by counter-history and counter-narratives. Such critical understanding is possible through our use of the CRT lens. CRT permits awareness of how racist ideologies create laws and structures that are utilized against minorities and, conversely, how the law and community conscientization can be utilized for social change (Yamamoto, 1997). The recovery and preservation of the history and stories of undocumented Americans of Mexican origin is an important step in this process and our main objective.

As noted by Valenzuela (1999), Acuña (2003), and other researchers, Mexican culture and language have been historically and systematically minimized through the legal system, educational policies, and institutionalized practices in the United States. At the turn of the millennium, they face great social challenges, while racial prejudices continue to spread under the disguises of a perceived immigration *threat*, the fluctuations of natural economic cycles, and the post-September 11th regime. As in other periods of U.S. history, racial chauvinism and anti-immigrant sentiments threaten the chances of educational achievement, social development, and economic progress for Mexican-Americans. Considering current socio-economic and demographic trends (see Chapter 2 for specific data), their marginalization has a great potential to affect the economic wellbeing of mainstream Americans and the future of the country (Massey et al., 2002). A successful answer to this challenge must include the voices that have been silenced by dominant narratives. Additionally, education is an indispensable part of the solution to almost any problem. Hence an educational component must be part of the answer to this quandary.

The counter-history of Mexican-origin Americans demonstrates their high regard for education. Their social struggles against colonization have repeatedly revealed their educational aspirations (Samora and Vandel-Simon, 1993). Therefore, an egalitarian dialogue that acknowledges their voices also must respond to such aspirations. Furthermore, it must be recognized that the education of undocumented Americans of Mexican origin, like for the rest of us, is a human rights and a civil rights issue.[12] Meanwhile, an increasing number of United Statesians of Mexican descent, Mexican immigrants, and undocumented Americans of Mexican origin are building a stronger civil society and developing a growing consciousness against legal violence, repression, and racial discrimination (Haney-López, 2001). This book aspires to serve as a modest inspirational instrument for this process of conscientization and decolonization. To do this, it is essential we learn and acknowledge our counter-history in all of its dimensions.

Navigating Borders

The following chapters challenge ahistorical, decontextualized, and one-dimensional narratives of Mexican-origin Americans in the United States. By focusing on successful undocumented American students, we highlight their dreams, their humanity, and their potential. At the same time, their personal life histories are situated in a larger historical context, a counter-history that emphasizes an alternative version of events and facts.

In Chapter II we seek to provide the counter-historical and counter-cultural backdrop to the book and set out to recover and rescue a version of Mexican history and immigration that challenges the Master Narrative of American History. The chapter also reflects critically on the "immediate history" surrounding the lives of Mexican-origin people and Mexican immigrants in the United States, including their current political, demographic, and socioeconomic circumstances.

Chapter III focuses on the educational contexts and challenges, both historical and contemporary, Mexican-Americans have to navigate in their quest for educational advancement. The literature discussed in this chapter reveals how as a colonized community, Mexican-Americans generally—and undocumented Americans of Mexican origin specifically—face unique, and sometimes enormous, challenges in order to attain educational achievement.

Chapter IV introduces the stories of the six participants in this study: David, Jesenia, Justo, Marina, Roberto, and Rosario. These six Americans of Mexican origin have been undocumented, although two of them have now normalized their status. Through their voices the chapter uncovers and recovers their poignant memories, images, feelings and experiences of what it has been like growing up and living undocumented lives. Their metaphorical and literal "navigating of borders" provides a significant insight into the lives of United Statesians who have solid educational goals but find themselves obstructed by racism, language barriers, lack of institutional support systems, poverty, alienation, and undocumented status.

Chapter V continues with these undocumented stories, reflecting on the obstacles these individuals overcame and the personal, familial and community resources and reserves upon which they drew in order to preserve their identity and survive. The chapter reveals how undocumented Americans of Mexican origin live in and create a "third space," both United Statesian and Mexican, but not entirely one or the other, where their renewed cultural and linguistic presence is growing. This chapter builds on the stories of resilience, agency and resistance to identify key measures educational institutions can adopt to meet the needs and civil rights of those students who occupy that space.

Chapter VI, the final chapter, shows how through a fusion of CRT, counter life history and critical arts-based research, the documented stories were transformed into a critical performance text. In so doing the chapter provides a summative reprise of the CRT approach as well as an insight into the methodology underpinning the book. The chapter's primary purpose however is to show how an artistic telling of the stories functioned as a means to legitimize, empower and promote the voices of undocumented American students; the evoking of their experiential and sensual knowledge helping to co-create, co-recover and interrogate a shared memory and history while simultaneously enriching an anti-colonialist critique of majoritarian structures and institutions. In this way, the authors were able to talk with (and back to) the undocumented participants, the Mexican-American community and beyond, to evocatively co-create and politically share their societal and educational experiences with a wider audience.

Notes

1. When referring to someone else's research we use the style of the author, with or without the hyphen.
2. In a list of 900 deportees, 229 are labeled "Mexicans," even though most of them were actually American citizens of Mexican origin (Arizona Board, 2000).
3. Fred Watson's oral history about the Bisbee Deportation was recorded on tape by Dr. Robert Houston of the University of Arizona on February 12, 1977.
4. The First Amendment of the United States Constitution guarantees freedom of religion, press and expression. It reads: "Congress shall make no law respecting an establishment of

religion, or prohibiting the free exercise thereof; or abridging the freedom of speech, or of the press; or the right of the people peaceably to assemble, and to petition the Government for a redress of grievances" (Library of Congress online: http://www.loc.gov).

[5] See for example FRONTLINE's investigative report "Lost in Detention" about the Obama administration's harsh immigration policies, totaling almost 400,000 deportations in 2010. http://www.pbs.org/wgbh/pages/frontline/lost-in-detention/

[6] After Arizona's extreme anti-immigrant legislation, states like Alabama, Georgia and North Carolina enacted tough immigration laws. The Alabama legislation, considered the most draconian, has caused great economic and human damage. As revealed in an editorial in *The New York Times*, "Hispanic homes are emptying, businesses are closing, employers are wondering where their workers have gone. Parents who have not yet figured out where to go are lying low and keeping children home from school" (*The New York Times*, 2011: A28). The agricultural industry of the state is one of the most affected. The new job openings that the laws have created are not being filled. As expressed by a businessman in the industry, "A crew of four Hispanics can earn about $150 each by picking 250–300 boxes of tomatoes in a day. . . . A crew of 25 Americans recently picked 200 boxes—giving them each $24 for the day" (Reeves and Caldwell, 2011). Alabama modeled its new laws after Arizona's legislation.

[7] Before the Mexican city of Juárez became to be known as one of the most dangerous cities in Latin America, Charles Bowden (1998), a photo journalist and activist from Tucson, published *Juárez: The Laboratory of Our Future*. In it, he documented the reality of violence and poverty in this industrial border city. Bowden's painful and disturbing photographs and narrative underscore some of the reasons for Mexican emigration. In what could be termed "economic violence"—a result of economic colonization—more than 300 foreign-owned *maquiladoras* (factories) employ over 200,000 Mexican workers in Juárez, while 2,820 *maquiladoras* across Mexico provide work for around 1,218,000 people (Instituto, 2006b). It is important to note however that *maquiladora* workers are predominantly women, who work 48 hours a week or more for about $9 per day. American mainstream perspective is that such inferior wages and labor standards are justifiable because the cost of living is less in Mexico and "they would not have work otherwise." In reality, prices in Mexico are highly incommensurate with wages, while the average American worker easily earns ten times more than a Mexican counterpart. Bales (1999) argues that this is in fact a new type of slavery, where people are disposable, and they are controlled by another person for the purpose of exploitation. In spite of having to pay wages (or rather "slave wages") and not having "legal" ownership, modern slavery gives slave owners the advantage of ownership without the legalities. "For the slaveholders, not having legal ownership is an improvement because they get total control without any responsibility for what they own" (*Ibid*.: 5). Paradoxically, those who have escaped this situation in Mexico and have come to the United States as undocumented immigrants can find themselves in similar circumstances, excluded from "the mainstream labor economy through racial labor segmentation, and thereby forced into ethnic enclaves where all labor laws are routinely neglected" (Ross, 1997).

[8] Freire (1970) has used the terms "Conscientization" and "Critical Awareness" to refer to ". . . reflection and action upon the world in order to transform it" (33). Also see Glossary for an expanded definition.

[9] Nelson Mandela has notably referred to "the violence of poverty" (quoted by Toh, 2004: 25). At the same time, Cahill (2004) has pointed out "the violence" of stereotypes on the lives of racialized minorities.

[10] For a comparative perspective on citizenship and nationality policies, competing models of citizenship, and a discussion of the concept of citizenship as membership, see Klusmeyer and Aleinikoff (Eds.) (2000).

[11] The Southern Poverty Law Center, a civil rights organization committed to racial equality, monitors hate groups and tracks extremist activity throughout the U.S. In its Spring 2007 Intelligence Report, the SPL Center informed that the hate group count in 2006 reached the unprecedented number of 844 organizations—an increase of 40% since 2000. Hate groups have been "energized by the rancorous national debate on immigration" and have been "increasingly successful at penetrating mainstream political discourse." Additionally, there is a fast growth of right-wing anti-immigrant groups that "stop short of the open racial hatred espoused by hate groups." In only two years, some 250 new nativist xenophobic organizations of this kind have emerged (SPLC, 2007). Furthermore, the mainstream media, right-wing talk shows, and politicians extensively disseminate the dominant anti-immigrant narratives, which have been taken to unbelievable extremes. For example, the *Wall Street Journal* quoted Republican Representative Steve King of Iowa who "regularly accuses illegal immigrants of committing sex crimes against 'eight little girls' a day as part of 'a slow-motion terrorist attack'" (Kronholz, 2006).

[12] This is clear in the United Nations *Universal Declaration of Human Rights* (United Nations General Assembly, 1948) of which the United States is a signatory. Article 26, specifically states that "Technical and professional education shall be made generally available and higher education shall be equally accessible to all on the basis of merit."

Navigating Historical Borders: Internal Colonialism and the Politics of Memory

We did not, in fact, come to the United States at all. The United States came to us.

— Luis Valdez (1972: xxxiii)

The root of oppression is loss of memory.

—Gunn Allen (quoted by Misztal, 2003: 15)

Internal colonialism is a form of inegalitarian pluralism where different ethnicities and cultures coexist, but ethnic relations traditionally follow an assimilation model, like in the United States (Blauner, 1972). It is also a form of racism where the dominant culture views the colonized ethnicities and cultures as alien and inferior, as is the case with Native, African- , Asian- , and Mexican-Americans in the U.S. Internal colonialism exists in the United States with or without the intention of individuals (Martínez, 1999) and can be found in all dimensions of life. Historically, governments have created, legitimized, and maintained subordination of colonized minorities (Fendrich, 1983), while "popular [dominant] culture" and the media reinforce racial stereotypes and exclusion (Harrison, 1994). Internal colonialism contradicts the notion of an integrated and democratic society where, some researchers argue, political and economic inequalities are not temporary, but necessary for the industrial, capitalist system (Konradi and Schmidt, 2004). The dominant society does not see such contradiction, which perpetuates their privileges and "the myth of American equality and democracy . . ." (Ibid.: 630). Racism, as defined in our previous chapter, is a central component of colonialism.

It is also important to point out that, while the traditional concept of racism involves an element of discriminatory action and a superiority-inferiority notion, it excludes unintentional or institutionalized racism (Gillborn, 1995, 1998). Through institutionalized racism, people and organizations carry out biased practices that are not intended to be racist but are discriminatory in their effects (Gillborn, 1998). Thus, as a mechanism of colonialism, racism can thrive without overtly racist individuals because it occurs "through social and cultural processes" (Pilkington, 2004: 15). In the United States, racist-colonialist elements are still embedded in our political system, economic structures, and socio-cultural practices, while reinforced by the majoritarian narratives of events, circumstances, and official history.

Americans of Mexican origin and undocumented Mexican immigrants alike are the victims of colonialism and institutionalized racism when they must reject their culture, language, and identity in order to succeed. As a community, and in spite of their numerous individual success stories, people of Mexican origin are colonized because they continue to be underrepresented in social and government institutions, remain the poorest minority, have the lowest educational achievement and, according to the U.S. National Research Council, have "an uncertain future" (Tienda and Mitchell, 2006). Further-more, by being colonized they are not allowed to make their own history (Córdova, 2005: 222).

Researchers have specifically criticized *anti-Mexican racism* in the United States (Mariscal, 2005; Pulido, 2007) and U.S. nativism, "distinguished by a pronounced *anti-immigrant racism* that [is] disproportionately directed against Mexicans . . . due to the hegemonic conflation of 'Mexicans' with 'illegal aliens'" (De Genova, 2005: 206). This appears to be part of the post-September 11 regime and one of the many dangers that assail the nation. The anti-immigrant discourse discards the socio-cultural memory of Mexican-origin United Statesians and attempts to build a monolithic truth to be embedded in official history. The counter-perspective is that cultural memory and history are versions of reality and, paraphrasing Ortega y Gasset, there are as many realities as points of view. Similarly, there are as many spaces in reality as there are perspectives on it (Kern, 2003). And, as noted by Michel Foucault,

> The external mechanisms influencing social memory are rooted in the forces regulating societies. "Each society has its regime of truth" and "types of discourses it accepts and makes function as true." So-called truth is bound to specific institutions, constantly exposed to political and economic incitements; 'truth' is the object of various forms of distribution and consumption, largely controlled by a few political and economic apparatuses (Foucault's *Truth and Power*, quoted by Eckstein, 2006: 22).

In this context, dominant/hegemonic stories are narratives of events, im-mediate and remote, as told and promulgated by members of domi-nant/colonizing groups. The dominant stories are interlaced with the values and beliefs that justify and legitimize the actions taken by the colonizers to perpetuate their hegemony. "The commonly accepted history of the United

States is one such story" (Love, 2004: 228–229). On the other hand, an alternative version of history that emphasizes different events and perspectives is a counter-story that attempts to democratize cultural memory. Such democratization "is an egalitarian dialogue that embraces the voices marginalized by dominant discourses" (Eckstein, 2006: 113) and enriches the politics of memory. The following section is a brief counter-history of peoples of Mexican origin in the United States.

The Memory of the Colonized

Mexicans became the first official "Hispanic"[1] Americans in the United States. They were incorporated into their new country by military conquest, after the US "deliberately provoked" the U.S.-Mexico War of 1847–1848 (Steinberg, 1981: 22). Abraham Lincoln, who became a congressman in 1847, vehemently opposed the war against Mexico (Damrosch, 2005; Monroe, 2000). So fervent was his opposition to the war that his inaugural speech in the House of Representatives was a condemnation of the invasion of Mexico (Lincoln, 2005). Lincoln denounced the invasion as "unnecessary," "unjust," and "unconstitutional," in other words, illegal (Lamon, 1895: 24; Lincoln, 1848). It is ironic that, in our day, the anti-immigrant fervor decries the "illegal invasion" of Mexicans coming to the U.S. It is also striking that contemporary Republicans who want the Mexican border sealed and militarized claim their affiliation to be "the party of Lincoln."

Many other prominent figures of the time denounced the invasion of Mexico and its injustice, but their critiques have been generally ignored by the dominant version of the story. Little-known perspectives include that of: John Quincy Adams, elected as a representative after being the sixth U.S. president, who strongly criticized the war with Mexico as an attempt to expand slavery (Stephenson, 1921). Ulysses S. Grant, another Republican president, recalled with shame in his *Memoirs* being one of the generals who fought in the U.S.-Mexico War, calling it "the most unjust war ever waged by a stronger against a weaker power" (Grant [1885–1886], 1995: 16). Henry David Thoreau was incarcerated for refusing to pay taxes to fund the war, and, while in prison, he wrote *Civil Disobedience*, where he established the principles that Gandhi and Martin Luther King would later use in their struggles. Nicholas P. Trist, the U.S. envoy who negotiated the peace treaty with Mexico, expressed feelings of shame and referred to "the iniquity of the war" and the "abuse of power" on the part of the United States (Meyer and Beezley, 2000: 368–369). Joshua Reed Giddings, a leading abolitionist, denounced "the murder of Mexicans upon their own soil" and "the robbing them of their country" in what he called an "aggressive," "unholy," "barbarous," and "criminal" war (Giddings, 1853: 17, 324). Decades later, even after Emancipation, members of the Republican Party still referred to the war as "one of the darkest scenes in our history . . . in pursuit of territorial aggrandizement of the slave oligarchy" (Dawson, 1880: 97).

As a result of this asymmetrical confrontation, Mexico was forced to recognize the U.S. annexation of Texas and what we know today as the states of Arizona, California, Colorado, Nevada, New Mexico, and Utah as well as parts of Oklahoma, Kansas, and Wyoming (Francaviglia and Richmond, 2000). These enormous territories were not "purchased" by the United States, as it is commonly believed, but acquired by "conquest," a practice that was not officially declared illegal by international law until the first half of the twentieth century.[2] There is an erroneous belief that, after the war, Mexico "sold" these territories to the United States for $ 15 million. After the repeated refusals of the Mexican government to sell territories to the United States, such a transaction would have been the equivalent of the "sale" of property as the buyer points a gun at the seller. In fact, the Treaty was not negotiated during a cessation of hostilities, but whilst both nations were still at war, with all Mexican ports and the capital of the country under the control of U.S. troops. Mexican historian Josefina Zoraida Vázquez asserts that the amount paid to Mexico was accepted as an indemnification for damages to the Republic and to help with the problems resulting from the loss of territory, while Mexican lands were taken by conquest (2000: 581). In the words of Manuel de la Peña, the Mexican president during whose term the Treaty was signed,

> The territories that have been handed over in the Treaty, are not sold for 15 million pesos,[3] but to recover our ports, and invaded cities; for the definite cessation of all kinds of evils, of all types of horrors . . . (quoted in Pescador Osuna, 1998: 198).

Clearly the Treaty was not a sale agreement but the only way for Mexicans to stop the aggression of a stronger invader and "to recover" at least part of the invaded territories. Article XII of the Treaty of Guadalupe Hidalgo states:

> In consideration of the extension acquired by the boundaries of the United States, as defined in the fifth article of the present treaty, the Government of the United States engages to pay to that of the Mexican Republic the sum of fifteen millions of dollars (Treaty, Article XII).

Therefore, the money given to Mexico was at best a "consideration," a "magnanimous" gesture of the conqueror after "the limits of the Mexican Republic" had been blatantly redefined by Article V of the same Treaty. Including Texas, Mexico lost 55% of its territory in what Thomas Sheridan (1995) has called: "the most monumental land grab in North American History" (50). Such "land grab" (not a land purchase) (see Map 1) was larger in extension than present-day Belgium, France, Germany, Italy, Luxemburg, the Netherlands, Spain, and the United Kingdom combined (1,996,752 sq km). This event alone consolidated the U.S. continental dominance (Meyer and Beezley, 2000) and became the catalyst for the United States' development into a new world power (Meed, 2002). At the same time, "Mexico's destiny was linked to its northern neighbor" (Meyer and Beezley, 2000: 369). At that point, the powerful U.S. could not imagine to what extent its own future would be linked to much-weaker Mexico.[4] The subsequent economic domination of Mexico would link the two countries in asymmetric interdependence in unforeseen ways (Fernandez and Gonzalez, 2003).

Before the U.S.-Mexico War, Mexico had already lost part of present-day Texas after the Anglo-American invasion that ended with the state's Declaration of Independence in 1836 (Hernández, 2001). Previous to the war, the U.S. took military possession of Texas and an enormous "disputed territory" (see Map 1) that, according to President Grant was done "apparently in order to force Mexico to initiate war" (Grant [1885–1886], 1995: 17). Prominent thinker and theologian William Ellery Channing referred to "the Criminality of the revolt" to take Texas from Mexico (1837: 6) and wrote that:

> The Texans in this warfare are little more than a name, a cover, under which selfish adventurers from another country [the USA] have prosecuted their work of plunder. Some crimes, by their magnitude, have a touch of the sublime; and to this dignity the seizing of Texas by our citizens is entitled. Modern times furnish no example of individual rapine on so grand a scale. It is nothing less than the robbery of a realm (20).
>
> . . . A nation, provoking war by cupidity, by encroachment, and, above all, by efforts to propagate the curse of slavery, is alike false to itself, to God, and to the human race (24).

Immediately after the war, Texas and the disputed territory were incorporated into the Union with the rest of the lands taken from Mexico. At the time, slavery and differential treatment based on race were official institutions in the United States. Subsequently, Texas became part of the Confederate South that practiced slavery. Many Mexicans chose to leave, while those who stayed were made into U.S. citizens overnight in accordance with the Treaty of Guadalupe Hidalgo between Mexico and the United States (Hernández, 2001). The new "Americans" of Mexican origin were officially United Statesians, but they were not in fact accepted as such. They relied on the Treaty to protect their civil rights, including their religion and language, but they had clashes with the Protestant Anglo-Americans and were treated as second-class citizens (Hernández, 2001; San Miguel and Valencia, 1998). Most of them had their rights violated; many lost their lands and properties and were not properly represented in politics (Acuña, 2003). Furthermore, the enormous territorial expansion afforded by the lands taken from Mexico put the issue of race and slavery at the forefront of the U.S. political debate. The slave oligarchy wanted the Mexicans to be enslaved, while the northern politicians feared southern expansion. This political struggle accelerated the crisis that eventually led to the Civil War (Monroe, 2000). In his memoirs, President Grant regarded the U.S. Civil War as God's castigation of the United States for the injustices it had committed against Mexico ([1885–1886], 1995). He specifically asserted that:

> The Southern rebellion was largely the outgrowth of the Mexican war. Nations, like individuals, are punished for their transgressions. We got our punishment in the most sanguinary and expensive war of modern times (Ibid.: 17).

Map 1: The Origin of the Southwestern United States

In 1837, even though it was still part of Mexico, Texas was recognized as an independent state by the U.S. In 1845, the U.S. annexed Texas in what Mexico considered an act of aggression and responded by breaking diplomatic relations with its northern neighbor. The light gray area in the map was not recognized by Mexico as part of Texas, but the Treaty of Guadalupe Hidalgo

forced Mexico to accept the annexation of the whole territory by the U.S. Later, individual military aggressions and pressures from the U.S. forced the sale of the territory known as La Mesilla, the so-called Gadsen Purchase of 1853 that gave the U.S. added lands along the border with Arizona and New Mexico (Meyer and Beezley, 2000).

Over a century and a half later, for many United Statesians of Mexican origin, the perception is that their ancestors did not emigrate from a distant country to a new promising land, as the U.S. Pilgrims did, but that a new, dominant nation came to them and transformed them into second-class citizens. This is embedded in the cultural memory of many Mexican-origin people in the United States but unrecognized by the dominant version of history. As expressed in the statement of a fourth generation Californian, "My great grandparents didn't cross the border; the border crossed them" (Felix Gutiérrez, quoted in J. Quiroga, 1997: 38). Researchers also have asserted that "a large share of the Mexican-Americans are here not because they crossed the border, but 'because the border crossed them'" (Alcoff and Mendieta, 2003: 99). Contemporary Mexicans might not know whether some of their ancestors resided in the former Mexican territories when they were taken by the United States, but the weight of history and their ample concept of family give them an inevitable connection with Mexican-origin people in the U.S. Many Mexicans would come to the United States for family unification or as economic migrants to the most logical place for survival, where their ancestors had lived or where many other Mexicans had later built a life as "Mexican-Americans" and United Statesians.

After the U.S.-Mexico War, the new border sliced Mexico in half and officially created the first United Statesians of Mexican origin.[5] Many Mexicans decided to move south within the new Mexican borders, but those who decided to stay—as the "immigrants" who came later—suffered ferocious attacks as a colonized community in the United States, most notably during times of economic decline (Acuña, 2003; Massey et al., 2002). After the War, which has been referred to by a Mexican researcher as an "Anglo-led race war against the people of Mexico" (Rojas, 2001: 17), internal colonialism came close to genocide (Carrigan and Web, 2003; Vélez-Ibáñez, 1996). Mexicans were robbed of their lands, cheated in commercial transactions, professionally diminished, utilized as commodities, and considered inferior in regard to language, customs, and religiosity (Acuña, 2003; Haney-Lopez, 2003; Vélez-Ibáñez, 1996). They were "subjected to multiple clearly racialized forms of displacement, disenfranchisement, exploitation, and oppression" (De Genova, 2005: 102).

Peoples in the territories taken from Mexico were very diverse. They were Native Americans, Mestizo (a mixture of many Native American and European ethnicities), and Mexicans of European decent. Thus the granting of U.S. citizenship to Mexicans, supposedly guaranteed by the Treaty of Guadalupe Hidalgo, was dependent on the Anglo-American perception of the "race" of a particular Mexican. Most of them were denied citizenship and "were not allowed to vote because of their race" (Wong, 2006: 19). Dispossessed Mexicans only could respond with the widespread claim: "We were here before you came" (McKenna, 1988). Their supplications and appeals would not be heard; they "simply did not count in the moral calculus of expansionism" (Frederick Merk quoted by Steinberg, 1981: 22).

Demographic History: Who Counts?

Demographics, the statistical data or profile of a specific population, continuously change due to fertility, mortality and immigration rates but also due to socioeconomic circumstances (Warf, 2006). In turn, these factors transform societies and populations and have an impact on their material, spiritual, and cultural circumstances. Consequently, the life histories contained in this research are in great part the products of such circumstances. Through them, the connections between immediate and remote histories are illuminated.

The 1850 population census revealed that more than 80,000 Americans of Mexican origin constituted about twenty percent of the population of the Southwestern United States. Most were natives of the former Mexican territories, and most lived in areas where they had been born. This was "the critical moment when Mexicans became Mexican Americans" (Nostrand, 1975: 378). Their greatest number was concentrated in the Territory of New Mexico. Nevertheless, research in the *Annals of the Association of American Geographers* shows that "Mexican Americans" were most likely significantly undercounted (*Ibid.*). People of Mexican origin were counted by the census as a kind of second-class white citizen, while Native American populations living in the former Mexican territories—who were previously Mexican citizens—were not counted as "Mexican-Americans." At the same time, many White Mexicans were ironically counted as "Americans."[6] Furthermore, many Mexican women and their children were excluded from the count if they had married a non-Mexican. In New Mexico Territory, Mexican-Americans could be excluded from the count if census takers noted "copper" under color or when their residence was a Native American town. In California, people of Mexican origin were not included in the "Mexican-American" category if the census taker noted "Indian" under "color" (*Ibid.*: 382). To make things worse, "some census takers undoubtedly were ignorant of Spanish and thus may have avoided Mexican Americans" (*Ibid.*: 383). At this point, the population of Mexican origin was being quickly overwhelmed by the massive numbers of immigrants from the East and from Europe after the discovery of gold in California (just before the end of the U.S.-Mexico War). In summary, the 1850 census was an extremely arbitrary caste system, with strong elements of internal colonialism, racism, and exclusion embedded in it.

During the second half of the 19th century, the new border between the two countries was unregulated, and movement across it was mostly unrestricted (De Genova, 2004). By the end of the century, the Southwestern economy grew rapidly and Mexican labor was actively recruited in mining, railroads, ranching and agriculture. Mexicans were encouraged to cross the border and work without any official documentation (Acuña, 2003; De Genova, 2004). Their population had grown steadily but invisibly. In 1910, after the Mexican Revolution spread throughout Mexico, a flood of refugees came to the United States, presenting the country with one of its first refugee crises. During this era Anglo-Americans, police, and the judicial system committed disproportionate abuses, civil rights violations, and violence against immigrants and Americans of Mexican origin (Rosales, 1999). On the other hand, the capitalist development of the Southwest demanded cheap labor, and employers did what they could to recruit Mexican laborers. According to Spener (2009: 99), in the period of 1888–1917,

> U.S. employers first accessed Mexican laborers in the interior of Mexico by hiring Spanish-speaking labor recruiters. known as *enganchadores* or *enganchistas* (literally, "hookers" from the Spanish noun *gancho*, hook, and verb *enganchar*, to hook), to convince them to accept jobs in the United States and accompany them on the new trains to the border. This system of labor recruitment, known as *el enganche* ("the hooking"), was already practiced extensively within Mexico as a way of mobilizing peasants in central Mexico to work in expanding factories and mines in the northern region of the country. Following completion of the railroad to the border, U.S. employers tapped in to the *enganche* system quite effectively. The *enganchadores* frequently induced rural men to travel with them by getting them drunk and would sometimes collaborate with local authorities to forcibly recruit vagrants and prisoners. The terms of employment offered by the *enganchadores* were often changed for the worse once workers were "hooked," and workers were commonly treated as chattel and held against their will until they could work off their transportation debts (Durand, 1994, 108–10). The thousands of men who traveled north with *enganchadores* during this period typically did so without signing a formal labor contract; rather, they would not be asked to sign a contract until they reached a contracting office on U.S. soil. In this way the *enganchadores* tried to give the appearance that they were not violating the foreign contract labor ban (Reisler 1976, 10).

After 1917 and continuing through the 1920s, more restrictive immigration laws made *traditional* migration from Mexico more difficult while free undocumented labor immigration was allowed (Bernard, 1998). A huge clandestine demand for Mexican labor throughout the Southwest and elsewhere in the U.S. led to a vast human smuggling industry (Wilson, 2000). Later, as economic conditions declined during the Depression of the 1930s, at least 500,000 Americans of Mexican origin, including many whose ancestors had lived in the former Mexican territories before the U.S. invasion, were "deported" to Mexico during the so-called "Mexican Repatriation" period. They were expelled with no regard to citizenship by birth in the U.S. but simply for being "Mexicans" (De Genova, 2004; Flores, 2003). Andrade (1998), argues that as many as one million people were expelled, in what became the largest expulsion of people in the history of the United States, only comparable to the relocation of Native Americans from their own land in the 19th century.

One hundred years after the 1850 population census, things had changed, although one could not see much difference in the census numbers. The 1950 census "revealed" that the U.S. was 89% white and 10% black (*The Economist*, 2000). This time, people of Mexican origin were hardly noticed. In 1942, however, new labor shortages had pushed the United States government to reach an agreement with Mexico to encourage unemployed Mexicans to work in the United States, under contract, as "temporary workers." The Labor Importation Program became to be known as the "*Bracero* Program," from the Spanish word *brazos* (arms). Most jobs were in the agricultural sector, where many *brazos* were needed as a result of the shortages created by World War II. Although the program was supposed to end after the War, it continued for years afterward, as farmers repeatedly demanded extensions from Congress. By 1956, 25 percent of all agricultural workers in the country were people of Mexican origin, most were working extensive hours for below-subsistence wages, living in poor conditions, and possibly suffering from exposure to dangerous pesticides (Rodríguez, R., 1997). The population of Mexican origin in the U.S. was inexorably growing due to the pull factors imposed by the capitalist expansion of the economy and the need for undocumented workers/cheap labor (Bach, 1978).

For a long time, although they were obscure statistics in most of the official documents that acknowledged their existence, migrant workers had been essential to the development of the agricultural economies of the Southwest (Joppke, 1999). In the middle of the twentieth century, as in other times in history, racist legislation tried to benefit from these immigrants and keep them away at the same time. In the Immigration and Naturalization Act of 1952, the so-called Texas Proviso (because it was endorsed by a group of Texan agricultural interests) stated that employing "illegals" (sic) did not constitute the criminal act of "harboring." Therefore, it was legal to employ undocumented workers, while it was easy to deport them when not needed (*Ibid.*: 30). The economy could count on them, but they only counted as "illegals," "outsiders," and "others." This type of institutionalized and *de jure* racism would perpetuate the human rights abuses, the exploitability, and invisibility of migrant workers.

Growing numbers, Growing Conscience, Growing Adversity

Between 1951 and 1965, at the peak of Mexican worker flows into the U.S., approximately 450,000 Mexican workers crossed the border contracted by the *Bracero* Program (Meier and Ribera, 1993). One of the terms of the Bracero Program stipulated that, "Mexicans entering the U.S. under provisions of the agreement would not be subjected to discriminatory acts" (Mize, 2006: 87). As in other periods of Mexican-American history, the official literature about the *Bracero* Program assumes that it operated under the guidelines established by the official agreement (*Ibid.*). Conversely, the counter-history of this era can be found in Chicano literature, like Rodolfo Acuña's classical *Occupied America: A History of Chicanos*, first published in 1972. Acuña (2003) exposes Chicano exploitation and oppression under a system of internal colonialism and racial differentiation. Other accounts have utilized open-ended life-history interviews, photos, and even family correspondence to document the economic push-pull pattern of Mexican immigration and economic oppression that precedes the *Bracero* Agreement and continues today (see, for example, Jacobo, 2004).

In 1954, ignoring the Mexican government's appeal for a minimum wage for *braceros*, the U.S. Congress allowed the Department of Labor to unilaterally recruit Mexican workers, and the Border Patrol itself actively recruited undocumented migrants (Cockcroft, 1986). At the same time, between 1954 and 1958, the United States government deported over 3.8 million "wetbacks," or *mojados*,[7] to Mexico under the Operation Wetback Program. This program, labeled with an overtly racist name, harassed Mexicans who for decades had been lured by the pull forces of a booming economy that voraciously demanded their labor. By then, they had built a life in the United States; some had married U.S. citizens, and many had children who were born in the U.S. Nevertheless, irrespective of their status in the country, whether "legally" or without documents, they felt constantly intimidated and in fear of being deported. The deportations of the 1930s were still fresh in the social memory of Mexican-Americans. The simultaneous existence of the Bracero Program and Operation Wetback made authorized and undocumented immigrants more submissive and even afraid of utilizing public services like health care, public assistance, and public education (Barclay, 2005; De Genova, 2004; Michelson, 2001). They were expected to be a tame and easily discarded workforce who could be used as scapegoats in times of economic decline (Bustamante, 1976). In spite of this, United Statesians of Mexican origin were increasingly challenging the status quo. In 1954, a ground-breaking case in the Supreme Court, *Hernandez v. Texas*, became one of the stepping stones of the American Civil Rights Movement and the fight against racial segregation in the U.S. At this point,

> . . . the law began to recognize the social reality of Mexican Americans in the United States, a development that occurred somewhat later than it did for other minority groups. A unanimous Supreme Court, in an opinion by Chief Justice Earl Warren, who also authored the unanimous opinion in *Brown v. Board of Education*, ruled that the Equal Protection Clause of the Fourteenth Amendment barred the systematic exclusion of persons of Mexican ancestry from juries, one of the institutions often identified as exemplifying the United States's commitment to democracy (Johnson, 2004: 5).

By the 1960s, United Statesians of Mexican origin became more politicized. The word "Chicano," previously a pejorative term, became a political term that expressed militant ethnic nationalism (Chávez, 2002). This period gave birth to the struggle for Civil Rights, which included an intense participation of Mexican-Americans, but whose involvement has only been included marginally, if at all, in most popular history books. One of their foremost battles was their fight for the unionization of farm workers led by César Chávez, Dolores Huerta and other leaders. The social movement that later became to be known as the Chicano Movement had emerged. There was an increasing perception among Mexican-Americans, Chicanos, and Latinos in general that they were acquiring political influence. The sense that their growing population and participation would lead to political power was to a great extent an illusion, but the numbers were real. At the beginning of the decade, the U.S. Census revealed that there were almost four million Americans of Mexican origin in the country, and 85% had been born in the U.S. (Acuña, 2003).

We Serve Whites Only

As late as the 1960s, it was common to see signs in establishments throughout the Southwestern U.S. that read: "No Mexicans or dogs" (Espinoza et al., 2005: 57), "no Mexicans allowed" (Ruiz, 2001), and others. This photograph was taken by Russell W. Lee in the small agricultural town of Dimmitt, Texas in 1949. The sign was directed to migrant workers, who mostly came from Mexico.

Courtesy of The Dolph Briscoe Center for American History. The University of Texas at Austin

Before 1960, the foreign-born population of any Latin American origin did not reach one million, but by the end of the decade more than one million additional Latin Americans entered the country through official channels (Gutiérrez, 2004). At the same time, the end of the Bracero Program in 1964 and the rapid population growth in Mexico promoted an expansion of undocumented immigration.

In the 1970s, Mexican-American political participation expanded in part thanks to the Civil Rights Movement. Raúl Castro and Jerry Apodaca, two United Statesians of Mexican origin, became governors of the states of Arizona and New Mexico, respectively. An increasing number of moderate Mexican-American politicians were able to be elected to public office. The mid-1970s to the mid-1990s has been defined as a time of transition that gave birth to the Post-Chicano/Hispanic Generation (Gonzales, 2000). Some achievements and many of the unfulfilled promises of the Chicano movement were now confronted with an era of rapid change. Mexican-Americans were more visible now than ever due to their explosive demographics and the new challenges they represented to the hegemonic concept of "America" such as bilingualism, Affirmative Action, and immigration. Yet, in spite of their increasing visibility as representatives, mayors, state legislators, and other appointed officials, they had little decision-making power in the larger political context and Mexican-origin United Statesians continued to be severely underrepresented in politics (Meier and Ribera, 1993).

Immigration flows grew more rapidly than ever during the 1980s. In this decade, an average of more than 100,000 Mexican immigrants per year were authorized to come to the country. Most of them already had family members residing in the United States. At the same time, myriad individuals and families from mixed immigration statuses had dual residency, living in both countries and supplying labor demand in the U.S. as needed. For the undocumented, going back and forth was relatively easy, since border enforcement was lax and a network of friends and family connections facilitated the journey. Crossing the border without documents was not treated as crime, but as being out of compliance with an administrative requirement, an infraction without major consequences. In 1986 the Immigration Reform and Control Act (IRCA) made it illegal to give employment to the undocumented and gave an amnesty to those in the country since 1982. Anti-immigrant critics argued that the IRCA never adequately punished immigrants who continued coming to the country without authorization. A decade after IRCA was enacted, the U.S. General Accountability Office (GAO) would uncover widespread IRCA-related discrimination. Research found not only higher discrimination but a reduction in Hispanic employment due to IRCA (Lowell et al., 1995). Nonetheless, by the end of the 1980s, Latin Americans and Asians accounted for almost 90 percent of all authorized immigrants. The complexities of Chicano, Hispanic, Latino, Latin American, Mexican-American and many other identities from the Spanish-speaking world were emerging as a multifaceted reality in the United States. Language was the social glue that gave them all a common quality as well as a commonly perceived threat by the dominant culture. The English-only movement emerged as a hostile response with the aim to abolish bilingual education. Such movement has been denounced as a "pedagogy of exclusion" and a form of colonialism (Macedo, 2000). The Spanish-speaking population in the U.S. was inexorably growing and challenging the exclusionary concept of "Americanness." Although the U.S. Constitution does not establish an official language, 28 states have enacted laws establishing English as their official language.

At the beginning of the 1990s, Mexican- and Latin American-origin United Statesians had made some visible progress in the political arena. At this point, there were an estimated 4,000 elected officials of Hispanic origin in the United States, about half of them in Texas and a majority of Mexican descent (Meier and Ribera, 1993). Between 1994 and 2000, the number of Hispanic voters would increase from 5.5 million to eight million. These realities and the demographic trends of the Hispanic population indicated that the ethnic composition of the country was experiencing important transformations. Immigration became a prominently contentious issue in the political arena, while warning signs were detected of a new form of nationalism based on fear and insecurity (see Dittgen, 1999). California Proposition 187, also known as the "Save the State Initiative" (SOS), was approved in November 1994, with support of 31% of the Latino voters. The law denied public education, health and social services to undocumented immigrants, although "much of the comfortable Californian way of life enjoyed by the middle class depends on cheap and frequently 'undocumented' workers" (Ibid.). A year later, most of the law was declared unconstitutional by a federal judge. The initiative became a national debate on undocumented immigration and made some conservative sectors of the population react belligerently. By the end of the 1990s, according to the Southern Poverty Law Center (2011), "anti-immigration xenophobia began to rise to levels not seen in the United States since the 1920s." As pointed out by De Genova (2005), such anti-immigrant racism has been markedly aimed at Mexicans who are commonly conflated with "illegals" and outsiders, despite the fact that most of them are U.S. citizens and authorized residents. Ironically, during this decade of increasingly restrictive immigration policies, the U.S., Mexico and Canada signed the North American Free Trade Agreement (NAFTA), which facilitated the free movement of goods and services across borders. Contrary to expectations, the displacement of peasants in Mexico was one of the consequences of NAFTA, and many of them felt forced to emigrate as a way of economic survival. But now things and consumer goods could cross the border much easier than human beings.

Meanwhile, the detested but necessary mojados inexorably kept crossing the border although some of them would never succeed in crossing. Some died in tragic circumstances, drowned, dehydrated, or even murdered (Eschbach et al., 1999; Scharf, 2006). Others were caught and sent back or jailed by the Border Patrol. In Arizona, undocumented immigrants were also called "aerialists," since they supposedly entered the state by climbing barbed wire fences. Immigrants risked dying of dehydration, venomous desert creatures, and sharp penetrating cacti by crossing through the desert, but they kept coming, pushed by rapid demographic growth in Mexico and pulled by much higher wages in the U.S. (Massey et al., 2002). Furthermore, for an increasing number of immigrants there was an even more powerful pull factor in the United States: since many of them had family members who had been living in this country for generations, emigration was the way to mend their fractured families (Rodriguez and Hagan, 2004). Many of their ancestors had been lured by the development of the state economy, the expansion of the railroad system, agriculture, mining, and construction booms. Eventually they too would be incorporated into the Mexican-American communities throughout the Southwest.

With the emergence of the post-September 11th antiterrorist state, border enforcement and immigration policies have been transformed "under the aegis of a remarkably parochial U.S. nationalism and an unbridled nativism" (De Genova, 2004). In March 2003, the Immigration and Naturalization Service was absorbed under the new Department of Homeland Security. Subsequently, immigration policies have been misused in the name of national security (Hing, 2006), while discrimination and abuses against immigrant workers have been documented after the attacks on the World Trade Center in 2001 (Bacon, 2004a). Romero (2006) notes the escalation of racial profiling that targets "Mexicanness," denoted by stereotypes of skin color and bilingualism. In 2004, however, the Bush administration proposed the temporary "regularization" of undocumented immigrants as part of a new Bracero-style labor system (*Wall Street Journal*, 2005). At the time, human rights advocates and critics feared that such a plan would establish a new scheme to perpetuate the availability of disposable, and still deportable, migrant labor (De Genova, 2004).

In the 21st century, the struggle that started with Mexican resistance after the U.S. dispossessed Mexico of half of its territory has reemerged as a growing aspiration for cultural recognition and equality. Today Mexican-Americans allegedly live in a more pluralistic society where multiculturalism, globalization, and human rights are common issues. Nevertheless, a disproportionate number of them live in poverty (Lichter et al., 2005), still experience discrimination (Stone and Han, 2005), and have high levels of attrition and failure in school (Kao and Thompson, 2003; McGlynn, 1999). Countless United Statesians of Mexican origin are inexorably linked to the flows of new immigrants from Mexico, where family members, friends, and cultural connections remain. Family reunification, business and shared interests constantly generate binational links that are a product of history and economic circumstances. In such a complex process, many Mexican-origin Americans have become integrated to the mainstream society and feel distant from their Mexican roots;

others are part of a racialized second-class citizenry that stubbornly preserve their language and traditions. There is also an enormous population of un-documented Americans, United Statesians of Mexican origin, who exist in a judicial limbo. Whether they are identified as Hispanics, Latinos, Mexicans, Mexican-Americans, or Chicanos, they coexist with the dominant American culture in an environment of racial adversity that perpetuates "white privilege" (Delgado, 2006) and internal colonization. Their material existence is an integral part of a political economy that is founded on such conditions.

The Political Economy of Mexican Immigration: "Those who own the present, own the past. Those who own the past, own the future."[8]

As pointed out by Bhattacharyya et al. (2002), an economic system "shapes our lives and our life chances, whoever and wherever we are" (36). It could be added that economic systems are inseparable from politics. Political econo-mists criticize mainstream economic models that ignore the historical contexts that shape all human events, while they assert that political power and eco-nomic activity cannot be understood separately (Schneider, Knoedler, and Sackrey, 2005). Thus, political economy differs from mainstream economics in its much broader focus, paying attention to the intertwined relationships of economic structures with societal institutions and social developments. A political-economic view is thus sensitive to the effects of factors seemingly outside of the economic arena such as political circumstances, social move-ments and organizations, values, ideology and others (Schneider et al., 2005). The impact of unauthorized and authorized immigration on the U.S. econ-omy has been the cause of acrid national debates, but it cannot be explained simply with a one-dimensional perspective. Evidently the discussion has grown into different dimensions, predominantly the political arena, as well as in socio-cultural and academic fields, but the interconnections are not always understood.

   Looking at a larger context, although less than 2% of the world's popula-tion resides in a country other than that of their birth, immigration is a prominent political issue in all developed market economies (Money, 1999). Industrialized nations tend to develop anti-immigrant sentiments when their economies shrink and are more inclined to support immigration flows when they grow (Ibid.). The U.S. is not an exception (Bustamante, 1976; Massey et al., 2004), but, in addition to the economic decline during the Obama ad-ministration, greater anti-immigrant sentiments have been sparked by the doctrine of the Anti-Terrorist State that emerged after the attacks on New York on September 11, 2001 (Bacon, 2004; Kay-Oliphant, 2005). In spite of this, nurtured by mass immigration, the U.S. economy could arise by midcentury as one of the most multicultural and wealthy nations in history (Kotkin, 2010).

One of the main concerns for the American economy is the fall in the participation rate of the labor force (*The Economist*, 2006). Economists recommend that the labor supply be revitalized by boosting immigration flows, especially since the proportion of immigrants who work is higher than that of native-born Americans (*Ibid.*). Paradoxically, political trends and legislation are going in the opposite direction. Conservative political leaders who oppose immigration vociferously preach about the "immigrant invasion" and are gaining followers. Paul Buchanan, a three-time presidential candidate, has written best sellers entitled *The Death of the West: How Dying Populations and Immigrant Invasion Imperil Our Country* (2002) and *State of Emergency: The Third World Invasion and Conquest of America* (2006). Congressman Tom Tancredo, former chair of the Congressional Immigration Reform Caucus, wrote *In Mortal Danger: The Battle for America's Border and Security* (2006), where he explained how Mexican immigrants endanger the future of the United States.

While immigration issues are used as either opportunistic or ideological tools to win elections, in an apparently schizophrenic move, the U.S. Federal Reserve has devised programs to extend banking programs to undocumented immigrants, and about 150 financial institutions have followed its lead (Jordan, 2006). Similarly, although undocumented immigrants cannot obtain a social security number to work "legally," the U.S. Internal Revenue Service (IRS) allows them to file taxes by applying for an Individual Taxpayer Identification Number (ITIN), originally designed for foreigners with a temporary authorization to reside in the U.S. but now widely used by undocumented immigrants. The IRS issued an estimated 1.8 million ITINs in 2009, up from roughly 900,000 issued in 1999 (DHS, 2010). The state governments also have started programs to allow undocumented immigrants to pay state taxes (Bartlett, 2006) and to obtain home mortgages (Huffstutter, 2006). These actions by the federal and state governments are pragmatic solutions to maximize the potential benefit from undocumented immigration (Porter, 2005). The National Academy of Sciences has estimated that immigrants pay an average of nearly $1,800 per person more in taxes than they claim in benefits while they contribute as much as $10 billion a year to the U.S. economy (Smith and Edmonston, 1997).

In 1995, the Cato Institute, surveyed 38 former presidents of the American Economic Association and the past chairmen of the President's Council of Economic Advisers. Eighty percent agreed that immigration has been "very favorable" for the nation's economic growth," while 74% agreed that undocumented immigrant workers have had "a positive impact" on the U.S. economy (Simon, 1995). The CATO Institute study concluded that, on balance, immigrants do not displace native workers, depress wages or abuse welfare (See Table 1).

Table 1: Survey of "the Most Respected Economists" (1995)

On balance, what effect has 20th-century immigration had on the nation's economic growth?	
Very favorable	80%
Slightly favorable	20%
Slightly unfavorable	—
Very unfavorable	—
Don't know	—

What impact does illegal immigration in its current magnitude have on the U.S. economy?	
Positive impact	74%
Neutral impact	11%
Negative impact	11%
Don't know	4%

Source: The Cato Institute and the National Immigration Forum (Simon, 1995).

The CATO Institute findings were further corroborated in June 2006 by an open letter to President George Bush and Congress from more than 500 renowned economists, including five Nobel laureates. The letter asserts that "immigration has been a net gain for American citizens," conceding that, "while a small percentage of native-born Americans may be harmed by immigration, vastly more Americans benefit from the contributions that immigrants make to the economy, including lower consumer prices. As with trade in goods and services, gains from immigration outweigh the losses" (*Wall Street Journal*, 2006). Finally, in the midst of economic decline in the United States, a new study from the CATO Institute contradicted the anti-immigrant discourse, once again warning of the potential economic harm of deporting the undocumented (Dixon and Rimmer, 2009). At the same time, the Immigration Policy Center and the Center for American Progress (2010) projected that a comprehensive immigration reform would benefit the U.S. economy over the next 10 years by a cumulative $1.5 trillion, while deporting just over half of the undocumented workforce would shrink GDP by $2.6 trillion over the same period (Hinojosa-Ojeda, 2010). The negative impact would have devastating multiplying effects on the economy.

Specifically regarding undocumented immigrants, *The Economist* (2000) has put it simply:

> The embarrassing secret is the importance to daily life of illegal immigrants. Every American politician claims to condemn their presence, but without them the domestic life of middle-class America would fall apart; food prices would climb steeply as produce rotted in the fields; hotel rooms would stand uncleaned; swimming pools would become septic tanks; and taxis would disappear from the streets. In short, the country would grind to a halt.

By the beginning of the century, it was estimated that undocumented Mexican immigrants alone contribute at least $154 billion to the U.S. GDP (Hinojosa-Ojeda, 2001).[9] Thus, the contributions of documented and undocumented immigrants go far beyond the benefits of cheap labor, since they are literally an engine of growth and economic vitality in many sectors (Ewing and Johnson, 2003). The service sector, the construction and extractive industries, and manufacturing are clear examples of areas where undocumented immigrants make significant contributions to the U.S. economy (see Graph 1).

Graph 1: Undocumented immigrants make significant contributions to the economy. Percentage of workers in different sectors is shown.

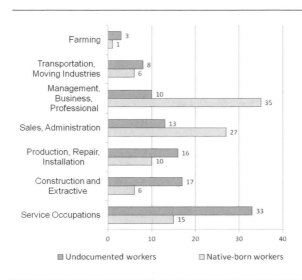

Moreover, the Ewing Marion Kauffman Foundation has reported that immigrants far outpaced native-born Americans in entrepreneurial activity (Fairlie, 2006). The U.S. Census Bureau reported that between 1997 and 2002, Hispanic businesses alone grew by 31%, equivalent to three times the national average for all businesses (Bergman, 2006). Finally, in addition to consumer spending and billions in direct tax contributions to the federal, state and local government, immigration can be the solution to the problem of the U.S. social security system, which is being strained by an ageing population and a declining labor force (Ewing and Johnson, 2003; Porter, 2005). Unfortunately, although they are overrepresented in entrepreneurship, Latinos are underrepresented in politics.

The U.S. currently has a larger proportion of undocumented immigrants than at any time in history (Massey, 2005; Gans, 2006), most of them from Latin American countries (see Graph 3). The full vitality and dynamism they could bring to the economy if they were "legalized" is not achieved due to political, ideological, and racial prejudices. These immigrants and their children, many of whom are U.S. citizens, by virtue of their "illegality"—or simply because they are the offspring of undocumented parents—are

> . . . marginalized from the rest of American society, economically vulnerable, politically disenfranchised, and fearful of contact with social institutions that deliver health care and education. Undocumented children who grow up in, but were not born in, the United States face an impermeable ceiling to economic mobility and strong barriers to their incorporation into mainstream society. If U.S. officials had set out to intentionally create a new underclass, they could hardly have done a better job (Massey, 2005: 2).

The magnitude of the Mexican diaspora to the United States will continue to create policy dilemmas and be perceived as a threat by some sectors of the population. As the product of historical, socio-economic, and geopolitical phenomena, Mexican immigration is unique and multi-dimensional. Even the figures for authorized immigration to the U.S. show that Mexican immigrants constitute the largest portion of it from a single country. Almost 25% of all authorized immigrants in the last decade of the 20th century were of Mexican origin (Graph 2). Considering their extended family structures, this fact alone increases the likelihood of continuous family ties across borders and may promote further immigration. A revealing fact of the era of telecommunications is the growth in calls from the U.S. to Meixco, which grew by 171% between 1995–2001 and is now "the largest destination of all outgoing American telecommunications" (Vertovec, 2004).

Finally, a survey taken by the Pew Hispanic Center shows that 82% of all Mexican immigrants have relatives in the United States (see Table 2). Undoubtedly, when they leave their country, they also leave relatives in Mexico. At the end of the 1980s, around half of the Mexican adult population were related to someone living in the U.S., and one third of all Mexicans had been to the United States sometime in their lives (Massey and Espinosa, 1997). This reveals an extensive network of relatives and friends that probably will have an impact on future immigration as well as on the Hispanic cultural phenomenon in the U.S. Undocumented immigrant residents, authorized immigrants, and Americans of Mexican origin have strong family structures that are being fractured by the political economy surrounding the immigration conundrum (Rodríguez and Hagan, 2004). Issues of family unification, human rights, and transnational economic survival[10] affect all of them, irrespective of their status in the country. By 2006, as a result of the national debate over immigration reform, 54% of all Hispanics in the U.S. perceived an increase in discrimination (Suro and Escobar, 2006).

Table 2: Survey of Mexican Immigrants in the U.S. (2005)

Do you have relatives in the US?		How much English do you speak?	
Yes	82%	None/a little	54%
No	13%	Some/a lot	44%

Source: Pew Hispanic Center (from *The Economist*, 2005)

Figure 1: Origins of 9.1 million authorized immigrants arriving in the United States between 1991 and 2000 (percentages)

Source: Department of Homeland Security, Office of Immigration Statistics, *2003 Yearbook of Immigration Statistics* (from Massey, 2005).

Figure 2: Origin of the undocumented population in 2010. Estimated population in thousands

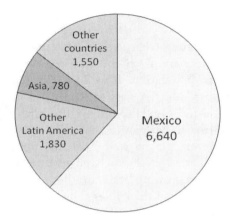

Source: Department of Homeland Security, Office of Immigration Statistics (Hoefer et al., 2010).

Demographics, Economics, and Immediate History

In the 21st century, over 20% of all Mexican-origin people in the world live in the United States, and they are an integral part of a diverse, complex, and very large Hispanic/Latino population. People of Mexican origin comprise 66% of this population (U.S. Census, 2010b), but new Hispanic immigrants also come from countries in Central America, South America, and the Caribbean, residing in many states throughout the country. The U.S. Hispanic population was estimated at 50.5 million in April 2010, not including the 3.7 million residents of Puerto Rico (U.S. Census, 2011), who are also U.S. citizens. With a birth rate significantly higher than the national average, Hispanics/Latinos constitute now 16% of the total U.S. population, 20% of all elementary and high school students, and 47% of all the foreign-born population (U.S. Census, 2010b). According to revised Census Bureau projections, the Hispanic population will reach around 133 million by the year 2050, or 30% of the total population (*Idem.*). Another projection shows that, at mid-century, non-Hispanic Whites will have dropped to half of the total population (Bergman, 2004).

Carlos G. Vélez-Ibáñez (2004), an American researcher of Mexican origin, director of the Ernesto Galarza Applied Research Center of the University of

California, Riverside, predicts a great emergence of the population of Mexican origin in the twenty-first century. Vélez-Ibáñez forecasts that, by 2100, the population of Mexican ancestry alone will make up slightly less than a third of the entire U.S. population, but could still face the challenges of economic inequality, sharp social stratification, and modest educational attainment (*Ibid.*). This population proportion is already true of Hispanics in California and Texas, the most populous states in the nation, where they represent substantially *more* than one third of the total population. If we look at birth rates as an indicator of Hispanic population trends, the state of Arizona is an illustration of astonishing growth. In this state, non-Hispanic White births have declined by 13% since 1983, but births to Hispanic women have increased by 256%. By 2004, more newborns in Arizona were Hispanic than non-Hispanic (See graph 4). Then, on December 22, 2006, the Census Bureau reported that Arizona had become the fastest-growing state in the nation (Bernstein, 2006), and Hispanics were having most of the babies. These trends are part of the reason ethnic tensions and anti-Mexican racism became exacerbated in the state throughout the first decade of the 21st century.

It is evident that the growing flow of documented and undocumented immigration to the U.S. will continue to have an impact on the demographic transformation of the country (see graph 2). People of Mexican origin in the U.S. are a clear example of this, since now 37% of them are first-generation immigrants (U.S. Census, 2010a). This reality represents new challenges and opportunities for building a nation in the future. People of Mexican ancestry in the U.S. have a median age of 25.7, compared to 36.9 for the total population, more than a 10-year difference. Incredibly, about one third of the Mexican-origin population is children, while their poverty rate is about 24% or higher (U.S. Census, 2007).

Graph 2. Number of births to women aged 15–44 in Arizona, 1983 & 2004

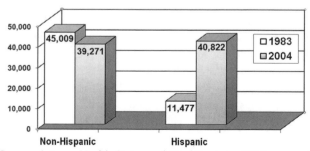

Source: Arizona Health Status and Vital Statistics 2004 report, Arizona Department of Health Services (2004).

Map 2: Nine states where 85% of all Hispanics lived in 1980

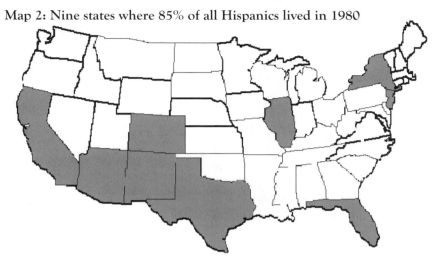

In 1980, the 9 states where the great majority of Hispanics lived were geographically and historically representative of U.S. expansionism and colonizing actions in Latin America. A clear connection was evident with the territories taken from Mexico, later migrations fueled by economic booms and the Bracero Program, as well as geopolitical and military interventions in the rest of Latin America. The nine states where 85% of Hispanics lived were: Arizona, California, Colorado, Florida, Illinois, New Mexico, New Jersey, New York, and Texas (Bean et al., 1987).

Map 3: The Hispanic expansion in 2010

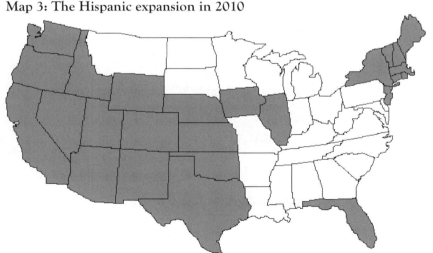

By 2010, states in which Hispanics were the largest minority group were Arizona, California, Colorado, Connecticut, Florida, Idaho, Illinois, Iowa, Kansas, Maine, Massachusetts, Nebraska, Nevada, New Hampshire, New Jersey, New Mexico, New York, Oklahoma, Oregon, Rhode Island, Texas, Utah, Vermont, Washington and Wyoming (U.S. Census, 2011).

The Pew Hispanic Center has estimated that, "Of the 29 million Latinos added due to post-1966 immigration, 17 million were immigrants and 12 million were their U.S.-born offspring" (Pew Hispanic Center, 2006b: 4). One of every five children in the U.S. is now an immigrant or a child of an immigrant, and 62% of those children are Hispanic (Perreira, Chapman, and Stein, 2006). This young generation represents an opportunity to have a more balanced fiscal system, where they will be an important part of the taxpayer base that will absorb the large number of baby-boomers retiring in the coming decades. The challenge will be to provide them with education and opportunities to grow and excel as productive citizens.

Graph 3: Portion of the last 100 million increase in population attributable to post-1966 immigrants and offspring, by race and ethnicity, 2006

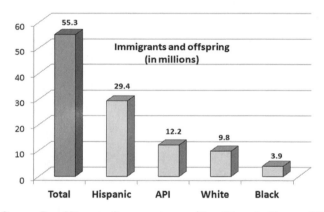

Source: Pew Hispanic Center estimates (Pew Hispanic Center, 2006b). Note: Race groups are for people of non-Hispanic origin. API refers to Asian and Pacific Islanders.

Undocumented Exploitation: The Economics of Death

The abuses against immigrants generally do not get media coverage, but an investigation by the Associated Press conducted in 2004 revealed that Mexican worker deaths were rising sharply, even as U.S. workplace safety was improving overall. According to the report, in the mid-1990s, Mexicans were about 30% more likely to die at the workplace than native-born workers, but this probability rose to about 80% in 2004. It is a "worsening epidemic" where Mexicans are almost twice as likely as other immigrants to die at work and four times more likely to die than U.S.-born workers, with an average of one victim per day (Pritchard, 2004).[11] AP's interviews with public safety officials and workers revealed that immigrants are hired to work cheaply in more risky conditions and without proper training or safety equipment. Their work culture and safety expectations do not discourage higher risk-taking and they are reluctant to complain. Moreover, in the case of undocumented immigrants, their "illegality" makes them fearful of attracting attention (Kittrie, 2006) and, even if they have legitimate grievances, they may be silent if they speak no English (Pritchard, 2004) (see Table 2).

As this goes on, the U.S. economy in general increasingly depends on immigrant labor. When the economy has grown rapidly, the pull factor attracting immigrants has been much stronger and has promoted undocumented immigration (Massey et al., 2004). Between 1996 and 2000, the economic boom in the U.S. created 14.3 million new jobs, but the country's population increased only by 12.3 million *including immigration* (Gans, 2006). Moreover, since not all the 12.3 million people were of working age, it has been estimated that 1.1 million more jobs were created per year than population growth during this five-year period (*Ibid.*). Generally, slower native population growth creates tight labor markets and raises wages, therefore attracting undocumented workers who are willing to take low-paying jobs (Hanson, 2005). Between 1990 and 2004 the foreign-born population in the U.S., both authorized and unauthorized, increased dramatically and immigrants accounted for over 50% of growth in the labor force (Gans, 2006). Even with a slowing economic growth, projections show that this trend will continue for other powerful reasons. The country does not have too many solutions to the fiscal and economic challenges imposed by demographic trends and an aging society. A baby boomer tsunami will expand the elderly population dramatically, and, by the year 2050, the foreign born will have a staggering national share of a 23% of the workforce, compared with 15% in 2005 (Passel and Cohn, 2008).

Absurdly, given this context, Mexican immigrants are dying in record numbers trying to gain access to the labor markets in the U.S. According to the Migration Policy Institute (2005), after September 11, 2001, as concerns about security increased and led to intensified border policing, border deaths increased by 41%. In 2005, a record 464 immigrants died trying to cross the U.S.-Mexico border. Incredibly, more than half of the deaths (260) occurred in the Arizona desert (Migration, 2005). By 2009, an analysis of recovered bodies determined that the risk of dying was 1.5 times higher than in 2004 and 17 times greater than in 1998 (Jiménez, 2009). Between 1994, when the North American Free Trade Agreement (NAFTA) was signed between Mexico, the U.S. and Canada,[12] and 2008, 5,607 immigrants died attempting to cross the border (*Ibid.*). The death toll has grown every year as a result of law enforcement policies that push immigrants out of more accessible areas into the remote desert. These deaths are larger in numbers to the human loses suffered in New York in the events of September 11th or in the attack on Pearl Harbor, but this almost silent mortality rate has not yet captured much political or public attention. In Arizona it has become an ignored humanitarian crisis of disturbing proportions. In the past nine years, more than 1,800 bodies of people who died trying to get into the United States have been recovered from the Sonoran desert (Robbins, 2010).

Paradoxically, as fears grow about the "unsafe" southern border and a possible terrorist attack coming through Mexico (see Malkin, 2002 and Tancredo, 2006), the U.S. depends on both undocumented Mexican immigrants and American citizens of Mexican origin for its "War on Terror." It has been reported through research and the press that an increasing number of people of Mexican origin, notoriously students, are recruited into the ranks of the U.S. military for economic reasons (Davis, 2007; Hil, 2005; Mariscal, 2005). The *New Internationalist* noted that "the green card troops" and the "poverty draft" were disproportionately made up of Mexicans and Mexican descendants, while their share of the deaths was also "disproportionately high" (Hil, 2005). In addition, it criticized the recruitment campaign that allowed recruits on active duty to apply for citizenship once they join up rather than having to wait years for the granting of a green card. The same year, the *New York Times* reported that there were increasing numbers of deaths among soldiers of Mexican origin recruited by the U.S. Army to fight in Iraq (McKinley Jr., 2005).

As explained in Chapter I, this is not something new. United Statesians of Mexican origin fought for their country and died disproportionately in World War II. Later, during the infamous Vietnam War, 19.4% of the casualties from the southwestern U.S. between 1961 and 1967 were Mexican-American. Although the great majority of Mexican-Americans lived in this region, they only comprised about 10% of the population in the Southwest in those years (Guzman, 1969). Thus, there is an obvious link between race and war but not of the type the anti-Mexican rhetoric preaches. These days, Mexican-origin Americans often enlist as a way to get an education and out of poverty. They are promised technical training and money for college after they serve. Undocumented immigrants can also become "green card marines" enticed by the massive publicity campaigns by the Pentagon targeting Hispanics/Latinos in general and by the recruiters who target high schools with heavy populations of Mexican origin (Landau, 2006). By March of 2006, when the UK announced that its troops would be reduced by 800 to 7,000 in the Middle East (BBC News, 2006), almost 25,000 undocumented Mexicans had enlisted for military service in the U.S. (Landau, 2006). Many of them had been brought to the country by their parents when they were children; they attended school in the U.S. and speak English, but they never had the opportunity to become citizens. These undocumented Americans of Mexican origin are undoubtedly United Statesians in their minds and hearts. By 2006, Mexican-origin people made up 13% of the Marine Corps, by far exceeding the proportion of Mexican-origin Americans in the total population (*Ibid.*).

Meanwhile, in Arizona, legislation imposes severe penalties on employers who hire undocumented workers, while it is estimated that one in ten workers in the state is undocumented. In 2007 *The Economist* predicted that if the law were applied, it would harm the state's economy; therefore it would not be strictly enforced (*The Economist*, 2007). Research by the Udall Center for Studies in Public Policy at The University of Arizona also supported the prediction, which has proved correct. The Udall Center has estimated that immigrant workers generate about 12 percent of Arizona's economic output and that immigrants, including non-citizens, make an important contribution to the state (Gans, 2007). For now, as other state laws that in the past have been found unfeasible or even unconstitutional, this type of legislation increases the exploitability and vulnerability of undocumented immigrants (see for example, Cacho, 2000 on the effects of Proposition 187 in California). Therefore, as hundreds of unsuccessful migrants die in the Arizona desert every year, the ones who make it through the border will continue to help boost economic growth, reduce inflationary pressure, and fill labor shortages (*The Economist*, 2001; *Wall Street Journal*, 2006). Such is the economics of death and hypocrisy surrounding the immediate history of the immigration phenomenon in the U.S.

The dominant stories, pieces of the colonizing "regime of truth," and the Master Narrative of American History exclude the other side of memory; the memory of those driven by historical, social, and economic realities in their movement across borders and cultures. They will continue to cross the border to reunite with their families and to meet the voracious demand for immigrant workers in the large services and agricultural sectors of the U.S. economy (Rozental, 2007; Hirsch, 2005). Their challenges will be many if they want to be part of an egalitarian and democratic society, but perhaps the most important will be educational development.

Notes

[1] U.S. agencies define *Hispanic* or *Latino* as "a person of Cuban, Mexican, Puerto Rican, South or Central American or other Spanish culture or origin regardless of race" (Martin and Gerber, 2005: 2). See Glossary for a more complete explanation.

[2] International law does not recognize the annexation of territories by conquest. Ironically, precedent was established in the twentieth century by the United States itself through the "Stimson Doctrine," in 1932, by which the U.S. government did not recognize the take-over of Manchuria by Japanese troops. "The following year, the Assembly of the League of Nations passed a resolution stating that 'it is incumbent upon the members of the League of Nations not to recognize any situation, treaty or agreement which may be brought about by means contrary to the Covenant of the League of Nations or to the Pact of Paris'" (quoted in Malanczuk and Akehurst, 1997: 152).

[3] At the time, the U.S. dollar and the Mexican peso had the same monetary value.

[4] Mexico is currently the third largest trading partner for the U.S., and, while China has become its second most important trade partner in total trade numbers, Mexico purchases almost twice the amount of U.S. goods as China (U.S. Census Bureau and U.S. Bureau of Economic Analysis, 2010). U.S. exports to Mexico are greater than U.S. exports to all Latin American countries combined (*Idem*). In 1995, the mighty U.S. financial system received a frightful lesson on how its destiny could be linked to the much weaker Mexican economy. At the time, the so-called "Tequila Effect," caused by Mexico's currency crisis, provoked a domino effect throughout the world's emerging markets and threatened to destabilize the U.S. and the entire world economy (*Washington Post*, 1996). On a different dimension, Americans of Mexican origin and Mexican immigrants are determinant factors in the "Hispanicization" of important regions throughout the United States. The U.S. now has a Hispanic population that surpasses the entire populations of Canada or Spain (CIA, 2010), while native and bilingual speakers now make the United States the second largest Spanish-speaking country on Earth (*Idem*.). As a market, Hispanic Americans in the U.S. represent the equivalent of the 10th largest economy in the world, with a purchasing power that surpasses the economies of Brazil or Spain (Wilmot, 2006).

[5] It is not a coincidence that large percentages of the population in the states of Arizona (31%), California (37%), Colorado (20%), Nevada (26%), New Mexico (46%), and Texas (37%) are Hispanic (U.S. Census, 2010b). Almost 60% of all Hispanics in the U.S. live today in these formerly Mexican territories. At the national level, the population of Mexican origin in the United States surpassed 30 million in 2009, while the total Hispanic population reached 48,400,000 (*Idem*). Additionally, also for historical and geopolitical reasons, the largest proportions of Cuban and Puerto Rican Americans live in the states of New York and Florida, which have Hispanic populations that surpass seven million (Pew Hispanic Center, 2010).

[6] When the Southwestern U.S. was still part of Mexico, Europeans, French-Canadians, and Anglo-Americans had settled there and become Mexican, as they did in other parts of the country (Nostrand, 1975).

[7] The term "wetback" alludes to the fact that many undocumented immigrants swim across the Rio Grande River in order to get to the United States. The words wetback and its equivalent in Spanish (*mojado*) are commonly used in a pejorative sense to refer to Mexican-origin people in the United States.

[8] Ronald Takaki, quoting George Orwell, in his answer to the question: *Who owns history?* (Takaki, 2007b).

[9] To put this figure in comparative perspective, when the size of the undocumented Mexican economy was estimated (2001) the Chilean and the Venezuelan economies were smaller. Chile's GDP was estimated at 115.6 billion at official exchange rates in 2005, while Venezuela's GDP was estimated at 106.1 billion for the same year (CIA, 2006). As an indicator of the economic activity generated by these hard-working people, just in a three month period in California, undocumented immigrants made bank deposits of $50 million (Renshon, 2005: 243).

[10] With the term *transnational economic survival*, we refer to the fact that, although families are increasingly divided by the U.S.-Mexico border, they have strong economic links across the political boundaries. For instance, according to the Inter-American Development Bank, in 2009, Mexicans living in the U.S. sent over US$21 billion in remittances to family members in Mexico (http://www.iadb.org/mif/remesas_map.cfm?language=English).

[11] Also in 2004, the *American Journal of Industrial Medicine* revealed that, between 1992 and 2000, Hispanic construction workers were nearly twice as likely to be killed by occupational injuries as their non-Hispanic counterparts (Dong and Platner, 2004). Similarly, California farmworkers—most of whom are people of Mexican origin—have high levels of leukemia and stomach, uterine and brain cancer, but most farmworkers have few options for other employment. Most of them are recent, non-English-speaking immigrants and more than half are undocumented. Thus, relatively few complain to state or federal agencies for fear of losing their job or being deported (Clarren, 2003).

[12] The North American Free Trade Agreement, or NAFTA, was signed by the governments of Canada, Mexico and the United States in order to liberalize trade relations among the three countries. The Agreement is a model of economic integration that facilitates the movements of capital, investment, goods and services across borders, and it was expected to boost employment in Mexico. However, as large multinational corporations have displaced Mexican small businesses, the country has not created enough jobs to keep up with demand (Moody, 2007). Paradoxically, the movement of labor across borders, a key component of economic integration in other parts of the world, has become more restricted for Mexicans who want to emigrate to the U.S. Meanwhile, the Mexican government has suppressed wages and labor organizations in order to attract foreign investment, which in turn has intensified the push factor that encourages emigration to the United States (Bacon, 2004b).

Navigating Educational Borders:
Barriers, Bridges and Paths

Colonialism imposes "distinction" as an ideological yardstick against which all other cultural values are measured, including language. On the one hand, this ideological yardstick serves to overcelebrate the dominant group's language to a level of mystification (i.e., viewing English as education itself and measuring the success of bilingual programs only in terms of success in English acquisition) and, on the other hand, it devalues other languages spoken by an ever-increasing number of students who now populate most urban public schools.

—Donaldo Macedo (2000: 16)

Deficit thinking exists when educators interpret differences as deficits, dysfunctions and disadvantages. Consequently, many diverse students quickly acquire the "at-risk" label and there is a focus on their shortcomings rather than their strengths. This thinking hinders the ability and willingness of educators to recognize the strengths of students from diverse ethnic, racial, and language groups

—Donna Y. Ford (2005: 381)

After the U.S.-Mexico War, the most generalized distinction of the new United Statesians of Mexican origin, including many indigenous and most *mestizo* and white Mexicans, was the widespread use of Spanish. The language of the first European colonizers had culturally connected the diverse peoples of Mexico during 300 years of Spanish domination. After they became United Statesians by conquest, the best historical example of how the new dominant system colonized Mexican-Americans was the restriction of their language. Through language, people not only perceive the world but understand themselves. Therefore, the prohibition of Spanish made it easier to socially and politically marginalize Mexican-Americans and subsequently served as a tool in their systematic denigration and racialization (González, N., 2001; Moreno, 1999). This process facilitated the establishment of the colonizer-colonized relationship where Mexican-Americans lost a large portion of their original culture and even began to view Mexicanness in a negative sense

(Delgado-Bernal, 1999). Consequently great numbers of Mexican-origin Americans began to be assimilated into the dominant society through the imposition of the colonizers' language.

N. González (2001), who has interviewed Mexican-origin women and children in Tucson, Arizona, places language in the context of social processes, hegemony, and power. She asserts that, since childhood, Mexican-Americans develop an "emotion of minority status." Such emotion is caused by a message of "foreignness" or "otherness" that is effectively transmitted through legislation—like English Only laws—the media, and multiple societal and institutional elements (*Ibid.*). Thus, although achieving citizenship has afforded some privileges to many immigrants, like the right to vote and free education, it also has brought great disadvantages, like having to deny their native tongue, struggling to learn a new language, and being subject to many forms of discrimination (Nieto, 1996; Raymond and Sesnowitz, 1983; Suárez-Orozco and Páez, 2002)—sometimes disguised in the process of "Americanization."

After the U.S.-Mexico War that forced Mexico to cede half of its territory to the United States, the Treaty of Guadalupe-Hidalgo guaranteed that those Mexicans living in the new United Statesian territories and who chose to become citizens of the U.S. would have ". . . the enjoyment of all the rights of citizens of the United States, according to the principles of the Constitution . . . ." as well as ". . . the free enjoyment of their liberty and property, and secured in the free exercise of their religion without restriction" (*Treaty*, Article IX: 13–14). Therefore, since the former Mexican citizens only spoke Spanish, they would justly have the "liberty" and "rights" to speak and preserve their own language and culture. Furthermore, as forms of cultural "property," Native American and Spanish languages from the former Mexican territories should have been protected in consonance with the Treaty as well as under the First and Fifth Amendments of the U.S. Constitution.

At that point, the only way to preserve the right to equity would have been to preserve the right to use their language in courts, economic transactions, public affairs, and education. On the contrary, the lack of respect for Mexican culture and language soon became evident as new laws and policies were enacted negatively affecting the first United Statesians of Mexican origin (Acuña, 2003; Hernández, 2001). As early as 1855, a law in California prohibited the translation of laws and regulations, while Texas forbade the use of Spanish interpreters at election polls (Stacy, 2003). In 1899 Arizona enacted a bill (Title XIX) establishing English as the official language of instruction in public schools in spite of the fact that Mexican children comprised over 50% of all school age children in the state (Ruiz, 2001). The Native American ancestry of most Mexicans made them a lesser dark-skinned race, while white

Mexicans had "an ambiguous position in the racial order" (Powers, 2008: 469); thus they were systematically segregated. Clearly, at a time when skin color determined people's opportunities in life, their language and culture were considered inferior.

Language was then, as it is today, an essential element of ethnic identity and

> English is a crucial symbol of the ethnicity of America's dominant core culture. Language can be a symbol of group status, a symbol of dominance, and a symbol of participation in or exclusion from the political process. Campaigns to make a language standard or official can thus be seen as attempts to create or reinforce the dominance of the culture of which the language forms an integral part (Perea, 1992).

At the beginning of the twentieth century, Americanization policies were aggressively implemented, while educational policies for Mexican children had the aim of making them ready for "Mexican" occupations (Lucero, 2004). This approach was based on the notion that Mexicans were culturally inferior and could not be acceptable American citizens without their culture and language being eradicated. Consequently, schools would place Mexican children in separate classes for "language deficiencies." The main objective of these programs was Americanization and not academic achievement (Aman, 2005; Lucero, 2004).[1] The highest educational opportunities to which Mexican-origin students could aspire were in vocational training, intended to prepare them for labor-intensive, low-paying jobs (Gonzalez, 1990, 2001).

The assimilation of Mexican children was the clear aim of educational policy in this period. At this point, Mexicans did not assimilate particularly well, but this had more to do with the fact that only whites could enjoy the benefits of full citizenship. Even white Mexicans stubbornly spoke a language and preserved a culture that were not considered "white." Moreover, even when many of them and their ancestors had been in the Southwest before it became part of the U.S., they were treated as outsiders and immigrants. Such racial differentiation was supported by a racist state and federal laws. In fact, racial obstacles to citizenship for immigrants were not eliminated until the McCarran-Walter Act of 1952, and white racial preferences remained until the Immigration and Nationality Act of 1965.

Today, many Mexican-origin Americans and new Mexican immigrants continue to live with low family incomes, low educational attainment, and great numbers of them outside of the mainstream society. One reason they are perceived as different involves a cultural conflict between the values they preserve and the values shared by the dominant society in the United States. Schools are a natural battleground where these divergent values collide

(Dotson-Blake, 2006) and, generally, where the dogmas of the dominant society are imposed (Córdova, 2005).

Education as a Battlefield: Counter-Memories from Combat Zones

Mexican-Americans have a long history of struggle for civil rights and educational equality. The exclusion of their legal fight for school desegregation from major law books has been criticized by Richard Valencia (2008), who points at thirty-five cases of desegregation lawsuits by Mexican-Americans between 1925 and 1985. Such scholarly omission is attributed to "the Black/White paradigm of race" that produces the misperception that Mexican-Americans, Chicanos, and Hispanics/Latinos do not need civil rights protections as much as African-Americans (Valencia, 2008: 1). Schools have played a significant role in the inculcation of dominant values, keeping Mexican students subordinated via the cultural relationships and belief systems indoctrinated through the curriculum (Valenzuela, 1999). Schools are a powerful instrument of indoctrination and, through this medium, Mexican culture and language have been systematically minimized through laws, educational policies, and practices (*Ibid.*).

Internal colonization through the official educational system engenders alienation, detachment from history and community, and even self-hatred (Córdova, 2005). Scholars, however, offer widely divergent interpretations of the colonizer-colonized analysis. For example, while Roberts (2000) recognizes the present era of neo-colonialism, he suggests that getting rid of the European legacy is not decisive. In contrast, Bowers (1983) sees even Freire's pedagogy of liberation as another form of cultural invasion. In any case, it appears that a racial component has consistently been an underlying ingredient in the struggle of resistance against colonization (Barndt, 2007; San Miguel and Valencia, 1998). A brief historical account of some of the struggles of Mexican-Americans in the educational arena clearly illustrates this.

Throughout the first half of the twentieth century, children of Mexican origin were publicly humiliated and abused physically and verbally for speaking Spanish on school grounds (Powers, 2008). Sheridan (1986) narrates the story of Carmen Villa, a resident of Tucson, Arizona who remembered how in the late 1950s, as a first grader, she had her mouth washed out with soap for speaking Spanish. She also recalled an Anglo principal telling Mexican children that they "would never amount to anything unless they forgot every word of their native tongue" (*Ibid.*: 219). These stories are very common among Americans of Mexican origin who lived through those years and among their children and family members who heard the stories. At the time, high school dropout rates for students of Mexican origin were extremely high. Educators would not encourage Mexican students to go to college because, in their eyes, they did not have the mental skills to achieve academic success and would not need a higher education for the kind of jobs they were expected to do.

In Texas, a renowned researcher in the field of intelligence measurement, Lewis Terman, exerted great influence in the educational arena. In 1916, Terman argued that the Spanish, Indian-Mexican, and Negroes of the Southwest should not breed. In his view, they were genetically unintelligent races and therefore

> No amount of school instruction will ever make them intelligent voters or capable citizens. . . . They cannot master abstractions, but they can often be made efficient workers (Terman quoted by Blanton, 2003: 43).

In Colorado, where the sugar beet industry created a voracious demand for cheap labor, the Great Western Sugar Company aggressively recruited workers in Mexico and child labor was a common practice (Donato, 2003). In a study of an agricultural community in northern Colorado, Donato (2003) concludes that "Mexican Americans were not expected to rise beyond their station in life beyond manual workers, they were not accepted into the local mainstream, and they were not expected to stay in school after the elementary/junior high school years" (84). In Arizona, laws mandated more severe segregation of African-Americans than those existing in most other western states, while school officials segregated Mexican-Americans without the sanction of law (Melcher, 1999). Officials based the segregation of African Americans on their desire to separate the races while they justified the segregation of Mexican-Americans of any ethnic origin by pointing to the need for English instruction and gradual assimilation. In both cases, racism was the true essence of segregation (López, 2004). These conditions were not always accepted without a struggle, even during periods when civil rights activists faced great challenges. Such is the case of the struggle of Mexican women in Arizona against segregation between 1925 and 1950, whose oral histories were documented by Mary Melcher (1999). Mexican-American women, with the support of African-American and Euro-American allies, challenged state laws that banned the use of Spanish in schools in order to bring greater intercultural understanding and racial equality. Like activists in other areas of the nation, they were motivated by a variety of concerns, including the desire to protect their children, foster racial support, or gain equal rights. Through this process, they resisted institutional structures that subordinated minorities through the educational system.

After World War II, the most important organizing efforts of Mexican-Americans have emphasized education (Samora and Vandel-Simon, 1993). From a Critical Race Theory approach, Valencia (2005) argues that most people in the United States are unaware of the essential role that Mexican-Americans have played in some of the most important struggles regarding school desegregation. The case of *Mendez vs. Westminster* (1946), a lawsuit filed on behalf of more than 5,000 Mexican-American students in Orange County, California, became the first successful constitutional challenge to segregation. The U.S. District Court ruled that Mexican-American students' rights were being violated under the equal protection granted by the Fourteenth Amendment. A number of legal scholars at the time saw this as a case that could have accomplished what *Brown vs. Board of Education of Topeka* finally did in 1954, reversing 60 years of legal segregation. *Mendez* and *Brown* were strongly connected, the former serving as a foundation for the latter (Valencia, 2005).

In the fifties and sixties, Mexicans actually witnessed legislation against segregation in schools, but judicial decisions also ignored desegregation (Melcher, 1999). In 1954, the same year the Supreme Court ruled that "separate educational facilities are inherently unequal," Hispanics won another legal battle in *Hernandez v. Texas*. In this case, the Supreme Court decided that the equal protection guaranteed by the Fourteenth Amendment not only included blacks and whites, but all racial groups. In reality, actual implementation of new laws was slow and sometimes careless, while *de facto* segregation of students of Mexican origin continued (Hernandez, 1995). School officials in general continued justifying it and, implicitly, furthering the concomitant colonizer-colonized mentality. Segregation continued long after it was found to be illegal by the courts (Melcher, 1999). Conflict between ideologies, confusion in the legislature, and delays in fulfilling the spirit of the law allowed the continuity of old vices and attitudes. There was an important part of the dominant society who still believed that Mexicans were culturally inferior. Mexicans were (again) proclaimed to be abnormal, ignorant, backward, unclean, and unambitious people (see Delgado-Bernal, 1999; Haney-López, 2003; Rendón, 1996; Weinberg, 1977).

At precisely the same time when *Brown vs. Board of Education* officially ended school segregation for African-Americans, Congress was enacting Operation Wetback. Critical Theory has referred to these historical contradictions as a form of scapegoating in which members of powerful groups discharge frustration on nonmembers who are not the cause of that frustration but who are safer to attack (Delgado, 2003). Indeed, a *de facto* segregation of children of Mexican origin, especially of immigrants, would continue to be the norm in public education, often justified with the pretext of language education (Van Hook and Balistreri, 2002). Roseann Dueñas González, a scholar who grew up in Arizona in the 1950s, has narrated how she realized at an early age that "Sorry I don't speak Mexican" became a cover for "Mexicans aren't served here," a common phrase in her youth (Dueñas González, 2000: xxii).

School officials took little interest in solving these problems until the League of United Latin American Citizens (LULAC), an organization founded by United Statesians of Mexican origin, became involved in the fight to end segregation for real (Hernandez, 1995). LULAC had been founded in 1929, but during the 1960s and the early 1970s, other organizations were formed for the express purposes of seeking recognition, justice, and better opportunities for Mexican-Americans and Chicanos. The aim was to empower these citizens to endorse candidates, to take stands on issues, to register them as voters, and to increase their political participation. From different fronts, Chicano and Mexican-American activism played a crucial role in the attempts to end school segregation and racism in the 1960s. In 1960, the American Coordinating Council on Political Education (ACCPE) of Arizona was founded in Phoenix to provide political support to elect a Mexican-American principal in the Phoenix Elementary School District (Samora and Vandel-Simon, 1993). This goal would not be achieved until 23 years later, when Louis P. Rodriguez became the first Mexican-American superintendent of the Phoenix Elementary School District (Ibid.). In 1965, the Association of Mexican American Educators (AMAE) was created in California in response to the educational inequalities experienced by Latino/Mexican-American students. Student groups like the Mexican American Youth Association (MAYA), the United Mexican-American Students (UMAS), and the Mexican-American Student Association (MASA) were also born in California; while the Mexican-American Youth Organization (MAYO) emerged in Texas. All of them had the common goal of obtaining access to fair and quality education (Delgado-Bernal, 1998). In 1968, Chicano students founded a chapter of UMAS at the University of Washington. The same year, the Mexican American Legal Defense and Education Fund (MALDEF) was born in San Antonio, Texas.

Clearly, by the end of the 1960s, students and educators of Mexican origin had become more politicized and reacted strongly to educational injustices. They protested and demanded educational change through the use of walkouts or "blowouts" (Chávez, 2002; Meier and Gutierrez, 2000). The changes they wanted included the right to have Mexican-American educators and administrators, bilingual programs, smaller class sizes, multicultural education for all students and educators, and other legitimate demands (Chávez, 2002; Meier and Gutierrez, 2000; Rendón, 1996; Weinberg, 1977). Most protests occurred in Los Angeles, but many other cities were involved, including Chicago and New York (*Ibid.*). Before the protests, in 1968, the government had begun to fund bilingual education through Title VII of the Elementary and Secondary Education Act of 1965. However, it appears that this endeavor turned out to be more a compensatory education than a way to solve inequality. Some educators maintain that this legislation was indeed a modest effort toward equality but believe that such legislation helped those in power more than the people it was supposed to help (Matsuda et al., 1993). Consequently, students themselves began to be directly involved in the socio-political movement for justice and organized and participated in protests. They were part of a larger ferment throughout the country that conjugated powerful forces like the Black Civil Rights struggle, the anti-Vietnam War movement, the Feminist Movement, the promises of the War on Poverty, and revolutionary struggles in other parts of the world (Delgado-Bernal, 1999; García, 1999). For the first time in the U.S., multitudinous young, forceful, and vociferous United Statesians of Mexican origin demanded change in the educational and sociopolitical arenas. Racial prejudice against the protesters led to police brutality and judicial discrimination that in turn incited Chicano militancy. Countless student leaders and community activists of the time deserve recognition for their relentless struggle for justice. Names, however, are omitted in deference to each and every one of those who participated in the struggle.

During the school blowouts in East Los Angeles, almost ten thousand students walked out of their classes to protest the inferior quality of their education. Organizations like MASA and UMAS played a central role in the organization of the movement. Nevertheless, it is also important to highlight the leadership assumed by Chicanas in the struggle. (Delgado-Bernal, 1998) interviewed eight key female leaders in a unique oral history project where she argues that, before this counter-narrative project, their story had only been told by males with a focus on males. As a self-defined Chicana, Delgado-Bernal recovers "the women's voices that have been omitted from the diverse historical accounts of the Blowouts—particularly those women who were key participants" (114). Despite the many boycotts, protests, and demonstrations by thousands of students, which occurred throughout the U.S. in this period, bureaucracy prevailed and educational injustices and racism were addressed very slowly, if at all (Chávez, 2002; Rendón, 1996). During the 1960s and 1970s, most scholars would highlight the African-American struggle for equal education during this period under the assumption that Mexican-American children were educated by a neutral system. Quite the contrary, public schools practiced widespread ethnic, linguistic and class prejudices.

During the early seventies, tensions continued regarding desegregation and bilingual education. There was a major funding cut in bilingual education, and school finances were drastically reduced for Mexican-American students (Delgado-Bernal, 1999). However, successful lawsuits during the same period, such as *Lau vs. Nichols* (1974) and *Serna vs. Portales Municipal Schools* (1974), have later served to assist students whose first language is not the primary language in the United States (Delgado-Bernal, 1999). Many Mexican-Americans began to question the high dropout rate and low achievement of their youth. *Lau vs. Nichols* became a landmark case establishing that failure to provide non-English-speaking Chinese students a comprehensive education denied them equal educational opportunities. This case triggered a renewed interest in ESL and bilingual education programs that benefited people of Mexican origin and other minorities. It was an important lesson for Mexican-Americans (Donato, 1997). In 1975, a Texas state law banned undocumented children from attending public schools and numerous lawsuits were filed in defense of the rights of the affected children. In 1982, the Supreme Court would rule against the Texas law because of its infringement of the U.S. Constitution. The Equal Protection Clause of the Fourteenth Amendment provides rights to all human beings, including unauthorized immigrants. In other words, these are not citizen or United Statesian rights but simply human rights. This ruling has been considered as an equivalent of *Brown v. Board of Education* in the Latino struggle for educational equality (Valencia, 2008). By then, Mexican-Americans had learned that legislative support was essential to win their struggle for equality and to transform the educational system.

The Chicano movement and communities around the United States had successfully put pressure on colleges and universities because of their failure to provide equal educational opportunities to students from different ethnic groups. In response to the pressures, educational institutions began to establish Black, Chicano, and other ethnic studies. In a way, ethnic studies were forced upon some colleges and universities by the actions and active demonstrations of minority groups and their supporters (Samora and Vandel-Simon, 1993), but this pressure was short lived. By the end of the 1970s, universities had diminished their initial commitment to equal opportunity. In order to minimize their failure to attract poor Chicano/Mexican-American students, universities selected from the socioeconomic elite of the Hispanic community, using Cubans, South Americans, and middle-class Mexican-Americans to fill their recruitment quotas. The target became Hispanics/Latinos in general with less attention paid to underprivileged students of Mexican origin (*Ibid.*).

Nevertheless, after the Civil Rights Movement of the sixties and seventies, much legislation has occurred in defense of minority students. Affirmative

Action, for example, provided opportunities to individuals who had histori-cally been denied opportunities because of discrimination by race, sex, disabil-ity, or national origin. Its policies have had a great impact in the educational arena, and it has been a hotly debated issue in many colleges and universities (Skrentny, 1996). Supporters of Affirmative Action cite as justification the historical instances when Americans of Mexican origin and Hispanics in general have been exposed to unequal, unfair, and separate educational re-sources (Rendón, 1996; Suárez-Orozco and Páez, 2002). Conversely, oppo-nents believe Affirmative Action quotas are morally wrong and a socially destructive form of "reverse racism" (O'Sullivan, 1995).

In the eighties, the conservative policies of the Reagan era had a negative effect on Mexican-American schooling (Delgado-Bernal, 1999). There was a widespread drive to do away with social equity programs put into place by President Johnson's War on Poverty (Fendrich, 1983; Rendón, 1996). Con-servatives began to increase military spending and reduce educational spend-ing (Rendón, 1996), while other reforms created more inequality among minorities (Fendrich, 1983). Among such reforms, Samora and Vandel-Simon (1993) point at the strong trend towards reversing bilingual and bicultural programs and legislation in favor of English-only education. The inequality created by these policies has been corroborated in a more recent study by Zavodny (2000), where it was found that male workers with limited English proficiency who live in states with English-only laws experience an earnings loss relative to other men. Zavodny concludes that, even if these laws are not intended to be discriminatory, they can have a discriminatory effect on people who do not speak or read English fluently. The same decade, it was recognized that economic competition was "the Sputnik of the 1980s" and that the nation had to acknowledge that "educational attainment of its people is an intrinsic element of national economic well-being" (Jennings, 1987: 104). Ironically, not enough attention was paid to the fastest-growing sector of the secondary student population, Hispanic-origin children.

In the nineties, anti-Mexican and anti-immigrant sentiments were exacer-bated in the Southwest and expanded to the rest of the country (Johnston, 2001; Michelson, 2001). In 1994, Proposition 187 passed in California deny-ing undocumented workers public education and public health care. Both Mexican-American citizens and undocumented immigrants were harassed and became the target of hate groups inside and outside California. Michelson (2001) hypothesizes that Mexican-Americans became more concerned about racism and discrimination and acted accordingly. Mexican-Americans and Mexican immigrants organized some of the largest demonstrations to occur since the Vietnam era and high school students in Los Angeles, once again, walked out of their classes in protest (Gutiérrez, 1999). They and their families had suddenly become "guilty" of all the economic troubles of the state. Later, the U.S. Supreme Court declared the proposition illegal.

During this period, a positive trend also emerged when many colleges in progressive states took on the socio-economic challenge posited by undocumented immigration by offering in-state tuition to undocumented residents. The rationale was pragmatically simple and it has had a life-changing impact on these young people: Education dramatically increases their average future earnings and, therefore, the amount of taxes they will pay to the states where they reside. At the same time, the argument goes, it reduces criminal justice and social services costs to taxpayers (Dervarics, 2006). By 2005–2006, at least nine states with high immigration flows—including California, New York, and Texas—would enact legislation allowing undocumented students to pay in-state tuition (Drachman, 2006). But not all states with a high proportion of unauthorized immigrants adopted the same approach. Arizona, with one of the highest proportion of undocumented immigrants (Passel, 2005), has never joined the states that offer in-state tuition to undocumented residents. The children of these taxpayers are allowed to attend public elementary schools and high schools but usually do not have the means to attend higher education institutions. In order to enroll in college they have to pay out-of-state tuition, even if they have resided and paid taxes in the state most of their lives.

After the turmoil created by Proposition 187, some states enacted legislation to deny bilingual instruction, higher education, and public services to undocumented immigrants. A new wave of twenty-first century racism, xenophobia and anti-immigrant sentiment was emerging across the nation (Redden, 2006; SPL Center, 2007). In the early 2000s, anti-immigrant racism has infamously attacked Mexican-origin people who, irrespective of their history in the country—or perhaps because of it—are seen as outsiders (De Genova, 2005). One of the reasons for their perpetual "otherness" is the growing flow of undocumented Mexican immigrants, though they are not alone. In 2006, hundreds of thousands of undocumented immigrants from different national origins and their sympathizers flooded the streets of major U.S. cities demanding immigration legislation reform. Their protests were perceived as a "new civil rights movement" (Robinson, 2006). Undocumented students and the children of undocumented immigrants also left their classrooms to demand regularization of their immigrant status (Fine et al., 2007).

In 2004, Proposition 200 passed in Arizona denying basic public services to undocumented residents. As a result of the negative coverage and intimidation, unauthorized immigrants and undocumented Americans were more hesitant to go through the formal process of enrolling at community colleges, even in basic adult education courses (Gabusi, 2005). In 2006, Arizona voters passed a law prohibiting undocumented immigrant students from getting state-funded scholarships, tuition and fee waivers and other financial assistance. The new law denied undocumented immigrants "in-state" college tuition, even if they had resided and paid taxes in Arizona all of their lives. Since they now have to pay like international or out-of-state students, the cost of attending higher education is inaccessible for the great majority of them (Billeaud, 2007). Traditionally, the community college had been the most accessible higher education institution available to immigrants (Bagnato, 2005; Szelényi and Chang, 2002). Thus these young people, who most likely will remain in the United States, are condemned to perpetuate a Mexican-American underclass. Their tragedy is that they grew up in the U.S. and graduated from U.S. high schools, but Arizona laws make it extremely difficult for them to enroll in community colleges and universities. In February 2007, another law (Proposition 300) banned immigrants from attending adult education and from obtaining child care assistance and scholarships provided by the state. The law did not ban undocumented residents from higher education but makes tuition unaffordable for the great majority by denying them in-state tuition (Community College Week, 2007). During the first six months the law was in effect, over 4,600 people in Arizona were denied state financial aid, prevented from paying in-state tuition, or rejected from adult-education classes (Hebel, 2007a). This clashes with the financial principle of community colleges by which the community subsidizes education for its residents from their own taxes. In return, the community becomes more competitive, skilled, and productive, hence creating a virtuous economic circle. Arizona, however, passed even harsher immigration laws that earned negative world attention and served as a models for other states. The states of Alabama, Georgia, and South Carolina specifically enacted laws that ban undocumented students from public higher education, even if they can afford to pay for it.

Optimists have pointed out that the conditions of Mexican-Americans have gradually improved during the past five decades thanks to the Civil Rights Movement (Grogger and Trejo, 2002; Lewis, 1988). Under the 1968 Bilingual Education Act, school districts have to assign resources for the training of teachers and development of instructional materials to help students who do not speak English; overtly racist administrators, teachers, and policies have been removed in many institutions; and diverse cultures are now included in school curricula (Salas, 2003). Thus, D'Souza (1996) criticizes the "neurotic obsession" with race that continues to divide U.S. society, while Sowell (1984, 2004) argues against affirmative action and the "civil rights establishment." Nevertheless, such arguments were uttered as a right-wing educational movement was trying to overcome deficits with "standards" (Pearl, 2002) and intensified efforts to lessen the hard-won gains of the Civil Rights Movement. In the twenty-first century, affirmative action for the disadvantaged continues to be under attack, while affirmative action for the privileged receives no serious scrutiny (Tierno, 2007). Other researchers point out that multicultural education, bilingual education, and affirmative action have been under attack by the U.S. neo-conservative movement since the Reagan era (Rhoads, Saenz, and Carducci, 2005; Valenzuela, 1999).

This debate has continued during the administration of the first African American president, but the roots of racism are still "embedded and intertwined in the life and history . . . of our nation" (Barndt, 2007: 13). Race is clearly an element in educational achievement. In 2008, 18.3% of Hispanics between the ages of 16 and 24 had neither completed a high school program nor were enrolled in high school, compared to 9.9% of blacks and 4.8% of whites in the same age range (Baum et al., 2010). A lack of money and resources limits educational opportunities, but money alone cannot eliminate all the obstacles faced by many of these minorities (*Ibid.*). In 2008, Hispanic college enrollment immediately after high school was 8 percentage points below the white enrollment rate. A short-term, optimistic view can point to the fact that eight years earlier, in 2000, the gap between Hispanic and white high school graduates enrolling in college was 19%. Hence an obvious progress has been achieved. However, "In the mid-1970s, Hispanic high school graduates were as likely as white graduates to enroll immediately in college" (Baum et al., 2010: 35). This shows that progress is not always linear and, notwithstanding significant improvements, regressions can occur as social movements, economic circumstances, and policy and fiscal prescriptions collide.

Regression appears to be the dominant trend for economically disadvantaged Americans of Mexican origin and for undocumented United Statesians. Even for the U.S.-born children of undocumented immigrants, the increasing anti-immigrant legislation and social exclusion of their parents translates into economic hardship and family stress, which, in turn, affect child development and educational achievement (Yoshikawa, Godfrey, and Rivera, 2008). Stereotyping, racial discrimination, intimidation, legal marginalization, and low academic expectations affect them all, citizen or not. Such is the educational climate that minorities and undocumented Americans of Mexican ancestry face, but educational inequality is only one of the elements of an unjust system that perpetuates the status quo. Race, socioeconomic status, language, and unfair institutional structures define the boundaries of success and social mobility (Kay-Oliphant, 2005; Rodríguez, R., 1997). In the following section we draw on research findings from key studies in the field in order to expand this perspective. We examine the multifaceted dimensions where the above-mentioned structures define the lives of immigrants and citizens who have been constructed as "perpetual foreigners" (Rocco, 2004).

Determinants of Failure and Achievement in Students of Mexican Origin

When seeking the determinants of academic success and failure among United Statesians of Mexican origin, it matters greatly whether students or their parents were born in the United States or in Mexico. A notoriously higher proportion of *Hispanic* immigrants drop out of school before earning their high-school diplomas (44% in 2003), compared with those born in the United States (Schmidt, 2003). In 2010, a report by America's Promise Alliance, Civic Enterprises, and the Everyone Graduates Center at Johns Hopkins University revealed that high school graduation rates had risen at U.S. schools. Nevertheless, the research also found that, on average, almost 40% of minority students (African-American, Hispanic, and Native American) continued to fail to graduate from high school (Balfanz et al., 2010).

In higher education, U.S.-born children of Hispanic immigrants have comparable college enrollment rates with their White peers, yet they are less than half as likely to graduate from four-year universities (Lane, 2002). Another salient difference about Hispanics in general is that 40% of Hispanic-origin college students between 18 and 24 are enrolled in community colleges and two-year institutions, compared with 25% of black and 25% of White students (Schmidt, 2003). However, the term "Hispanic," officially utilized by government agencies, conceals important demographic differences. For example, Mexican-American students 18 to 24 are about half as likely as their Puerto Rican or Cuban-American peers to be enrolled in community colleges (*Ibid.*). "Students of Mexican descent are dropping out of school at nearly three times the rate of their Cuban American counterparts, while also scoring significantly lower on Stanford achievement tests than Cuban, Nicaraguan, and Colombian Americans." (Ream, 2005: 7). The majority of college students of Hispanic/Latino origin are U.S. citizens, but Mexican-origin Americans in general have more difficulties, while those without documents have enormous challenges. These realities mean that the six Americans whose stories are told in this book were among the most vulnerable students in their quest for educational achievement. With the goal of explaining salient challenges and vulnerabilities faced by these students, the following section provides a summary of issues identified in the literature. The examples by no means represent a comprehensive literary review but are illustrative of what could be termed "counter-research." They demonstrate alternative perspectives that challenge the Master Narrative of American History and support the counter-narratives in this book.

Race, Class, and Discrimination: "Mexicans Are Dirty"[2]

Throughout U.S. history, the racial denigration of people of Mexican origin has had both inward ramifications, facilitating the subjugation of immigrant and American citizens of Mexican ancestry, and outward, toward Mexico and Latin America (De Genova, 2005). From a variety of perspectives, contemporary researchers utilize *racism* as a category of analysis because, as pointed out by Ladson-Billings (1998), racism is "normal," not aberrant, in U.S. society. In his review of books on race, Delgado (2006) concurs with this premise and points out that

> Much racism today is unintentional, unstated, quite polite, and even normal. Embedded in a host of behaviors, attitudes, expectations, rules of the game, and norms is a system of advantage and exclusion that constantly places whites on top at the expense of others (1275).

Race and class are independent concepts, but they have been interlaced throughout history. From one approach, racism is a consequence of capitalism, "which splits the working class, creates hierarchies of privilege among waged workers and ensures an industrial reserve army of less-enfranchised labour" (Sivanandan, quoted by Bhattacharyya et al., 2002: 36). From that perspective, class, like citizenship, is part of a structure that legitimizes social inequality (Marshall, 1998). The interlacing of race and class factors also has been studied in connection with the underachievement of students of Mexican origin. In a pioneering study in Tucson, Arizona, Bender and Ruiz (1974) explored the links between race and class in determining underachievement and underaspiration among Mexican-American and Anglo high school students. In their study, they stressed the importance of belonging to a particular social class. They found that class membership is more critical than race in determining levels of achievement and aspiration of Mexican-Americans. Their conclusion was that, when developing curriculum aimed at improving the achievement rates of this population, "class membership should be seriously considered in program development" (54). The implication is that, by not paying attention to this factor, schools may be promoting student underachievement.

López and Stanton-Salazar (2001) suggest that Mexican-Americans may react to the "quasi-racial stereotyping" and their low class status with reduced motivation and achievement. Specifically with regard to immigrant communities, their class status becomes a relentless obstacle because "they lack the web of organizations and social practices that have allowed specific groups to utilize traditional culture to help children achieve" (Ibid.: 57). Over generations, class and socio-economic status create networks that consolidate the accumulation of economic resources and financial advantages (Grant, 2005). It has been argued that such "cumulative advantages" enhance children's educational outcomes (Ibid.). Thus, some researchers emphasize the role of "social capital" in their explanation of achievement differences between rich and poor students (Gibson and Bejínez, 2002; Stanton-Salazar and Dornbusch, 1995). Social capital refers to the students' access to the social relationships and resources they need to be successful within a context of unequal economic and power relations (Gibson and Bejínez, 2002).

> Students from middle and upper class households, whose parents are college educated, not only have greater access to but also greater ability to draw from the kinds of social relationships that facilitate academic success than do children raised in less affluent surroundings (Ibid.: 157).

Therefore, since immigrants are excluded from mainstream networks and practices, it is important that they create their own support systems. In tandem with this proposition, from a Critical Race Theory approach, Villalpando (2003) analyzes the findings of a longitudinal study of Chicana/o college students that involved 200 Chicana/o and 200 White college students from 40 universities across the United States. Villalpando criticizes the racial barriers institutionalized by universities and, contrary to the "racial balkanization myth" (619), finds that Chicana/o college students benefit from association with their Chicana/o peers. He emphasizes that race and racism are essential characteristics of U.S. society, but they also intersect with other identity determinants such as language, gender, and class (Ibid.). In order to strengthen his analysis, Villalpando (2003) utilizes the "counterstorytelling method" to tell the stories of two undergraduate students and a college professor of Chicana/o origin. Through the counterstories, and the data that emerged from his research, he reveals important themes that converge with other research, namely: the need to maintain a strong critical Chicana/o cultural consciousness; students' dependence on spirituality; students' strong commitment to Chicana/o communities; influence of language on students' lives; and the influence of family (Idem.: 639–640).

In another CRT study, Arizona State University professor Holguín-Cuádraz (2006) explores the life histories of three narrators of Mexican origin who enrolled in doctoral programs at UC Berkeley. She analyzes these narratives from different interpretive perspectives and finds that educational achievement by people of Mexican descent is conditioned by what she calls "a politics of exceptionality" (83). Holguín-Cuádraz points out that high academic achievement is not considered typical of students of Mexican origin; thus, people who achieve are seen as exceptions to the supposed meritocracy. She also criticizes social policies that attempt to improve educational achievement but remain focused on the individual and not on institutional structures. From her interviews, Holguín-Cuádraz infers that there is a rich and varied cultural legacy in which the narrators' stories are inscribed. This legacy should not be ignored "but rather acknowledged and utilized, as in the tradition of borderlands and critical race theorists, to illuminate the process by which these individuals and/or their families relate to and pursue their schooling" (104).

Sarther (2006) has explored the experiences of seventeen first-generation, Mexican-American female students (ages 18 to 25) in a community college. Through semi-structured interviews, she analyzed the participants' narratives, their experiences, and future plans. One of the foci of her analysis is the influential constructs of society and history, where the issues of racism, ethnicism, and gender are crucial. The influences of racism and ethnicism are analyzed in the context of the participants' personal experiences. Sarther argues that, living in the United States "illegally" and taking English as Second Language (ESL) classes have influenced the participants' ethnic identity. Many of the participants in this study had developed an ethic of caring and justice to help others in similar circumstances and to correct the inequities experienced as Mexicans. This sense of purpose was a powerful motivator for academic achievement. Furthermore, Sarther found that, while "the student development literature recognizes the college years as a time of exploration," the participants in her study were "generally more focused on getting through school, not in engaging in new experiences" (318). With regard to class and race, she found that some participants were able to give up their ethnicity in order to succeed in certain social worlds. "Others, because of their physical characteristics, or characteristics related to being poor like the look of their old cars," were not able to do so (337–338). She concludes that racism has a "profound impact" on people of Mexican origin in the United States.

Ponce (2002) conducted research on the high academic achievement of Chicana and Chicano doctoral graduates who earned their Ph.D.s prior to 1965, before affirmative action legislation was enacted. Her study explored the academic experiences of 20 Chicana/o "Pioneers" and how they advanced and succeeded in the U.S. educational system. Most of the participants came from traditional Mexican, Spanish-speaking families with low incomes and nearly all of them expressed having experienced racism during their educational experiences. They were able to overcome racial adversity and achieve educational success by their "resilience, integrity, and belief in self." An interesting finding was that nearly three quarters of the participants in the study possessed Anglo characteristics (fair skin color), and all express awareness regarding the privileges that their physical appearance provided in certain circumstances. Thus, the stories in Ponce's research reinforce other studies on phenotypes and life chances in the U.S. that have found a correlation between academic and socioeconomic achievement and physical appearance (Arce, Murguia, and Frisbie, 1987; Holleran, 2003). Murguia and Telles (1996), for example, found that skin color and physical features have an effect on educational achievement among Mexican-Americans. With data from the 1979 National Chicano Survey, they found that Mexican-Americans with European-looking features had about 1.5 years more of schooling than the darker and the more indigenous-looking majority (*Ibid.*). Ponce (2002), however, concludes that racism appeared "to serve as a catalyst" in making the successful students in her study want to achieve (201).

Duncan-Andrade (2005) argues that a history of discrimination affects Chicanos perceptions of schooling. He analyzes the Treaty of Guadalupe-Hidalgo as a historical counter-narrative of colonialism and argues that, although circumstances evolve, some fundamental aspects of a colonial relationship continue to exist. The destructive impact of dominant narratives, Duncan-Andrade claims, affect the academic performance of Chicano youth. His research supports the premise set forth by other researchers (Elenes, 2002; Valencia, 2002; Valencia and Solorzano, 1997) that, for educational reform to promote Chicano achievement, it must abandon pedagogical approaches that propagate dominant cultural ideologies and attribute blame for failure to perceived deficiencies (deficit thinking) in Chicano culture. Elenes (2002) specifically refers to the border culture and advocates a "border pedagogy," critiquing the limited access to non-racist institutional "spaces" and educational empowerment for the linguistically diverse Chicano-Mexicano communities. She criticizes the illogical spaces of belonging and non-belonging that have been created for Chicanos and Chicanas. From a similar perspective, Duncan-Andrade (2005) recommends the creation of a caring academic environment through the use of a critical pedagogy that empowers students and provides them with a sense of cultural pride, purpose, and positive identity.

Immigrant Origin: "No migratory children wanted here"[3]

The literature on higher education of immigrants of Mexican origin is limited, but it is growing in the twenty-first century. A report by the Pew Hispanic Center in 2002 (Lowell and Suro, 2002) revealed that fewer immigrant Latinos[4] than natives completed college. The report also pointed out that the number of young immigrant Latinos who come to the United States and go to school here is growing. This growing segment of the immigrant Latino population has a better educational profile than immigrants who are educated in their countries of origin (*Ibid.*). A study by Fry (2002) found that native-born Latino high school graduates enroll in college at a higher rate than their immigrant counterparts. This is not surprising in Arizona and other states where anti-immigrant legislation has made higher education financially inaccessible to undocumented students and even legal immigrants are affected by hostile environments. The same study found that immigrants are far more likely to enroll in community colleges than any other group. This is not surprising either, since community colleges often enroll "the neediest students, the most academically underprepared, and the economically disenfranchised" (Hebel, quoted by Perin and Charron, 2006: 155). What was startling in Fry's (2002) findings was that about 10 percent of all Latino high school graduates enroll in some form of college, compared to seven percent of the total population of high school graduates. However, Latinos lag behind every other group in attaining college degrees, thus their college dropout rate is extremely high.

In "We ARE Americans: Undocumented Students Pursuing the American Dream," Perez (2009) investigated the oral histories of sixteen undocumented students between high school and graduate studies, as well as four formerly undocumented college graduates. Perez discusses immigration policy, socio-economic realities, and educational issues in the lives of these young people. His focus on the stories of people of Mexican origin, as in this book, alludes to the most controversial immigrant population in the United States at this point in U.S. history. He also reminds us that, historically, anti-immigrant forces have opposed Scandinavian, Japanese, Korean, Vietnamese, Central and South American immigration. "Yet the United States ultimately made a place for these immigrants and was enriched by their cultural contribution, talents, and hard work" (xxxiv). To this rejection-acceptance cycle, we could add Germans, Jews, Italians, Irish, and practically any group resembling "otherness" including Catholics, Muslims, communists, and atheists. As expressed by D.G. Solorzano in his foreword to Perez's research, "The framing of the debate around 'immigration reform' has focused primarily on immigrants themselves, void of any significant discussions about the forces or structures that create the international migration of people" (*Ibid*.: xii). We contend that such forces and structures are the historical foundations created by a racist, colonizing state apparatus. Hence our emphasis on socio-economic and historical contexts from a CRT approach. Ultimately, Perez's stories, like the counter-narratives in this book, reveal the humanity and values of incredibly resilient, hard-working, and courageous undocumented Americans.

Alvarez-McHatton et al. (2006) studied the characteristics of 57 students from migrant[5] farmworker families who were successfully attending a four-year university. Very often, the need to work in order to supplement their poor family incomes, their high mobility, and a myriad obstacles force migrant students to leave school. Among adult farm workers in the United States, only about 15% have completed high school or more (26). In spite of their high risk of academic failure, many of these students finish high school and make it into higher education. The researchers found "a strong sense of determination and self-reliance on the part of these students as well as the strong role of families played in their decision to pursue higher education" (*Ibid*.: 25). Mothers, predominantly, were credited by participants as their main source of inspiration. Among other recommendations, the researchers advise continuous efforts "addressing systemic and institutional discrimination to ensure equitable access to a high quality education for all our students" (38).

Also through in-depth interviewing research, Bohon, Macpherson, and Atiles (2005) have explored the educational experiences of new Latino immigrants in the state of Georgia, where immigration from Mexico has grown tremendously after the 1990s. The state of Georgia, like the state of Arizona, consistently ranks low in most educational measures (*Ibid*.). The interviews in this study included 68 participants from the public and private sector who work with Latinos, but the research focused mainly on the responses of eleven participants who work directly in education. The researchers identified six barriers to educational achievement of immigrant *Latino* students: 1) lack of understanding of the U.S. school system, 2) low parental involvement in the schools, 3) lack of residential stability among the Latino population, 4) little school support for the needs of Latino students, 5) few incentives for the continuation of Latino education, and 6) barred immigrant access to higher education. Furthermore, this research confirms the importance of an educational environment where immigrants can find role models, counselors and administrators properly trained to educate Hispanic students. Finally, the researchers conclude that the educational barriers experienced by Latino immigrants are due to the reproduction of ethnic stratification. "Additionally, the social inequalities present within race and ethnicity, class, and gender categories continuously intersect, compounding the disadvantages felt by the Latino population" (56).

In a different study conducted in California, Gibson and Bejínez (2002) found that, despite the high risk of failure, students of Mexican origin from migrant farmworker families persevere in school in significantly higher numbers than native classmates of Mexican origin. The research focused on 105 migrant students, considered the most vulnerable and disadvantaged among all immigrants. Generally, these students have special education needs related to their families' mobility, since many follow the crops seasonally. Many of them live below the poverty level, and they "often have high levels of absenteeism, due to family and work responsibilities, as well as to migration" (156). Other impediments of academic achievement "emerge from the structure of school programs, from their interactions with mainstream classmates, and with their relationships with teachers and other members of the school staff" (*Ibid.*). The explanation for the unexpected finding of high perseverance of these immigrant students is the academic and social support provided to migrant students by the Migrant Education Program (MEP) established by the federal government in 1966. The MEP also sponsors the Migrant Student Association, an inclusive student-run club with a large membership and a good reputation for student engagement. In contrast with the lack of institutional support found by the research conducted in Georgia by Bohon et al. (2005), the research by Gibson and Bejínez (2002) corroborates that the implementation of support systems like the MEP for students at risk can significantly promote academic achievement.

In a similar approach, the Hillsboro school district in the State of Oregon also has implemented a federally financed migrant program to help families meet basic needs so immigrant children are more likely to attend school. Most immigrant students in this region come from poor farm families in Mexico who have moved to the countryside of Oregon seeking the backbreaking work of picking berries, cucumbers, or grapes (Zehr, 2002). Many of them come from the Mexican states of Oaxaca and Michoacán and are of indigenous origin. School officials have noted that the discrimination that indigenous Mexicans face in their own country continues when they reach Oregon, where other Mexican immigrants tend to look down upon them. Because of this, the poorest Indian immigrants tend to stay in the 21 migrant-labor camps in the district. Thus, under the federal Migrant Education Program, Hillsboro home-school consultants visit the migrant camps and the homes of immigrants to assure the families that their children are entitled to a free, public education in the United States, even if they are undocumented (*Ibid.*). The school consultants accompany Spanish-speaking parents to school meetings and help them understand the system and, in many cases, they become advocates of immigrant students. The rationale behind these programs is that the creation of caring environments can be an antidote for academic attrition, even for the highest-risk immigrant students (Alvarez-McHatton et al., 2006; Gibson and Bejínez, 2002).

Gibson (2003) further explores the factors that contribute to the academic achievement of high-school migrant students in a California school. She notes migrant children are among the most disadvantaged in the country due to the combined effects of poverty, malnutrition, deficient health care, and high absenteeism from school. The author utilized qualitative and quantitative methods to follow the school performance of 160 migrant students from 9th through 12th grades. She implemented participant observation, student surveys, and interviews with students, teachers, and the Migrant Education Program (MEP) staff. She gathered data on students' grades, their academic progress, and college preparatory courses completed. Gibson (2003) emphasizes that a sense of belonging in school seems to be an essential factor for the motivation, participation, and academic achievement of immigrant students. The creation of such a sense of belonging was promoted through school and community activities developed by the Migrant Student Association (MSA). Moreover, this study found that caring relationships between migrant staff, educators, and students are essential in promoting academic success. Migrant educators can more easily understand this student population and can build and maintain friendly relationships with the students. Furthermore, institutional and academic support were synergistically reinforced by services such as constant academic guidance, after-school tutoring, placements in paid after-school jobs, ongoing advocacy and mentoring, connections to other school resources, and others.

From another perspective, White and Glick (2000) have found that immigrant students of Mexican origin who arrive in the United States as adolescents are more likely than those who arrive earlier or those born from immigrant parents to persevere in high school. In spite of lower previous academic achievement and lower levels of "human capital," these immigrant students tend to graduate. However, once they graduate, they are no more likely to engage in additional educational goals than other students. For immigrants who leave school early, socioeconomic status and language background determine many of the activities they pursue. Glick and White (2004) have also found that structural background and family support, such as parental involvement and parental expectations, translate into differential participation in post-secondary education by first- and second-generation youth from different racial and ethnic groups. According to their study (2003), longitudinal data from the 1988–1994 panels of the National Education Longitudinal Study (NELS) reveal that the vast majority of immigrant parents expect their children to go to college or beyond (See section on *Family and Parental Involvement* below). Additionally, they found that immigrant and second-generation youth are more likely than their third- or later generation peers to complete secondary school and go on to post-secondary education (*Ibid.*).

Finally, the notion of deficit thinking merits special attention when attempting to understand the educational achievement, or underachievement, of Mexican immigrants. Deficit thinking is evident in the prevalent idea that immigrants are a burden or a threat to society (Buchanan, 2002, 2006; Huntington, 2004a, 2004b; Tancredo, 2006). In a subtle form of deficit thinking, conventional wisdom in the U.S. assumes that, in order to progress, immigrants need to learn how to "become American" and overcome their deficits with respect to the new language and culture (Rumbaut, 1997). Therefore, deficit thinking is not just an individual problem but a structural and societal one (Shields, 2004). Thus, if educational institutions are a reflection of society, educational practices and assumptions emerging from the deficit thinking paradigm can further affect Mexican immigrant students who are linguistically and culturally different. From this approach, educational bureaucracies frequently attempt to "fix" underperforming students, placing the blame on them, their families, and their cultures (Weiner, 2006). Such deficit thinking prevents any real institutional change and tends to ignore the "social ecology" of the school and classroom (see also Fong, 2004).

From a critical perspective, Shields (2004) reproves institutionalized deficit thinking and its "pathologies of silence." She argues that such pathologies "are misguided attempts to act justly, to display empathy, and to create democratic and optimistic educational communities" (117). She also criticizes liberal multiculturalists who believe differences are unimportant, since we are all part of a single human race. Shields notes that children with family cultures that diverge the most from their social and organizational school structures tend to be the least successful in the U.S. educational systems. She proposes to replace deficit thinking with deep and meaningful relationships with students. This, Shields argues, is the best way to overcome our pathologies of silence about differences, including those of ethnicity and class (*Ibid.*). Similarly, Rumbaut (1997) argues that ethnocentric assumptions and orthodox expectations about immigrants' self-identity and education must be debunked. What immigrants most need is the opportunity to openly participate and contribute to society, not by the suppression of old memories but by their incorporation into common life.

Specifically regarding undocumented Mexican immigrants, cutting them off the receipt of social services and education, like the Arizona legislature increasingly attempts, will be counterproductive to U.S. society (Massey and Espinosa, 1997). Such measures will not produce a reduction in the size of the undocumented population but will create an underclass of excluded residents "disconnected from the rest of society—unhealthy, poorly educated, with little stake in the future of the country, its government, or its way of life" (*Ibid.*: 992). Recent research in human geography also warns that the current demographic and economic trends indicate that a Mexican-American underclass might be forming (Allen, 2006). This situation, in turn, will perpetuate the pathologies of silence and the deficit thinking that facilitate colonization, oppression, and institutional racism.

Family and Parental Involvement: "Those Mexican parents don't care at all . . ."[6]

A recent national poll found that Latino voters have extremely high aspirations for their children. An astounding 96% would like their children to earn a college degree (impreMedia, 2011). For students of Mexican origin, parental influence appears to be of great importance in their motivations and inspirations. This factor seems to be as essential for students in elementary education as for those in college, whether they are immigrants or they have been in the U.S. for many generations (Bohon et al., 2005; Ramirez, 2003). In different research studies, parents and family are consistently identified as essential sources of support and encouragement promoting educational achievement in students of Mexican origin (Alberta, Castellanos, Lopez, and Rosales, 2005; Alvarez-McHatton et al., 2006; Bohon et al., 2005; Gándara, 1995). In a study on the effect of mentoring on the career aspirations of Mexican-origin high school students, Flores and Obasi (2005) found that 78% of them identified parents, brothers, sisters, aunts, or other family members as mentors. They also found that, "as in previous studies, mothers are highly influential in Mexican American students' lives" (159). Other research suggests that racial and gender similarities among the mentors and the mentees can lead to favorable outcomes (Ensher and Murphy, 1997). Hence, the importance of family role models is clear, but the role of educational administrators, faculty, and staff of Mexican/Hispanic origin who interact with families and students should not be ignored.

Different studies show that minority students from disadvantaged backgrounds and single-parent families are more likely than their mainstream counterparts to leave school (McGlynn, 1999; Warren, 1996). The many obstacles these parents face in being involved in their children's educational development contribute to their children's failure. Additionally, as noted by Segal and Kilty (2003), there is "a significant historical correlation" between race, ethnicity and poverty (55). Thus, in the case of parents of Mexican origin, the compounding effects of poverty, the caste system, and racial hegemony intensify the challenges they face. However, in situations when they are not involved in their children's educational affairs, it does not necessarily mean they do not care about their children's education (McCollum, 1998; Shannon and Latimer, 1996; Valencia, 2002). Shannon and Latimer (1996) have concluded that, while most parents of Mexican origin have a high regard for education and teachers, many do not believe they can provide any significant input. If parents appear not to be interested, it may be because of their self-perception of educational limitations. Shannon and Latimer's research also found that Mexican parents who are first or second generation in the U.S. may not even be aware that educators in this country expect parental involvement (*Ibid.*). Furthermore, as Bohon et al. (2005) have found, language barriers make it difficult for immigrant parents to communicate with teachers and administrators.

Glick and White's (2004) study of post-secondary school participation of immigrant and native youth found that students whose parents have high expectations are more likely to graduate from high school and enroll in college than students with parents holding lower expectations, "even in the face of controls for previous academic performance and family resources." Significantly, they also found that parents of immigrant students express higher expectations for their children than U.S.-born minorities of the third and later generations (*Ibid.*). The high aspirations of some immigrant parents may be related to studies that show that a strong relationship exists between high parental expectations and academic achievement, explained as the result of the intense motivation encouraged by these parents and, consequently, the adjustment of the child to such expectations (Portes and Rumbaut, 2001). An earlier study by Stanton-Salazar (1997), also found that some immigrants may achieve higher educational levels than their native peers thanks to family environments that tenaciously nourish academic achievement with high expectations, school involvement, and communication with children regarding school-related issues.

The connection between parental expectations and academically successful students of Mexican immigrant origin has been studied in a doctoral dissertation by Montoya (2006). In her study of five families, she explores the characteristics of parental involvement that helped their children graduate from a university. As in this book, Montoya utilized in-depth interviewing as a research method. The immigrant parents in her study came from relatively advantageous backgrounds: they owned their homes when their children were young; they had very stable jobs; they did not allow their children to work during high school, and helped them financially while in college. Moreover, the immigrant parents in Montoya's study "were in constant communication with the school," and they were part of their children's support networks during their college years. Other research shows that these are precisely the structural characteristics that encourage students to enroll in college (Thompson, Alexander, and Entwisle, 1988). However, in most Mexican immigrant families, low parental education, poverty, and single-parent structures hinder educational achievement by shaping the surrounding opportunities available to students (*Ibid.*). Most Mexican immigrant students have high rates of poverty (Schmidt, 2003) and generally have to spend scarce resources within the family in order to go to college.

In other words, high parental expectations alone will not necessarily guarantee academic achievement. A report by the *Chronicle of Higher Education* (Schmidt, 2003) notes that Hispanic families are well aware of the value of education. Family surveys have shown that more than nine out of ten Hispanic parents expect their children to enroll in college, but Hispanic children are much less likely than White children to have a parent who attended college (*Ibid.*). The dropout rates of students of Mexican origin, in particular, are "scandalously high" (Valencia, 2002: 365). Glick and White's (2004) discussion of the high academic expectations of immigrant parents also acknowledges the important role of structural variables like socioeconomic status, family structure, and language background. Additionally, they recognize the importance of parental attitudes and behaviors, such as their level of involvement in their children's education.

Very little research on parental involvement has been conducted on immigrant communities of Mexican origin. Bohon et al. (2005) and Schmidt (2003) suggest that the limited support and low parental involvement of immigrant parents in their children's schools is in part due to the poor understanding of the U.S. school system. Additionally, a mixed methods study by Grzywacz, Quandt, Arcury and Marín (2005) has found that recent immigrants experience higher levels of work-family strain associated with stress and anxiety. These findings reinforce Duncan-Andrade's (2005) argument that the claims that Chicano parents are less involved with schools and/or the political process are based on shortsighted class values. Such claims "fail to understand economic limitations requiring a parent(s) to work multiple jobs, or shifts, differing from the middle class cultural norms of 9 to 5" (584). Additionally, a case study by Espinoza-Herold (2007) challenges the idea that working-class immigrant families do not care about the education of their children. Her research links Mexican oral traditions to the resilience and motivation that counter the lack of resources and knowledge to guide their children in an unknown educational system (*Idem.*).

Finally, Ramirez (2003) interviewed immigrant parents of Mexican origin in a community with strong Latino roots in California. He found that immigrant parents believed the schools are not interested in listening to their input. The parents expressed a strong interest in being part of their children's education, but schools were not conducive to their involvement. They could not find interpreters to help them communicate with school officials, teachers would not be available or able to speak with them, and they received no communication from schools when their children were in need of academic support. The parents interviewed by Ramirez felt excluded and frustrated because of their inability to obtain information regarding their children's education (*Ibid.*). On the other hand, Shannon and Latimer's (1996) research suggests that most parents of Mexican origin respect the teachers' professional position and fear their involvement could be perceived as interference. Unfortunately, this view is often perceived by teachers as lack of concern for their children's education.

Supportive and Undermining Environments: "We need people who don't just speak Spanish, but also understand Mexican culture"[7]

Parents, siblings, and other family members of students of Mexican origin are important sources of motivation in their academic success, but a supportive family environment alone might not be enough to help students persist in their academic goals (Alberta et al., 2005). "Latina/o student perceptions of their college environment have considerable impact on their social and academic lives" (*Ibid.*: 203). In a study by McWhirter et al. (2007), they found that Mexican-American high-school students perceive many more barriers to college than do their White peers. The research surveyed 140 Mexican-American and 296 White students and analyzed 28 internal and external barriers. In general, Mexican-American students expect to encounter more barriers related to abilities, preparation, motivation, support, and separation from their families than did their White counterparts. They also expected such academic obstacles to be more difficult to overcome. Finally, Mexican-American females were more likely than males to anticipate financial barriers to their college education (*Ibid.*).

Research also has found that, regardless of undermining environments, enormous barriers, and negative prognostications some students of Mexican origin achieve academic success. Gándara (1995) observed cases of low-income Mexicans from homes with little formal education who have attained high academic achievement. Using a qualitative approach, she examined how these students became successful despite disadvantages and poverty. Her study is significant because it attempts to better understand the factors that help "Chicano" students succeed despite the fact that they were born and raised in environments that more typically produce academic failure. She studied 50 people (20 women and 30 men), all of whom had earned Ph.D., M.D., or J.D. degrees from prestigious U.S. universities. What she found was that these people had achieved success despite the odds because of their internal drive and expression of "social self-consciousness." Additionally, Garza, Reyes, and Trueba (2004) have found that, when at-risk students succeed academically, they develop coping strategies that become part of their personal characteristics. Such characteristics include determination, persistence, a strong work ethic, responsibility, commitment, resourcefulness, cooperation, and a sense of hope (114).

In a five-year study of Hispanic students, Romo and Falbo (1997) identify diverse variables that affect students' academic progress. In an effort to motivate others to make necessary changes in schools and communities to enhance student achievement, they incorporate the voices and experiences of parents and students into their work. Their research focused on the narratives of students who graduated from high school against all odds. Their research tracked the progress of one hundred students in Austin, Texas, from 1989 to 1993. They found that the reasons students drop out of school have less to do with ethnicity and more to do with school and community environments. According to this study, Latino families and students see education as a way to improve living standards, but schools are not necessarily conducive to the achievement of this goal. In fact, many students choose to leave school because they believe it is a waste of their time (Ibid.). These findings are reinforced by Espinoza-Herold's (2003) research on student and teacher experiences in two urban high schools in Arizona. Her study involved in-depth interviews with two "at-risk" Mexican-American students, one of whom was an immigrant. Espinoza-Herold also surveyed 31 educators and two administrators from the interviewees' schools. She concluded that the voices of students are ignored when educational policy is made. Thus, a major disconnection exists between the official goals of educational institutions and the goals of those who are ostensibly being educated.

Romo and Falbo (1997) also argue that, despite evident civil rights gains, many of today's school policies and practices tend to undermine student motivation and participation, discourage parental involvement, and deter community involvement. These negative institutional elements have been linked to low academic achievement of students of Mexican origin (*Ibid.*). Other studies have identified specific practices contributing to low student achievement, such as tracking and ability grouping, mainstreaming, grade retention, achievement testing, the hidden curriculum, meritocracy, and teacher attitudes (Fendrich, 1983; Kao and Thompson, 2003; Ortiz, 1996; Sosa, 1993; Valencia, 2002). Valencia (2002) further argues that Chicano educational failures are not just an educational problem; thus, he advocates "deep-rooted systemic reform . . . in broad economic, political, cultural, and school curricular contexts" (365). Nevertheless, research also shows that student achievement is linked to much simpler educational strategies (Romo and Falbo, 1997).

In a study by Donato and de Onis (1995), they found that a positive attitude toward students, commitment to help them succeed, and support services in general were essential to their overall achievement. Thus, Donato and de Onis recommend: hiring minority staff in leadership positions to act as role models; providing courses that do not limit students' choices or trap them in low-level curricula; offering students basic and advanced courses through bilingual and "sheltered" methods; and engaging parents in the planning of their children's academic schedules. Although this research focuses exclusively on middle school students, it confirms that helping minority students succeed involves services and attitudes beyond the instructional arena. Supporting this perspective, Valenzuela (1999) discerns how "caring" is an essential element in the schooling process and how Mexican-American students interpret, experience, and are aware of this factor. She found that schools she observed in Houston, Texas are structured to destroy student identities, while their underachievement is a form of passive resistance. Students, she argues, are divided socially, linguistically, and culturally from each other and from the staff. It can be inferred that strategic changes that nurture the students' cultural identities and a caring environment will help students succeed (*Ibid.*).

In a case study of two students of Mexican origin who graduated from Stanford University, Cabrera and Padilla (2004) found that both participants (a male and a female) attributed their success to personal motivation and support from their mothers. Furthermore, by in-depth interviewing these graduates from extremely impoverished and adverse backgrounds, the researchers found that their educational achievement was also possible because they learned the "culture of college." These students learned about college opportunities from their counselors and tutors who emphasized that they were persons of worth (*Ibid.*). Research by Salas (2003), Stewart (1998), and Tinto (1987) also supports these findings and suggests that the role of student counselors and administrators is important in preparing Mexican-American students more appropriately for educational achievement in college.

Educational institutions have the power to shape their organizational cultures to create environments that promote "a share vision of success and a fundamental belief that opportunities, not barriers, exist" (Reyes, Scribner, and Paredes-Scribner, 1999: 209). Institutions also can make a commitment to alter "deficit thinking" in order to create "new ways of thinking" (*Ibid.*). According to Yosso (2006), deficit thinking permeates U.S. society, and both educational institutions and those who work in them mirror these beliefs. Therefore, this is one of the great obstacles in the creation of educational environments that are conducive to the educational achievement of people of Mexican origin. Educational institutions driven by deficit thinking, she argues, "most often default to methods of banking education critiqued by Paulo Freire" (23). Such a banking concept of education very often results in institutional practices that aim to fill up supposedly passive recipients (students) with pieces of knowledge that are regarded as legitimate by the dominant society because they perpetuate the *status quo* (*Idem.*). Therefore these practices ultimately become an instrument of oppression (Freire, 1970).

Deficit thinking, negative organizational environments, and perceived barriers by students can compound into insuperable obstacles (McWhirter et al., 2007; Valencia, 2002). Some researchers look beyond the school environment and argue that, in order to encourage and retain at-risk youth in school, an interactive approach that combines diverse strategies and dimensions is necessary (Sanders and Sanders, 1998). To facilitate such an approach, parents, educators, community members, businesses, and public and private agencies must work together in a cohesive way (*Ibid.*). Thus, Rumberger and Rodríguez (2002) remind us that "too much emphasis has been placed on 'at-risk youth' and their families, and not enough on the high risk settings in which they live and go to school" (122).

Nevertheless, the power of educational institutions should not be minimized. Institutions that disregard immigrant student's ethnic, cultural, and linguistic identities generally adopt unsuccessful deficit thinking practices. According to Pearl (2002) and Valencia (2002), one of the most harmful effects of deficit thinking is that it results in unequal encouragement to succeed in the classroom, establishing different expectations that lead to different student performances. Allen (2006) goes further and argues that the children of immigrants do better in school when their educational institutions provide an environment that builds upon their cultural heritage and when they "avoid certain detrimental aspects of American culture" (27). The following section expands the discussion on the issues of acculturation and cultural preservation as they relate to the success of students of Mexican origin.

Acculturation and Cultural Preservation: "I speak *Spanglish* because I stay in the middle."[8]

Can cultural preservation be an obstacle in the way of educational achievement for immigrant students? Or, as Gibson (1998) has asked: When trying to promote academic success among immigrant students, "Is acculturation the issue?" Some researchers argue that people of Mexican origin are unable or unwilling to acculturate because we are a native minority that began as a conquered population in our own land, who later became an immigrant population with extensive and continuous contact with our country of origin (Hurtado, 1997; Huntington, 2004a, 2004b; Schaefer, 2005). Gibson (1998) argues that

> The children of immigrants who remain strongly anchored in their ethnic cultures and communities while also acquiring skills in the dominant language and culture generally do well in school. Most at risk are those who acculturate at a pace faster than their parents, who lose the ability to speak their parents' mother tongue, and who have no strong ties to an ethnic community that can buffer the negative forces that immigrant students from low socioeconomic status backgrounds often encounter in their peer and school worlds. The danger, thus, is not that immigrant children are not learning English fast enough, but rather that they are too rapidly losing knowledge of their parents' and grandparents' tongue and, as a result, are at risk of losing their connectedness to their parents culture and emotional support than their parents and other older members of the community can provide (629).

Other researchers have found that schools that choose to build on their students' cultural pride, history, and language have better results with these students (Gibson and Ogbu, 1991; Gibson, 1998; Romo and Fabo, 1997; Valenzuela, 1999). On the other hand, students who feel they must hide parts of their cultural identity at school, or who feel pressured to diminish their home cultures, are likely to experience alienation at school (Gibson, 1998). In one study of acculturation of Mexican-American community college students, the researchers hypothesized that subjects of the study with the lowest levels of acculturation in the U.S. majority culture would also have the lowest level of goal-oriented competitiveness (Lucas and Stone, 1994). Nevertheless, the researchers found that the results did not support their prediction that Mexicans at higher levels of acculturation would exhibit significantly more interpersonal competitiveness. On the contrary, it was concluded that students of Mexican origin with low levels of acculturation are as competitive, if not more competitive than students from the majority culture. Similarly, Cummings (1981) and Fordham and Ogbu (1986) agree that, when students accept who they are and embrace their roots, they can confront challenges more successfully and academic achievement is more feasible.

It appears that the population of Mexican origin in the U.S. is in an unprecedented historical position. Hurtado (1997) points out that the concepts of acculturation and assimilation assume that the group who is expected to adapt to the dominant culture constitutes a numerical minority and they have very limited contact with their country of origin. She notes that, in the case of Latinos in the U.S.—most of whom are of Mexican descent—they have become the majority in California and they have extensive contact with their countries of origin. Thus, California has become the first state in the U.S. with a "minority majority" (Wilson, 2004) while an unprecedented number of first-generation Mexican immigrants reject dominant culture values. Nevertheless, this minority majority has the highest numbers of low-income students, school poverty, dropout rates, and underachievement (Orfield and Lee, 2005). Even as their numbers have increased dramatically, they continue to live in a system of internal colonialism (Martinez, 1999; Vélez-Ibáñez, 1996) that disdains their culture.

Throughout their history as a minority, people of Mexican origin have had to adjust, acculturate, and assimilate into the dominant European-American cultural majority. Recently, however, one of the intellectual apologists of the anti-Mexican discourse, S. P. Huntington (2004a), has argued that the great flow of Mexican immigrants will not *assimilate* like others have done in the past. In a study with clear racist overtones, he laments that "Mexican Americans no longer think of themselves as members of a small minority who must accommodate the dominant group and adopt its culture" (44). Huntington also expresses his concern that more than 90 percent of second-generation Mexican-Americans speak Spanish. While they also speak fluent English, he notes with alarm, they fail to reject their ancestral language. Moreover, many second- or third-generation Mexican-Americans who were brought up speaking English have learned Spanish as adults. In plain English, Huntington warns that Mexican-Americans in the Southwestern United States soon will have enough power "to do what no previous immigrant group could have dreamed of doing: challenge the existing cultural, political, legal, commercial, and educational systems" (Ibid.: 40). Strongly reinforcing the colonizer-colonized relationship, this important scholar from Harvard University explicitly concludes that the most serious challenge to America's Anglo-Protestant identity comes from Mexican and Latin American culture (Ibid.).

Many years before Huntington, research found that many Mexican parents relied on their children to interpret for them, both linguistically and culturally. Padilla (1980) observed that, "even into the fourth generation there are individuals who have not completely acculturated and who still possess some marked degree of cultural awareness and/or ethnic loyalty to their culture of origin" (75). However, according to Trueba (1993), the children learned English much faster than their parents and served as translators and negotiators for them in diverse circumstances, including legal, financial, and social situations. In the educational arena, some research suggests that low levels of parental acculturation—and education—may have a negative effect on their children's academic achievement (Stein, 1990). Similarly, a study by Castillo, Conoley, and Brossart (2004) suggest that comfort with dominant cultural values and perceived support from family, including support for such values, are related to lower perceived distress in some college students. However, in a life-history study Shannon (1996) reveals the story of a Mexican-American mother who narrates how she adapts to mainstream practices of parental involvement, while preserving her own Mexican ways of parenting. This research exposes different challenges the narrator faces, such as the teacher's resistance to the mother's intervention in school and the absence of culturally sensitive mediation between the school and the mother (Ibid.). Nieto (1996) also claims that, when students themselves resist assimilation and preserve their culture and language, they are more academically successful. Cultural preservation, even if the student faces cultural conflicts, may eventually have a positive effect on academic achievement (Ibid.).

Gecas (1973) investigated the self-conceptions of Mexican immigrants and "settled" Mexican-Americans. He found that immigrants were more firmly attached to cultural identity structures like family, religion, and ethnicity than were Americans of Mexican origin. This was interpreted as a consequence of acculturation, which is probably higher for Americans of Mexican origin than immigrants. Additionally there was a very significant finding in this study regarding the self-conceptions of these two groups: immigrants had a more positive view of themselves than did Americans of Mexican origin with regard to self-esteem, sense of moral worth, competence, self-determination and altruism. Finch, Kolody, and Vega (2000) discovered equally surprising findings after surveying 3,012 people of Mexican origin, ages 18–59, in Fresno, California between 1995 and 1996. Their purpose was to find the relationship between perceived discrimination, acculturative stress, and mental health among adults of Mexican origin. They found that discrimination was directly related to depression and, more significantly, that less acculturated immigrants did not suffer discrimination as often as their more acculturated counterparts.

In a study that contradicts Huntington's (2004a, 2004b) arguments, Alba, Logan, Lutz, and Stults (2002) have found strong evidence of language assimilation among people of Mexican origin. Language is a major indicator of adaptation to mainstream culture and, according to this research, two thirds of third-generation Mexican-Americans do not speak any Spanish. This appears to follow a traditional model of language assimilation where the immigrant generation makes some progress but mainly uses its native tongue; the second generation is bilingual, and the third generation speaks only English (*Ibid.*). Nevertheless, in a study of children of Mexican immigrants, St-Hilaire (2002) has found that fluent bilingualism in Spanish and English is positively associated with educational aspirations and expectations. This research also found that the great majority of students of Mexican origin value education as a superior means of socioeconomic advancement. However, as they become assimilated, measured by length of residency in the U.S., they tend to aspire to lower levels of education. Furthermore, the author argues that immigrants who deliberately preserve their native culture and maintain solidarity within their ethnic community in the United States make rapid socioeconomic progress. Thus, for these immigrants full assimilation to mainstream cultural norms is not necessary to achieve upward mobility, as it was for immigrants in earlier decades (St-Hilaire, 2001, 2002).

There are many students who have succeeded within the framework of assimilation. Most have chosen to go along with mainstream values and programs in order to succeed. Because of the amount of confrontation involved in battling the system, they have—at least superficially—denied their culture in order to fit in and to be accepted. As in Kornblum's (1994) perspective, these students believe that assimilation is the only way to gain equal status in mainstream social groups and institutions. Assimilation, however, entails frictions within their own cultural group. Sometimes, these students are accused of "acting White," and they are treated as outsiders by members of their own group because they are thought to be disloyal (Gibson and Ogbu, 1991). Their dilemma is that if they are successful in the dominant world, they may be rejected by their culture of origin. Thus, when we hear educators and policymakers claim that assimilation is the only way to ensure the educational achievement of minorities; we suggest they step back and reexamine this philosophy. Instead of attempting to erase the culture and language of these students, perhaps schools could encourage the uniqueness of every culture and language as a foundation for their academic success.

Concluding Thoughts

As we have expounded in this chapter, previous research has identified a myriad of social factors that are responsible for the educational under-achievement of people of Mexican origin in the United States. Such barriers include: low education of parents (Shannon, 1996); negative stereotypes (Villenas and Deyhle, 1999); teen pregnancies (Méndez-Negrete, Saldaña, and Vega, 2006); lack of role models (Rodríguez, C.E., 1997; Yosso, 2002); language barriers (Alva and Padilla, 1995; Stanton-Salazar and Dornbusch, 1995; Wright, 2005); dysfunctional families (Hovey, 2000); curricular and classroom inequalities (Darder, 1991); low expectations (Glick and White, 2004; Warren, 1996); racism and discrimination (Delgado, 2003, 2006; Kay-Oliphant, 2005; Fendrich, 1983; López, 2004; Ogbu, 1986; Parker, Deyhle, and Villenas, 1999; Stone and Han, 2005); lack of teacher training to educate multicultural populations (Battle and Cuellar, 2006); lack of institutional resources (Berlinger and Biddle, 1995; Stanton-Salazar and Dornbusch, 1995); and immigrant status (Bohn et al., 2005). Finally, at the root of many of these problems, the basic reality of poverty subjugates an enormous proportion of students of Mexican origin (Bohon et. al., 2005; Lichter et al., 2005; Orfield and Lee, 2005; Stein, 1990). And poverty, some scholars argue, is in part the result of racial differentiation (Lichter, 1988; Lichter et al., 2005; Segal and Kilty, 2003).

Academic failure in students of Mexican origin can also be exacerbated by the harmful effects of "deficit thinking" that places the causes of failure on individuals, families, and cultures (Valencia and Solorzano, 1997) and, consequently, blames the victims of unjust socioeconomic and political structures. Certainly many of the challenges discussed in this chapter can be interconnected with the negative consequences of deficit thinking. Nevertheless, not much is known about students who have succeeded in spite of such challenges. Research about disadvantaged immigrant students who have been successful in higher education is practically nonexistent, particularly in the case of undocumented students. Even less is known about the successful experiences of undocumented Americans of Mexican origin in higher education. More research is needed about the influences that have helped these involuntary immigrants succeed academically in spite of great obstacles and racial adversity. The history and voices of this under-researched but vast and complex minority must be heard if we want the multicultural society of the future to be a just one.

As a colonized community, undocumented Americans of Mexican origin and Mexican-origin Americans in general face great challenges that must be overcome in order to attain educational achievement and greater socioeconomic mobility. However, there is also some evidence that, as the Latino population grows and Americans of Mexican origin multiply, educational success and economic prosperity appear to be more feasible, even without full assimilation (Andrade, 1998). It is clear that students of Mexican descent have unique and complex educational needs which must be met to ensure academic success. Meanwhile, the failures of Mexican-American schooling are blamed on a large number of reasons, but school dropout rates continue to be dramatically high and students of Mexican origin enrolled in higher education in disproportionately low numbers. Consequently, researchers propose that educators, parents, and communities need to discover new ways to keep Mexican-origin students in school (Sanders and Sanders, 1998; Shields, 2004; Valencia, 2002).

Undocumented immigrants' main obstacle is not their attachment to divergent cultural values, but structural, legal, and institutional constraints imbued with racial prejudice (Bendersky, 1995; Haney-López, 2001; Kay-Oliphant, 2005; Wright, 2005). Thus, as unintentional, *de facto*, and *de jure* racisms persist in the quotidian lives of people of Mexican origin, new research will need to explore beyond official memory and institutional structures. That is why our research strives to hear the voices of those who have succeeded in spite of great obstacles, defeating the odds and preserving their cultural identity. We propose that, by revealing what successful undocumented Americans of Mexican origin have to say about their educational achievement, we will oppose the "pathologies of silence" deplored by Shields (2004). The more their stories, their dreams, and their successes are exposed, the better the dominant society can recognize our common humanity.

Notes

[1] As aliens in their own land, Native Americans were the first to be targeted by the racist policies of internal colonialism, "Americanization," and forced assimilation. Dr. Johnson Bia, a Native American of Navajo origin, and an administrator in an Arizona community college, told Ricardo Castro-Salazar the story of his family name. After the Navajo people were dispossessed of their ancient lands and relocated to a much smaller territory, his father was sent to a mandatory boarding school in the 1920s. As noted by Lindauer (1996), such boarding schools were part of a plan by the federal government "to bring about the disappearance of North American Indians, not by military means, but by Americanizing their children in the hope disappearance would occur through assimilation" (37). At the boarding schools, the children were forced to change their Navajo names to "American" names. Dr. Bia's father, as all the other students, had to draw random names from a hat and thus his first name became *Andrew*. In a second draw, he pulled what would become his surname: *Bia*.

The word is actually an acronym that came from "Bureau of Indian Affairs," the agency in charge of Americanizing Native Americans in the state. Like in the case of other Native American cultures, Navajo customs, practices, institutions and language were the object of cultural genocide (or "ethnocide," according to Clemmer, 1995). The failure of the U.S. government's attempt to exterminate Navajo culture proved felicitous during Second World War: Andrew Bia became one of the Navajo Code Talkers who were crucial in the U.S. campaigns in the Pacific between 1942 and 1945. Fifty years later, in 1992, thirty-five veteran Navajo marines were honored at the Pentagon for their contribution to the defense of the United States. (This narrative comes from a personal conversation with Dr. Johnson Bia on January 24, 2007. References to internal colonialism, cultural genocide, and research by Lindauer and Clemmer are the author's).

[2] McKenzie (2004) reports that 90% of Texas schools were segregated by 1930, while some schools were designated exclusively for Mexicans. Supporters of segregation claimed that "Mexicans are dirty" and pointed out poor housing and other conditions of poverty to support their views (76–77). The stereotype of the "dirty Mexican" has not disappeared in the 21st century. In her analysis of internalized oppression and racism, Padilla (2001) relates a conversation with a college classmate who was delivering a tirade about the detriments of undocumented Mexican immigration. When she interrupted, informing him that she was an American of Mexican origin, the classmate's response was: "But you're not a dirty Mexican," and continued his diatribe (59). From another perspective, Hill (2006) argues that the environmental concerns raised about Mexico when the North American Free Trade Agreement was signed (1994), propagated the belief that immigrants were the pollutants. Hill claims that the environmental debate and media reporting intensified the American stereotype of Mexicans as "dirty" and "unhygienic" (Ibid.).

[3] In the first decades of the twentieth century, children of immigrant farm workers in California could go, if they were lucky, to special "migratory schools." In violation of state laws on the required number of attendance hours, immigrant children only attended school in the morning and then joined their parents in the hard work of fields. In some schools, immigrant children were denied all forms of education; signs reading "No Migratory Children Wanted Here" were posted on some Californian schools (Aman, 2005).

[4] The term Latino, preferred by these researchers, has the same connotation utilized by the U.S. Census Bureau, which uses the term as synonymous of Hispanic. See the Glossary for a more complete explanation.

[5] Broadly speaking, the term "migrant" refers to someone who has to move from one geographical location to another in order to work. Migrant workers are not always immigrants, but many immigrants become migrants when they do seasonal farm work or perform certain remunerated activities only during certain parts of the year. For additional information and a more detailed definition, see the United Nations International Convention on the Protection of the Rights of All Migrant Workers and Members of Their Families. Available online at: http://www2.ohchr.org/english/law/cmw.htm.

[6] The phrase is quoted by Z. Cline (2001) in an analysis where she recalls conversations with school principals. She reflects on her divergent views, influenced by her poor immigrant childhood experiences. Cline concludes that it is in the telling of her story that she can begin to understand herself and make sense of the community of which she is a part (Ibid.).

[7] Comment from a migrant education specialist in a rural county in Georgia, whose school district lacks enough certified bilingual and bicultural educators to serve the growing Hispanic population (Bohon et al., 2005: 52).

8   D. Luna of San Francisco State University conducted interviews with six Mexican immigrant female students who shared their educational experiences. One of the students explained that she could not really speak Spanish fluently but felt she should be bilingual because her parents speak Spanish. The student stated: "I think I speak Spanglish because I stayed in the middle, not a lot of Spanish, not a lot of English. I can't speak Spanish in a whole sentence. I throw a couple of English words in there" (quoted in Luna, 2004: 24). Spanglish, or *Espanglish*, is a spoken hybrid of Spanish and English that Professor Ilan Stavans, from Amherst College, has codified and analyzed in *Spanglish: The Making of a New American Language* (2003). Stavans, a Jewish-Mexican immigrant, examines the historical context of Spanglish, tracing it to the U.S. annexation of Mexican territories. His work includes a controversial Spanglish translation of the first chapter of *Don Quixote* and a lexicon of 4,500 words. From another perspective, Morales (2002) has referred to the "Spanglish people," arguing that the term can be used as an all-encompassing socio-cultural designation that can substitute the words Hispanic, Latino, Mexican-American and others. In this sense, to become Spanglish "is a sometimes violent, sometimes delicate rethreading of two parallel story lines, of long separated siblings and hated enemies. Becoming Spanglish is inextricably linked with history and issues of race and class . . ." (32).

Making History

Navigating Personal Borders: Recovering Memories of Identity and Culture

Today only the dissidents conserve the sentiment of continuity. The others must eliminate remembrances; they cannot permit themselves to keep the memory. . . . Most people have an interest in losing memory.
—György Konrad (quoted by Coser, 1992: 22)

The ability of life history to focus upon certain moments, critical incidents, or fateful moments that revolve around indecision, confusions, contradictions, and ironies, gives a great sense of process to a life and gives a more ambiguous, complex, and chaotic view of reality. It also presents more "rounded" and believable characters than the "flat," seemingly irrational, and linear characters from other forms of qualitative inquiry.
—Andrew Sparkes (quoted by Hatch and Wisniewski, 2003: 116)

As discussed in previous chapters, the contemporary demographic, socio-economic, and political contexts surrounding the narratives of undocumented Americans of Mexican origin are part of a counter-history (both remote and immediate) that is commonly ignored by the official memory. The following stories are infused with the social experience and community memory of an enormous "minority" of Mexican origin in the United States. These counter-memories, with the contexts and realities that underlie them, have an impact on many Americans of Mexican origin and United Statesians in general but have been diminished and denigrated by the majoritarian narrative. From its inception in the United States, a large part of Mexican-American social memory has been a counter-memory, sometimes a dissident memory and an alternative version of history. The anti-immigrant and anti-Mexican narrative that has reemerged in different parts of the country, the growing cases of violence against Latinos, and the dehumanization of unauthorized immigrants as "illegals" are confronted in this chapter with the stories of six exceptional individuals who have been undocumented students. Higher education has been for them a form of redemption as they broke barriers and borders in order to achieve the aspiration of the great majority of Latinos in the U.S.: a college degree (impreMedia, 2011). Their stories humanize and illustrate the complex circumstances behind their struggle to be recognized as worthy Americans. Some of them have been successful in their quest for "legalization," and some still live in a judicial limbo that precludes them from developing their full potential.

Jesenia's Story: "We are like the foundation"

Jesenia came from a poor family in northern Mexico. Her parents divorced when she was six, and her mother decided to emigrate to the United States as a way to survive economically after the separation. Jesenia was only seven when she was brought to the U.S., and when she told her story to Ricardo Castro-Salazar, the interviewing author, at age twenty-seven, she could hardly remember Mexico. Her cultural roots, however, were as profound as her family memories; her identity was as intricate as the life dimensions she had to navigate. When she was asked what language she would like to use for the interview, she gave an unexpected answer. Jesenia preferred to do it in "Espanglish." She also had a unique approach to her narrative. She felt words were simply not enough to express all she had inside; hence she decided to use a complementary form of expression to tell her story: photographs she had collected throughout her life.[1] Jesenia started her narrative with an album that she had put together when she was nineteen years old. It contained photographs of her baptism, her childhood, and her teenage years. She showed images of the town where she was born in Mexico, her mother and older sister, her grandmother, her relatives, the town where her mother was born, her little brother. . . . With those images, Jesenia wanted to express what she felt was impossible to express with words.

Jesenia's memories were clear and full of colors, like her photographs. She told the story of how her mother first migrated alone, staying with relatives in southern Arizona until she could secure a job and a place to stay in order to bring her children with her. Jesenia was brought to the United States without documents, through "the hole," with her mother, her sister, and the wife of the person who drove them to the town where they would live. She remembers how the experience was assimilated by her child's mind:

> There was mud when we crossed the fence, and I was behind my sister, and we slipped.

Once they arrived in the city, everything seemed so different, "shiny," "fancy." Jesenia could tell she was in a wealthier society. She remembers being impressed with the vehicles, the lights, fancier stores . . .

> To me, it was as if we had come here to play. . . . To me the most important thing was that we could live with my mother. So . . . everything else didn't matter.

Jesenia's mother worked hard to make ends meet and struggled to give her children a stable environment. They changed residences four times in approximately two years. As the family moved, Jesenia was enrolled in bilingual programs in different public schools. In spite of the challenges, she excelled in her studies. Starting third grade in the U.S., she loved the art and music classes, which she had never had before. She also participated in the school folkloric dance group. However, one of the challenges she faced in one of the middle schools she attended was a lack of bilingual programs. Although Jesenia could survive with her knowledge of English at that point, she felt the Spanish-speaking part of her had been shut down. At the same school, she remembers seeing things she had never seen before: gangs, violence, and a negative educational environment. Consequently, she remembers losing the motivation and desire to attend school. Nevertheless, Jesenia finished eighth grade in this school. She found sources of support and inspiration in her mother and in a new friend:

> Margo was from Guanajuato (a region in Mexico). A super intelligent girl. She was good academically, very intelligent. If she did not go to school, I did not want to go to school. . . . I went, but without enthusiasm, because my mom would not let us miss school. Grades always had to be good.

Jesenia's mother has a domestic partner who became Jesenia's stepfather. He also was a source of encouragement and motivation in her life, both economically and emotionally. Another inspirational figure for Jesenia was her uncle. She became sentimental as she showed a photograph and spoke about her uncle and his support for all things that had to do with school. In spite of Jesenia's family support for her academic goals, things were far from easy as she went through her high school and college years. Jesenia had disagreements with her mother and stepfather as she assimilated some feminist values and rebelled against the home responsibilities of the Mexican family structure. Nonetheless, she always felt support from her uncle. At certain point, the culture clash at home made her decide to move out and live first with a boyfriend and later with her sister and husband. She now interprets that conduct as an immature teenager attitude.

Jesenia reflects on the nature of her teenage rebellion:

> My mom worked a lot. That's why I had so much to do taking care of the children. Since she and my stepfather worked so much, I had to take care of [my younger siblings]. . . . My sister always cooked for us and I would do the cleaning. . . . Then, my sister, when my sister married, boom! Her responsibilities fell on me. . . . And, since I grew up here . . . well, I had . . . ideas that were more liberal, and she [her mother] did not approve . . .

Jesenia grew up thinking that she was like other children and teenagers around her. She discovered that she was an undocumented resident when she was in high school, when she attempted to get a job. She realized that she could not work without a social security number. She still submitted some job applications without the number, but the employers never called her. Jesenia did not want to be a burden to her parents and discouraged herself to participate in extracurricular activities because of the cost involved. However, she graduated from high school at seventeen and decided to enroll immediately in the community college. A counselor helped her enroll as a minor, with her mother's tax return forms, showing that she had been paying taxes in Arizona for a number of years[2] in order to fulfill residency requirements. Jesenia loved school, but she also had doubts:

> I wanted to learn, but then I thought "Why am I studying if I won't be able to do anything with it?" . . . But . . . that was what I wanted to do, you know . . . I knew what my family expected from me.

Tragically, Jesenia was so motivated to be a productive member of her family and of society that, in her worst moments of desperation, her frustration translated into suicidal thoughts. Her voice broke as she explained:

> I reached the point of saying that it would be easier if I was not here. . . . Being like this, I feel that I am just giving my mom a heavier load.

Undocumented immigrants face depression and stress associated with factors like stigmatization, exclusion, restricted mobility, feelings of blame and guilt, vulnerability, and exploitability. Unfortunately, "very rarely are the psychological implications of 'illegal' identity considered" (Sullivan and Rehm, 2005: 240). Researchers have pointed out that social isolation and separation from family may provide insight into stress and its contribution to significant anxiety and depression among immigrants (Hiott, Grzywacz, Arcury, and Quandt, 2006). These were situations that were also experienced by Jesenia. However, research also has shown that strong family and cultural ties contribute to the more positive mental health profile of foreign-born Latinos (Hayes-Bautista, 1997). Jesenia obviously had a strong family and cultural values, but her undocumented status kept her from being more involved in student activities at the college and perhaps from becoming a student leader.

> I attended the meetings [of Student Council], but I tried not to get involved, or stand out, as I would have done if I did not have that limitation (being undocumented).

Finally, Jesenia not only graduated from the community college, but she was able to transfer to the university. Jesenia was lucky to be invited to participate in a program designed to help minority women who were struggling to achieve their educational goals. This allowed her to afford the university and not be so economically stressed. However, Jesenia was always aware that going to school was a "privilege" that should not be taken for granted. While many college students view their studies as the most difficult thing they face, for Jesenia school was the easy part:

> I earned good grades, that is not difficult. The difficulty was outside school, when . . . uh . . . money . . . food . . . being able to rest, um . . . that was hard. School was not hard.

In addition to these challenges, Jesenia's narrative reveals that she has been surrounded by negative elements like gangs, violence, and drugs. Fortunately, she could separate herself from such influences, but her twenty-one-year-old brother has been in trouble and was sent to jail once. Ironically, Jesenia's brother and younger sister were born in the U.S., therefore they are American citizens. She hopes they will have better opportunities in life because of it, but she is painfully aware of the limitations they have due to their socioeconomic environment:

> In the neighborhood where my mom lives . . . ah, there were a lot of drugs when we lived there. There were gun shootings in the middle of the night . . . in the house behind. You know, little by little we've been surviving all this. There is still drugs, but it's . . . a community where . . . the majority of the people are *illegals* or . . . they are . . . you know, struggling; so my brother and sister live in the middle of all that. . . . They have the potential, but they are in a community where other people can't, so they also believe they are limited.

Jesenia graduated from the university with a baccalaureate degree in Elementary Education with a concentration in science. She is also certified in bilingual education, but her immigration status prevents her from putting her knowledge to work for her community. Ironically, in 1998, the New York City Department of Education announced that, in this metropolis with millions of Spanish speakers, a shortage of Spanish teachers would be filled with imported teachers from Spain (Smith, 2002: 428). Similarly, in 2006, CBS reported that the City of Dallas was bringing in bilingual teachers from Mexico and Chile, and that at least 10,000 teachers from abroad were needed in the U.S. every year (CBS News, 2006). In 2007, the State of Utah's schools districts sent a delegation to Mexico to recruit Mexican teachers. At that point, Utah was willing to import as many as 50 teachers from Mexico due to teacher shortages in the state (Benson, 2007).

Jesenia tries to resign herself to accepting her situation. She expresses her sadness and frustration about her immigration status, but she also reveals a profound sense of history. She places herself historically with other people she does not believe were recognized in their time. Jesenia also places herself with the discrimination against other immigrants in the past. She believes that

> we are the like the foundation for our kids *que van a nacer en el futuro* (those who will be born in the future). . . . And at this time, you know, we are like those Irish people that . . . they gave them the hardest work . . . we're kind of like that. We're evolving.

Jesenia, however, has a difficult time thinking of herself as an immigrant:

> I sometimes don't feel like I immigrated . . . immigrated here to the U.S . . . it sounds like they're talking about someone else. . . . Because I grew up in Arizona, and this is my home.

But she expresses ambivalent feelings as she experiences the dehumanizing designation of "illegal alien." The rancorous immigration debate in the U.S. appears to affect her sense of place and identity:

> Because sometimes you get . . . you get numb, you know? You hear all this, and then you feel like, oh, I'm not . . . *te sientes como* . . . (sighs) . . . I'm like an alien! *Como dicen* (Like they say), "illegal alien." You do feel like an alien out of space. You're not a person anymore. . . . You just feel like less than a person. At a point, I think that's what happens to a lot of us. Cuz it has happened to me too.

One of the things that helped Jesenia succeed academically was her fortitude and determination to finish school. One of the reasons she left home was her relationship with an Anglo-American boyfriend of whom her family did not fully approve. He was in the military and was very supportive of Jesenia's academic goals. She lived with him for a while on the military base (a place where only U.S. citizens are supposed to have access). He even gave Jesenia access to his boss's office in the middle of the night so she could use the computer to work on her homework. Nevertheless, when her boyfriend finished his service, seven months before Jesenia's last year at the university, she decided to stay in school instead of following him to Texas, where he had a job offer.

Letting her boyfriend go was a very painful decision for Jesenia. Paradoxically, while for most people staying in school is their pass to a better life, for her, staying with him could have lead to marriage and, consequently, to citizenship. But Jesenia knew what she wanted and she chose to stay in school . . . despite the fact that she could not fully achieve her dreams because of her "limitation." Thus, even though Jesenia appears to have a timid personality, she possesses tenacity and a strong identity that reflects her bicultural character. And she is not easily stopped by conventionalisms. As she shows more photographs in her album, she explains a picture where she wears a black dress:

> This was my *Quinceañera*.[3] It was . . . it was a scolding because my dress was black. One of my aunts scolded me because of my black dress, since . . . well, "it must be white."

Jesenia remembers that she could not always wear what she wanted. When she was a child, her family was poor and did what they could to maximize resources. Once, her stepfather sat with her and explained that they could not buy new clothes for her because she would be able to wear her sister's dresses as they grew up. Now she appreciates all the sacrifices her parents made for her, and she wants to demonstrate to them that she can be self-sufficient and successful. She wants her parents to be proud of her.

Jesenia now works for a family as a domestic worker, cleaning their home and taking care of their children. Surely not too many American families can afford to have an elementary school teacher, certified in bilingual education, as a domestic aide. Jesenia loves their children and she has a good relationship with her employers, but she is also aware of her reality. She explains, as she shares a photograph:

> This is the family I work for. They also said I'm, like, part of their family, I'm not just a worker there. And it does feel . . . but sometimes it feels like: "wait, I'm just a maid." . . . So I'll clean the restrooms, make the beds, clean floors, dust, vacuum, you mention it, anything that there is to do at home, I do it. . . . Pick up the kids, bring them home, um, help them with their homework . . . then I make dinner, ah, *les sirvo dinner a todos* (I serve dinner for everyone) . . . I pick up the dishes and wash the dishes while they sit around and watch TV or, you know, have family time . . .

Jesenia takes comfort in the fact that she is working at least a little in what she studied, even if informally, when she helps the children with their homework. Jesenia's day ends between 8 and 9:30 at night. For all this work, she was originally hired for $150.00 per week. Then her employer's sister, a single mother, came to live in the household with her child. Jesenia was also expected to take care of this new child, so she asked for a raise. She now receives $220.00 per week. However, her employers have found another way to benefit from her:

> I was asked to write a letter for them [for the Department of Economic Security] . . . for the mother of the child. . . . She receives help from the government. So I had to write a letter saying that she gives me much more money than what really . . . than what they really give me.

By stating that she is being paid money that she is not receiving, Jesenia is actually subject to higher taxes on her meager salary. Therefore, she is doubly subsidizing an American citizen's welfare. Clearly in this case, as Massey et al. (2004) have pointed out, immigrants raise the living standards and privileges of the middle class in the U.S. in apparently both legal and illegal ways. Jesenia sometimes feels she does not get the respect she deserves working for this family, but no matter what others think, she is a productive member of society. In fact, as a tax payer, a university graduate, and a hard worker she contributes to her community more than many official citizens do.

Jesenia has so much to say, so many memories, so many stories. She goes back and forth with anecdotes. She alternates between English and Spanish or she mixes both throughout her narrative. She finds pictures of some of her classmates and teachers. She goes back and forth in time and does not particularly care to follow a chronological narrative. But she seems to find the positive even in some painful memories. At one point she remembered how she was tortured by the English-speaking children in her class, "especially the boys." She would try to understand what the English-speaking children were saying, but the bilingual boys would "translate":

> "She said you are very ugly." Or, "She said your dress is very ugly." And . . . and . . . they tortured me, you know?

Jesenia smiles as she remembers that some English-speaking girls wrote her notes that she could not understand. She was not sure what to make of them, but she kept them for years.

> I kept them . . . When I was able to read them, I thought, whoa! . . . It felt very nice . . .because one of them wrote something like: "When you can read this . . . I am just saying I hope I see you next year . . ."

We hope many years from now Jesenia will be able to read this story and smile with the serenity of someone who has received what she deserves in life.

David's Story: "I am always learning"

David was the only participant in this study who wanted to interview entirely in English. He speaks with almost no accent and wanted to emphasize his competence in English. He came to the United States in 1993 at age seventeen after graduating from high school. He does not match the stereotype of the quiet and submissive Mexican immigrant. In Mexico he had been a student leader, participating in school demonstrations against a corrupt principal. He planned to continue his education and knew he could achieve great things if he only was given the opportunity.

David came from a broken family and did not speak English before immigrating to the United States. His mother started a new relationship with an authorized resident of Mexican origin in Arizona. She also became an authorized immigrant through this relationship, and, later, she submitted an application to the U.S. Immigration and Naturalization Service to permit David to become a U.S. resident as well. Unfortunately for David and his younger brother, residency permits for family members of authorized residents do not have the same priority as requests made by U.S. citizens. Residency permits for children, parents and siblings of authorized residents can take many years to be approved and are sometimes denied (see Suárez-Orozco, Todorova, and Louie, 2002).

Optimistic, David entered the U.S. legally, with a visa and the hope of becoming a legal resident in the country. From the beginning, he had educational goals in mind:

> I chose to come with my mom to the United States because I wanted to go to a good college. That was . . . my first goal. To go to school. That's why I came to the United States to begin with.

David's dream was to attend a university in the United States, but he could not speak English, and he was not an official resident of the State of Arizona. For students to pay cheaper in-state tuition fees, public higher education institutions in the U.S. have state residency requirements. In the past, the qualifying condition for in-state tuition was a demonstrated permanent residency in the state for over one year. The rationale was that, as workers and economic members of the community, residents pay taxes and, in this way, subsidize such public institutions. In return, they would become more productive and pay higher taxes, therefore benefitting the community in different ways. In Arizona, residency could be established with a driver's license, utility bills, bank statements, or other official documentation. When David went to college, higher education institutions were not obliged to request proof of citizenship. However, after recent laws passed by the Arizona legislature, anyone attending a public higher education institution must produce both proof of residency and proof of "legal" status (e.g., U.S. citizenship or an authorized residency permit) or pay out-of-state tuition fees. This has made it impossible for many undocumented students who have graduated from Arizona public high schools to continue their education. Additionally, twice a year, Arizona community colleges are required by law to report to the legislature the number of undocumented students who have requested admission. The collection of this information has the effect of intimidating potential undocumented students, even when they are able to pay the more expensive tuition fees. Moreover, the new laws make it impossible for undocumented residents to obtain a driver's license, which makes them more vulnerable and limits their mobility.[4]

David enrolled in the community college only two months after his arrival. Since he was not a U.S. citizen and could not establish Arizona residency through other means, his family helped him pay international student fees. As he attended college and waited for his immigrant visa, he recognized the meager conditions his family lived in and felt pressured to start working to help improve their situation.

> I noticed that there wasn't enough money for the family. So, so . . . I was the oldest. So I had to work!

The family was anxiously waiting for David's immigration permit to be processed, but he ran out of patience. It was painful to see his family struggling financially while he was attending college. Thus, he decided to work without the proper immigrant authorization. He soon found work washing dishes at a restaurant.

> . . . the need for food and the need to sustain yourself is bigger than your patience.
> I basically got a job as a dishwasher because I didn't speak English. Obviously, they didn't care about paperwork. All they said was, "Do you have a Social Security Card?" "Yes, I do." That's all they cared. So I got the job.

At the time, David had a legitimate social security card that he had requested as a family member of an authorized resident. He was not allowed to work with this social security number, but his employer accepted it as valid in spite of the label on the card that forbade employers to do so. David's immigration status was ambiguous and he was, in fact, authorized to be in the country. As he waited for his immigration permit, paying out-of-state tuition at the college was an enormous sacrifice for David and his family, but he enrolled for a second semester. After a year of English classes and long hours at the restaurant, he met the residency requirements for in-state tuition. He enrolled at the community college as an in-state student utilizing the same social security card and copies of his bills.

At the college, David joined an organization called Future Hispanic Leaders of America (FHLA). He was surprised to learn the Hispanics in the organization only spoke English, but he decided to participate anyway. He was determined to learn the language at a proficiency level.

> . . . obviously I didn't speak English much. But, all they spoke was English. So, you also learned that way because, you know . . . you have to speak English.

At the FHLA, David learned about affirmative action and the struggles the Hispanic community faces in the United States. He was not convinced that race had anything to do with school failure, but he realized that not all students had the same opportunities in life.

> How do you expect a guy that's working sixty five hours a week have the same GPA as a guy who does not work and has the latest technology for, ah, writing . . . I mean, programs, software, money to pay tutors . . . and yet, you are admitted to business school based on GPA average. I understand that if people want to be successful, they have to try . . . to the hardest of their abilities. But that's . . . you do not have an equal playing field.

David decided the difficult workload and limited hours of study were simply the reality he would have to face, so he focused on his studies and work. He also faced pressure from his family. At one point during his studies, his mother was disappointed because he was "only" working one full-time job. Although she encouraged him to study, she also expected him to work more. After all, his stepfather had three jobs and was looking for another one.[5] David circumvented the pressure and completed enough credits at the community college to transfer to the university to pursue a baccalaureate degree. A counselor at the community college helped him to submit his credits for transfer to the university but, at the university, David was faced with an insurmountable dilemma. He was asked to produce proof of citizenship and, when he could not, he was told he could attend only if he paid international student fees. At that point, he had been in the U.S. for over three years, waiting for the INS to normalize his status and his ability to study, work, and advance his full potential. The INS, however, had not returned any of David's phone calls. Finally, around the same time he was trying to transfer to the university, a devastating communication arrived in the mail:

> I got a letter from INS saying that my application . . . that I put in many years prior
> had been denied because my mom and my stepdad married um . . . two days after my
> birthday. My eighteenth birthday.

David's younger brother was under eighteen at the time of the wedding and did qualify for residency and, later, citizenship. Their family is now facing a common phenomenon in the Mexican immigrant community: fractured families across and within borders comprised of citizens, authorized residents, undocumented members, and dependants simultaneously (see Rodríguez and Hagan, 2004). Communities and families of Mexican origin in the U.S. are being impacted socio-culturally, politically, economically, and even psychologically due to this phenomenon (see McGuire and Martin, 2007; Vertovec, 2004). They have an ambiguous sense of belonging, and, like many immigrants in similar situations, David's family members live in constant fear that one day he could be deported.

David is aware of the injustices that may ensue from his immigrant status. For years, he has averaged over fifty work hours per week, sometimes more than sixty. His checks invariably included the mandatory tax deductions, but he was never paid the legal overtime rate for working over 40 hours a week. He also felt intimidated by the overwhelming presence of the immigration police:

> . . . you got more stations of the INS here, or the Border Patrol . . . than you got
> McDonald's.

David decided to leave that environment. In 1995 he left for Colorado, where he worked several unskilled jobs. At one point he became a pizza delivery driver, accepting more responsibility when it came his way, and working his way up to shift manager. Two years later, he was promoted to assistant manager. Then he decided to return to the town in Arizona where his family lived. He was hired as an assistant manager at a newly opened pizza restaurant and eventually became the general manager. His boss encouraged him to study, but David knew the university was not accessible to him, so he decided to go back to the community college "just to learn something." Then something unexpected occurred. A counselor from the university came to the community college and invited the students in David's class to apply to transfer their credits to the university. David applied, and, this time, he was admitted without further requirements.

At the university, David took as many courses as he could while continuing to work long hours. Paying for tuition continued to be a struggle, but his situation became even more difficult when he married an undocumented

Mexican and they soon had a daughter. At that point, even in-state tuition was difficult to pay and his combined work and study load began to affect his family life. He withdrew from the university eight classes shy of earning his bachelor's degree, but he did not give up his academic dreams or his passion for learning.

> I'm always learning. And I'd like to learn more . . . I think that . . . if this whole immigration debate ends and things get settled, I should be able to even apply for . . . citizenship, or even more, I don't know. I could even start . . . my own business. Or go back to school, and . . . I don't know, I think I may have to start all over. But I don't care. I will.

As a manager, David works for a large restaurant chain that has a managerial performance ranking system. He is always at the top ten in southern Arizona, sometimes in the top five. In his position, he also realizes he has the power to do positive things for the community through donations and relationships with non-profit organizations. He has raised funds for the Muscular Dystrophy Association and for the Miracle Network, an organization that helps babies who are born prematurely. He has given donations to different churches and has organized events to support diverse causes, including rehabilitation of drug abusers. Thus, David feels he is an integral part of the community in many ways, but as an immigrant he has ambiguous feelings that he describes with metaphors and analogies:

> It's like . . . being in a . . . in a limbo. 'Cuz you don't know. I mean, you are there, but you're not."
> I am in a golden cage.

David does not have a visa anymore and this entails another dilemma. He loves his father, but he cannot go to Mexico to see him. Crossing the border without documentation is now very difficult. Nevertheless, David realized that his physical features could be an advantage in a racialized society that operates with stereotypes. He actually was able to cross the border twice to see his father and returned to the United States. He was able to do this pretending he was a U.S. citizen, showing his driver's license and his university identifications at the border. "All I got is my face," he explains, referring to his white complexion and blue eyes. "And my English . . . that was my passport."

The last time David crossed the border was 2002. He has not seen his father since. His wife is in a similar situation. At the time of the interview, her father was sick in Mexico, but she could not travel to see him for fear to not be able to return to her home in the U.S. David and his wife are now afraid to cross the border without documents because the anti-immigrant, anti-terrorist movement has intensified and they have a daughter to care for in the U.S. Their situation highlights the phenomenon pointed out by Massey et al. (2004) that "migrants" stop migrating when they have more barriers. They stay where they have the hope of improving the quality of their lives. David's story also illustrates how, as immigration barriers have grown and the undocumented become criminalized, he has been forced to take more risks and fall in the perils of "illegality." He rationalizes his actions with a personal sense of history and justice:

> Blacks used to be the property of whites, not citizens . . . Asians were not allowed to immigrate to this country . . . and it was illegal to marry a different race. Things will change for the better.

David has recurrent nightmares about being caught and sometimes his stress soars. Ironically, at the restaurant where he works, border patrol agents regularly stop by and purchase pizza. However, David looks Caucasian, speaks English very well, and is a manager. He is under the racial radar . . . for now.

Marina's Story: "I am an American in the shadows"

Marina grew up in Mexico City, living there until the age of twelve. Her family was extremely poor. She lived with her parents, her maternal grandmother, and two brothers in a single room dwelling. Her father had constructed another room for the kitchen out of plastics and other discarded materials. Both of her parents worked, but the income was barely enough to survive. Then her father lost his job. Her mother's meager income was not sufficient to support the family. Desperate, the family decided to take drastic action for survival and the hope of a more secure future. Her father decided to look for work in the United States.

Marina's father left the family to find work in the U.S. To make things easier on her mother, Marina was sent to stay with her paternal grandparents while her mother continued to work and care for the two boys. Marina's dad was able to provide for his family with his job in the United States, but the family was paying too great a price. All seemed to feel the family was disintegrating. Marina's parents decided to reunite the family and start a new life in the United States. They casually asked their children what they thought about living in the U.S. The response was not very cheerful. Thus, they told their children that, since they all had earned good grades, they would take them to Disneyland.

We were very excited as we packed, but my mother was crying as she said goodbye . . .
And my father also. As a twelve-year-old, I did not understand. Why the sadness?

Once the family reached the border, Marina's father told the children to wear comfortable clothes because they were going for a walk in the dark.

I remember we were getting close to a barbwire. And that barbwire . . . (her voice breaks). My mom was pregnant. . . . Then, my father held down the barbwire and helped my mom cross. Then my older brother crossed. And then the little one. . . . He was only six years old then. My older brother was fifteen and I was twelve. I remember my older brother was holding the barbwire down so I could cross, but my pants got caught. Then I pulled and my pants ripped.

The family walked through a deserted region and finally reached a store's parking lot on the outskirts of town where Marina's father had parked his vehicle. They drove to their final destination in southern Arizona and arrived without trouble. The next day they woke up in a little one-room apartment that would become their home, but the children did not understand that they were in another country. They wanted to know when they would go to Disneyland. Their father explained to them that he would have to make a little more money first, and then they would go. He also explained that they were now in the United States and they might have to stay there for a while.

The neighborhood where we were . . . it was not very pretty. We were in an apartment . . . like in Mexico, it was just one room, where we lived . . . I . . . my older brother and I slept on the floor. But it was carpeted, so . . . it wasn't so ugly. My mom, my dad and my little brother slept in the bed. Later, my dad found a sofa and I slept on the sofa, and my older brother stayed on the floor, on the carpet.

Marina's father enrolled the children in school.

He told us that we could be here and go to school, so we would know what it was like to go to school in the United States, and then we would go back to Mexico. . . . And up to this day, I am still waiting to go to Disneyland.

Marina's transition to an American school was difficult. She discovered that most Spanish-speaking children came from the northern part of Mexico and they considered her a *Chilanga*.[6] The English-speaking children, especially the girls, did not like her either. Marina remembers that she was good in sports and she often came ahead of her peers, but this only caused her more trouble.

Even though I did not understand what the instructor was saying, I watched, so I knew I had to do exactly what the other girls were doing. But better. . . . So, the English-speaking girls did not like that. They did not like that a girl who could not speak English was better than them in sports. . . . When it was time to change clothing, they would hide my clothes, they would push me . . . they would say things that I did not understand. It was a time that . . . was very difficult for me.

A year later, in seventh grade, Marina learned to stand up for herself. She fought with some of the girls and earned a reputation as a troublemaker. She still could not speak much English, but she was already spending time in detention. She did not successfully communicate with her counselors and would often go home with bruises and other physical signs of her battles. However, by the end of the year Marina had improved her English, and her grades were also improving. She joined the Honor Society, the folkloric dance club, and a Hispanic club. But the group of girls who hassled with her continued to harass her and would even look for her after her dance class. Marina, continued to earn high grades and still was sent to detention due to her altercations.

Marina's last two years in high school had much less conflict. She became more adapted to the school environment. Marina and many other students were enthusiastic about enrolling at the university. They filled out the applications to matriculate, but Marina's application was returned due to incomplete information. A university recruiter asked her if she was a legal resident.

I told him "yes," that I was a resident. I am a resident of Arizona. I had been living in Arizona for six years, so I was a resident. And when they asked me for papers, I said "what papers?"

Then, when I asked my parents, they told me I was *illegal*.

Marina was now eighteen years old and she did not understand what being "illegal" really meant, but she did not give up her educational dreams. She filled out an application for the community college, but it was also rejected because of her immigration status. However, luckily, one of the community college counselors decided to help Marina achieve her educational goals. He put her in contact with another person at the institution who invited her to apply to a summer program to help high school students' transition into college. Marina enrolled in the program and started taking college classes. She had no vacation that summer, but she was finally attending the community college.

For some time, Marina experienced some negative feelings about her immigrant status. She internalized the acrimony of the immigration debate and the negativity in the media and turned it against herself. In Freirean terms, she had internalized the consciousness of the colonizer (Freire, 1970; García, 2004). She experienced self-deprecatory feelings and depression about her undocumented status. When she watched the news on T.V., she would cry when the issue of immigration was addressed. For a long period, she did not want to be active and did not want to go out.

> To me, illegal . . . to be an illegal immigrant was the worst thing. It was worse than being a thief, worse than a drug dealer.
> I have seen cases on T.V. where they treat them very bad. Simply because they are *illegals* . . . I mean, they treat them worse than animals.
> I think a drug dealer is treated better in prison than an illegal.

During her college years, Marina discovered some of the implications of her undocumented status. Arizona driver's licenses require a social security number, so she could not register for one. As a consequence, she could not drive nor be admitted to places that required identification. She could not go out with friends to night clubs and could join them on their trips to Mexico (a very popular place to visit among college students in border states like Arizona). Marina was afraid to answer questions like "where are you from?" and declined invitations to go out. Marina felt "limited" and several times she considered leaving college. In spite of all this, she did not leave school and gradually overcame her depression.

Marina was well aware of the sacrifices her parents had made for their children and she did not want to disappoint them. Her parents and her family were her greatest sources of inspiration to finish college. Marina remembered when she was a small child her parents did not have enough money for provisions, so they would give the little food they had to their children, while they went without eating. They also uprooted from their family in Mexico to give their children a better future, knowing they might never again see their parents, siblings and others dear to them. As she related her story, her eyes teared up as she explained:

> I try not to disappoint them because . . . because they want the best for us. That's why I continued studying. The community college was not easy for me. It was hard. I had to show my parents that what they did was right.

Extended family is very important in the Mexican culture. Thus Marina's parents made a big sacrifice by leaving their own parents and other family members in Mexico so their children could have a better future in the United States. The price they paid was extremely high. Marina's great-grandfather, her grandfather, and her uncle on her father's side died, but her family was not able to attend the funerals. Her father did not want to take the risk of being separated from his wife and children by not being able to cross back into the U.S. Thus, Marina's father was not able to say goodbye to his father and could not accompany his mother during these painful times.[7] Perhaps the void created by their missing extended family is the reason Marina's parents place extra importance on keeping the family together in Arizona. It appears that this sense of loss has magnified the importance of the nuclear family for them. Marina's parents also have an extremely strong work ethic. Her father began working when he was six years old, shining shoes in Mexico City. Ever since Marina can remember, he has held two and sometimes three jobs. Marina has followed her parents' example. While studying at the community college, she helped her mother as a domestic worker, cleaning houses, a job commonly held by undocumented immigrants (see Chang, 2000 and Hondagneu-Sotelo, 1994). She would get up very early to help her mother; then would change clothes and go to class. Some days she would also help her mother after her classes. Later she would help in their home with the chores, cooking, and taking care of her two younger brothers.

Marina, like her parents, is a hard worker and was a good student at the community college. Yet she has faced adversities that not all students in her situation are able to overcome. Her undocumented status has been a constant cause of stress and has limited her ability to interact normally with the rest of the world. Without documents, she could not apply for employment that was commensurate with her studies; she was ineligible for most scholarships and could not apply for work internships. A deficient public transportation system in the city where Marina resides also limited her ability to get to college or work, and she could not drive for lack of a driver's license. For the same reason, she frequently had difficulty meeting with other students to work on group projects. It was the cumulative effect of the obstacles Marina confronted day after day that almost made her leave college, but she persevered.

Marina has held jobs that are typically held by undocumented workers. She worked as a domestic worker, as an office cleaner, and in a couple of service sector jobs where she was eventually dismissed because of her invalid social security number. Marina had to try to reconcile the discordant reality of an upbringing in the United States, where the ideals of equality and justice for all are constitutional rights, yet finding herself excluded from that world:

> They are exploiting you . . . you know they are exploiting you, but you do nothing. . . .
> It's not because you can't, but because you feel impotent and you're afraid.

Finally, Marina found employment in a little store that belongs to the community college counselor who helped her enroll in college. Marina and her mother had already worked for him and his wife as domestic workers. At first, the hours were minimal, but as the business improved she was able to work more. At the time of the interview, Marina was working about forty-nine hours per week with no insurance and no overtime pay. Nevertheless she felt very grateful to her employers because they treated her with respect and she earned above the minimum wage.

As the store attendant, Marina has found that some clients do not like her accent. She has experienced some insecurity and self-doubt because of this, but she has also become more resilient. In fact, she has a hard time thinking of herself as an immigrant:

> What I know about Mexico is very vague. I grew up here. My friends, my first boy-friend, my education . . . I have had everything in the United States. It is a little diffi-cult for me to say I am an immigrant.
> I am an American in the shadows.

Marina participated in the immigrant protests of 2006 that took place throughout the United States to demand immigrant rights. When she arrived at the first gathering, she saw the thousands of people who were participating and could not contain her tears. Marina realized her cause had the support of many people. Marina took part in three marches and after her first experience, she began encouraging friends and other undocumented people to participate. On May first, 2006, the date of a major pro-immigrant march, one of her undocumented friends was offered a $200 bonus if she agreed to work rather than protest. The friend rejected the offer. Marina's employers did not oppose her participation in the protests. Marina was proud to see war veterans and some of her high school teachers in the march. Suddenly, her hopes for "legalization" were more optimistic.

Marina has wisely stated: "It is better to be persistent than to be naturally smart." Incredibly, she has earned four associate degrees from the community college, but she cannot do much with her degrees as long as she remains undocumented. Recently, an e-mail from Marina confided that she had not been paid for several months. The business is not doing well; sales are down, and she is starting to feel desperate. At the same time, the anti-immigrant sentiment is running high in Arizona and immigration reform is stuck in Congress. Her courage and determination are being tested once again.

Roberto's Story: "Racism is an excuse for failure"

Roberto came to the United States as an international student in 1991 in more advantageous circumstances than the other participants in this study. He first enrolled at the community college in English classes and a year later in the International Business Program. As he was working on the second year of his associate's degree, a family crisis almost brought his studies to an end. His father would no longer be able to support his studies. Roberto decided to get employment to finish his studies and was hired, without documents, at an international collections agency that collected overdue debts for American Express. Roberto was a natural at this kind of work

> They would give us [collection] goals. My first month goal was about $30,000 [U.S.] dollars and I collected $120,000.

Ironically, Roberto became a valuable employee because he could communicate very effectively with Mexican people who were in default of their international debts. A debt crisis had developed in Mexico due to the currency devaluation that devastated the Mexican economy in 1994–1995. The national economic slump provoked personal and corporate bankruptcies throughout the country, a deterioration of wages, and increased emigration from Mexico to the United States (Barkin, 1997; Morris and Passé-Smith, 2001).[8] Roberto's work in the U.S. provided him the income to pay for his studies and thus he was able to earn an associate's degree in International Business Studies. Completing his degree was a big challenge for him, since he did not have a lot of time to study and his family was going through a difficult time. Although he graduated from the community college, his dream of studying international relations at Grand Canyon University had to be put on hold.

Roberto's story is not the story of a poor immigrant who escaped poverty in Mexico but illustrates the multifaceted phenomenon of immigration and the complex reasons why individuals become undocumented residents in the United States. It is also evident from Roberto's story that the obstacles that immigrants have to face have not always been as difficult as they are currently:

> One day, my friends and I went to the office [the Social Security Administration] because we wanted to have a driver's license. And, in order to give you the license, they would ask you for a social security number. And if you wanted to open a bank account, they would ask you for the social security. And for everything else. . . . So we went to request the number. And they gave us the number. In some cases the card would read: "Valid only for work with INS permit," or something like that . . . and some would not.

Undocumented immigrants in Arizona no longer have access to the kind of advantages Roberto enjoyed (being able to obtain employment with a noncitizen social security number and obtaining a driver's license is not possible anymore). Such advantages, combined with his determination and boldness, helped him secure jobs where he was be able to use his Spanish skills, including Hispanic customer service jobs with MCI and AOL.

> I was very lucky. But, being positive helps you the most. Because the whole world would tell me, "it's not possible, it's not possible." . . . When you are positive, you have completed half of the journey toward your goals.

In contrast, most immigrants now feel harassed and intimidated and even U.S. citizens of Hispanic or Mexican origin perceive an increase in discrimination (Suro and Escobar, 2006). Anti-immigrant legislation and anti-Mexican racism are on the rise (De Genova, 2005; Mariscal, 2005). Nonetheless, though he has not normalized his status to date, Roberto still has a driver's license, a business license, a bank account, and he uses his non-citizen social security number to pay taxes every year (see Porter, 2005). In 2006, his earnings were higher than expected, and he did not deduct sufficient payroll tax throughout the year, thus he paid an additional $4,500 U.S. dollars at the end of the fiscal year.

Roberto has a network of immigrant friends who came to the U.S. under different circumstances. One of them crossed the border through the desert. Another one is a U.S. citizen raised in Mexico, but he left medical school in Mexico to come to the U.S. "for a better future." Another undocumented friend is a mechanic who started a successful business. After Roberto's family's economic debacle in Mexico, his sister came to Arizona and stayed with him for a while. She used to walk about eight miles every day, in the extreme heat of southern Arizona, so she could take care of a baby for a family that paid her 50 dollars a week. As pointed out by Massey et al. (2004), immigrants contribute to raising the living standards of the middle class and the returns to capital. Roberto and his friends are examples of this phenomenon.

Interestingly, Roberto's brother and sister have become U.S. citizens and his parents also reside in the U.S. The whole family resides now in the same town. Roberto's father has become an authorized resident while his mother has not yet normalized her immigration status. Family unification is a powerful trend among all Mexican immigrants. Their challenge, as in the cases of participants in this research, is the different immigration statuses held by the family members. Undoubtedly family unification is an impetus for immigration, while family maintenance serves as motivation to succeed. Like David, Roberto finds that being responsible for his family is a great motivator to succeed in spite of adversities.

> My family is an encouragement. I have two children. They are young. I want the best for them.

Roberto is aware of the disdain that exists toward Mexican immigrants in some sectors of the population. He blames some of this disdain on the "sensationalist press." To be sure, it is common to read and see images in the U.S. media that refer to horrific isolated events that involved undocumented immigrants. They are easily transformed into hate targets and referred to with dehumanizing adjectives like "aliens" and "illegals" (sic).[9] On April 4, 2006, for example, radio host Brian James of KFYI-AM in Arizona advocated murder as a way of dealing with undocumented immigrants. Among other things, he suggested that the National Guard shoot illegal immigrants and receive "$100 a head." The remarks prompted Arizona Attorney General and the U.S. Attorney to send a complaint to the Federal Communications Commission (Associated Press, 2006). Roberto believes a lack of education plays a role in these prejudices:

> That disdain exists because of a lack of culture. A lack of knowledge, more than anything. . . . Learned people are very polite, the great majority. And learned persons are very understanding people.

Roberto displays an interesting mixture of pragmatism, realism, and optimism. He appears to discount or ignore all of the negativity and tension currently surrounding the immigration debate. The structural forces that stop undocumented immigrants from advancing are evident in the limitations he faces. He expresses frustrations about them, but he believes those who cannot succeed create their own barriers. Despite his own limitations, he expresses admiration for the cultural values of the United States and sees them as an avenue for success.

> Here, those who want to get ahead will get ahead. Those who do not want. . . . Well, they make their own barriers.
> American culture is more individualistic. That's why they are successful.

At the same time, he expresses pride about his Mexican origin and is critical of perceived cultural differences between his native and his adopted county:

> Here your word is not worth anything. Here you have to write everything. And Mexicans don't do that. If someone tells you something will be done in a certain way, that's the way it will be.

Irrespective of conflicting perspectives, Roberto truly believes in the American Dream. In fact, ironically, he is the personification of the American Dream: economic improvement by his own ingenuity and hard work. He has become an entrepreneur and owns a franchise business that provides services to stranded vehicles. He contracts with insurance companies and receives calls twenty-four hours a day. He makes very good money compared to other first-generation immigrants, but he is always on call. His work ethic and determination have helped him succeed and provide for his family, but he still lives at the margins of mainstream society in many ways.

> We do not have our own house because. . . . If I buy a house, who will benefit if I am not here? [implying the possibility of being deported]

Roberto's undocumented status has been a great disadvantage, but he has demonstrated great resilience against all odds and adversities. He is an example of the entrepreneurial spirit, tenacity, and hard work that immigrants bring to the U.S. in spite of great obstacles. Like other undocumented immigrants, Roberto knows that his dreams have limits. He has become a little cynical and prefers not to waste time reflecting on explanations of immigrant disadvantage and racial inequality. In Roberto's own words, "racism is an excuse for failure"

Rosario's Story: "If you don't make your own way, no one will make it for you"

Rosario's story illustrates the drama of many Mexican families who have seen their economic conditions deteriorate throughout the past three decades. Cajeme, the municipality where Rosario comes from, was a major agricultural economy from the time immediately after the Mexican Revolution through the 1970s. The Mexican government started implementing neoliberal economic policies in the early 1980s and, in 1994, signed the North American Free Trade Agreement (NAFTA) with the United States and Canada. Since then, different sectors of the Mexican economy have been impacted in different ways by this new competitive model. Large portions of the agricultural sector have experienced a constant decline because of the impossibility of competing with the large, highly industrialized North American corporations and because of the enormous subsidies the U.S. grants to its producers (see De Janvry and Sadoulet, 2001). Many people in the countryside, unemployed and finding little to no other option, have become undocumented immigrants to the U.S. Many urban families, like Rosario's, who used to be connected to the agricultural sector, have been forced to find new ways to make a living (see Bacon 2004a, 2004b).

Before that, Rosario's plans in life were very different:

The easiest thing would be to study English in the U.S. and then maybe I would go to Guadalajara to study Tourism. That was, as a woman, a typical career in those days. Because in Mexico they [well-to-do young ladies] had the mentality that you would get married, and then what would your studies be good for?

Before Rosario was born, her father resided, studied, and worked in the U.S. as a single man. As a young couple, her parents also lived in the United States for eight years. Like many Mexican immigrants, her mother saved money from her husband's wages and sent it to Mexico to build their first house (see Massey, 2005). When they returned to Mexico, Rosario's father established what would become a prosperous business in the agricultural transportation sector. Rosario's parents had a cautious admiration for the United States and, like other well-to-do families in Mexico, they would make trips to shop in the nearest U.S. malls. They had had some rough times while in the U.S., but that was part of the past.

My parents experienced racism when my dad worked in the United States. My mom tells me that, when they lived in Texas, they saw establishments with signs that read: "No Mexicans."

Rosario grew up in an upper middle class environment where it was not uncommon for children to be sent to the United States to learn English during the summers or, in some cases, for one or two school years. They knew that learning English was important advantage in the Mexican classist societal structure. Thus, in the early 1980s, like some of her teenage friends, Rosario was sent to Arizona as an international student to learn English. By this time, however, her father's business was declining. Rosario was sent to stay with friends of the family who resided in the poorest part of town, where a large population of Mexican origin lives. As explained before, the connections between Mexicans on both sides of the bother are very extensive. At the end of the 1980s, around half of the Mexican adult population were related to someone living in the U.S. and one third of all Mexicans had been to the United States sometime in their lives (Massey and Espinosa, 1997). Rosario was a clear example of these transnational bonds.

Around 1981, with her father's permission, Rosario moved in with three friends of her age and shared living expenses. Her roommates were upper middle class Mexican students who also had come to Arizona to study English. At the time, her parents were going though an increasingly difficult economic situation and their marriage was failing. In spite of this, Rosario's parents came to Arizona very often "to check" on her. In 1982, her parents finally divorced. The same year, Mexico had the dubious honor of triggering the international debt crisis (see Soros, 1998). Many middle class and upper middle class families suffered irrevocable financial losses during this time, in what would prove to be one of the most challenging economic debacles in the country's history. The Mexican currency devalued by 100%, and many affluent families went bankrupt. Rosario's friends had gone back to Mexico and her family could not pay for her studies anymore, but she refused to go back to a fractured family in financial ruin. She was now eighteen years old and on her own.

> The Peso exchange had jumped from twelve Pesos, fifty cents to twenty-something. We did not know what was going on. We did not know what inflation was![10]

Rosario kept her student visa, but she stopped going to school. She suffered the rigors of poverty and found herself falling into a spiral of negative events. She experienced the rejection of a Jewish boyfriend because his mother did not like Mexicans, she had a relationship that ended in physical abuse, and, when her visa expired, she became an undocumented resident.[11] She experienced isolation, depression, and even food deprivation.

> In those days I suffered a lot. I suffered much loneliness. I even suffered from hunger. Even hunger, when I was alone . . .

Despite these challenges, Rosario never stopped trying to get ahead. She sold homemade Mexican food and jewelry to friends to support herself. In the mid-eighties, forced by their moribund economic condition in Mexico, her mother, sister, and a teenaged brother also came to Arizona. The four of them lived together in a modest apartment in a poor area of town. On one occasion, they were assaulted in the middle of the night, inside their own home, by three criminals who forced their way into the house by breaking a glass door. The malefactors made the family lie on the floor at gunpoint and tried to get money from them. They were unsuccessful and left without hurting anyone, but the family continued to live with terror. The incident was never reported to the police. As noted by Political Research Associates (PRA), a think tank devoted to racial justice, "fear keeps undocumented immigrants from reporting dangerous working or housing conditions and other community concerns." Apparently, this is not only true of the undocumented, but also in some cases where authorized immigrants are the victims of abuses or crimes (PRA, 2002). Under the stress of living in unsafe conditions, Rosario started to work two jobs as a nanny and as a housekeeper and, with the combined effort of the family, they were able to move to a different apartment in a nicer area of town.

Rosario wanted to be a teacher and was encouraged by a friend to attend the local community college. She was able to register without citizenship documents by proving residency in the state of Arizona, but she dropped out of her classes because of economic difficulties. In the late nineteen eighties, with the help of one of her domestic employers, Rosario applied for the amnesty offered by the Reagan administration to undocumented workers. After normalizing her residency status in the U.S., she worked in a restaurant as a food preparer. She met a Mexican-origin man and married him in 1989, but he was not the responsible husband she expected. Only five months after their wedding, he left her. Rosario had to leave the apartment where they lived and, once again, work in a restaurant. Her husband came back sporadically and she became pregnant twice in the following six years. Rosario had a daughter in 1991 and a son in 1996.

While working in the restaurant, Rosario did not have health insurance, but she managed to pay for her daughter's health policy with her meager salary. She did not know that, being a legal resident living under the poverty line, she was entitled to federal programs that could help her.

> I did not know those programs existed . . . I had been paying for my daughter's insurance, and now that I was pregnant I was paying 300 dollars per month.

In 1996, after her son was born, she was fired from the restaurant where she had been working for years. She was openly told she could not work there while having to take care of two children.

> "You know what?" he [her employer] tells me, "We've been talking and, well, you already have two children . . . why don't you stay home and take care of them? . . . How could they leave me without a job knowing that I had two children to feed?

Rosario then suffered an intense post-partum depression but was not aware of this at the time. She struggled through a very difficult time where she could barely get up in the morning. She felt worthless and isolated. Adding to her sense of worthlessness was her eventual decision, though reluctant, to ask for public aid. A friend persuaded her to ask for this benefit, which she did not know she was entitled to. Rosario thought such aid was for "the lazy people of this country." To make things worse, she fell ill and had to spend 15 days in the hospital. The hospital served as a time of reflection for her, a turning point where she decided to take positive action to improve her situation. She decided to go back to college. Rosario thought the university "was very big" for her. Once again, she enrolled in the community college.

I got out of the hospital with hunger . . . I was hungry to be someone. I told them [the counselors at the community college], "I want to go to school, I don't know what I want to study, but I want to do something. Something in life."

At the community college, Rosario was invited to participate in a program called Women in Progress (WIPA), specifically designed for single mothers who were struggling to earn an education. Her mother supported her educational goals and helped her take care of her children while she went to school. The influence of Rosario's parents in her decisions is omnipresent throughout her narrative. She expresses a mixture of fear and respect toward her father and enormous deference toward her mother. Financially, it was only possible for her to attend the college because she was granted a scholarship from WIPA. It was still very challenging; her mother could not always take care of the children. One of Rosario's instructors would allow her to attend class with her daughter if she would sit with her at the back of the classroom. Her daughter colored quietly through the class.

In the classroom, the instructor would tell me: "I don't see her" [her daughter]. Then I would try to cover her with some binders. And she would duck and stay there. She would not even make any noise.

Rosario obtained a job as a student aid for the community college as she completed her associate degree in Business. Later, she worked in a temporary position for the college as a clerical assistant. By the time Rosario graduated in 2003, she was actively involved in the WIPA program and had taught keyboarding to some of the participants. She now works for a school district in an adult education program where she is helping other immigrants. Rosario also has formed a new family with a U.S. native of Mexican ancestry who has become a putative father for her children. He has given her the choice to stay home to be a full-time mother, but she has decided to continue her work for the community.

Rosario remembers with sadness the period when she was undocumented and how afraid she was of the police, even when she had done nothing wrong. In those days she "did not know about the great racism [against immigrants], that you can now see every day." She explains that the undocumented immigrants she works with live in a constant fear of being deported. She understands that fear very well:

In the mornings, when they leave to work, their families do not know if they will see them again. . . . Simply traveling from point A to point B is very scary when you do not have documents. . . . You cannot trust anyone.

Before the draconian laws that institute barriers to higher education for undocumented students (see Billeaud, 2007), noncitizens who could demonstrate local residency could attend the community college like any other community taxpayer. In our interview, Rosario explained that, even before these cruel laws were enacted, there were many people who wanted to attend the community college but were afraid. They felt intimidated, even after many years of residing and paying taxes in the community, because they did not have documents. Thus, like Marina, Rosario participated in the national marches for immigration reform in April and May, 2006. At the time, the protests were seen by some scholars as part of a "new civil rights movement" and as a phenomenon of mass, trans-national economic migration engendered by globalization (See Robinson, 2006).

> A residency permit takes a big burden from you. Because you feel you have more liberty. Simply moving around the city. . . . Simply going from point A to point B is very frustrating. That's why I support the marches and the boycotts. I support their struggle.

Rosario is also an active member of the Parents Association in her children's school, where she has taught some Spanish courses to children. She and her children are bilingual, but she always speaks to them in Spanish. She feels totally integrated in the community. Rosario reflects on her life in the United States and realizes that, after 25 years, she finally feels she has a stable life. She has become more spiritual and acknowledges God as her greatest support in life. She believes that God made her go through hard times and helped her become familiarized with the community college and other community organizations so that she could help others succeed. But she is also very pragmatic. In her own words,

> When you are hungry to do something, or you want something in life, you break barriers down; you remove the stones from the road. If you don't make your own way, no one will make it for you.

Justo's Story: "There are no limits"

Justo's family, like Rosario's, was the victim of one of the recurrent Mexican financial crises. Justo's father was a prosperous businessman in the state of Sonora until he lost everything during the economic crisis of 1994. From a position of relatively high socioeconomic status, his father lost his businesses, the family house, and his vehicles. His parents considered the options: staying in Mexico, with the national economy in ruins, and coming to the U.S. Their situation was so desperate that, even without work permits, the U.S. seemed to grant them the greatest chance for success. In the end, the family came to the U.S. for the same fundamental reason that pushes the great majority of Mexicans to emigrate: economic survival.

Growing up, Justo was a timid child who stuttered and did not have friends to play with during his school breaks. However, he was born in a more privileged environment than most immigrants. At twelve years of age, Justo had the benefit of attending a bilingual (Spanish/English) school in Mexico, so language was not the main challenge he would confront in the U.S. Justo's family also had an advantage that most destitute immigrants do not possess. Although they did not have work permits, the family had traveled in and out of the U.S. many times in the past, so they used their passports and visitor's visas to cross again. Nonetheless, this time it was very different. The traumatic experience of losing everything and then moving to an unknown environment in search of an uncertain future was only the beginning of the new challenges they would face.

Justo's family story could exemplify the argument that self-selection by migrants usually means that they are especially resourceful, entrepreneurial and ambitious (*The Economist*, 2001). They also corroborate a study at the University of Chicago (Chiquiar and Hanson, 2005) that utilized the 1990 and 2000 Mexican and U.S. population censuses, where it was found that Mexican immigrants in the United States are more educated on average than nonmigrants in Mexico. Research also has found that "when Mexican economic crises occur, they lead to more out-migration and to relatively more skilled immigrants" (Orrenius and Zavodny, 2005: 237).

Justo's father had managerial and administrative skills that he could not use in the United States, but he and his wife continued to work as volunteers for a chapter of their church in Arizona. He had owned a car-washing business in Mexico and his brother-in-law owned a similar business in Arizona. Thus, the first job Justo's father found in the U.S. was as a car washer. He went from being the owner of the same type of business to a less-than-minimum-wage-earning laborer. The family found themselves living under the official poverty line in their adopted country. The minimum wage in Arizona was $4.15 per hour. Justo's father was paid $2.15 per hour. That was a very painful situation to witness for Justo, who expresses great admiration for his father's determination and stoicism. This is one source of Justo's inspiration:

> He would never . . . complain. He would get home after working fifteen hours . . . After that job, he had another one at Jack in the Box for three years, and he once had one shift of twenty-two consecutive hours. So, my dad is the type of man who'd never complain. And I did not want to inconvenience him; I would never talk about how I

> was aware that he . . . suffered, when he went into his room and, obviously sore after the day's work . . . especially during the winter, when he had to wash cars. And . . . and my uncle would lose many workers, except my dad. Because he needed the work. Then, well . . . he [his uncle] would take his tips, half of them . . . In other word, it was a complete abuse.

Justo witnessed how his father suffered the plight of many undocumented immigrants, being abused and exploited but feel like they cannot do anything about it. Justo felt frustration but focused on the best choices he had as a seventh grader in a new country: school and sports. By ninth grade he was running track and playing football and basketball. He was good in sports, he became the captain of his football team, and began receiving scholarship offers from different universities, including Washington State University. However, without "legal" residency status in the U.S., Justo could not dream of accepting them. Nevertheless, Justo thought football could be a way to regularize his immigration status and he trained hard . . . until he suffered a career-ending injury to his shoulder.

After three years of hard training, Justo was devastated to learn that his football dreams would never be. But he was able to find motivation in new activities. He kept working hard academically and, with other five high school friends, founded a club they called *Voces de la Juventud Hispana* (Voices of Hispanic Youth). The objective of the organization was to inform Hispanic students about their choices in higher education and to encourage them to stay in school. Then, Justo reveals an amazing fact: The six founding members and many students in *Voces de la Juventud Hispana* were undocumented students.

> The leaders . . . We were six leaders, the board members, it was six of us who founded the club, and . . . none of them had documents.

Justo's internal drive, his advocacy and agency to help others, appear ironic. He was creating a positive effect in the community irrespective of his or their status. He was only sixteen or seventeen years old then. He had a fearless determination to make something of himself. But Justo was not exempt from the constant fear and stress experienced by undocumented immigrants:

> When you don't have documents, even the guards in the mall make you nervous. That is, you think . . . everybody is looking at you. You don't want to argue about things, you don't want to be noticed . . . more noticed that what it's necessary. Because . . . because you feel vulnerable to everything.

Finally, the church Justo's parents attend helped the family immigrate as religious workers, and the whole family became "legalized" in December of 1999. Up to that point Justo's father had been doing side jobs like washing cars and fixing the vehicles of church members, handyman jobs and gardening . . . and he was also paying taxes. Justo kept working hard academically, with the added incentive that he could now go to college. But even after regularizing his immigration status, Justo was not exempt from the subtle influences of institutionalized racism. He felt ashamed of his accent and was quiet in class, but two of his teachers encouraged him by focusing on his strengths.

> "I see something in you," he told me. "I see something . . . something you have not taken advantage of."
>
> And sometimes I did not have an A, but he would tell me: "I know you can." So, he pushed me. He pushed, and pushed, and pushed. . . . He was always well dressed. He was a leader in his Baptist church. He was . . . he was someone you would not expect would care so much for an immigrant student from Mexico.

Justo graduated from high school with honors and received the recognition of Business Student of the Year. He has developed the ability to extrapolate experiences from different dimensions of his life and turn them into inspiration in other areas. His main positive influences in life, he reveals, are his parents, his church doctrine, and sports. He switches his narrative to English and explains to the interviewing author how his football coach taught him a lesson that he now applies in all areas of his life:

> He [the coach] said, "You know why I'm yelling at you?" I answered, "Because I went the wrong way." Then he said, "No, because you did it half speed." He said, "In my team, you do everything full speed. If you go the wrong way, I don't give a shit," he said, "you go full speed. If you go the right way, you go full speed. I would rather you go the wrong way full speed, than go the right way half speed. You never do things half speed in my team.
>
> I have never forgotten. Then, I thought . . . if I'm not going the right way with this college thing, at least I'm gonna' go at it full speed.

Justo earned a scholarship to start his higher education at the community college. Like Marina and Jesenia, he started taking college classes in a summer program designed to help students transition into college. In one of his developmental education classes,[12] he experienced his first big challenge in college. It had nothing to do with his academic skills or with his ability to do the work. His Reading class instructor accused him of giving the answers to another student—his girlfriend at the time—when Justo was borrowing a pencil from her during a test. The instructor even accused a third Mexican student who was sitting next to Justo and his girlfriend during the test. Justo tried to speak with the instructor, but she refused to talk with him

> "I'm gonna' write a letter to the president of this campus," she told me. "I will make sure everybody knows what kind of a person you are, and make sure your ass never comes back here again," she told me.
>
> And I was very scared because she said, "Your academic life is over." She said, "Once it's on your record, you can't come back here or any college in this state. I'm gonna' make sure that happens." *She told me,*[13] "I'm gonna' make sure your ass never comes back to college again."
>
> "I don't talk to people your kind," she said. "So leave my office now. Leave my classroom now."

Justo did not understand processes at the college and assumed that he was going to be expelled. As this was happening, he had an interview for a job as a maintenance worker at the college. He was going to withdraw his application, but his mother encouraged him and insisted that he should not miss the interview. He was hired. At the end of the semester, students in his Reading class met with the instructor so she could explain their final grades. The three students involved in the incident were summoned by the instructor. She had asked a campus police officer to be present in the classroom while she spoke with the students. Justo still gets disturbed when he remembers the incident:

> And she told us, "I'm giving you an F for the course because you cheated in the class." And we explained again, "We didn't cheat." "Well," she said, "After this meeting, you're going to be escorted out of the college by this police officer . . ." "And . . . he's here for my protection" . . ."and to make sure that you leave the campus and you don't come back," she said. And then she called the police officer. She had the officer in the room, next to us. Like if we were criminals . . .

The instructor added a statement that was supposed to appear magnanimous to the students, but it was probably meant to assure that they would not appeal her decision:

> She told us, "What I'm gonna' do is I'm going to give you the F," she said, "and not report the incident." "I'm not going to report this incident."

Justo felt embarrassed and felt that everybody was looking at him and his two friends as cheaters. His first thought was that he was disappointing the people who helped him get to college, his parents, his teachers, his counselors. They tried to go straight to one of their counselors to explain to him what was happening. The police officer followed them around campus and he finally told them they had to leave. Justo's friends were crying and he felt like his future was crumbling in front of him. They felt humiliated, intimidated and powerless as they left the campus escorted by a police officer. Their instructor was not only working against them but trying to remove any recourse they could have to appeal her actions. Once again, Justo's parents were a source of support that encouraged and helped him go through an exhausting appeal process that lasted many months. He was "terrified" of his instructor, but he submitted a grade appeal and filed discrimination charges against her.

Justo had to cope with the appeal process as he went through the following semester and worked in his new job. Initially, the division dean reviewed Justo's work and the parties were convened with supporting witnesses. Justo's witness was a Chicana instructor who made it clear he was an outstanding student. The dean decided that Justo deserved an A in the class, but the Reading instructor disagreed and appealed the decision to the chief academic officer. The division dean's decision was upheld, which apparently hurt the instructor's pride. She appealed once again, this time to the campus president. Eight months after the case was open, the president himself reviewed Justo's work and ruled in his favor. By then, Justo had straight As in all his classes and he had become a member of Phi Theta Kappa. After all, it appeared his instructor had chosen a very studious immigrant to persecute.

In retrospect, Justo sees this ordeal as a "blessing" because it helped him meet other college staff and administrators. The campus president invited Justo to be part of a campus renovation committee representing the students' perspective. Later he ran for and was elected campus student president (the first immigrant to hold that office), and finally he became the student representative for the whole district at the community college board of governors meetings. Through these activities, he earned scholarships that helped pay for his tuition and materials. It took Justo three years to finish his associates degree at the community college, where he earned six scholarships, one for each semester. Not surprisingly, Justo graduated with honors.

In Justo's view, if you work hard enough, you can do anything. It is difficult to think of someone who could be a better exponent of what the media sells as "American values." His spirituality has been a strong support for him, but he does not expect God to resolve issues for him.

> There are no limits. If you truly want something, you can achieve it in this country. This is the country of opportunity.
> I have learned that . . . God blesses those who work hard (I: 594–595).
> Since I was a little boy, I would tell God, "Father," I used to say, "I will do my part, and I hope you do yours. Let's go fifty and fifty on this." (I: 1003–1005).

In his last year of community college, Justo was selected for the All-Arizona and All-USA Academic Teams, for which each year two graduating students are selected to represent the college. The students earn state-wide recognition in the media and are awarded a two-year scholarship to the student's choice of one of the three state universities. Justo earned a full scholarship to attend the University of Arizona. Additionally, through his activities at the university and through his own perseverance, Justo was able to secure other small scholarships from diverse sources including the Hispanic Scholarship Fund, Congressional Hispanic Caucus Institute (CHCI), and Phi Beta Kappa.

Once in the university Justo went "full speed" into his studies and activities. He was a speaker at the National Conference on Race and Ethnicity, (NCORE). The community college invited him to do several motivational speaking presentations to potential students. He also became involved in Students in Free Enterprise (SIFE), a student organization where he participated in national competitions promoting entrepreneurial innovations with a social perspective. His desire to help others is reflected in the activities he chose to be involved in, for example, a SIFE program that taught university students smart personal finances and how to use credit wisely. In the midst of all his successes, Justo remained attached to his culture and identity. As he was starting his university experience, one of his acquaintances of Mexican origin, who was not particularly proud of being of Mexican descent, approached him:

> He was teasing me and he said, "Hey, you're proud of being Mexican, right?" And I
> said, "Yes, I am." Then he said, "Well, here's something for you Hispanics." He gave
> me an application for CHCI. The Congressional Hispanic Caucus Institute. And he
> said, "It's due in a week. . . . I saw it, and . . . I know that you're all proud, and you're
> all *raza*. So, uh, you know, so you go ahead and try it out. Maybe you'll like it."

A summer internship program in the US Congress sounded like an exciting idea to Justo. He was not accepted the first time he applied, but his mother encouraged him to apply the following year. Justo rewrote his essays and resubmitted his application. He was accepted.

> All the people there were from Stanford, Harvard, Yale, all of them. And me, from
> the community college. . . . The only community college and, well, almost no one
> from state universities, they all came from Ivy Leagues. . . .

Justo was the only immigrant and the only non-citizen in the group. That year, he was chosen by his student cohort to represent them in addressing the Congressional Hispanic Caucus. Later, Justo applied for a CHCI scholarship and he received it. He also became the president of SIFE, where he participated in international projects teaching computer skills and entrepreneurial principles to children in Mexico. In 2004, he was one of four students selected by the U.S. Department of State to assist in the development of a SIFE team in Egypt. In 2005, Justo graduated Cum Laude with a baccalaureate in Political Science. In 2006, he was selected to become a public policy fellow at the CHCI. He was part of an exclusive group of 20 students from across the United States who worked as legislative assistants for nine months in the House of Representatives.

Recounting all of Justo's successes and adventures would take more than a few pages. Interestingly, his voyage to Egypt, representing the US Department of State, was as an authorized U.S. resident, but he had to travel with a Mexican passport because he was not yet a U.S. citizen. In 2006, Justo was the first in his family to become a U.S. citizen. He makes clear his admiration and love for the United States in our interview. However, his identity and sense of family are inextricably influenced by his Mexican culture. As the oldest child, he feels responsible to and for his family, especially for his younger sisters and even his cousins:

> . . . my little cousins, they look up to me, you know. And when I go to their birthday parties, they want to take a picture with me, and that's exciting for them. I always felt that . . . it's not only about me [alluding to the responsibility he feels toward his family].

Justo reveals that he does not really feel like a foreigner, but he does not mind being seen an immigrant. He is proud of his Mexican roots. He thinks people of Mexican origin and immigrants have much to contribute to the United States.

> To be an immigrant is to be different, always going against the tide . . . But that is my normal lifestyle. I have a strong heritage. I know where I come from. And because I know where I come from, I have a strong culture, I know where I'm going.

At the same time, Justo's strong determination and confidence do not blind him to the reality of prejudice and bigotry. Perhaps even he, at times of weakness, has been the victim of internalizing a colonizing, racialized conscience:

> Sometimes, in college, when I was about to enter an elevator, and I saw only Anglos inside, I felt . . . insecure. . . . I used to think "How is a Mexican going to stop that elevator and make it late?" . . . Even the word "immigrant." You don't even have to . . . say illegal, or undocumented, or . . . whatever term they use, it's just that word, I think it has a negative connotation to it. It's just saying . . . you are an outsider. They stereotype it as, what are you doing here? You know, "you may study, but you're probably on a Hispanic scholarship" kind of thing, or . . ."if you're not," you know,

"you should be working somewhere else," . . . there're some fields where they're not used to seeing Hispanics.

Justo believes that prejudice and racism are simply "ignorance." He has experienced that ignorance within the Hispanic, the Mexican, and the Chicano communities as well. He feels it is useless to dwell on this and complain about it. He just pushes forward and fights it where he can. He focuses on the positive, on his goals, and his commitment to the community where his family lives.

If we always would dwell on discrimination . . . Ugh! Where would we be now? We would be in a hole, crying and . . . nothing. Because it's everywhere. I have high goals. I'm . . . not even halfway done with what I want to do. Sometimes I look at me and I say, "I'm twenty-four and I'm behind . . . behind schedule here."

Unquestionably any community in the United States would benefit from Justo's presence. For him, there is one thing that reaffirms his belonging to the community where he now lives with his wife. He explains with pride:

There is nothing that makes you more part of a community than having graduated from the community college.

Notes

[1] As an amateur photographer, the interviewing author found this idea very exciting. Photographs can contain powerful stories and messages. Photography is a universal language that can reflect truthfully life and events in ways that words cannot. It also can be utilized as a visual pedagogical tool to challenge the status quo. For example, Ramírez (2002) has described the artistic photography of Alma López as a "visual language" that has contributed to the process of decolonization of peoples of Mexican origin. With her photographs, Jesenia was allowing the author to penetrate her world both visually and through her narrative.

[2] As explained in "The political economy of immigration," in Chapter II, the U.S. Internal Revenue Service (IRS) allows undocumented immigrants to file taxes by applying for an Individual Taxpayer Identification Number (ITIN). Jesenia's mother, like the interviewees in this research and hundreds of thousands of undocumented immigrants (Gorman, 2006), pays taxes but is not officially entitled to their benefits.

[3] In the Mexican and Latin American tradition, the *Quinceañera* is a young woman's celebration of her fifteenth birthday. It is considered an important event and is celebrated differently from other birthdays. Traditionally there is a lavish *fiesta* with dance, food, and drinks, where the birthday girl wears an elaborate white dress.

[4] See Drachman (2006) and Varsanyi (2006) for different perspectives on citizenship rights and access to higher education for undocumented students.

[5] In contrast to the stereotypes and the dominant narratives, research has found Mexican-American workers to be productive, cooperative, and possessing a strong sense of teamwork and work ethic (Weaver, 2000). Interestingly, research also has found the perception that European Americans and Jewish Americans hold regarding the work ethic and intelligence of Hispanics improved significantly between 1990 and 2000 (Weaver, 2005).

[6] *Chilango/a* is a Mexican slang word used to refer to a person from Mexico City or its surrounding areas. The *Chilango/a* adjective is usually associated with the sing-song Spanish accent spoken by people from southern Mexico. The term can have a negative connotation.

[7] Restrictions on travel are not only faced by undocumented immigrants but also by authorized permanent residents. For an excellent review on such restrictions and their potential consequences, see Morawetz (2006). Her research refers to such restrictions as an inhumane "invisible border," which is a product of anachronistic laws that place restrictions on a wide variety of situations and immigration statuses. She argues for a more humane approach that does not place noncitizens in the situation of having to choose between family responsibilities and their residence in the U.S.

[8] Arguably, the main cause of the Mexican currency crisis was the hegemonic economic influence of the U.S.—and U.S. dominated international financial institutions—over Mexico. Pressure for neoliberal economic policies, currency speculation, unregulated foreign capital flows (mainly involving U.S. investors) (see Armijo, 2001), and excessive and irresponsible lending by international banks "desperate to put money to work" (Soros, 1998: 116) provoked one of the worst economic crises Mexico has seen.

[9] Andrés Oppenheimer (2007) has criticized "the U.S. xenophobic anti-immigration hysteria" and the widespread labeling of undocumented immigrants as "illegals." He argues that, "You may have violated a rule but that should not make you an 'illegal' person. You may have gotten a ticket for speeding, but that doesn't make you an 'illegal' human being, even if the potential harm of your reckless driving is much greater than anything done by most of the hard-working undocumented immigrants in this country" (*Ibid.*).

[10] Between the 1940s and 1970s, Mexico had experienced one of the longest periods of economic growth in the Developing World and was a "paragon of political stability" in spite of dramatic population growth. In the 1980s, Mexico's economic and political systems started to decline (Smith, 1996: 83–84).

[11] Over 40% of all undocumented immigrants to the U.S. are believed to have entered with passports and simply overstayed their visas. In 2001, the Immigration and Naturalization Service found that 10% of foreign students had overstayed their visas (Hall and Sutton, 2002).

[12] Among other things, developmental education courses are designed to address academic preparedness and to help students overcome affective barriers to learning. Developmental education is supposed to be sensitive and responsive to cultural differences and special needs among learners. One of the main goals of developmental education is to enhance the retention of students in college (National Association for Developmental Education: www.nade.net).

[13] Most of Justo's interview was in Spanish, but he switched to English when it felt more comfortable. Like Jesenia, he inserted small Spanish phrases in the middle of his English narrations, or vice versa. However, unlike Jesenia, he would try to speak completely in English or fully in Spanish. His diction was more sophisticated in English and he did not want to speak *Spanglish*.

Navigating Institutional Borders: Resilience, Agency and Resistance

> Race, class, and gender still matter because they continue to structure society in ways that value some lives more than others. . . . They matter because they remain the foundation for systems of power and inequality that, despite our nation's diversity, continue to be among the most significant social facts of people's lives.
>
> —M. L. Andersen and P. Hill Collins (2007: 1–2)

> Making history is a way of producing identity insofar as it produces a relation between that which supposedly occurred in the past and the present state of affairs. The construction of a history is the construction of a meaningful universe of events and narratives for an individual or collectively defined subject.
>
> —Jonathan Friedman (1992: 837)

As discussed in previous chapters, counter-story telling has been utilized by critical race theorists as a method of telling the stories of those whose voices have been marginalized by the dominant discourse and to challenge the stories and dominant ideology of those in power (Love, 2004; Nebeker, 1998; Solorzano and Yosso, 2000/2001/2002). The following analysis examines selected excerpts from the stories elicited by this research in the context of the themes explored in Chapter III and other readings. The narratives of the participants represent counter-stories of survival, perseverance, struggle, and success as they navigated economic, linguistic, social, and cultural challenges in a community college in Arizona and in the larger societal context. Their memories corroborate and augment previous studies and reveal new perspectives that may stimulate further qualitative research on undocumented students.

The narratives in this book demonstrate that great adversity does not necessarily lead to educational failure. The denial of formal citizenship, subsequent stigmatization, and lack of resources did not stop these persevering students from earning community college degrees. Nevertheless, their achievements were possible because they did not face the new legislation in

Arizona and other states that deny undocumented students instate tuition, special college programs, and driver's licenses. Furthermore, for most undocumented Americans, educational achievements cannot be openly utilized in the labor market and higher educational aspirations are banned to them.

Race, Class, and Discrimination:
"*Ni de aquí ni* from there"

The Volume Library, an encyclopedia published in New York in 1928, confidently explained: "One reason for Mexican poverty is the predominance of its racial inferiority" (quoted by Fuentes, 2004). Later, successive waves of anti-Mexican and "legally sanctioned racism" would rise and wane with the fluctuations of the political economy. The anti-immigrant movement that started in southern California in the late 20th century (Bandhauer, 2001; Johnston, 2001) would spread nationwide in the dawn of the 21st century (De Genova, 2004, 2005; Mariscal, 2005; Pulido, 2007). In 2010, United Nations human rights experts expressed great concern over the "disturbing pattern of legislative activity hostile to ethnic minorities and immigrants" in Arizona (Office of the High Commissioner for Human Rights, 2010). The apologists of anti-immigrant legislation argue that their rhetoric is not anti-immigrant but only "anti-illegal." Nevertheless, race-based prejudice, racial profiling, and immigrant scapegoating abound in the media and in statements from prominent public officials. Governor Jan Brewer of Arizona infamously stated that most unauthorized immigrants "are bringing drugs in" (Davenport, 2010), while former presidential candidate John McCain blamed "people who have crossed our border illegally" for Arizona's forest fires. No factual evidence was ever found to support such claims, which were soon rejected by the Border Patrol and U.S. Forest Service (Katrandjian, 2011).

It may be argued that prejudiced or false statements are not necessarily racist, but as pointed out by Stoler (2002), we must distinguish between the "seen" and the unseen" in a new type of racism that is more "insidious" and "silently sophisticated" (371). A racial essence also involves the subtle dimensions of "cultural competencies, moral civilities, and effective sensibilities" (*Ibid.*: 372) that are not always seen as racial battlegrounds. As a presidential candidate, Barack Obama appeared to be aware of this when he recognized that "the immigration debate took a turn that was both ugly and racist in a way we haven't seen since the struggle for civil rights" (Obama, 2007). Arizona's bans on Affirmative Action, Ethnic Studies, and teachers with accents in English classes (see Chapter I) are part of this neo-racism. At the same time, gross violations of human rights and criminalization of unauthorized immigrants and undocumented Americans are acceptable to, even supported by, large, often vocal, sectors of the population.[1]

Living in these increasingly adverse surroundings, the participants in this research have revealed different levels of awareness of their racialized environment. Clearly Rosario has inherited the memory shared by many people of Mexican origin through her parents:

> My mother and father lived through racism when my father worked here in the United States. . . . my mother tells us that, when they lived in Texas, they had signs saying "No Mexicans" . . .

Rosario realizes that survival is not becoming easier for immigrants, and anti-Mexican prejudices make it more difficult:

> When I was studying in the community college, I had the opportunity to get a driver's license. That was my only I.D. when I did not have any papers . . . that made me feel a little less stressed. But, I remember in 1982 I was stopped by a police officer, my first ticket . . . I was shaking. He gave me a ticket and I was terrified. And in those days there wasn't so much racism . . . (breathes deeply) . . . These days, if the police stop you, they can call immigration. There wasn't this great racism you can see day to day.

In 2005, the voters of Arizona passed Proposition 100, a law that allows local police departments to detain undocumented immigrants without the right to bail. One of the consequences of this law was that undocumented people could be incarcerated indefinitely for any reason (like a minor traffic violation) as they wait to be remitted to the USCIS jurisdiction. Thus, if a detained immigrant wants to appeal the charges for a minor offense, he or she would have to go through the appeals process while incarcerated (Ramos Cardoso, 2007). The Arizona Public Defender Association (APDA) has released an official comment (Arizona, 2007) criticizing Proposition 100 for its "violation of [the defendants'] due process rights" (9) and for its "constitutional infirmities" (12).

In contrast to Rosario, however, Roberto did not appear too concerned about the racial frictions in the state of Arizona. He is a firm believer in the "American Dream":

> Interviewer:
> Are you sometimes concerned about your children . . . growing up in this environment, where we have these situations . . . ?
> Roberto:

No, because everybody can have their own beliefs and everyone thinks differently.
And that's what makes this country great . . .

Roberto has a strong personality and he is determined to succeed. He is
not afraid of challenges and prefers not to reflect too profoundly on racial
issues or abstract concepts. He is pragmatic and resolute. As it became evident
throughout our interview, his entrepreneurial spirit is a powerful force that
emerged in many of his answers. At first, he appeared to be mostly aloof to the
institutionalized or legally sanctioned forms of racism that have hindered his
dreams to continue his higher education and to work for a multinational
corporation. Nevertheless, at one point in the conversation, Roberto made a
remark that revealed his own perception of racism as he criticizes the legal
barriers to gay marriage.

> Racism is very strong because marriage "has to be" (in ironic tone) between a man and
> a woman . . . It is something that flows throughout this country . . . religion is a very
> powerful force.[2]

Interestingly, researchers have pointed out the effort of progressive gay
and lesbian political movements to link the struggle against homophobia to
social movements against racism, sexism, and economic injustice (D'Emilio,
2000: 46). It appears that they would find an advocate in Roberto, who apparently does not fit traditional stereotypes of Latino religious conservatism. He
also is aware of the power of the media, the manipulation of images, and
perceptions surrounding the immigration debate. He illustrates this referring
to the pro-immigrant marches where thousands of people, including junior
and high school students, took to the streets of many cities across the nation:

> For example, in the case of immigrants, what did they do? The interviews focused on
> the white people who were supporting the immigrants . . . I did not go, but those you
> saw in the news were the white people. . . . Then, there was a group who gathered in
> front of the Mexican Consulate and burned the Mexican flag. It was like six or seven,
> but they got a lot of coverage.

For Roberto, this is just the way things are and "those who want to get
ahead will get ahead." As pointed out by Delgado (2006) and Ladson-Billings
(1998), Roberto feels this is possible in an environment where some of the
societal actions, expectations, and norms that disadvantage him appear "normal." He sees racial tensions as the result of political maneuverings and
machinations:

Roberto [about racial tensions]:

More than anything it is a political issue. It's a tool for reelection.

In a society that is "obsessed with racial/ethnic politics" (Fina, 2000: 155), Roberto's perspective is not surprising. As narrated in his life-history, he also views racial conflict as the result of ignorance rather than a manifestation of oppression. From a CRT perspective, whether it is recognized or not, the concept of "race" has become a metaphor for "disguising forces, events, classes, and expressions of social decay and economic division far more threatening to the body politic than biological 'race' ever was" (Toni Morrison quoted by Ladson-Billings, 1998: 8). In that sense, David made some conceptual connections that revealed his understanding of class and race relations while unveiling his personal process of conscientization about inegalitarian educational opportunity:

David:
. . . in Mexico most people think that if you're a good student you should have the opportunity to go to school. Rather than if you're a Native American or a minority, you should go to school. In Mexico it's more towards [people's aptitudes]. . . . In America, it is different. I mean, it is like if they were saying, "you know what? Not everybody has the same chance in America. We are not all the same." And I kept thinking, well, that's the stupidest thing I ever heard. Why would they do that? [referring to Affirmative Action policies]. Not knowing the history of the country, um . . . I thought of that and it did not make sense. 'Cuz I kept thinking, well, it should be based on grades and effort. But once I went to the university, I lived and learned, I understood . . . they were right.
Interviewer:
So you changed . . .
David:
'Cuz we are not all the same! I changed my . . . my perspective.
Interviewer:
Tell me what you think about affirmative action.
David:
Well, I'll tell you . . . uh, maybe it shouldn't be based on race. I think it should be based on income. Because what I did learn in college was that there were other Mexicans . . . I mean, it was real minimal, compared to the [Whites] . . . I believe when I was there maybe six or seven percent were Hispanic . . . students at the university. And um . . . I remember that some of those Hispanic students were pretty rich. They were pretty well off. Well, I mean, I worked at . . . that pizza place [as a manager], where I had students . . . where I had my cooks, that were working their butts off to go through high school. But when they graduate, they're not going to have money to go to the university. . . . A lot of the students at the university were pretty well off. I mean, they're driving these brand-new SUV's, the BMW's . . . it's not fair to say that we have the same opportunities . . . for a guy that's working sixty-five hours a week.

David also understands that students are the beneficiaries of preferential treatment for other reasons besides socioeconomic class:

> I remember I was in a class with Professor Wilkinson, and uh, there was a student from Mexico. And he was a diver for the university team . . . the university team. He was never in the classes. Never. And he got a B. And I worked my butt off to get a B in his class.

Students from Mexico represent one of the largest groups of international students in the nation's community colleges and the eighth-largest foreign group in all types of educational institutions combined (Institute of International Education, 2010). The great majority of international students of Mexican origin in the US are likely to come from private educational institutions in Mexico and from economically prosperous families that can afford the expense. This fact adds to the complexity of the student population of Mexican origin. In the southwestern US, for example, the large population of Mexican descent sometimes inadvertently perpetuates racial and class divisions that exist in Mexico (Rojas, 2001).[3]

Jesenia, Justo, and Marina, who graduated from high schools in Arizona, made reference to perceived class differences among students of Mexican origin as they navigated through the educational system. Marina, who came from Mexico City and had a distinct southern Mexican accent when she started school in Arizona, narrated the difficulties she had trying to be accepted by her peers of Mexican origin:

Marina:
When they asked me where I was from and I said from Mexico City (sighs). . . . At that time, most of the kids here came from Nogales, Agua Prieta, Hermosillo, Magdalena [cities in the northern part of Mexico] . . . and I am from Mexico City. I am a hundred percent Mexican, but I was a weirdo for them.
Then . . . I am a weirdo for my own . . .
Interviewer:
Co-nationals . . . [the original word I used in Spanish was: *connacioneles*]
Marina [rectifying]:
Mexican co-nationals.
. . . For a while I was struggling, trying to . . . to be accepted. First by the Mexicans. . .
. . . And then, I tried to be accepted by the English-speakers, but they never accepted me. I always had a problem with the girls.

Marina's use of emphasis when specifying that she was not accepted by her *Mexican* co-nationals was meant to indicate that she also has US co-nationals, which is a revealing aspect of her dual identity to be discussed below. Jesenia also experienced a similar duality and class divisions:

And you would see the Mexicans gathering over here. Over there you would see the blacks, and over there the Chicanos. And the preppies would gather somewhere else. The preppies were the ones who had money. Sometimes there would be Chicanos, there were some blacks, and they would gather apart somewhere.

The importance of belonging to a particular social class has been studied by Bender and Ruiz (1974) in explaining underachievement and "underaspiration" among Mexican-American and Anglo students. In their study, they refer to "demographic research" that shows a correlation between belonging to "lower socioeconomic classes" and poor performance in the educational arena. Bender and Ruiz do not arrive at definite conclusions regarding this interrelationship. Nevertheless, they conclude that, regardless of race and class, one of the strongest variables to predict educational achievement is the measure of students' "internal control" (53).[4] Interestingly, Jesenia, Marina, and Justo disclosed feelings of non-belonging and difficulties being accepted by different groups, while David was a loner focusing on his work and studies. The six participants, however, appear to have a strong internal locus of control, judging by their determination, positive attitude in the face of adversity, and determination to be successful in school and beyond. At the same time, there is awareness among the participants that they operate in a racialized environment, where phenotype and other racial categories can be important factors in their sense of belonging. David expressed it simply when narrating how he once escaped being detected by immigration officials:

. . . the fact that I look kinda' white helped me.

It also became evident from the narratives in this research that Mexican immigrants can potentially be judged and discriminated against from all sides, including those they consider part of their own group, creating a perception that they do not fit anywhere. Justo touched on another dimension that illustrates the perceived differences among people of Mexican origin and the challenges immigrants face in their effort to reconcile class and race divisions. He expressed his discomfort and frictions with Mexican officials in one of the Mexican consulates in Arizona when he requested a passport. When Justo was invited by the Department of State to travel to Egypt with three other students, he was already an authorized resident in the US. However, since he was still not eligible for a U.S. passport, he had to request a Mexican passport in order to travel abroad. Going through the process to obtain his passport made Justo aware of socio-cultural cleavages he did not know existed:

Justo [referring to racial divisions]:

... that exists everywhere. In all kinds of people, not only in other races against us. Unfortunately you can see it a lot in our own people. And then you have those situations that happen because ... for example, my Spanish is not perfect ... I don't know all the proper words and so, many times ... to be perfectly frank with you, where they have made me feel the worst is in the Mexican Consulate. When I've been there and I have used the wrong word, I have been corrected. I have been told that's not the way it's said in Spanish. "That's incorrect Spanish." "Are you sure you're Mexican," they've asked me.

This experience was obviously hurtful for Justo and perhaps it damaged his sense of identity as a *Mexican*. He felt discriminated against by those he thought felt equal to him.

And they corrected me one time after another ... You know, when you encounter these situations, it feels like discrimination coming from your own people, you know what I mean? So, a friend and I had a joke; we used to say: "Ni de aquí ni *from there*," because many times you feel attacked from two fronts.

The phrase "*ni de aquí ni from there*" (neither from here, nor from there) is a clever way to combine English and Spanish in a play with words that paraphrases a popular saying in Spanish: *Ni de aquí ni de allá.*[5] The phrase captures the sense of "otherness" that some Americans of Mexican origin face on both sides of the border and offers a glimpse at the multifarious contexts they have to navigate. As the dominant society imposes a "second border" on immigrants based on their differences (Morales, 2002: 117), frequently Mexican-origin people in the U.S. impose barriers on themselves based on socioeconomic status, birth origin, and language. Since about a third of Mexican origin people in the U.S. are first-generation immigrants, Mexico's social structure is a powerful point of reference for many of them. Their societal reference is an enormously inegalitarian country[6] where people—and notoriously the indigenous populations—face great socioeconomic and educational disadvantages based on class, gender, and race prejudices (Castellanos, 2001; Flores-Crespo, 2007). Although she was a teenager when she emigrated, Rosario could remember the classist and genderized inequalities in her Mexican community:

... there in Mexico they [young well-to-do women] used to think that they would get married, so what would education be good for? Then, as a woman one always has a dream, right? You will find your prince charming. ... One doesn't think about the future, especially when you are sixteen.

Interestingly, the two participants who have been able to normalize their immigration status and citizenship, Rosario and Justo, came from the upper middle class in Mexico. Their families became financially bankrupt before they came to the U.S., but as suggested by López and Stanton-Salazar's (2001) research, they may have developed the social practices, attitudes, and relationships that have helped them achieve this aspiration. More research would be necessary to explore this connection, but social capital certainly appears to be a factor in the facilitation of educational achievement (Gibson and Bejínez, 2002; Grant, 2005; Stanton-Salazar and Dornbusch, 1995). Conceivably, some of the social networks and practices that have served as "capital" for Justo and Rosario operate transnationally (Hinojosa-Ojeda, 2003). The role of Justo's church in his "legalization" and his reaction and determination to fight against a perceived injustice when he was threatened by his instructor further illustrate his use of social capital.

> I could have become depressed. But to fight, to struggle for what is right, always gives you good results. . . . It always will give you some kind of positive result. In this case, it brought me a great number of blessings.

Obviously, in spite of great faith and determination, young Mexican immigrants not only could face the racially hegemonic system in the United States but racism, sexism, and classism within their own Mexican-American communities. In Freirean terms, many of them have internalized the conscience and the value system of the colonizer and reproduce their own oppression (Freire, 1970; García, 2004; Mullaly, 1997). In the dominant community, immigrants trying to improve themselves through education may face overt bigotry—as in the case of Justo, who was almost unjustly expelled from college by one of his instructors—and covert, institutionalized discrimination. In his counter-narrative and analysis of Chicana/o college students, Villalpando (2003) argues that cultural consciousness and commitment to their communities help these students navigate institutionalized racial barriers. In spite of this, Duncan-Andrade (2005), points out that the power of the dominant narrative may have a destructive impact. In this regard, Jesenia made an amazing analogy that reveals her racial insecurities:

> You can see it in nature, you know? I was telling a friend the other day: Why don't dogs have (laughs) (inaudible)? Why? Because they discriminate. When I took biology classes we learned how species, like zebras or insects, discriminate . . . That's how they evolve. . . . You won't see red frogs having babies with green frogs [jokingly] . . . Maybe it happens, but the great majority of species get together with their own groups.

It appears that Jesenia has internalized the racial conscience of the colonizer, which in essence is "a consciousness that is motivated around that group's [the racially hegemonic White society] self-interest" (Dennis, 2003: 16). In Freirean terms, this is a colonizing consciousness that validates the story and the paradigms of the oppressor; it represents the duality that is established in the innermost being of the oppressed, who inadvertently become the oppressors (Freire, 1970). Rosario also had a revealing realization as she reflected during our interview:

> Many people, as soon as they know you come from the other side, they want to pay you less. Even we [Mexican origin people] do it. Even I, I believe I have done it with gardeners in my house. I think we can be racists too. . . . And we are without realizing it because sometimes it happens and we don't think about it.

Thus, the participants may have internalized the conscience of the oppressor, but despite their internal and external struggles, and against all odds, they have been academically successful and contradict Huntington's (2004a, 2004b) anti-immigrant theses. More importantly, the participants in this study, as the participants in Sarther's (2006) research, have developed a powerful sense of purpose that became a motivator for academic success in spite of adversities. Jesenia, for example, sees herself "like the foundation" for further generations. Similarly, Rosario and Justo illustrate the development of a sense of caring and justice to help others and to rectify the inequities experienced as "Mexicans" (also found in Sarther's study). And, as it has been found by other researchers (Alvarez-McHatton et al., 2006; Bohon et al., 2005; Flores and Obasi, 2005; Gándara, 1995), all of them see their families as an inspiration and purpose for academic achievement.

López and Stanton-Salazar's (2001) claim that the "quasi-racial stereotyping" and low class status of Mexican-Americans may result in reduced motivation and achievement was not true in the stories elicited in this research. However, all the participants have encountered racial challenges that they have successfully overcome. Justo, the most academically successful, reflects on another incident he experienced as he and his cousin waited in line at the theater. They were called racial names by a woman who thought his cousin had cut in line.

> . . . for at least that whole day I was self . . . self conscious of my race. I was self conscious of my . . . my *status*. I wasn't a citizen that day; I mean I had just become a citizen three months before. I wasn't a citizen that summer and now I was. But that didn't make any difference. I just felt . . . I just felt different. I felt singled out. Even though this person who has no . . . manners, no authority, no nothing. It was just an argument from an ignorant individual. Because that's what racism is. It's ignorance.

Racism can, indeed, be a pathological form of ignorance. Furthermore, Sullivan and Tuana (2007) argue that such type of ignorance is actually produced and reproduced for the purpose of domination and exploitation. Ignorance produces stereotypes, bias, intolerance, and hate, which in turn generate barriers between people. Undocumented Americans of Mexican origin, Mexican-Americans, and Mexican immigrants understand this very well.

Immigrant Origin: "In a golden cage"

For many Mexican-origin people in the United States, whether they are citizens or undocumented residents, "the border is everywhere" (De Genova, 1998: 106). They face an invisible barrier, an omnipresent border that has historically defined their social position as "illegal" outsiders and racialized others (Villalpando, 2003). Their racialization is inseparable from their colonized and subordinated status, "whose singular role is to provide cheap and tractable labor" (De Genova, 1998) at the service of a white, racist ideology (Villalpando, 2003). As noted before, "When the economy is strong and jobs are plentiful, employers are eager to hire immigrants with little concern over the legitimacy of their green cards, but when the economy is weak, immigrants quickly become scapegoats" (Taylor Gibbs and Bankhead, 2001: 155).

Since historical memory is short and limited in the majoritarian narrative, these great injustices are easily forgotten or become only footnotes in the Master Narrative of American History. In April 2005, California Congresswoman Hilda Solis refreshed the nation's memory by introducing The Commission on Mexican American Removal During 1929–1941 Act to "investigate the removal of as many as two million Mexican Americans from the United States during the Great Depression" (Weider, 2006). Ironically, under the mantle of new anti-immigrant legislation, a similar possibility to force legitimate inhabitants of the U.S. out of the country has been promoted by conservative politicians.[7] In the specific case of undocumented students, legally sanctioned racism and anti-immigrant legislation make achievement in higher education extremely difficult and increasingly risky. For a number of years, societal attitudes and beliefs about Mexican immigrants have become gradually more hostile and, unfortunately, mirrored in school culture (Shannon and Escamilla, 1999). Justo also experienced this hostility at the university, where he was invited to participate in a student club of College Republicans:

They were discussing whether they should place a drinking fountain in the middle of the university courtyard . . . as a mockery of the water stations that they [human rights groups] put in the desert for the immigrants. "If we are putting water in the desert for those who are here illegally," they said, "why don't we put a drinking fountain in the middle of the university to mock the Democrats?". . . and I protested immediately, and well, obviously we had a big argument. Then it evolved into a discussion about Affirmative Action and, you can imagine, yet another argument. Then we continued with bilingual education . . . imagine that! They almost kicked me out of there.

These types of incidents are examples of "symbolic violence," which can translate into real barriers to just and equal education for all students (Shannon and Escamilla, 1999). To be sure, Paulo Freire's concept of violence (1970) does not only pertains to the wars, massacres, and conflicts that plague our world "but also the violence of the status-quo, of an unjust society which distorts and limits the possibility of full humanity to masses of people—people who are not even seen as human by those in power" (Weiler, 2003). In Arizona and other states with anti-immigrant policies, undocumented Mexican immigrants and their families—who may or may not be undocumented—live in an environment that, to paraphrase Charles Bowden (1998), could be the laboratory of our future,[8] where violence and oppression against perceived "outsiders" exist in all conceivable forms.

Freire refers to "the disguised or hidden violence: hunger, the economic interests of the superpowers, religion, politics, racism, sexism, and social classes" (1996: 185). From a similar philosophical perspective, Lee (1996) argues that once it is appreciated that the essential causes of poverty emanate from the institutional structures that determine wealth and power distribution, it is clear that poverty is caused by violence. From this perspective, poverty "is an institutional injustice causing or tending to cause significant harm" (Ibid.: 69). Thus, violence does not necessarily mean "physical violence," or the application of "vigorous force," but it does involve a constant threat of force in order to maintain such structures. Poverty is created and maintained when individuals are denied the resources they need for a minimally decent life (Ibid.: 70). In this sense, discrimination and exclusion are also forms of violence. Hence, violence is more closely connected with the concept of *violation* (the Latin root of the term) than with the use of force. "What is fundamental about violence is that a person is violated" (Newton Garver quoted by Lee, 1996: 71).

It is in the midst of such violence that undocumented Americans of Mexican origin have to attempt economic survival, cultural adaptation, and educational progress. Another challenge they face is the complexity and diversity of the immigrant experience among people of Mexican origin, which is enormous and cannot be captured with simple categories. As Jesenia's and Marina's narratives show, even within a similar social class, the difference between someone who comes from northern Mexico and someone who comes from southern Mexico is enough to make a difference in how immigrant children socialize in the United States. The diversity revealed by the narratives in this research involves:

- Mexican immigrant families whose members include naturalized citizens, authorized residents, and undocumented inhabitants of the same community.[9] Many, like Rosario, have gained citizenship by marrying U.S. citizens but have members of their family who remain undocumented.

- Families whose members were born on both sides of the border and include U.S.-born citizens and undocumented members. Such is the case of Jesenia's and Marina's families, who have been fractured by their different immigration statuses.

- Undocumented residents who have been in the country for many years—sometimes decades—have learned the language, participate in community organizations, and have relatively stable jobs, as in the cases of David and Roberto. As it is evident in their stories, by the time they came to the U.S. they were aware of immigration issues impacting their families. Nevertheless, they were still minors and went through extensive acculturation and adaptation processes. Although David and Roberto do not mind being categorized as immigrants, their ethos is distinctly United Statesian. Their admiration and love for the United States, their work ethics and educational achievements are examples of the great potential of undocumented Americans. Interestingly, they have married other undocumented residents of Mexican origin, which suggests the existence of networks and communities of undocumented.

- Undocumented Americans who are practically indistinguishable from U.S.-born people and, in some cases like Jesenia and Marina, do not even see themselves as immigrants. They are an integral part of U.S. society and, in many cases, speak English better than Spanish. They were brought to this country as children, as in the cases of Marina, Jesenia, and Justo, and would have much difficulty adapting in Mexico because they have spent most of their lives in the U.S. Even though they are labeled as "illegal aliens," if the concept of citizenship is understood as membership in societal structures and possession of cultural values, they cannot be told apart from other United Statesians. They are, in fact, cultural, social, and economic beings and *de facto* citizens of the U.S. (Del Castillo, 2002; Flores and Benmayor, 1997).[10]

Mexican immigrant communities also have been fractured in more profound ways, culturally and socially within the same family. Jesenia bitterly conveyed her frustration about her brother's wasted "legality" and disinterest in education. She explains in *Espanglish*:

> . . . I'm sorry to say that one of my brothers, the one who was involved with drugs . . . He is not *illegal* . . . and I used to get angry when I was in college because . . . there are all these kids with the opportunities . . . they have the opportunities, but they don't take them. They don't finish school. And here I am, struggling. I want what they have. But I can't have it. What's keeping them from doing it? And when I look at my brother . . . He has the opportunity! Why does he waste it?

According to Fry (2002), immigrant *Latinos*, are much more likely to enroll in community colleges than any other group. All the participants in this study enrolled in the community college because they perceived it as their most accessible option. Additionally, all of them wanted to attend a four-year university as part of their educational goals. Nevertheless, as Bohon et al. (2005) have argued, banned access to higher education is one of the greatest barriers faced by undocumented immigrants.

> I was a senior at the university. I almost made it! Um, and I plan on going back if I have the opportunity (David).
> The main obstacle [for immigrants to get an education] is the lack of documents (Roberto).
> I want to have more education. I want a better life for me and for my parents (Marina, II: 33-34).

It is very likely that David, Roberto and Marina would have gone further in their higher education had they not had the obstacle of being undocumented. However, they were fortunate to complete their studies at the community college at a time when it was still feasible. With the growing perception of Mexicans as "illegals" and "aliens" (De Genova, 2005) and increasing anti-immigrant legislation, it is not surprising that native-born Latino high school graduates enroll in college at a higher rate than their immigrant counterparts (Fry, 2002). This is particularly problematic considering the high percentage of first-generation immigrants as a proportion of the total population of Mexican origin. Among them, there is

. . . a substantial "shadow population" of *illegal* migrants—numbering in the millions—within our borders . . . whose presence is tolerated, whose employment is perhaps even welcomed, but who are virtually defenseless against any abuse, exploitation or callous neglect. . . . The existence of such an underclass presents most difficult problems for a Nation that prides itself on adherence to principles of equality under the law (Kittrie, 2006).

In spite of such adversity, all the participants in this research have defied the odds by enrolling in college and completing their degrees. Similarities were found with the research by Alvarez-McHatton et al. (2006) on successful university students from migrant farmworker families. As in that study, the participants in this research were found to have "strong determination" and "self-reliance," supported by the positive influences from their families in their pursuit of higher education. Marina's determination is clear when she expresses that she *is* struggling to have an education, implying that she is looking for ways to get further, notwithstanding that she has earned four degrees from the community college.

Desperation was always a negative factor. I always had my parents' support. I always wanted to be someone. But it is not the same when you do not have papers. Even when you are part of here, of the United States, go to college, interact with people . . . you know you have obstacles, like struggling with transportation when you have to meet with your College peers to work on group projects. So, if you have to meet with your group at 7:00 P.M., there is almost no public transportation here. So, those kinds of things. . . . Now who do I ask for a ride? Sometimes you do not have a lot of money to spend if your peers decide to go to a restaurant . . . you have to spend money if you want to work with them. And, well, I was struggling, *I am struggling*, to have my education, but I cannot have the luxury of spending what I don't have. Also, by being "illegal" . . . after the group finishes your College project, they want to go to a night club. And, although I was twenty-one years old, I did not have an identification card. So I could not go with them . . . How would you explain to people? How could you tell them your story? It's very wearing . . .

Jesenia finds it difficult to cope with the fact that, even though she managed to earn a higher education degree, she cannot use it to improve her economic and material conditions. She feels fortunate that she was able to obtain a university education in spite of her undocumented status, but she also reveals frustration and doubt:

Having an education is a success. Though it's hard to describe success, because like I said, living in a society where you're not successful if you don't have some money . . . I went to school, and I still sometimes don't feel successful.

Internalizing the guilt and stigma of being an undocumented immigrant can certainly lead to feelings of desperation and confinement. Even after she has become a citizen and graduated from the community college, Rosario referred to her painful experience as an undocumented resident as "being in a golden cage." Remarkably, the same expression was used by David and Roberto. The expression probably comes from the popular Mexican saying: *Aunque la jaula sea de oro no deja de ser prisión* (Even if the cage is made of gold, it is still a prison).[11] The six participants' sense of belonging in this country and in college, so important for academic motivation in Gibson's (2003) research, has been continuously challenged. They have been constantly told, through the media and the dominant discourses, that they are "illegals" and therefore do not have a right to the space they occupy. Rosario, who now works at a literacy community center helping immigrants who are trying to get ahead, reflects on this:

> In the Center, where we have so many undocumented people, they walk around in fear, but they are studying, they are doing something positive, because they do not come here to do harm to anyone. They are studying, they are learning English, and I am there as a coordinator . . . they want to get ahead. So now, with the raids they are doing [the immigration police] . . . they feel very fearful, they walk around in fear . . . I think about this, and I know what they feel, because I've been there. Many women want to have a vacation with their husbands when they have a little extra money. So they would like to go to Disneyland, for example, but without documents they are afraid they could be stopped by the immigration police in the way . . . or, in the mornings, when they leave home to go to work, their families don't know if they will see them again. So, they are, and I was too, in a golden cage, right? You can have many comforts, yes, but if at the same time you don't have freedom, well . . . Now I have it and I can go out with less worry, but I remember. In the summer of 1999, I started having many depressions because of it . . . I felt a great loneliness. It was the kind of loneliness that, even if I could be accompanied by thousands of people in a room, I felt alone inside.

Justo also remembers his feelings of vulnerability as an undocumented American. He switches from Spanish to English when he explains how he felt at school before he obtained his residency permit:

> I didn't want to ask questions because that's to show weakness. That shows lack of knowledge.
> I felt that I just had a big thing on my head that said "Immigrant" . . . and I didn't. And many times people said "you have something special, you can go far." And this was back in high school when I didn't see that. All I saw myself as was as an immigrant student that was just there. I mean, when you're here and you're not here legally, the least thing that you want is attention on you. You don't want that . . .

Someone like Justo, with so many talents and confidence in his own potential, is hardly the person one would expect these revelations from. At that point, in Justo's mind, society's negative construct of the immigrant became his primary label, superseding all other talents and skills he has, even when others were telling him otherwise. His insecurities as an undocumented American were a manifestation of the fear of exposing himself and of the intimidation and alienation experienced by undocumented, and sometimes even authorized, immigrants (Groody, 2000; Massey, 2005; Ramos, 2007; Veranes and Navarro, 2005).

Another challenge immigrant students, both authorized and undocumented, have to face is their lack of understanding of the U.S. school system (Bohon et al., 2005). This even appeared to be true for Justo, Jesenia and Marina, who were brought to Arizona as children and graduated from U.S. high schools. Although they are United Statesians for all practical purposes, their parents were not familiar with U.S. institutions and could not help them.

> Justo:
> One of the challenges . . . was actually not knowing the system. That is because I did not have anyone to turn to. I did not have . . . my father was not able to guide me.
>
> Like when I was a freshman, they asked all these kids, "Where are you going to school?" And I was thinking, "I'm going to Cross." You know, like Cross High School. That's what I was thinking! They were thinking college. I didn't know what Stanford was. I had a jacket of Stanford when I was in eighth grade, and then when I graduated from Middle School, I thought I couldn't wear it anymore because I was going to be wearing it at a high school, and it was the wrong name. I didn't even know what Stanford was! And . . . all these kids grow up knowing what college they want to go to because their parents went to College in the U.S . . . so for me the question was, "Are you going to school?" And if I said no, then they're like, "Okay." And if I said yes, they would be like, "Which one?" And I didn't know which one. And I said, "Maybe." And they're like, "So why . . . why don't you know?" So it was a hard question when you're growing up. And for other kids, it's like, "Hey, which one are you going to?" "Oh, I'm going to this one my parent went to. I'm going to the U of A. I'm going to whatever."

All the participants in this study faced similar obstacles, even as they entered community college. They had to learn a "college culture" (Cabrera and Padilla, 2004) unfamiliar to them and sometimes they had to find a difficult balance among their academics, family responsibilities, and work. All the participants worked as they navigated through their community college experiences. For undocumented students, this is particularly challenging. Cacho (2000) argues that racial prejudices in the United States limit our understanding of unjust capitalist relations, serving to artificially augment the white middle-class wealth, opportunities, and power while making undocumented immigrants even more vulnerable and exploitable. Massey and Espinosa(1997) also has argued that immigrants improve the standards of living of citizens. The participants' stories substantiate these claims:

David:
Here you work, you go home, and the next day you get ready to get back to work. When I started school, it seemed to me that work had a little more meaning. It had a little more meaning because it was work that I did as something secondary. . . . It did not mean . . . I did not feel as a machine. As a robot that only does that. I felt there was something for me ahead.
Marina:
The community college was not easy for me. It was hard. And sometimes I would tell myself "I don't want to study anymore." The pressure of higher education is very intense and difficult. And not everyone has the capacity to handle such pressure, much less if you work, because that's another problem . . . I went to the community college, but since I could not work in just any place, I would help my mother to clean houses. Then, I would go very early to clean homes with my mom and after that I had to run to get changed and go to school. Then it was coming back from school and, if I had another house to clean, I would clean a house. So, after the classes, after cleaning houses to make some money, I would get home and help my mom with our home, cooking, taking care of my two younger brothers, helping her with my brothers' school issues. . . . After that it's not easy at all.
Roberto [about the many hours he has to work to support his family]:
I don't have a life.
Jesenia [about the family that enjoys her services as a domestic worker with a university degree, but pays her substandard wages]:
They also said I'm like part of their family, I'm not just a worker there. . . . but sometimes it feels like, wait, I'm just a maid.

As it has been revealed in the counter-history of Mexican immigration included in this book, and as found in more recent research (Johnson, 2003), the lack of civil and human rights protection for immigrants is a historical and contemporary reality. The abuses they encounter exist in all dimensions of life: economic, educational, cultural, and legal. This is particularly troubling when one in every five children in the United States is an immigrant or a child of an immigrant and 62% of these children are Latino (Perreira et al., 2006). The violence of poverty[12] afflicts about 24% of the population of Mexican origin (US Census, 2007) and Mexican immigrants are the most economically vulnerable (Crowley, Lichter, and Zhenchao, 2006). This is a more subtle violence, condemned by Paulo Freire, which does not only pertains to the wars, massacres, and conflicts with which we are now so familiar, "but also the violence of the status quo, of an unjust society which distorts and limits the possibility of full humanity to masses of people—people who are not even seen as human by those in power" (Freire quoted in Weiler, 2003). Additionally, most low-income immigrants live in unsafe neighborhoods where crime, access to drugs, and alcohol abuse are prevalent and have a quotidian impact on their lives (see for example Alaniz, Cartmill, and Parker, 1998). Thus, violence against immigrants can be symbolic, implicit, overt, and very real.

> Jesenia:
> In the neighborhood where my mom lives (sighs) . . . there were a lot of drugs when we lived there. At midnight, there were shootings in the house behind. Bit by bit we've been surviving. There are still drugs, but it's a community where the majority of the people there are illegal or they are . . . you know, struggling, so my brother and sister live surrounded by all that. They have the potential [to study and get ahead], but they are in a community where the rest of the people can't, so they see themselves limited. They believe they are also limited.
>
> Once, some young men with guns broke into our house. And they held my brother with a gun.

Although no one in the family was psychically harmed in this incident, obviously overt violence and other adversities have surrounded Jesenia and other participants in this study. Jesenia makes a powerful observation about her younger siblings: even though they are not undocumented, they are still affected by their community environment as if they were. Thus, in spite of holding U.S. citizenship, her siblings face similar limitations but from their shared reality and socialization rather than from their immigration status. Furthermore, Jesenia realizes that being "legal" is not necessarily a guarantee of success.

> . . . there are immigrant students that are *legal*, but they're still, like, left behind. They can't do well . . . you don't see a lot of role models, or heroes, or icons that are successful from our culture, even though they're *legal* and all.

Therefore, undocumented students face a double risk: the already well-documented problem of underachievement of students of Mexican origin compared to other demographic groups in the U.S., plus their documentation issues (Bohon et al., 2005). Furthermore, if as argued by Glick and White (2004), immigrants are more likely than their third- or later-generation peers to complete secondary school and go on to higher education, anti-immigrant policies are probably aggravating the underachievement problem. Anti-immigrant legislations, like the laws excluding undocumented immigrants from public education, are relegating a large number of people with great educational—and therefore economic—potential. From such perspective, the warning by Allen (2006), that current demographic and economic trends predict the formation of a Mexican-American underclass, appears more ominous.

> Marina:
> You cannot find work, you cannot find a job . . . is frustrating. So, only cleaning houses. That was the only thing I can aspire to . . . the best thing, if you are lucky, (inaudible) houses. So, I came to expect that I would never find another job.

Marina actually found other jobs, but they were all similar to the ones held by other undocumented people. She has worked at a restaurant, as an office cleaner and, eventually, in a little store that belongs to the college counselor who guided her into college. A little luck, knowing the right person at the right time, and making a good impression have helped Marina find a little better employment. However, not all the undocumented are so fortunate, as demonstrated by Jesenia's story. Marina is not reaching her full potential either, and she would certainly strive for more if she had the opportunity. She also realizes with frustration that her father, after so many years of working for the same company, and in spite of having a temporary work permit, earns almost as low wages as she does.

> How is it possible that he makes about the same wages I do? . . . And I only have been in this job for three years! So, I see some discrimination. It doesn't matter how many years you've been employed . . . if you do not speak English and you do not fight for your rights, you will never get out of there.[13]

Fighting for their rights is not easy for undocumented immigrants, even through the massive national protests of 2006 in demand of immigrant rights, in which Marina and Rosario participated, and considerable sympathy from some parts of mainstream society. When Justo finally obtained his residency permit, much of his lack of confidence and many of his fears began to disappear and he gained a sense of security that he did not have before. Also, as recounted in Rosario's story, she expressed very similar feelings.

> Justo:
> Certain things in my life started to give me confidence. The one I can tell you was the greatest was to have obtained the residency [his official permit as an authorized resident]. It gave me a sense of security.
> Rosario:
> Your residency permit takes a big burden from you. Because you feel you have more liberty. Simply moving around the city. . . . Simply going from point A to point B is very frustrating. That's why I support the [pro-immigration] marches and the boycotts. I support their struggle.

Obviously, Justo would have not been able to fight against the discrimination he suffered from a college instructor, especially in the tenacious way he did, without his documents. Rosario would not be helping immigrants in the same way she does. In other words, a "legal" status gives immigrants the ability to fight for their rights in a way they do not necessarily have without their documents. For the participants in this study, it is clear that legal status can eliminate the fear of discovery and allow students and their family members to fight unfair treatment. Otherwise, they try to fly "under the radar," undetected and voiceless. Nevertheless, the inspiring pro-immigration marches and the political activism of Marina and many immigrants show the growing aspiration of undocumented people to be seen and heard.

When Marina was asked what would be the first thing she would do if she could obtain her citizenship documents, she immediately responded:

> The first thing I would do is to get into the university. [14]

As De Genova (1998) and the participants have stated, "The border is everywhere" in "the golden cage," but it still allows them to dream and believe in the myth of the "American Dream" while they might be, in fact, being transformed into an underclass. Meanwhile, the undocumented will continue to be exploited as cheap labor, taxed by the government without access to the benefits, and criminalized without full human rights. Masses of them will remain in a perpetual state of poverty, like Marina's father. At the same time, the Master Narrative of U.S. history assures us that, "poverty is a temporary condition of immigrants or persons who have fallen willy-nilly on evil days, but who will eventually become beneficiaries of the American Dream if only they have the will" (Sieber, 2005: 24). An alternative explanation that is not popular among mainstream Americans is that societal structural conditions produce and perpetuate racism, class privilege, and power, while they impose barriers to social mobility and even extend poverty (*Ibid.*), as is the case of many second- and third-generation immigrants. In the midst of such adversity, there is one institution that gives many Mexican immigrants strength and inspiration: the family.

Family and Parental Involvement: "Strength . . . trust . . . love"

Even when immigrants of Mexican origin do not understand the academic system in the U.S., or do not speak English, they can have a powerful influence on their children's academic motivation and achievement (Sather, 2006). Espinoza-Herold (2007) argues that oral traditions within families of Mexican origin can create a powerful environment that encourages academic achievement. The narratives elicited in this research corroborate Cabrera and Padilla's (2004) case study and Flores and Obasi's (2005) research regarding their strong personal motivation and the influence of their parents in their academic achievement, predominantly the positive influence of mothers. Similarly, in Alvarez-McHatton et al.'s (2006) research of 57 successful students from migrant families, they found that participants predominantly credited their mothers as their most important source of motivation. All participants in this research alluded repeatedly to the positive influences and support they received from their families. Five of them referred specifically to the influence of their mothers.

Jesenia:
. . . my mom would not let us skip school. Our grades always had to be good.

When I came here, my mother was the most important person in my life. . . . So, everything that was important to her was important to me. And for my mom it always has been very important that we go to school because she only made it to third grade.

David:
. . . my mother, on the other hand, kept telling me, "Always go to school, work (laughs) as much as you can." But my brother, my brother that made it through the legal papers thing, he barely graduated from high school.

If my mother were not here, I think I would have not achieved this. Because my mother always would tell me: "You have to go to the university, study, get as far as you can. . . ." And my mom would tell my brother: "See? He [David] does not have what you have [citizenship] and see where he is" [going to the university].

Rosario:
I always talked with my mom first.

Alejandra [Rosario's daughter] was taken care of by her grandmother until she was four years old, when she started kindergarten. She was basically raised by my mother! [this allowed Rosario to go to community college].

Marina:
When my mom saw signs that I was going to throw in the towel, she said: "just one more little push, just one more push . . . because you only need one more class, and you can . . . you have the ability. One little step at a time."

My parents did not have a lot of schooling. My mom went to school up to sixth grade.

So she said her children would not go through the same path she did, the situations she had to face, the economic problems . . . She educated herself as much as she could. Not in school, but she purchased many books. She reads a lot.

Justo:
"That's not enough, you have to shine among the stars," my mom always said. "If a star shines among rocks, that is not difficult, but, when a star shines among other stars . . ." she said, "that's what defines a person."

Clearly the participants' mothers were sources of inspiration to them, both indirectly and directly in their educational achievement. Mothers encouraged the participants to persevere and helped them in important ways, regardless of their lack of knowledge about the U.S. educational system and their level of education. Mothers with little formal schooling, like Marina's and Jesenia's mothers, were relentless in their academic expectations from their children. Marina's mother did not let her lack of education and economic circumstances discourage her. When she could not study in the schools, she studied outside of the school and demonstrated to her children how valuable it was to read and learn. Mothers implanted a sense of responsibility, instilled positive words, reminded their children where they came from, and did not let them quit in their path toward academic success. Mothers also were lovingly demanding, since they would overtly expect their children to work and be students at the same time, as in the cases of David and Marina. They were extremely supportive, as in the case of Rosario, whose mother took care of her granddaughter while Rosario worked and went to college. In summary, the role of mothers appears to have had a great effect on the participants' ability to succeed in the face of adversity.

Justo brings up an important perspective that has not been explored in this book, but it does have precedent in research:

[Education] . . . is what immigrant parents come in search of for their children.

From this perspective, the "better life" immigrants come in search of not only includes a better income and better standards of living for the immediate future but also education for their children so future generations can continue improvsing their standard of living. Perreira et al. (2006) argue that the decision of Latino parents to emigrate from their countries could be understood as a parental decision to help their children achieve a better education. In interviews conducted by Perreira et al. (Ibid.), the desire to obtain a better education for their children was ranked as the most important reason behind parents' decision to immigrate to the U.S. Remarkably, the opportunity to offer their children better schooling was ranked above better economic conditions, safer environments, and family reunification. Clearly, the participants who were brought as children to the U.S. understand the sacrifices made by their parents and make a conscious effort to pay their parents back. Throughout their narratives, Justo, Marina, and Jesenia identify three main motivations in their lives: 1) The sacrifice their parents made for them and the need to validate that sacrifice, 2) their own desire to have a better life than their parents had and to achieve this through education, and 3) their own future children, and their desire for them to be able to succeed academically and in life.

Justo:
He [his father] got here thinking about my education and about his job. But I don't think like that. I think about my education and the education of my children, and I think about helping my parents also.

Marina [who cannot drive legally in Arizona, but makes payments on her mother's vehicle]:
I don't need a lot . . . I do not need much right now. I don't have an ambition for things because I know I will have things in the near future. So, since I know my mom won't have some things, then I give her that satisfaction. That is, for my mom and my dad, and for the kids [her siblings] because . . . I did want things when I was a kid. And, since I don't have children, and I wanted so many things when I was little, I don't want my little siblings to long for things and not have them. So, if my parents cannot give them what they want, I give it to them, so they are not left wanting them.

Marina [about her indebtedness to her parents and what she would tell them about their decision to emigrate from Mexico to the United States]:
" . . . you did a lot for me, so what I give you is minimal. That is, you gave me life, you gave me education, you gave me happiness . . . the best I am, you gave it to me. So, what I give you is a fraction of what you gave me."

Jesenia:
When you're little you know your parents expect things from you. I knew they expected that I finish school . . . and that I would do something with my schooling. So, even though they did not tell me, I knew they knew that I could, and . . . they didn't tell me, but they instilled it in me.

Although institutionalized racism and classism exist in Mexico, once in the United States, many parents encounter overt racism for the first time. They also face economic and social segregation, but they are able to help their children develop coping mechanisms to succeed in their new social context (Perreira et al., 2006). In spite of the multiple challenges immigrant parents encounter in their new country and the barriers they experience trying to help their children in the U.S. school environment (Bohon et al., 2005), most of them have a high regard for education (Shannon and Latimer, 1996; Valencia, 2002), have high academic expectations of their children (Glick and White,

2004), and can be surprisingly well equipped to foster academic achievement in their children (Stanton-Salazar, 1997). They do not capitulate very easily.

> Jesenia [talking about how she used to be incredulous regarding her mother's perceptions of discrimination]:
> When my mom worked under an Anglo supervisor, she would tell me that she [the supervisor] was a racist. "You don't see it because you don't work there, but she is racist against us. She does not let us drink water. No, no, no . . . you don't know because you're not there." So my mom felt discriminated against in the factory, and she used to say: "the Gringo and the other person who can speak English do get permission to drink water. They get to go to the restroom more often." "They don't tell them anything and we are under the whip" (noise of snapping fingers), my mom said. . . . And she would tell me: "you don't know what it feels like." And we would start an argument, and I would say: "Okay, ma. Okay. If you say so, ma. . . ." But she was the one who worked there, and that lady probably did discriminate against her. My mother was very angry, but with her work we had enough money for me to start at the community college.

Lamentably, the state where the participants in this research reside, in Arizona, has gradually imposed tougher legal barriers that affect both documented and undocumented Americans of Mexican origin (Menchaca, 1993; Rodríguez, R., 1997; Romero, 2006; Veranes and Navarro, 2005), and those who can potentially be the most academically successful generation of Mexican-origin students.[15] Immigrant parents not only have linguistic difficulties (Bohon et al., 2005) and lack of knowledge of the U.S. school system (Shannon and Latimer, 1996; Schmidt, 2003) as barriers to support their children, but they also have to struggle financially (Schmidt, 2003). Nevertheless, high parental expectations and relentless support for their children's academic goals can make a great difference in their success. Justo's story illustrates this when he was about to be expelled from the community college by a prejudiced instructor. His parents supported him and accompanied him throughout the eight painful months of the appeals process.

> Justo:
> And my parents did not give up. They said, "Let's talk to people. Who do we talk to?" We were sent to Alexandra Ryan [a counselor] and she helped us with the appeal process. She said, "there are two things to address: your grade appeal and her discrimination." You have to go to Joan Sanders for the grade appeal and to Dr. Jameson for the discrimination grievance. That's how I learned that there was an instructional area and a student development area in the community college. And it was a very long process because I had to face her [the instructor] again. And there I was waiting in the hall next to her office, with Dr. Michaels, on a little chair against the wall. Then I could hear her steps and I was in agony because I was afraid. I mean, I was . . . I was terrified of that lady who intimidated me so much. And she knew that she intimidated me, so she would give me a very ironic smile, a cynical smile, like

when she expelled me from campus. The process took place throughout the semester. So I was coping with classes, my new job, and this issue. It was constantly drilling in my mind. I mean, I was tired coming out of our meetings [with college officials to resolve the issue]. I was exhausted, but I had to bring a character witness . . . uh, she also brought her witness, a math teacher . . . Valerie [the instructor] brought her as a witness of what a good teacher she was. And my witness was Ms. Gutiérrez, a top notch Chicana Power instructor. So they had an argument and I was simply there. Joan Sanders [the Dean] reviewed the case and, I'm not sure how it works, but she wrote a report explaining that I deserved an A in the course: "After reviewing his work, I rule that he deserves an A." But Valerie Frost appealed to Dr. Michaels [the Chief Executive Officer]. Then I had an interview with Dr. Michaels, and there was another round of meetings among the parts. Dr. Michael's report upheld the Dean's decision: "Justo deserves an A after my review." And Valerie Frost appealed again, this time to Dr. Royce. This time, Dr. Royce stopped it. He said, "It stops here. He deserves the A and there is no question about it. Even if you take points off, his work is 'A' quality. . . ." He [the Campus President] agreed with me, but how I agonized! It was painful for me and for my parents. It lasted about eight months.

This story demonstrates a great deal of fortitude and stamina on Justo's part. He had to appeal not only once, but three times, while the instructor kept insisting on pushing her side of the case. Justo's parents supported and encouraged him from beginning to end, which very possibly made a difference in the outcome of this story. However, the family had obtained residency authorization at that point, and it is quite likely they may not have offered such strong support to Justo had they not had an authorized residency in the country. Their residency status gave them the strength to have a voice, and even the confidence to go against the system. They were willing to put themselves under scrutiny by the system because they no longer had an ultimate vulnerability that could have legal repercussions and take away their hopes for a better future. That single fact gave them the ability to fight for their rights in a way they could not necessarily have done as undocumented immigrants.

Justo credits his parents' and community college officials' support in helping him cling tenaciously to his cause. At the same time, Justo's strong internal locus of control (as defined by Bender and Ruiz, 1974), his perseverance, and motivation cannot be ignored. Furthermore, Justo's story has other important elements that played a role in his development as a successful student. This experience actually helped Justo understand the community college system in a way that most students never do. Through his ordeal, he met the campus administrators and won their admiration for his perseverance, which later translated into Justo's involvement in campus activities and the student government body. Also, Ms. González's powerful support in Justo's defense can be an indicator of the importance of having ethnic minorities in the faculty ranks. In essence, the combination of all these factors created a cumulative effect that helped Justo win a battle where he was greatly disadvantaged. After years of academic and professional accomplishments, Justo's main inspiration still comes from his parents:

> My dad went back to school, he's at the community college now, you know, learning English, and doing this and that. They're taking turns between my mom and him so they're not both at school at the same time.
>
> Every time I start feeling tired, I remember my dad washing cars for $2.15 in January weather, when it's thirty-five degrees. Getting his hands wet, you know, and then having someone rip off half of his tips. I mean, I remember that and I think, am I going to complain about having to study until twelve or one A.M.? No, no, no, you keep going. You keep going. And you keep going. And I remind myself of my parents, and that's what keeps me going. I mean, they're my heroes.

All the participants appear to have very positive and solid family values. Perhaps their family structures became more solidified in the United States, as they became isolated from their culture and communities of origin. When Marina was asked what was the meaning of family for her, she answered laconically, with three nouns:

> It is strength . . . it is . . . trust and love.

The high levels of stress and family strain experienced by immigrants (Grzywacz et al., 2005) are magnified by undocumented status and challenge the health of family structures (Rodríguez and Hagan, 2004; Sullivan and Rehm, 2005). Nevertheless, the family remains as the main enclave of support and strength for immigrant students (Delgado-Gaitan, 1991, 2001). Even Jesenia, whose family has experienced divorce and remarriage, has a strong sense of loyalty to her family and a conviction that they have deeply impacted her in a positive way, despite all of the problems they have experienced. Rosario also came from a split family, but she still adheres to the importance of family and uses her children as her motivation to keep moving forward. In addition to family circumstances, external forces created by the community and school environments surrounding undocumented Americans and immigrant students can be decisive factors in their achievements (Trueba, 1983). The next section explores these dimensions.

Supportive and Undermining Environments: "I do not exist here"

Romo and Falbo (1997) have found that the reasons Latino students do not persevere in school are connected with their school and community environments. These researchers argue that school policies and practices have a propensity to undermine the motivation and educational achievement of Latinos (*Idem.*). Similarly, Stone and Han (2005), argue that school climates are clearly and consistently related to academic performance and perceptions of discrimination. In addition, undocumented students experience structural barriers related to their immigration status. Jesenia and Marina, the two participants who were brought to Arizona as children and remain undocumented, encapsulate the impact of the hostile environments they live in as undocumented Americans in lapidary and devastating phrases:

Jesenia:
I am limited. I am like a spectator: sitting, looking at others do the things I'd like to do some day.

Marina:
I do not exist here.

Some undocumented Americans, like the participants in this research, have been able to achieve educational success in spite of these demoralizing feelings. As it was also found in research by Cabrera and Padilla (2004), Gándara (1995), and Garza et al. (2004), the six participants in this study revealed their strong internal motivation, responsibility, strong work ethic, ingenuity, and hope. Additionally, their stories reiterated that internal and external barriers, real or perceived, can be alleviated by felicitous college environments, supporting individuals, and helpful programs (Alberta et al., 2005; Trueba, 1983). These factors can potentially counter the effects of negative influences such as poverty. For example, the programs for struggling women, transitioning high school students, and others utilized by the participants provided a small financial relief but, perhaps more importantly, they became a support system that encouraged them to persevere. This is important considering that, on average, students from low-income backgrounds—as are most Mexican immigrants—are less likely to graduate from college than affluent students. To be precise, when students come from families with annual incomes of $25,000 or less, slightly more than 25 percent of them earn bachelor's degrees. In contrast, when students come from families with annual incomes of $70,000 or higher, 56 percent earn college degrees (Hebel, 2007b).

Roberto [referring to Mexican immigrants in general]:
Many people do want to go to school to learn English, but they either pay for school or pay the rent, utilities, all that . . . just their basic needs.

Almost four in every ten (38%) foreign-born Hispanic adults are high-school dropouts, almost triple the rate (13%) for Hispanics born in the U.S. (U.S. Department of Education, 2007). Nevertheless, notwithstanding their precarious economic conditions and poor statistical prospects, all the participants in this study graduated. Their academic success, their personal fortitude and resilience, make their counter-narratives particularly important and the reason why they were chosen for this research. It appears that they will not take "no" for an answer, and they will readily undertake challenges and face adversities:

David:
So I usually would get up really early in the morning. I would average about an hour, an hour and-a-half before the class, so I could study . . . I remember all my classes were back to back, so I didn't have time between classes. So, my first class usually started at seven fifty or eight A.M., and then they would be done by two P.M., sometimes by twelve, depending on the day. Then at four o'clock I go to work. I go to work at four o'clock and I get home by twelve-thirty, one A.M. That's what my routine would be on a daily basis.

One time I . . . I was taking this [history] class. And the lady . . . the first day of the class, she said, if English is not your first language, you might as well drop this class. That was the first thing she said.

. . . there was a couple of Japanese girls, too. They were there in the class too. I knew them because I was taking, I think it was Writing for International Students [with the Japanese students], something like that. And so the Japanese girls dropped out. And I said "No, I'm staying."

But I still got a B. And I remember her [the instructor] telling me, "I never thought you were going to make it." And I said, "Why don't you let me take your next class, too?" And you know what? I took the next level class and I got an A . . . in the higher level.

An auspicious environment, support services, and institutional commitment will certainly be conducive to academic success (Donato and de Onis, 1995; Trueba, 1983). Additionally, personal resilience and the ability to turn adversities into opportunities, factors identified in all the narratives elicited by this research, appear to be essential attributes for facing adversity:

Jesenia:
[Education] has shaped my life and taught me to look at situations from different perspectives. You don't have to look at things all the time as a negative fight [referring to the adversities she faced throughout college]. You can choose to look at them that way, or you can choose to look at them from another perspective. I think that is what education does to you.

Roberto [referring to his goal to work in international business, his college degree, and using his language skills in spite of his undocumented status]:
What I do is temporary. It's good, right? But it's temporary. I don't see myself doing this until I am fifty, sixty years old . . .

There is a lot of opportunity. Much opportunity. It's what we do not lack here. . . . and everybody talks about wanting to be bilingual, but there aren't many bilingual people in this field.

Rosario [referring to how she graduated and achieved goals after her painful marriage failure]:
You know what experience has been the best in my life? What made me become a woman and started to teach me who I was? My divorce.

David:
They [at the university] require you to spend more time reading books, spend more time with a tutor, spend more time with your peers . . . I remember they [students] always had meetings about homework and I didn't have that time. So I had to deal with whatever hours I had available and make the best out of them.

Justo:
. . . being singled out, what puts some people down . . . for me it has been encouragement to do better. If I'm singled out, if you're looking at me, and you're expecting me to do something either good or bad, it doesn't matter . . . but I know my actions are being noticed. So I can't . . . I can't mess up. I mean, I have to do everything that I can to excel.

It appears that the students' resilience and internal drive was noticed by key individuals who motivated them and helped them in their struggles. As some research has shown, commitment to help students (Cabrera and Padilla, 2004; Donato and de Onis, 1995) and truly caring for them (Valenzuela, 1999) can make a great difference. Marina narrated the powerful impact a high school teacher, a community college counselor, and an Economics instructor had on her academic trajectory:

Then, in my freshman year, I struggled a lot. The next year, I continued to struggle, but I had the same teacher and he was really good. He would stay extra time after school hours if I did not understand him, he would explain again, and then he would explain in Spanish. He would teach one person, or several, just in Spanish because it was after *educational time*, after the hours during which he had to be a teacher. And so, when he taught us in Spanish, I learned very quickly. In Spanish I only needed him to explain . . . for five minutes, but in regular classes he would have to repeat three, four, five times.

. . . when I was not allowed to enroll at the community college and I was totally disappointed because I knew I would not go to college. He [the counselor] told me . . . He knew where I lived, he came to my home, knocked, and said: "I will take you" [to enroll in the community college]. Then he took me and, even though they had already told me "no" because I was . . . I did not have papers, because I did not meet all the requirements, he told me I was a resident because of all the years I had lived in Arizona. I was considered a resident.

My Economics instructor [at the community college] also supported me a great deal. I frequently said it was too difficult, but she would tell me: "you can do it, you can do it." She would tell me: "you've done well; you are the student who dedicates the most time to your studies." Sometimes my assignments were wrong and she would give me two or three assignments to redo, and I always redid them . . . she knew that when there was a review I always would be there, and I always would do the work. Then she would tell me that there were very few people like me, that there were not many students like me, so persistent. She told me to be always like that, that I would get very far. So, when your instructors see that . . . even when they know you have limitations . . . She did not know what my limitations were. She knew I had limitations; maybe she thought it was language. But she would say: "you have potential." Then, when your instructors *see* you, you say: "Yes, I have it in me!" Then, I simply need a little more determination, keep on working, keep on the same direction because I am on the right path. So you realize that what you're doing is worth the grief. And you start feeling fulfilled.

A solid work ethic and sense of responsibility helped Marina to complete her academic goals at the community college. Positive words from academic mentors and a college counselor gave her the incentives she needed to persevere at difficult times. Jesenia also expressed the idea of following the "right path," even if the future is uncertain. Thus, struggling through their educational experiences was worth it because of their personal growth and satisfaction, even at the risk of not being able to use their education in the U.S. in the future. As in Cabrera and Padilla's (2004) research, these students were introduced to the "culture of college" by committed counselors and tutors who inculcated in them that they were worthy people and could achieve great things. Justo also remembers crucial individuals in his academic growth (beside his parents), like his business teacher in high school:

Sometimes I did not have an A, but he would say: "I know you can do it." So he pushed me. He pushed, and pushed, and pushed. . . . He was a personality. Always very well-dressed. He was a leader in his Baptist church, someone you would not expect to have so much esteem for a Mexican immigrant student. And he had a lot of esteem for me . . . he always told me that I could do it. I had my difficult days, like the typical high school student, frustrated and sometimes rebellious, when I did not want . . . and he would tell me: "I know that you can" and "this is just a front you're putting." He would say: "do the work." And he would make me write, and he would turn the light off so I would not see the keyboard. In other words, he pushed me. And then, I had another lady teacher. She taught me how to use *Print Shop* and *PowerPoint* and different things, but she would tell me the same things. She used to say: "you are not even doing two percent of what you can do." And sometimes I didn't like the pressure.

Sometimes, the people who supported these students had unorthodox approaches and bent the rules in order to help. Interestingly, the individuals who went beyond the accepted practices in order to help these students succeed were minority counselors, faculty members, and administrators. This reinforces recommendations by Donato and de Onis (1995) to hire minority people in leadership positions. The instructor who allowed Rosario to attend class with her daughter was an American of Mexican origin, and so was the counselor who encouraged her to enroll in the program for struggling mothers, which helped her through her most difficult moments in college. The counselor who went to Marina's home looking for her in order to enroll her in the community college was also of Mexican origin. He was the same counselor who encouraged Jesenia and Justo to be enrolled in the Summer Bridge program to help them transition successfully into the community college. In other words, alongside supportive programs and conducive environments, there have been key individuals who helped these students to take advantage of them.

> Rosario:
> I did not have any money. I went to the community college because *Women in Progress* granted me a scholarship for two classes.
>   An afternoon I came to the computer lab where I was taking classes and I mentioned to one of the ladies in charge that I was looking for a job. She said: "we need a student aide." And Bingo! It occurred to me that I would love to do that. The money was very little, the minimum, but if you think about it, it was better for me to be working on campus than going back and forth. And so I became a Student Aide in the Computer Lab.
>   The summer of 1998 came and Nadia [Rosario's Mexican-American mentor] saw good skills in me . . . I am not sure what she saw in me, that she asked me to work with her as an assistant, coordinating the summer academies. That was a great experience for me.

All the participants in this research found help and support from specific people within the educational system. This appears to corroborate Gibson's (2003) findings that caring relationships between staff, educators, and students are essential in promoting academic success for immigrant students. Another part of the explanation for the high perseverance and academic achievement of the participants in this study is consistent with Gibson and Bejínez's (2002) research on Mexican students from migrant farmworker families, where the support provided by specific programs was found to be crucial. Initially, Rosario was able to afford college thanks to the small scholarship granted by the Women in Progress program and, more importantly, she benefited from a network that provided her with emotional and social support. Similarly, the

Summer Bridge Program helped Justo and Marina with their transition from high school to college. David took advantage of a program that promoted transferability between the community college and the university and was able to enroll at the university. Jesenia was able to start classes at the university thanks to Project Class Arizona, a program aimed at helping struggling women to get a higher education, where she was not questioned about her lack of documents. Therefore, the opportunities and_caring environments created by these types of programs can be part of the antidote for academic attrition, even for the highest-risk students (see Gibson and Bejínez, 2002; Alvarez-McHatton et al., 2006).

When the educational environment permitted, the participants even found sources of agency and support among themselves. Marina became a member of a student club, *Hispanos Unidos* (Hispanics United) made by and for Hispanics to support Hispanics. David became involved in a group called Future Hispanic Leaders of America. Justo himself was the founder of a student club, *Voces de la Juventud Hispana* (Voices of Hispanic Youth), that engaged undocumented students and encouraged Hispanics in general to take advantage of opportunities in higher education:

Marina:

Hispanos [Unidos] was a club we had. The group would raise funds for the members and . . . Let's say that those who were in sports could not afford soccer shoes, like myself, *Hispanos Unidos* would help me and I could have my shoes. I also was in the Folkloric Dance club and once I really wanted to go to the Mariachi Conference. But I had to pay to be there. *Hispanos Unidos* would sponsor us. That is, you would work doing carwashes, selling candy, giving presentations, and later, from that money, they would give you funds if you needed them.

David:

. . . when I arrived at the community college, I remember I joined a group called FHLA. Most of them were Mexica . . . ah . . . Chicanos, they call themselves Chicanos, they're born in America, but proud of their Mexican roots. It was called Future Hispanic Leaders of America. And I was in there. And I mean, obviously I didn't speak English much. But, all they spoke was English. So, you also learned that way because, you know, you only . . . you have to speak English. So . . . from there, I remember a lot about, um . . . affirmative action. They kept saying that it should be enforced . . . and I kept wondering: "what is affirmative action?"

Justo:

The majority of the members did not have documents . . . It was a Spanish club . . . it was in Spanish, and we would show . . . open their eyes to different opportunities.

We have a community college, we have a university, here you are . . .

Where we focused our efforts the most was on a change of mentality. That was the focus. Because there were many, many . . . [students who needed motivation] We also focused on those who had the opportunity: "you have the chance. Give it a good go!" And if they did not have the opportunity [alluding to undocumented students], we would not exclude them. Our attitude was never to say: "Too bad, this is not for you." We did not have all the answers. We were just sixteen-, seventeen-year-old kids. . . . I would not say anything about their [immigration] status, but I would say: "You know what? That is not a big deal. You set your goals. What do you want to achieve? There will be a way to do it." When you crave something, it's like Beethoven; he could never stop writing, until his last melody, when he was deaf. You know what I'm saying? That is, there are no limits. If you truly want something, you can achieve it in this country. This is the country of opportunity.

Now that Justo has a normalized immigration status, the system seems to be working well for him. Moreover, he has a powerful drive to succeed no matter where he is. Even when Justo was an undocumented teenager in high school, and organizing other undocumented students would seem to be an intimidating task, he persevered. Evidently, a favorable school environment helped Justo and his friends to achieve this. Today Justo is the incarnation of the "American Dream." However, Jesenia and Marina are struggling with the very same "dream," since their realities appear to be showing them the American Dream may be out of reach. For undocumented inhabitants of the United States, and particularly in Arizona, the possibility to "rise above" their socio-economic reality—as the American Dream implies—has become more difficult. David and Roberto are also experiencing truncated versions of the "dream." In addition to their undocumented status and the anti-immigrant movement, increases in income inequality, cost of living (housing, medical expenses, consumer debt), and the cost of higher education make many immigrants, and the poor in general, increasingly disempowered (Sieber, 2005). It appears Jesenia is the closest to giving up on the dream, while the other three who remain undocumented still hang tenaciously to the idea that their realities will change some day.

Marina:
. . . looking into the future, I want my children . . . if I was able to finish the community college, I want my children to have a university education. I want my children to have masters degrees, I want them to have a doctorate. And so, all this is for them to be able to achieve that; that's why I have to get a little bit ahead of my parents. So I have to . . . sometimes that was the only thing that motivated me to finish the community college. I know I could get a little bit further than the community college and I know they [her children] will get much further than me. [16]

The vital sense of optimism and hope expressed by Marina can be enhanced in college by organizational cultures that emphasize opportunity and reduce barriers (Reyes et al., 1999). Rumberger and Rodríguez (2002) criticize the lack of attention to the high-risk settings where disenfranchised students live and go to school. Colleges cannot do much about the poverty and violence that some of the participants, like many immigrants, experienced on a daily basis. Nevertheless, positive organizational environments and role models of Mexican origin may reduce the unequal encouragement to succeed experienced by minorities (Donato and de Onis, 1995; Pearl, 2002; Valencia, 2002).[17] Jesenia also experienced the positive influence of one individual who helped her to break barriers in order to be able to enroll in the community college.

> They gave me some tests and I made it into college. But it was Vicente Suarez[18] [a counselor of Mexican origin] who helped us [she and her sister] to get in. Because they previously had given my sister trouble when she tried to enroll at the community college before . . .
>   . . . he [Vicente] was a counselor. He took his time, he sat with us, helped us enroll and told us where to go and what to do. In order to enroll in any college, you had to be an in-state resident, right? Since we did not have in-state residency, he . . . I don't really know how he did it. He asked us for certain papers, like taxes . . . my mom's tax identification number. My mom claimed us in her tax forms, so we showed him my mother's tax forms. Then he asked us for school papers, our grades, the transcripts and things like that to be able to demonstrate that we qualify as in-state students.

Caring individuals and support programs can potentially create the environments that counter academic attrition, even for immigrant students living in adversity (Alvarez-McHatton et al., 2006; Gibson and Bejínez, 2002). If, as Shields (2004) proposes, deficit thinking in higher education is replaced with profound and meaningful relationships with students—as those developed by the staff, faculty, and administrators who help the participants—academic achievement will be more feasible for others like them. With the rising tuition at four-year colleges and the complex lives of immigrant students, community colleges seem to be propitious for those who need financially accessible educational opportunities and flexible options that allow them to work and be part-time students (Bailey and Smith Morest, 2006). Judging by their high enrollment rates (higher than the national average), higher education has a great value for Latinos (Fry, 2002). Paradoxically, in spite of such high enrollment, their graduation rates lag behind all other ethnic groups. Thus, "Much of the Latino achievement gap is the result of what happens after Hispanic students begin their postsecondary studies" (Ibid.: 4). In the specific case of the participants in this research, they obviously needed the financially accessible opportunities provided by the community college. Perhaps even more importantly, the support programs, role models, and caring individuals who helped them appear to have been essential in their academic achievement. In other words, access is important, but "access without support is not an opportunity" (Hebel, 2007b).

Finally, public education is not a Mexican or a citizenship issue, but a human rights and an economic issue. Therefore, the traditional concept of citizenship must be challenged and replaced by a multidimensional, humane notion of membership in a community (Heater, 1999). Thus, undocumented students who live in the U.S. permanently should have access to academic, financial, social, and legal support. In fact, it is in the public interest that these members of society be allowed to develop their full academic and economic potential. The states that allow undocumented students to pay in-state tuition have taken a step in the right direction.

Acculturation and Cultural Preservation: "Let's do it in *Espanglish*"

As explained above, Mexicans in the United States are a very diverse population ethnically, politically, and culturally. Some of them reject American culture to the point of refusing to speak English (apparently a minuscule minority) while others become assimilated by the dominant culture to the point of rejection of their own Mexicanness. In the first case, Ronald Takaki (1993) refers to the term "Occupied Mexico" used by some people of Mexican origin living in the United States. On the other hand, in her analysis of "subtractive schooling" and Mexican youth, Angela Valenzuela (1999) sees the schooling process as a "state-sanctioned instrument of cultural de-identification, or de-Mexicanization" (161), that deepens divisions among students of Mexican origin. As a consequence, many students of Mexican origin experience negative identity conflicts, feelings of guilt, and even self-hate. Along this wide spectrum of identities and realities, many immigrants have been able to create a cultural and linguistic space where they feel safe, or what historian David Gutiérrez has called a "Third Space" (quoted by Smith, 2005). Jesenia, like the other participants, appears to constantly navigate in that Third Space, somewhere between Occupied Mexico and de-Mexicanized America. Thus, when she was asked what language she would prefer to use in our interview she candidly responded:

Let's do it in *Espanglish*.

The historical prohibition of Spanish as an inferior language has been an instrument of political and socio-economic domination (González, N., 2001;

Perea, 1992). However, in our time, Stavans (2003) argues that Spanglish, or *Espanglish* as some Spanish speakers call it, represents the emergence of a new American language, a third space of resistance. Arredondo, Hurtado, Klahn, and Najera-Ramirez (2003) argue that this hybridity is a type of oppositional consciousness of "resistance to the repression of language and culture, a recognition of a 'third space' located within intersecting structures of power . . ." (5). Jesenia does not conceive the use of *Espanglish* as a statement of resistance to the hegemonic culture and language but rather as a convenience and as a sense of belonging:

> . . . since I know you speak both, I feel more comfortable [speaking *Espanglish*], although I know it's not a language . . . I used to have an English teacher in high school who always gave us a hard time about it. We [Jesenia and her friends] would sit in a place to talk, and that's how we talked [in *Espanglish*], and he would say, "Okay, you either talk to me all words in Spanish or English. No *Espanglish*, because I am training you for the real world. When you have to work, you will have trouble if I let you speak like that." And we laughed, "But sir, c'mon, sir . . ." It was fun.
>   I never spoke English in school. In high school, I spoke it only when I had to with teachers.

Although Jesenia's English is very good and certainly allowed her to function in school, she used it in high school only when necessary. She was able to do this because she resides in a large Hispanic community, but her use of *Espanglish* is an indication of her complex identity. Morales (2002) describes the use of *Espanglish*, and the state of *being* Spanglish, as living in "multisubjectivity" and as a link with history and issues of race and class (31–32). The participants in this study have lived and experienced multiple dimensions and subjectivities in the process of acculturation. Clearly all of them have adapted to the dominant culture and speak English well. At the same time, all of them feel proud of their background; they do not want to forget their native language, and those with children of their own emphasize Mexican culture as part of their family values. Gibson (1998) argues that when immigrants' children preserve their ethnic cultures while acquiring the dominant language and culture, they have a good chance to do well academically. This certainly appears to be the case of the six participants in this study. Their experiences also reinforce St-Hilaire's (2002) finding that fluent bilingualism is positively associated with educational aspirations and expectations. Justo and David express this in perfect English:

> Justo:
> I consider myself an immigrant, as I was telling you, proud of my [Mexican] roots, and I know we have a lot to contribute here.

David [narrating his experience in a Public Speech class, nervously speaking Spanish to his peers]:
. . . I remember, I started my speech with the same "*¿Cómo estás?*," as when I speak Spanish. And everybody's staring at me like, crazy. And then I told them, that's how I feel when you speak English to me. My point was, it's important to learn another language. And I was trying to tell them that, you know, I'm learning, I'm trying, you should too.

I don't speak Spanish as much as I speak English anymore. . . . A lot of people always tell me that I speak English like a university grad.

The participants' attachment to their Mexicanness and their solidarity with their ethnic communities also appear to be positive factors in their development. It could be argued that, because the participants reside in an urban community with a large population of Mexican origin, they have been able to develop more effective social networks and support structures that increased their social capital and encouraged their educational achievement (Gibson and Bejínez, 2002; Grant, 2005; Stanton-Salazar and Dornbusch, 1995). Takaki (1993) observes how Mexican-Americans who are U.S. citizens by birth are often reminded by their parents that they are still Mexicans "by blood" (354). Rosario has followed this tradition of pride, but differences have emerged among her family members:

I always have told my children that they are Mexican . . . because their parents are Mexican. They were born in the United States, but they come from Mexican parents, therefore they're Mexican. And so my sister always gets angry at me and tells me, "They are actually Americans," she says, "Why do you tell them they are Mexicans?" . . . her son never says "I am Mexican." I guess we are Mexican-American.

According to De Genova (1998), Mexican immigrants "have a remarkable heterogeneity of experiences," but "the terms 'Mexican American' and Chicano/a' have virtually no currency for self-identification; the pervasive category is 'Mexicano/a.'" Heterogeneity is definitely evident through the narratives in this research. However, self-identification can be a very complex endeavor. Roberto, for example, is also very proud of his Mexican background and is not very fond of the term "Chicano," as De Genova's research suggests, but he defines himself and his children as "Latino." Rosario does define herself as *Mexicana* (or Mexican), but she contradicts De Genova's (1998) research. Her statements show her adaptation and evolution in the United States:

I am an immigrant, a Mexican, *Mexican-American* . . . Hispanic . . . When they ask me, I always say: "I am Mexican," but I also feel American.

I am learning to be a better Mexican here in the United States . . . I've been learning more about my own culture . . . and I am a better American too.

And, in spite of her profound Mexican pride, Rosario can be very critical of Mexican culture and society:

> [Mexican] society imposes so many bad things, where we are all supposed to be equal . . . it's a big lie.
>
> It's a great cancer that we Mexicans have [referring to inequality in Mexican society]. And I brought that cancer with me . . . but, when I came to this country I was already a teenager; I did not want to stay here at the beginning. I felt that the *güeros*[19] were not part of my society, my natural environment. I thought Americans were dirty. . . . Then, I think God wanted things to happen this way, I was proven wrong.

Jesenia has a much more complicated, but inclusive concept of identity. She explains to me as she mixes phrases in Spanish and English:

> I am *México-Americana* because Mexico belongs to America.[20] Even though society, or . . . people in general, everybody thinks that America is only the United States. It's not. America is bigger. So, I am *México-Americana* because Mexico is also part of America. I am Latin because I speak Spanish and Spanish comes from Latin . . . I am also Hispanic because I speak Spanish. I was brought to the United States when I was a child and I learned English . . . so, I guess I am a little bit Chicana too. My little sister [who is a U.S. citizen] is Chicana, she struggles with her Spanish . . . but sure, I also have learned a little *Chicanismo*.

Interestingly, notions of space and identity merge in a subtle but powerful expression used by Jesenia and Rosario as they refer to Mexico as "the other side." Nugent (1993) has noted that the expression *El Otro Lado* (the Other Side), very commonly used by Mexicans to refer to the United States, alludes to "the other side . . . of The Same Space, of a single space" (6). Obviously, for Rosario and Jesenia, *the Other Side* is a valid expression on either side of the U.S.-Mexico border. The expression reveals their sense of belonging to both sides of the same space, while they connect with the counter-memory of their ancestors. Historically, "they did not cross the border; the border crossed them." Conversely, in the United States people are told that the inhabitants of the rest of this shared space are potential "aliens," the official term used by the U.S. government to refer to immigrants. These participants, however, share a clear counter-memory, a Mexican "community of memory" that contradicts the colonizing version of history. Implicit in it is a tacit claim and a sense of history and identity that is missing in the dominant immigration discourse.

> Jesenia [reflecting on the meaning of being an immigrant]:
> To migrate, you know, to migrate to another place, to another culture . . . that's immigrating to me. And I don't feel like I immigrated here to the U.S . . . it sounds like

they're talking about someone else. . . . Because I grew up in Arizona, and this is my home.

Marina:
I grew up in this country. So, it is difficult to say I am or feel as an immigrant. The only thing that makes me hit the wall is that I am an *illegal*, but I was *born* here. Many friends tell me, "You are not illegal. You were brought up here. You are a *Unitedstatesian*."[21] So, I grew up here, all my education has been here, but simply because of the lack of some papers I am not . . . (voice breaks) The way I feel about being an immigrant is that I am not one.

Marina and Jesenia utilize the term *illegal* to refer to themselves, a sad indication that they have internalized the racist discourse of the dominant narrative. They, like millions of undocumented immigrants, are victims of colonization who have internalized the consciousness of the colonizers (Freire, 1970; García, 2004). However, Marina also has a slip of the tongue and refers to herself as "born here," instead of "raised here." It is clear that she feels as "an American in the shadows." She is convinced that her children will grow up in the United States and will get "much further" than she has. Similarly, Jesenia expresses that "we are like the foundation for our kids" and places herself historically with other people she does not believe were recognized in their time. Specifically, she places herself with the discrimination against the Irish immigrants. Justo also shows historical perspective and a vision of the future when he explains that his educational accomplishments and hard work will benefit "those who come after me, my children." The participants' place in history, their dreams, and their identity are inexorably linked to their sense of belonging in the United States.

Roberto expresses great admiration for the United States and is a firm believer in its meritocratic system. He expresses some criticism to his adopted country, revealing a personal perspective about American culture:

Here your word is not worth anything. Here everything has to be on writing. And this is not true with Mexicans. If someone [in Mexico] tells you things will be a certain way, they will be that way.

Galindo, Medina, and Chávez (2005) point out that *Latinos* in the United States create new and manifold identities, while retaining past cultural forms. These "border identities" are hybrid, constantly evolving, "and may imply multiple loyalties" (81). The bilingual and transnational identities of Mexican-origin people, and Latinos in general, have historically been construed as "foreign" by the dominant narrative in the United States, which propagates the myth of a uniform American identity. Throughout their history as a minority, people of Mexican origin and all Latinos have been under attack "by subtractive assimilationist policies developed to eliminate Latino culture[s] and the Spanish language" (*Ibid.*). Schooling has been one of the main mechanisms utilized to achieve such objectives and, as stated by Valenzuela (1999), "the history of public schooling for U.S.-Mexicans shows schools to be key sites for both ethnic conflict and the production of minority status" (162). Nevertheless, the counter-narratives in this research show the complexity of hybrid identities and their dual loyalties.

> Justo:
> It's absolutely a blessing to have come here. And that's why I would not hesitate to defend this country if I have to do it.

With this assertion, Justo completely contradicts Huntington (2004a, 2004b). He is still connected to his Mexican roots and very proud of them. He still speaks Spanish and sees that as an advantage. However, he is also very proud of being an American and is extremely patriotic in this sense. As seen in "the political economy of immigration," Justo's energy, enthusiasm and high aims are the type of attributes many immigrants bring with them and the U.S. benefits from. Justo's narrative is extraordinary, as is the way in which he conceives his own identity. He does not identify himself with Chicano culture. He feels most comfortable with the term "Mexican-American," but he is well aware of the symbolism and power behind *Chicanismo*:

> I consider myself Mexican-American. But I see a lot of value in the Chicano movement, back in the sixties and . . . many of the rights that we have now are because of that movement. So I respect it. You know? I admire it. I mean, it took guts to do what they did back then. What people did back then . . .
> [The term] Latino is the safest one, because that's a geographic term. You know, it's Latin America.
> . . . I feel proud of who I am. I feel proud of where I come from. And, because I understand where I come from and where I am now, I know I can get to a place in the future. To be an immigrant is an identity for me. It's a constant way of life. . . . And I don't think of me as a disadvantaged immigrant, but I see it as an advantage. It's like when people laugh at someone with an accent, but that means that person speaks at least two languages.
> . . . being Hispanic doesn't only mean that you can lead the Hispanic club, that you can lead the Spanish club . . . the Hispanic, the Latino fraternity or sorority. No, no, no. You have the ability to be the . . . the Attorney General of the United States. You know, you have the ability to be the Surgeon General of the United States. And I'm naming those positions because they're occupied by Hispanics/Latinos. . . . We can be Speaker of the House, we can be . . . Senate Majority Leader!

Evidently Justo has a solid sense of self and of his own culture. However, in his narrative, he also revealed his insecurities and struggles as he navigated school environments both in Mexico and Arizona. Justo talked about the process of intense acculturation and challenges he faced when he first came to the U.S. He appears to thrive in the face of adversity, and, even when he struggled to adapt to and understand the U.S. school system as an undocumented student, he succeeded in achieving different goals. Justo's counterstory, as well as the other counter-narratives in this study, appear to corroborate Lucas and Stone's (1994) findings that students of Mexican origin with low levels of acculturation are as competitive, if not more competitive than students from the majority culture. Additionally, their counter-stories reinforce the claim that encouragement and nurturing of Mexican/Hispanic/Chicano pride, cultures, and language will be conducive to the academic success of immigrant students (Allen, 2006; Gibson, 1998; Nieto, 1996; Valenzuela, 1999). Ethnic pride, acculturation, and evolving identities are salient features in these stories:

Roberto [answering the question "Do you identify more with the U.S. flag or with the Mexican flag?"]:
With both!

Justo:
So, we have had to learn a lot of things after we came here, not just as immigrants, learning a different life style. . . . You also learn to respect differences. You learn how to appreciate different things. And you learn how to identify, in different ways, with people you never thought you would identify.

David:
Your way of thinking does change and you feel like a Mexica-Ame . . . like an American. And sometimes I don't feel like a foreigner. I always say "we" referring to the United States. . . . So, for example, when I debate about the war [in Iraq], I don't just talk about "the United States," I say "we" . . . referring to the United States. "I think *we* should do this," or "*We* should not go there . . ."or "*We* shouldn't do that . . ."

Marina:
I do not think like they do in Mexico. I adore Mexico, I am extremely proud of my Mexican roots, but I cannot change Mexico. And . . . it is very possible that, because of my ideologies, I would have many problems living there.

These statements go against some detractors' simplistic idea that Hispanic immigrants do not want or do not intend to acculturate to the United States (see, for example, Huntington, 2004a, 2004b). Perhaps it could be argued that, contrary to other minorities and immigrant groups, great numbers of people of Mexican origin have not been fully "assimilated" into the dominant U.S. culture and continue to speak Spanish (Huntington, 2004a, 2004b; Perea, 1992). This is probably due to the fact that more than 40% of them are first-generation immigrants (U.S. Census, 2007), rather than to their unwillingness to assimilate the dominant norms and language. In fact, Rosario's sister prefers to call her child American, rather than Mexican; Justo's parents go to school to improve their English; and David prefers to utilize English in our interview, rather than his native language. It would be difficult to accuse these people of reluctance to adapt to their new country.

If, as concluded by Gecas (1973), immigrants' loyalty to Mexican cultural values is stronger than in the case of Americans of Mexican origin, the six participants clearly show dual loyalties. Their identity structures appear to be malleable and fluctuate between two worlds. Their evolving minds demonstrate the complexity of cultural identity, which is far from being stagnant. The participants' strong English-language assimilation appears to corroborate Alba et al.'s (2002) research. Their adaptation to the dominant culture is unquestionable, but their socioeconomic advancement, as predicted by St-Hilaire (2001, 2002), is uncertain for those with an undocumented status. At the same time, Justo and Rosario, who have become formal citizens of the U.S., support the argument that immigrants who deliberately preserve their native culture and maintain solidarity within their ethnic communities make rapid socioeconomic progress (Ibid.). It is also possible that, especially in densely Hispanic areas of the U.S., educational success and economic prosperity for people of Mexican origin are feasible without full assimilation (Andrade, 1998). Ironically, for undocumented Americans of Mexican origin, who are clearly assimilated and possess the advantage of full biculturalism, prosperity and academic achievement are much more difficult to reach.

In conclusion, all participants in this study appear to navigate in that complex "Third Space" between Occupied Mexico and de-Mexicanized America. Since they were born in Mexico and are rejected by the majoritarian narrative, they do not always identify themselves with Chicanos and Mexican-Americans. They do not always feel the pride of the Chicano movement and culture because they came to the country after that struggle. And yet, they can feel the historical pain of the "native strangers" who have inhabited the Southwest since before the United States crossed their border. At the same time, they have been acculturated as United Statesian-Americans to the extent that they would not feel complete living only as Mexicans. The reality is that cultures are in a constant state of flux and transform each other. The narratives in this research show that people can actually embrace two or more cultures and languages as they are transformed by cultural cross-pollinization.

The participants appear to be, as defined by Stavans (2001), "a transitional group, living in the hyphen" (19).

Notes

[1] See for example Provine and Doty (2011), who denounce "The Criminalization of Immigrants as a Racial Project" and the "institutionalized racial violence embedded in our current immigration regime" (261).

[2] For an analysis on the importance of religion in Latino activism, see Espinosa, Elizondo, and Miranda (2005).

[3] Mexico has a population of 113 million (CIA, 2011) and a society that self-defines as *Mestizo*, a word from Latin meaning "mixed." The country has 56 officially recognized autochthonous ethnic groups (*indios*). The Spanish Conquest of Mexico and subsequent Colonial period (1521–1821) brought the first European settlers. Later came immigrants from other European nations (French, Germans, Greeks, Italians, Russians, and others) and from other continents (Africans, Arabs, Asians, Jews). About 60% of Mexico's population is *Mestizo* with a wide range of phenotypes, about 30% Native American (*indios*) or predominantly Amerindian, 9% white, and 1% other (CIA, 2011). During the Colonial period a *de jure* and *de facto* caste system was established in the "New Spain" (Mexico), where racial classification was defined based on the purity of European whiteness in each individual. This system, which Ramón Gutierrez has referred to as "Pigmentocracy" (quoted in Ruiz, 2004), categorized citizens in over 100 different castes, each one with different privileges and restrictions. Today, racism against *indios* is still widespread in Mexico, and they constitute the poorest and most disadvantaged minorities in most parts of the country (Castellanos Guerrero, 2001). Currently, the net migration rate in Mexico is −3.24 migrants/1000 population (CIA, 2011). The majority of those migrants come to the U.S.

[4] Bender and Ruiz utilize the concept of internal locus of control "to describe the extent to which an individual believes—or does not believe—that he is able to exercise control over the direction of his personal life" (51).

[5] *Ni de aquí ni de allá* (1987) is the title of a border film produced in Mexico, focusing on the immigration problem and emphasizing abuses against Mexican immigrants in the U.S. (Iglesias, 2003: 192). Similarly, *Ni de aquí ni de allá* (translated as "not from here, not from there") is also a popular Mexican-American rap song by Jae-P. The CD cover reads: *Dos mundos, dos lenguas, una voz* (Two worlds, two languages, one voice). The song is online at: http://www.youtube.com/watch?v=DJUBGa9Faps.

[6] Based on the three most utilized income distribution measures (the Gini coefficient, the Theil index, and the General Entropy index), Mexico is one of the most inegalitarian societies in the world (Brandolini and Smeeding, 2006; De Hoyos, 2005). Although Mexico is a relatively rich country among developing nations, extremely unequal wealth distribution perpetuates problems of malnutrition, substandard living conditions, and lack of access to services (*Ibid.*). Mexico has the highest number of children living in poverty (about one in every three) among the OCDE countries, while the richest 10% of its population has an income that is equivalent to that of 70% of Mexican households (Instituto, 2006a). In 2005, 47% of the population did not have full access to basic nutrition, housing, and education

(*Ibid.*). Paradoxically, in 2011 Mexico is among the the 15 richest economies in the world and is prolific in billionaires, including the richest person on earth.

[7] In a bold reinterpretation of the Fourteenth Amendment, Republican legislators in Arizona introduced a bill to deny citizenship rights to U.S.-born children of undocumented residents. The bill, as well as other anti-immigrant initiatives, was defeated in March 2011 after pressure from the business community and citizens from different communities. The bill was rejected in a public letter from 60 CEOs from major corporations and companies operating in Arizona, while children held symbolic sit-ins in Flagstaff and Tucson as a form of protest (Condon, 2011). Other states are also considering the same measure.

[8] Bowden, a photo journalist and activist from Tucson, Arizona documented the reality of violence and poverty in the industrial border city of Juárez, Mexico. Bowden's painful and disturbing photographs and narrative underlie some of the reasons for Mexican emigration. In what could be termed "economic violence"—a result of economic colonization—more than 300 foreign-owned *maquiladoras* (factories) employ over 200,000 Mexican workers in Juárez, while 2,820 *maquiladoras* across Mexico provide work for around 1,218,000 people (Instituto, 2006b). It is important to note however that *maquiladora* workers are predominantly women, who work 48 hours a week or more for about $9 per day. American mainstream perspective is that such inferior wages and labor standards are justifiable because the cost of living is less in Mexico and "they would not have work otherwise." In reality, prices in Mexico are highly incommensurate with wages (see footnote 28), while the average American worker easily earns ten times more than a Mexican counterpart. Bales (1999) argues that this is in fact a new type of slavery, where people are disposable and they are controlled by another person for the purpose of exploitation. In spite of having to pay wages (or rather "slave wages") and not having "legal" ownership, modern slavery gives slave owners the advantage of ownership without the legalities. "For the slaveholders, not having legal ownership is an improvement because they get total control without any responsibility for what they own" (*Ibid.*: 5). Paradoxically, those who have escaped this situation in Mexico and have come to the United States as undocumented immigrants can find themselves in similar circumstances, excluded from "the mainstream labor economy through racial labor segmentation, and thereby forced into ethnic enclaves where all labor laws are routinely neglected" (Ross, 1997).

[9] A report by The Urban Institute for the National Council of La Raza notes that there are about 5 million children in the U.S. with at least one undocumented parent (Capps, Castaneda, Chaudry, and Santos, 2007).

[10] There are at least 1.8 million children in the U.S. who are indistinguishable from other American children and speak mostly English but are undocumented (Passel, 2005).

[11] David specifically refers to the song entitled "*La Jaula de Oro*" by Los Tigres del Norte (The Northern Tigers), a popular band from northern Mexico. The lyrics of the song read: "Here I am, still living in the United States. It's been ten years since the day I became a wetback. My situation is the same. I remain an undocumented immigrant. I have my wife and children, who came with me when they were little. They have forgotten about Mexico; I haven't, but I can't return to it. What good is money if I'm being held in this great country against my will? Remembering this I cry, realizing that although the cage may be made out of gold, it's still a cage, nonetheless." Los Tigres del Norte have released dozens of records in Spanish in the U.S.

[12] Here, we refer again to the "violence of poverty" denounced by Nelson Mandela (quoted by Toh, 2004: 25) and Paulo Freire (1996).

[13] Utilizing data from the 1989 Legalized Population Survey, Powers and Seltzer (1998) found that occupational status and earnings of undocumented immigrants between their first jobs in the U.S. and their last employment before legalization, as an average, improved. In a more recent study by Toussaint-Comeau (2006), she concludes that socioeconomic status of immigrants is determined by a complex combination of human capital, immigration factors, and demographic characteristics. "Human capital characteristics are represented by education, English-language fluency, and years of labor market experience. Immigration factors are estimated by number of years in the U.S. and the period of migration. Demographic characteristics include gender, racial group, and membership in a specific Hispanic ethnic subgroup" (519). The findings also suggest that less-educated Hispanic immigrants will never reach the socioeconomic status of U.S.-born Hispanics or non-Hispanic Whites (Ibid. 531).

[14] The stories in this book corroborate a number of factors affecting the academic achievement of undocumented Americans. Their narratives confirm that their undocumented status translates into a number of barriers to college enrollment and fewer opportunities to afford education through federal and state scholarships and loans. In some states, they are not allowed to enroll in public colleges, while in many states (like Arizona) they have to pay out-of-state tuition irrespective of the number of years they have resided in the state. Undocumented students like Marina also lack easy access to transportation; including the ability, in most states, to obtain driver's licenses. Driver's licenses in most states require a social security number, so undocumented students cannot drive to and from college. Being pulled over without a driver's license is one way to be detected; hence many undocumented people do not take this risk. Finally, these students have to live with the permanent stress and fear of deportation and the concomitant negative impact on their academic and personal lives. In contrast, those with formal citizenship, regardless of community attachments, can easily establish residency to register as in-state students, making their education less costly. Many out-of-state students reside in their chosen university state for one year before starting their studies. After a year, they are considered "residents" and at that point they can pay in-state tuition. Many will leave the state as soon as they finish their studies, and hence the state will not receive any economic benefit from their education. Conversely, undocumented students have resided in their states where their families have lived for many years and, for the most part, intend to remain there.

[15] Grogger and Trejo (2002) have found that "an enormous educational improvement takes place between first- and second-generation Mexican Americans" (13). The average schooling for the second generation improves about three and a half years. After that, intergenerational school progress of Mexican-Americans slows considerably, lagging behind the academic achievement of whites "by an alarming amount" (Ibid.). However, Grogger and Trejo define the second generation as natives who have at least one foreign-born parent. In the case of undocumented Americans—like Marina, Jesenia, and Justo—who have successfully graduated from U.S. high schools, we would argue that they have the same potential as U.S. natives of Mexican parents. We also would question the categorization of "native" which, culturally, is not acquired by being born within a specific demarcation but by a sense of belonging and navigating successfully within a given environment.

[16] In 2003–2004, 64% of all Hispanic undergraduate students in Arizona were enrolled in community colleges (Excelencia in Education, 2004). By the school year 2013–2014, more than 40% of public high school graduates in Arizona will be Hispanic, predominantly of Mexican origin (Ibid.). Lamentably, higher education is less affordable in Arizona compared

to other states (*Ibid.*) and Hispanics have a high rate of poverty. The state lags behind the nation in the educational arena. A report by the National Center for Public Policy and Higher Education (2006) has graded Arizona and only four other states with a "D" in student preparation. Arizona is 50th in the nation with only 73% of 18–24-year-olds holding high school diplomas and shows no improvement in the percentage of students enrolling in higher education after high school (28%), ranking 47th in the Union. Additionally, the racial gap in college participation has widened. Whites are twice as likely as non-Whites to be enrolled in higher education, while college affordability continues to decline (*Ibid.*). It is in this context that community colleges must be instrumental in developing the state's human capital, and, contrary to the anti-immigrant rhetoric, that educational process should include undocumented permanent residents. This is necessary for pragmatic and economic reasons (Dervarics, 2006; Gans 2007) but, more importantly, human rights and dignity demand it.

[17] Lack of encouragement to succeed and barriers to educational achievement also have color. In 2007, the *Chicago Tribune* has revealed neglected data from the U.S. Department of Education for the 2004–2005 school year that shows African-American students are disciplined disproportionately more rigorously for the same offenses, even when compared with White students from the same socio-economic background. Similarly "Hispanic students are suspended and expelled in almost direct proportion to their populations, while White and Asian students are disciplined far less" (Witt, 2007). This research corroborates that racial factors are more important than the dominant society is willing to admit. Interestingly, the *Chicago Tribune* analysis found that some of the highest rates of racially unequal discipline are found in states with the smallest minority populations (*Ibid.*). Historically, this research reveals that we have not overcome the deep racial divisions and prejudices in American society. In a historical analysis of racial repression experienced by people of Mexican origin, Menchaca (1993) reviewed records of court cases between 1848–1947 and found that Mexicans of Indian descent were more severely discriminated against than Mexicans considered White.

[18] The counselor's real name has been changed for his protection.

[19] *Güero* is an adjective Mexicans commonly use to refer to people of fair complexion. However, many Spanish-speaking people in the U.S. also use this slang to refer to Anglo-Americans.

[20] As explained in Chapter I, this is a widely held opinion by Mexicans and Latin Americans in general. According to Levi (1991), "To millions of West Indians, Canadians and Latin Americans, America is more than the United States: it is North, Central, and South America and the Caribbean—the Western Hemisphere" (486). In his Presidential Address to the American Studies Association in 2003, Kaplan (2004) referred to the "the imperialistic appropriation of the name America" (10). This appropriation is something many Mexicans, and Latin Americans in general, feel resentful about. Jesenia's perspective probably came from her parents and the Mexican educational system. In Mexico, as in other Latin American countries, children are taught that America encompasses the whole American *continent*. Interestingly, the American continent was named after Amerigo Vespucci in 1507. Vespucci was an Italian explorer who, in 1502, was the first European to realize that the Americas were completely disconnected from Asia. However, neither Columbus nor Vespucci ever set foot on the land that would become the United States of America. Martin Waldseemuller, a German cartographer was the first person to print a map using the name "America." Paradoxically, he only used the word "America" for South America. In 1538, Gerardus

Mercator was the first person to make a map that included both the names "North America" and "South America."

[21] In the interview, Marina utilized the Spanish adjective *estadounidense*. In academic literature, Del Castillo (2002) refers to "the Unitedstatesian side of the border" (12). See Chapter I for further discussion.

Navigating Experiential and Sensual Borders: Toward Transformation and Empowerment[*]

> . . . the historical, political, cultural, and economic conditions of each context present new methodological and tactical requirements, so that it is always necessary to search for their actualization.
>
> —Paulo Freire (1997: 316).

> *El arte no es un espejo en el que nos contemplamos, sino un destino en el que nos realizamos. En eso radica su valor subversivo y creador.*
>
> (Art is not a mirror where we contemplate ourselves, but a destiny in which we discover ourselves. In this resides its subversive and creative value.)
>
> —Octavio Paz (1982: 224).

In this chapter we theoretically situate and ground our methodological work with undocumented Americans, to reflect on the evocative use and synergetic power of critical race theory (CRT), counter life history and critical arts-based performance for political recovery and empowerment.

Increasingly over the last 30 years methodological assumptions around epistemology and the nature of qualitative research have been questioned and reconfigured (Cahnmann-Taylor, 2008). Lincoln and Denzin (2003:17), speaking in relation to ethnographic work within the qualitative paradigm, highlight three key "understandings"—firstly, that "lived experience cannot be directly captured or represented by qualitative researchers." Secondly, that,

---

[*] A substantive part of this chapter draws on Bagley, C. & Castro-Salazar, R. (2011). "Critical Arts-based Research in Education: Performing Undocumented *Historias*. Copyright © British Educational Research Association, reprinted by permission of Taylor & Francis Ltd (http://www.tandf.co.uk/journals) on behalf of British Educational Research Association.

texts in the past have been "written as if an objective accounting of the world could be produced," and thirdly, that texts have been written "in the absence of thought given to praxis" or textual impact.

Arguably, in encountering and striving to come to terms with the complex, changing and contested societal contexts of 21st century living, researchers are posed with significant and evolving methodological questions for undertaking research. In particular, to what extent does this challenge require a move beyond simple recognition of a problem or reaffirmation of rigorous traditional approaches and lend itself to an interdisciplinary call for a reworking or shifting of methodological boundaries?

This chapter explores the possibilities afforded to educational research through an approach which finds inspiration and draws on the evocative and sensuous power of the arts. An aesthetically informed arts-based approach to education which acknowledges the issues highlighted above by Lincoln and Denzin (2003) to "offer researchers new pathways for creating knowledge within and across disciplinary boundaries" (Leavy, 2009: ix).

What do we mean when we say that an approach to educational research is arts-based? In addressing the question Barone and Eisner (2006) suggest the following two criteria:

> First . . . arts-based research is meant to enhance perspectives pertaining to certain human activities . . . educational in character. Second, arts-based research is defined by the presence of certain aesthetic qualities or *design elements* that infuse the inquiry process and the research "text" . . . the more pronounced they are, the more the research may be characterized as arts-*based* (95).

The design elements used in arts-based research have been predominantly word based in character and include short stories, poetry, and drama, but also include non-linguistic art forms such as music, dance and visual and performance art (Barone and Eisner, 2006). In essence arts-based research constitutes a range of arts-derived tools used by qualitative researchers at different phases of the research process which may encompass data collection, analysis, and representation (Leavy, 2009).

It needs to be acknowledged that the use of these research practices is well established in other academic disciplines such as the arts and humanities; however, it is their application within the social sciences and education that is relatively new and evolving. In this regard arts-based researchers in education are not so much creating new research tools as borrowing and adapting them from other disciplines (Leavy, 2009). As a consequence, utilizing the arts involves the researcher in a performance ethic (see Bagley, 2009), an important aspect of which includes attention and respect being paid to the traditions of the art form they are borrowing. For certain arts-based researchers this involves working across disciplinary boundaries in collaboration with colleagues skilled in a particular artistic craft. (For example, see later in this chapter how we take life history data and work with practicing artists from a number of fields) In so far as collaborative endeavors are undertaken to ensure an element of artistic integrity and avoid an overtly avant-garde "anything goes" mentality, so equally if "arts-based research culminates in little more than a delightful poetic passage or a vivid narrative that does little educational work it is not serving its function." (Eisner, 2008: 23). In effect arts-based research "should not become so enchanted with novelty that we forget about matters of meaning and the need to communicate" (Eisner, 2001: 140).

The findings arising from arts-based research however are not intended to explain or predict outcomes (Barone and Eisner, 2006), the purpose "may instead be described as the enhancement of perspectives" (Barone and Eisner, 2006: 96), providing an audience with evocative access to multiple meanings, interpretations and voices associated with lived diversity and complexity. Arts-based research in education is thus in the main a genre "capable of persuading the percipient to see educational phenomena in new ways, and to entertain questions that might have otherwise been left unasked" (Barone and Eisner, 2006: 96).

The fusion of the arts with qualitative research has the critical potential in (re)presentational terms to "create multi-vocal, dialogical texts" which illuminate emotions and experiences (O'Neill et al 2002:71) and which may "move" the audience through what can be described as "sensuous knowing" (O'Neill et al., 2002: 71). The ability to "move" is meant not only in the sense of an artistic (re) presentation or performance "imbued with 'spirit', with sensuousness, with feeling and emotion" but also in the sense of spurring the "other and self to action" (O'Neill and Bagley, 1998: 12). Further, in relation to the crucially important notion of praxis, we contend that more critically informed arts-based research practices—such as the work presented later in this chapter—have the potential to speak and engender understanding amongst a wide and diversified audience beyond the confines of the academy. It has the potential to harness the critically reflective, empathetic and evocative capacity of the arts to transpose researchers, performers and audience "into new, critical political spaces" (Denzin, 2003: 19) of cultural awareness and resistance.

The Undocumented *Historias* Project

In the same way that it has been claimed critical ethnography is ethnography with a political purpose (Madison, 2005) so we contend critical arts based research is arts-based research with an explicit political purpose. Arts-based work of this kind has been termed "outlaw" by bell hooks (1994) and in essence is overtly political work that challenges the dominant discourses and conventional ideas within society, placing the critical arts-based researcher in a position of tension and antagonism towards the status quo.

Madison (2005) in her critical ethnographic work talks of accessing "the voices and experiences of subjects whose stories are otherwise restrained [and] out of reach" in order to publicly offer "emancipatory knowledge and discourses of social justice" (5). Similarly, for us, the desire of critical arts-based research is for a methodological alignment with subjugated peoples and voices, to uncover unequal power relations and the disproportionate impact these relations have on certain groups marginalized because of their ethnicity, disability, sexual orientation, gender and class. Critical arts-based research seeks to harness the artistic representational qualities of the genre to share the results of academic scholarship with as wide and diverse an audience as possible. The approach aims to open up to public scrutiny and debate the social inequities and injustices of a status quo that has directly or indirectly, implicitly or explicitly, personally or institutionally perpetuated prejudice, discrimination and disenfranchisement.

The approach is thus conceived as a means to access, legitimize, empower and promote the borderland voices of the marginalized and dispossessed, to evoke their experiential and sensual knowledge, and to co-recover and interrogate a shared memory and history while simultaneously enriching a social critique of the dominant social order. The ultimate goal of critical arts-based research is through audience engagement and capture to raise consciousness and facilitate educational and social change.

Our critical arts-based research practice with undocumented United Statesians of Mexican ancestry involves a fusion of Critical Race Theory (CRT) (Ladson-Billings, 1998), to theoretically position and frame our standpoint and thinking, a life history or person-centered ethnographic approach (Wolcott, 1999), as the primary means of data elicitation, and live performance as the artistic means to disseminate our findings. In so doing our critical arts-based work strives to move theoretically and methodologically from a "context of discovery" to a "context of presentation" (Plath, 1990: 376) in order to co-create with research participants, performers and audience a transformative performance text entitled "Undocumented *Historias* in the Desert of Dreams."

Critical Race Theory

As critical arts-based research practitioners working with undocumented Americans we chose to adopt CRT as our politically informed standpoint as it provides an interpretive theoretical frame in line with our beliefs and thinking that racism is "normal," not aberrant, in U.S. society (Ladson-Billings, 1998).

Further, "race" must be categorized not as a biological, but a socio-historical concept that allows researchers to analyze the sources of ethnic and "racial" identity in society, the role of cultural differences, and diverse forms of subordination (Ladson-Billings, 1998). CRT assumes that "race" differentiation exists in institutional policies, programs, and practices that interfere with ethnic minority students" rights and abilities to obtain the same educational opportunities available to the dominant majority white society (Villalpando, 2004).

For example, in the case of students of Mexican origin not only do they have lower rates of college enrolment compared to other US ethnic groups (Bohon et al., 2005), but they are not succeeding academically in the same proportion as the rest of the U.S. population (Alva and Padilla, 1995; Kao and Thompson, 2003) with a disproportionate number dropping out before high school graduation (Battle and Cuellar, 2006; Stone and Han, 2005; Valencia, 1991, 2002). Research suggests students of Mexican origin encounter a range of racialized socioeconomic, cultural and political challenges that include: unsupportive teaching climates (González et al., 2004; Stone and Han, 2005); teachers who have not been professionally prepared to support students of Mexican origin (Battle and Cuellar, 2006; Valencia, 2002) exclusion of the Mexican-American culture from the curriculum (Valencia, 1991, 2002); conflicting values between home and school (Dotson-Blake, 2006); financial difficulties (Battle and Cuellar, 2006); and in particular subtle and more overt forms of racism which are encountered and experienced throughout schooling and in the wider community (Bell, 2003; Delgado, 2003, 2006; Espinoza-Herold, 2003; Kao and Thompson, 2003; Kay-Oliphant, 2005).

The majority of students of Mexican origin who manage to graduate from U.S. high schools and continue on to higher education tend to go not to traditional four-year institutions but to community colleges (Lowell and Suro, 2002). Those who do attend a university usually take longer to complete their degree than other ethnic groups (Ream, 2005).

For undocumented United Statesians with a legal federal right to be educated in the U.S. up to the end of high school (an estimated 65,000 graduating each year), the subsequent educational challenges they face are particularly harsh. Undocumented people of Mexican origin in particular, on a number of grounds not least the educational, are positioned as one of the most vulnerable and subjugated groups in the U.S. (Chávez, 2005; De Genova, 2004). As a group, constituting about 58%, or 6.5 million of all "unauthorized" residents in the U.S. (Passel and Cohn, 2011) they are increasingly excluded from public services like education, health care, housing, and the protection of labor laws (Archibold, 2006; Associated Press, 2005; De Genova, 2004). They are subject to human trafficking, economic exploitation, and cultural marginalization (Sarther, 2006), and live in fear of being deported and separated from their families (Feldblum, 2000; Kittrie, 2006). Consequently, and despite still paying taxes and contributing substantially to the economy (Gans, 2006, 2007), they constitute one of the poorest and educationally disenfranchised sections of United Statesian society (Lichter et al., 2005).

For us, CRT enabled a critical examination and positioning of the educational experiences and lives of undocumented Americans of Mexican origin as social constructions of inferior or even criminal "other," embedded in the dominant xenophobic culture of U.S. society (Rivera, 2006; Salas, 2003; Villenas and Deyhle, 1999). CRT as a means to uncover and understand the oppressive mechanisms of society utilizes storytelling, or "counter-storytelling," through a (counter) life history approach as a means to engage, legitimize and support the voices of ethnic minorities, and to incorporate their experiential knowledge—including that from education—into critiques of the dominant social order (Nebeker, 1998). Our critical arts-based research thus sought to engage, acknowledge, and give a political voice to lives of undocumented American students, as they encountered and traversed racialized boundaries, barriers and contexts in their path toward academic success.

Counter Life History

Counter life histories of racialized groups—who are not the subjects of official history and are largely excluded or marginalized in society—provide a legitimizing narrative voice to the victims of unjust structures and institutions. As such their narratives are intrinsically political and deeply embedded in relations of power and they challenge the Master Narrative of American History. They also remind us that history is about cultural and collective memory, shaped by intricate contexts and those who tell the story. As expressed by Kennedy (2002):

> . . . the data of the historian are not facts. That is, the historian always begins with a system of postulates. History, like every other form of human thought, ends and does

not begin with facts. That is, the historian always begins with a series of postulates and with a specific view of the course of events, a view consonant with his postulates (87).

Thus, as noted in Chapter I, what matters about a particular narrative is the meaning it gives to the collective subjectivities and identities of a particular people at a particular time (Friedman, 1992). In essence counter life history narratives feature as an alternative understanding of the official version of history and represent a counter-rhetorical recovery of history. As bell hooks (1990) observes, oppressed "people resist by identifying themselves as subjects, by defining their reality, shaping new identity, naming their history, telling their story" (43).

Villenas and Deyhle (1999) argue that critical ethnographic studies have proven that communities, families, and individuals armed with this knowledge can effectively resist oppression by reclaiming their language and cultural identities. In collectively creating such counter-history, immigrant children and adults are able to survive the violence of a "xenophobic nation" (*Idem*) and establish a more profound understanding of the socio-historical context of the colonizer-colonized/oppressor-oppressed relationships. Thus, researchers working together with oppressed individuals and groups are able to co-create "counter-hegemonic narratives of dignity and ethnic pride" (*Ibid.*: 437) and to look for answers and imagine an ideal world with different socio-political structures, institutions, values, and practices (Matsuda et al., 1993). In our study, in order to recover the counter life history narratives and educational experiences of undocumented American students, six individuals participated. The process of identifying these six undocumented individuals, given their immigration status, was a difficult and challenging process which involved cautiously and sensitively talking with individuals within the local Mexican-American community known to Ricardo. These initial contacts in turn suggested the names of students who "may or may not be undocumented" and who "may or may not be willing to talk." The recruitment process was laborious as some suggested contacts that were willing to be interviewed were found not to be undocumented, while some who were undocumented did not want to talk at length about their experiences. Eventually however six undocumented individuals for the purpose of conducting life history interviews were identified.

In line with CRT, their counter life history narratives were explored in their multifaceted contexts and dimensions, not simply as individual productions, but also as the product of cultural and ideological contexts (Bell, 2003; Delgado and Stefancic, 2001). The narratives were elicited by prolonged unstructured in-depth interviews. In the case of our research a minimum of two interviews were conducted with each participant, culminating in the grounded analysis (Glaser and Strauss, 1967) of 30 hours of taped transcript. (For a detailed analysis of the interview findings, see Castro-Salazar and Bagley, 2010)

Seidman (2006) emphasizes the purpose of in-depth interview is to understand the experience of other people and the meaning they make of that experience and is characterized by an extensive effort on the part of the interviewer to explore the perceptions and dynamics of the participants. In research with undocumented Americans of Mexican origin, the interview process involved extremely delicate matters of legality and vulnerability, and so the level of trust and rapport between interviewer and participants needed to be very high. In this instance, it was particularly important that the interviewees were able to ask questions of the interviewer, explore intent, seek clarification, and come to trust and value the interviewer's motives. Through this process the interviewer and interviewee were subsequently able to co-participate in the process of seeking understanding, to co-recover and "reveal the meaning of lived experience" (Raleigh Yow, 1994: 25) as an undocumented American and United Statesian of Mexican origin.

On this methodological note it is important to mention that Ricardo, who conducted all the life history interviews, is a U.S. citizen of Mexican birth and political activist in the community where the study took place in Arizona. The interviews were conducted mostly in Spanish and subsequently translated. Nevertheless, there was frequent code switching and English was utilized when it was easier to express an idea. Only one participant chose to be interviewed fully in English to demonstrate his fluency, but frequently this was forgotten and Spanish was introduced. During the research process transcripts were shared with interviewees for accuracy and, if necessary, modification. At the end of the initial pre-performance fieldwork period, the analysis of the data—located in its wider CRT-informed socio-political, historical and economic context—was also shared and discussed with interviewees.

Seidman (2006: 95) stresses that 'interviewing relationships exist in a social context' and that, even when a researcher makes a conscious effort to keep the relationship within strict interview parameters, social forces affect the process. The forces of gender, race, ethnicity, and class influence the relationship between the researcher and the subjects of the study, even when they try to eschew such influences (Ibid.). Similarly, the role or status of the researcher as an 'insider' or an 'outsider' can carry with it advantages or disadvantages in the interviewing process, while the boundaries between the two positions can be difficult to define (Merriam et al., 2001).

For example, Merriam et al. (2001) illustrate the possibility of becoming an outsider even among 'your own' ethnic group with the case of a Korean researcher who struggled to obtain cooperation from her own documented and undocumented compatriots in the U.S., who viewed her doctoral student status as more prestigious than theirs and, therefore, treated her as an outsider to their community (*Ibid.*). For us, as a Mexican-American and a white British 'gringo' researcher working together, we strove to appreciate that any assumptions of easy access to participant's narratives based on commonalities or differences of culture, class, gender, and ethnicity could be more complex than anticipated.

Critical theorists acknowledge that insider/outsider issues exist in a complex context that involves the researcher's positionality, power and representation in relation to race, class, gender, culture, and other factors. Therefore, positionality is "determined by where one stands in relation to the other" (*Ibid:* 411). Arguably, in this regard, the role of a researcher who utilizes a CRT perspective for conducting a critical ethnography is different from a researcher engaged in a more 'traditional' interviewing process (Delgado-Gaitan, 2001). CRT researchers seek to challenge white privilege, reject notions of neutral research and objective researchers (Solórzano and Yosso, 2002) and in sharing this perspective with the 'researched', believe at some point, researcher and interviewees can "become actors in a common culture" (Delgado-Gaitan, 2001: 8), against racist discrimination and oppression. From a critical arts-based research perspective the counter life-history interviews with undocumented Americans were thus perceived not simply as a means of culturally and politically co-recovering lived educational experience but as "a vehicle for producing performance texts. .about self and society" (Denzin, 2001: 24), focused on the manifestation and resistance to individual, institutional and structural racism.

Performance

The performing of ethnographic data to a live audience requires researchers to be politically and culturally sensitive. As Bagley (2009) states,

> . . . . the relational positioning of the researcher towards content (what is selected to be performed), art form (the maintenance of the integrity of the genre), artists (who is selected and their role), audience (to whom we perform), interviewees (how much and what is revealed), and staging of the performance (how it is structured to communicate meaning) are all integral to the enactment of a meaningful performative endeavor and collectively speak to a performance ethic (285).

In this instance a decision was taken to ground the performance within the local Mexican-American community; the undertaking perceived as a collaborative venture encompassing grassroots community organizations, local artists and academia. For example, the Mexican American Studies and Research Center and the Center for Latin American Studies at the University of Arizona provided support in the search for the artists. Other organizations involved in the promotion of the performance included the Arizona Association of Chicanos for Higher Education, Border Action/Acción Fronteriza, the Consortium for North American Higher Education Collaboration (CONAHEC), *Derechos Humanos*, EDUCAMEXUS, Fundación México, Los Samaritanos, the Mexican Consulate in Tucson, and the University of Arizona Binational Migration Institute.

A local community theatre, Beowulf Alley, in downtown Tucson was selected and hired as the venue to stage the performance. The performers—chosen following discussions about their commitment to the undertaking and the cause of undocumented Americans—were themselves all of Mexican birth or heritage. Each artist was paid a nominal fee as were the individuals responsible for stage lighting, sound, and filming of the performance.

The texts in the form of interview transcript, along with other contextual CRT-informed data were shared with the artists, who came from the fields of dance, music, poetry, photography and art. The performing artists were given a free hand to interpret and create a performance text to be staged as vignettes in a two-hour live performance. The visual artwork derived from the data was to be exhibited in the entrance to the auditorium.

On the evening of the performance the small theatre with official seating for 110 was overcrowded with an additional 60 people sitting on the floor, in aisles and even the sound and lighting room behind the seating area. Approximately 100 people had to be turned away. The theatre manager, a community activist herself, was very supportive of our effort and allowed the overcrowding, even though it was a violation of city codes and nullified our insurance! The audience was predominantly of Mexican origin including undocumented individuals, community activists, representatives of the Mexican Consulate, and students and academics of Mexican origin. Importantly, however, the audience also included non-Mexican individuals and groups sympathetic to the political cause of undocumented peoples.

The power of performance as a mechanism for portrayal "is ultimately linked with the immediacy of art" (Leavy: 12) and as such has an ephemeral quality which cannot be textually captured in print form "without losing the very essence the method seeks to reveal" (*Ibid.*:12). Ideally, the reader of this chapter needs to see the performance live to gather its real impact, and we are extremely aware of the apparent irony in advocating performance-based work, with the practical necessity of making our case here in print. Nonetheless, and while nothing can substitute for being there, an abridged audio-visual record of the performance can be viewed with subtitles at: http://www.tinyurl.com/bagley-salazar/performancelong.wmv

Further, as way of providing a very partial flavor of the event, we offer below four examples of artistic work presented and displayed on the evening: the poem *LIBERTAD* (Liberty) composed (in English and Spanish) by Dulce S. Encinas; the painting *Jaula de Oro* (Golden Gage) by artist Marisol Badilla; the dance and movement piece *Clandestina* (Clandestine) by choreographer-dancer Yvonne Montoya; and the sculpture *La Frontera Está en Todas Partes* (The Border Is Everywhere) by Ricardo Castro-Salazar, also shown on the cover of this book.

A poem: *LIBERTAD* (Liberty)

Dulce S. Encinas, illuminated by a single spotlight, read the following poem standing on stage facing the audience. The poem, structured in six chapters, is derived from each of the life history narratives of the six undocumented American student interviewees. The poem was written and presented in a mix of Spanish and English, a style commonly referred to as "Spanglish," mirroring the tendency of many Americans of Latin American origin to communicate and play with language in this way. To assist non-Spanish speakers, the poem while intended for a bilingual audience, has been translated, the English text placed in brackets next to the original Spanish.

CADA UNO TIENE SU HISTORIA Y CADA UNO TENEMOS NUESTROS SENTIMIENTOS, PERO HAY UNA COSA EN COMÚN . . .
TODOS SOMOS VÍCTIMAS DE UN FACTOR, UN SENTIMIENTO, UNA ANSIEDAD, UNA NECESIDAD: ¡LIBERTAD!

(Everyone has a story and every one of us has feelings. But there is a thing we have in common. We are all victims of one thing: a feeling, an anxiety, a need–Liberty)

Chapter 1: Jesenia

Identity? *¿De qué me sirve eso?* (What is it good for?)

No soy de aquí, (I am not from here)

I mean, I grew up here but I'm not *from* here

¿Pero de allá? . . . (But from over there?)

Ni lo conozco, (I don't even know the place)

Half of the things I say

son de allá y la otra mitad de aquí (are from there, and the other half are from here)

I'm confused! No, no, no, I'm focused . . . *Pero ¿de qué me sirve?* (But what is that good for?)

My mentality *ya no es de mexicana* (is not that of a Mexican)

Mi mentalidad es de americana (My mentality is of an American)

Ha, the American dream!

¿Pero cuál americana? ¡si soy de allá! (But what an American, if I'm from there)

A certified elementary school teacher,

certified in bilingual education,

Limpiando casas y cuidando niños por $220.00 a la semana (Cleaning houses and babysitting for $220 a week!)

Si es que ya ni persona soy (I am not even a person anymore)

Soy Jessenia, una extraterrestre de no sé dónde (I am Jesenia, an extraterrestrial from who knows where)

México le dicen. Ya ni me acuerdo de él (Mexico, they call it. I don't even remember it)

I grew up in Arizona! I am from here!

Aparte de alienígena soy ilegal (Besides an alien, I am illegal)

Y con mi país "lleno de oportunidades" (and my country "full of opportunities")

¡Mi país! ¡Mi país! (My country! My country!)

Estoy añorando una vida, pero con mi libertad interrumpida. (I am longing for a life but with my liberty interrupted)

Chapter 2: David

After 3 years of waiting, I was denied my resident status . . .

My stepfather and mom got married too late

2 DAYS after my 18th birthday!

But it's O.K . . . It's fine . . . it's O.K.

Y así me fui, (I kept going like that) I mean, I made it like this

Working hard, pushing through!

I got to the university! They couldn't stop me.

But because I got married and I am not from here,

I couldn't get financial aid

I had to drop out

But it's O.K. . . . It's fine.

I'm always learning

I am a manager now,

without any "papers," but I am the manager.

And I put the restaurant in the top 10, top 5 in southern Arizona.

So I'm here but *soy de allá* . . . (I am from there).

Aún sin papeles (still without papers)

My light skin and English can blind the border patrol

Pero quién sabe más adelante . . . (But who knows in the future)

Es como si viviera la vida añorada pero con mi libertad interrumpida. (It is like if I were living the life I long for, but with my liberty interrupted)

Chapter 3: Rosario

I was stable in Mexico, *pero la economía nos ganó* . . . (but the economy defeated us)

¡Y aquí sufrí más de lo que allá sufrí! (And I suffered more here than what I suffered there)

They call it isolation, depression and even food deprivation . . .

-Ation, -ation, -ation . . . *Inglés,* English and work

No college, no job, no money, no food

More hunger, more stress, more sadness . . .

¡ME VOY! (I'm leaving!)

I woke up of that nightmare when I went back to school . . .

And I've pushed through *toda mi vida!* (all my life)

Push through! Push through! Work, work!

Y *mírame,* (and look at me) I work with the boycotts,

the marches, my people . . .

Y si me agarran algún día, a ver quién ve por mis hijos. (And if they catch me some day , we'll see

who takes care of my children.)

¡Pero échale ganas! (But do your best) You have to make it your own way . . .

Ándale, the American dream!

I'm making it here, I am here . . .

I am from here! Am I?

But it's like I have the life I long for but with an interrupted liberty.

Chaper 4: Roberto

As an international student, I had it done here . . .

I came here for different reasons,

But next thing you know, I stayed . . .

I mean, I had to stay.

I was lucky though.

En mis tiempos nomás ibas y preguntabas por (In my days you simply went and asked for)

a social security card.

Y ya, la usabas, sin papeles (And that was it, you'd use it, without any papers).

Todos nos vinimos, (All of us came here). I mean, eventually.

Y ahora mi familia ya está aquí legalmente (And now my family is here legally).

Ya somos de aquí . . . (Now we belong here).

Mis hijos son ciudadanos (My children are citizens)

and I want the best for them. The best.

I have an Associate's Degree in International Business Studies!

I am a *realista,* a pragmatist, and most importantly an optimist!

Push through . . . the American Dream!

I am the American Dream! I have my own business.

Pero todavía no soy persona (but I am still not a person).

Soy un extraterrestre . . . (I am an extraterrestrial)

¿Y cómo darle la mejor vida a mis hijos? (And how can I give my children a better life?)

If I buy a house, who will it benefit?

I am not even here . . .

Yo vivo en las sombras (I live in the shadows).

Soy parte de los que no existen (I am part of those who do not exist)

y parte de los que se fueron (and part of those who left)

Yo soy hijo de una vida añorada con una libertad interrumpida (I am the child of a life that I have longed for with my liberty interrupted).

Chapter 5: Marina

Me decían chilanga! (They used to call me Chilanga)

Y es por donde vengo (It's because of where I come from)

Mexico City, *el Distrito Federaaaaal!* (the Federal District!)

Waiting for a trip to Disneyland that my parents promised

Que dizque ibamos a Disneyland (supposedly we were going to Disneyland)

por eso nos vinimos a Estados Unidos (That's why we came to the United States)

But I'm still waiting . . .

Y aquí estoy todavía (And I am still here).

Por defenderme de los bullies en la escuela (Because I defended myself in school)

me dijeron desma . . ."buscapleitos" (they called me jack a . . ."troublemaker").

Ahora al ver las noticias de mi gente hasta me pongo mal (When I hear the news about my people I even become ill).

I'm worse than an animal here . . .

I live in the shadows, *en la noche, no existo* (in the night, I do not exist)

I am an alien, from another planet . . .

No, no, no. From another country.

Worse than a thief, worse than a drug dealer . . .

They *do* illegal stuff, I am ILLEGAL

I'm impotent, afraid, abused and exploited

Ya se que me lo hacen (I know they do it to me)

Me doy cuenta con mis ojos, me duele la espalda (I can see it with my own eyes, my back hurts).

¿Pero qué hace uno cuando no tiene papeles? (But what can you do when you have no papers?)

What I know from Mexico is vague.

I came here when I was six. How am I supposed to remember?

I have an accent, but I grew up here!

Yo soy de aquí (I am from here). I have everything here!

My family, my friends . . . My job and my work with the boycotts and marches.

My people.

But I am not here. I am not from here.

I should belong here.

I am on the wrong side.

¡Pero yo soy parte de aquí! (But I am part of here!)

¡Yo estoy aquí! (I am here)

Persistent, persistent, persistent I have to be.

The American Dream I have to be.

I am the wanted life,

but I have an interrupted liberty

Chapter 6: Justo

Economic Survival they call it . . .

I came speaking English already, bilingual schools in Mexico.

The wealthy can have it.

Well, from wealthy to nothing . . .

That's my dad's story

Abused, but never complained.

Ni con futbol la hice en high school (I couldn't make it in football in high school).

My dreams of playing professionally got shut down.

When you don't have papers, no documents,

No se puede (you can't).

Even the guards at the mall make you nervous . . .

Y el acento en inglés me daba vergüenza (And my accent in English made me feel ashamed)

Hasta si te miran feo te sientes mal (Even if they look at you the wrong way you feel bad)

You are, you are, you are, YOU'RE ILLEGAL!

Pero por mi futbol entendí que: (But through football I learned that)

whatever you do, you go full speed.

Even if it's wrong, you go full speed!

Y aunque me dijeron: (And even though they told me)

"Your ass will never come to college again"

La hice con honores y todo . . . (I made it with honors and everything)

¡Mírenme! (Look at me!)

Ahora de ciudadano voy cambiar al mundo! (Now as a citizen I will change the World!)

Hay que cambiar al mundo. (We must change the world)

I'm strong heritage, I know where I came from,

I know who I am, and I know where I'm going.

FULL SPEED, FULL SPEED!

Yo soy de aquí: americano (I am from here, American)

Yo soy de aquí: mexicano (I am from here, Mexican)

American, Mexican, Mexican-American!

¿Identidad? ¿De qué la necesito? (Identity? What do I need it for?)

Estoy orgulloso de quien soy (I am proud of who I am).

Aunque no es definido como una identidad (although it is not defined as an identity)

Is it?

Entiendo lo que soy (I understand what I am)

Y yo soy la vida añorada (And I am the life I long for)

A painting: *Jaula de Oro* (Golden Gage)

The painting by the artist Marisol Badilla (Figure 1), was displayed in the entrance to the venue and viewed by audience members both prior to and following the event. The work entitled *Jaula de Oro* (Golden Cage) although presented here in black and white was in color and features a self-portrait of the artist sitting naked inside a golden cage holding an opened book.

The choice of the golden cage is significant as several interviewees in telling their stories in the narratives given to Marisol expressed their *undocumented* existence in terms of 'being in a golden cage.' Notably, there is a popular Mexican saying: *Aunque la jaula sea de oro no deja de ser prisión* (*even if the cage is made of gold, it is still a prison*) and a song entitled "La jaula de oro" by Los Tigres del Norte (The Northern Tigers), a popular band from northern Mexico. For Marisol the use of self-portraiture and the golden cage was in her own words "a visual way of saying that their story is also my story. That I am an undocumented woman and also every undocumented woman."

Figure 1: *Jaula de Oro* (Golden Cage) by Marisol Badilla.
Source: Bagley, C. and R. Castro-Salazar (2011).

In the foreground of the painting is a concrete barbed wired wall constituting a border for the artist in the cage and signifying the border between the US and Mexico. The configuration of the wall places the artist on the Mexican side of the border gazing into the US. The wall contains graffiti derived from actual graffiti present on the real border and states 'Murderers' (directed to the U.S. immigration police), 'Deport the Migra' (Migra is the nickname Spanish-speakers use for the immigration police), 'Frontiers, scars on the Earth' and 'Visual Terrorism' (referring to the wall and the display of police power at the border). The background to the picture is a reworking of the US flag the Stars and Stripes. The stars have been replaced with white crosses and the red stripes are portrayed as dripping into the white. According to Marisol,

> I wanted to present the stars as crosses found in graveyards to symbolize the death of those who have lost their lives crossing the border, and the red of the stripes as the blood on the hands of the US immigration police and other white racists who operate at the border.

A dance: *Clandestina* (Clandestine)

The lights go up and there are three dancers on the stage. One stands on a table with her head bowed, a second has her back to the audience and stands in the shadows at the rear stage, while a third dancer sits stage left of the table. The dancer on the table speaks, simultaneously stating (in English) and physically signaling with arm and leg movement, text derived from actual Homeland Security forms (see Figure 2):

Form I 425A Application to register for permanent residence or adjust status
I 864 I 765 AR 11 I 797 C
Notice of Action I-130 Biometrics Processing data
I 485 Department of Homeland Security
(With arms behind her back and chest out in a quasi-military pose)
You are hereby notified to appear for the interview as scheduled below:
Number A 047 0847912
Application denied. Failure to establish legitimacy based on 8CFR 247A 12C

The stage goes dark and when the lights are raised a dancer is seated on the floor next to the table, staring out towards the audience eyes wide open and looking scared. This time the sequence of words spoken is in Spanish, interspersed with a series of powerful movements of the head, upper torso, and arms. A second dancer stands in the shadows at the rear of the stage, simultaneously twisting and turning in a series of balletic movements.

Figure 2 *Clandestina* by Ivonne Montoya

> *Clandestina, Clandestina* (clandestine, clandestine)
> *Reprimida* (repressed)
> *¿Por qué nací yo de lado equivocado?* (why was I born on the wrong side)
> *¿Por qué te adelantaste? ¡adelantada!* (Why were you born in advance? Advanced!)
> *Escondida* (hidden)
> *Clandestina* I remain

The stage goes black.

A sculpture: *La Frontera Está en Todas Partes* (The Border Is Everywhere)

The sculpture by Ricardo Castro-Salazar was displayed at the Undocumented *Historias* event as a three-dimensional expression of emotions and data derived from the qualitative research. It is an allegory of the invisible barriers faced by undocumented Americans, emerging as linguistic, cultural, judicial, economic, psychological, and symbolic borders (see Figure 3). It symbolizes the pain and struggle of those regarded as outsiders and "others" in spite of their roots in their communities and the country they grew up in. The surrounding barbwire represents barriers and violence, but the roots of the tree go deeper, inaccessible to destructive forces.

Subtle body parts in the trunk of the tree insinuate sexuality and sensuality. They symbolize the inexorable propagation of humanity, the inevitable *mestizaje*, the fusion of peoples and cultures that make the tree of life grow and bear fruit. Its green color symbolizes life (only green; black, brown or white are irrelevant). Only the red of blood indicates the violence and hostility that is suffered by each new branch that grows from the trunk. Some of the branches have been broken. The hand reaching up to the sky denotes what we aspire to be, painfully growing beyond the borders that cannot imprison our essence.

Growth is not possible without struggle, but only attached to our roots can we disseminate our seed. A flower grows beyond the confines of the barbedwire as a symbol of human evolution and beauty in spite of adversity.

Figure 3: "La Frontera Está en Todas Partes" by Ricardo Castro-Salazar
Photograph by Alejandro González.

Attendees to the exhibit and the performance did not have to pay for admission but were expected to contribute a donation to Fundación México (a not-for-profit organization that awards scholarships to undocumented students) according to their means. Fundación México organized a reception at the theatre and provided free food and drinks after the performance. In addition an auction was held following the performance in which the artists' paintings, and photographs were sold along with personally signed books by the prominent Mexican academic and author of Chicano literature Miguel Méndez. Professor Méndez gave the audience his "Testimony of a Self-Taught Immigrant," in which he emphasized the importance of education and life-long learning. He also donated twenty-three of his books to Fundación México, which were all sold after the performance.

The event subsequently raised enough funds to support two scholarships for undocumented American students of Mexican origin to defray college expenses for two semesters. In this important regard the research project was able, in a small away, to have a material impact on real lives. The coalescence of the academic and the political went to the heart of critical arts-based praxis.

Transformative Reflections

Madison (2005) reflects critically on the staging of ethnographic performances referring to "a performance of possibilities" to elucidate "a movement culminating in creation and change" (172). She considers the potential of performance from three vantage points, namely the "subjects, whose lives and words are being performed . . . the audience who witnesses the performance and . . . the performers who embody and enact the data" (172). To these we would add the need to consider the researcher(s) who chose to adopt a critical arts-based approach.

To elicit the viewpoints of those involved interviews were conducted with ten members of the general audience (unsolicited email feedback from audience members was also received). Interviews were also conducted with four of the undocumented Americans on whose voices the performance was based, and who were in the audience, and all the artists involved in the production.

In reporting the feedback and experiential data following the performance (a very important but sometimes neglected aspect of arts-based research endeavors) we can only report what we found from the interviews we conducted and emails we received, which was—as we reveal below—an overwhelmingly positive and emotionally charged response. Admittedly, in determining the efficacy of the critical arts-based method, these findings may be tempered by the context in which the event was staged, namely to an audience culturally and politically pre-disposed to the issue. It was, however, precisely to such an audience that our work—with equally committed artists—aimed to speak, the performance seeking "to evoke and invoke shared emotional experience and understanding" (Denzin, 2003: 13), and reach out passionately and intellectually to an audience capable of conveying *undocumented* realities to a wider U.S. community.

All the performers stated that in receiving the transcripts and reading the stories that they felt an exceptionally strong bond to the experiences being recounted. As one performer remarked "it was like reading my own story." Undoubtedly, the use of artists of Mexican origin facilitated an emotional and political tie between performers and the subjects that could not otherwise have been achieved. As one observed:

> I wanted to do a good job not just because I am an artist but because I related to these stories, and I wanted to tell them to an audience in a way which let them see not only the educational problems and the pain but also the hope that together we can do something.

In this regard all the performers were highly motivated in their desire to do the most professional job they could in communicating the subject's lived experience to a wider audience. To this end each artist spent a great deal of time and critical reflection on the best way to utilize their artistic talents to maximum effect and impact. For several of them this was a particularly moving and emotional experience as they became closer to the voices and lives in the data they sought to portray; a connection in this instance heightened by the artists' personal or familial experience of the same issues. For example, the artist Marisol was herself until relatively recently undocumented. Madison (2005) eloquently describes the artistic process in the following terms:

> Since the performer is transported slowly, deliberately and incrementally at each rehearsal and at each encounter toward the knowledge and life world of the subject, the performer is creatively and intellectually taking it all in, internalizing and receiving partial maps of meaning that reflect the subjects consciousness and context. This receptiveness, however, is never completely without the generative filter of the performers own knowledge and location. The process of being transported of receiving meanings and generating meanings, is more intimate and potentially a more traumatic engagement for the performers than for the audience members, because the transportation is mentally and viscerally more intense than travelling to the world of Others. It is making those worlds your home place. The performer is only engaged, but also strives to become. For the performer, this is an endeavor not only to live in an individual consciousness shaped by a social world, but also to live in that social world as well (177).

There appeared to be a clear appreciation amongst the artists that " . . . the form of representation one uses has something to do with the form of understanding one secures" (Eisner, 2001: 139), and the artists in the process of choreographing the dance, painting the picture or writing the poem were not only concerned with being technically accomplished but substantively grounded so as not to lose the political message of the lived experiences they wanted to get across. Clearly, the artists shared with us as researchers a desire and felt an obligation to create something that an audience would find meaningful. Morrison (1994) reflects on the relationship between aesthetics and politics in the artistic process in the following way:

> I am not interested in indulging myself in some private, closed exercise of my imagination that fulfils only the obligations of my personal dreams. . . . It seems to me that the best art is political and you ought to be able to make it unquestionably political and irrevocably beautiful at the same time (p. 497) (cited in Madison, 2005: 175).

One of the undocumented American interviewees who was in the audience and witnessed the performance described her feelings about it in the following terms:

> The poem . . . Dulce . . . personally she had me out there, she did me, an awesome job. Every chapter you feel related . . . I am not from here I'm not from there. . . . I was proud of what she did. I talk Spanglish and she caught that and that is how I talk and who I am. I was sitting there next to my mother and holding my boyfriend's hand and it at first shocked me and I was crying and she was crying, it was so powerful and so strong . . . I was so excited . . . it was my feelings about being American . . . and a Mexican. I was listening and watching and thinking this is my story, how I experienced it how I lived it.

In terms of strong performative capture of an interview subject's voice Madison (2005: 173) refers not simply to 'the representation of an utterance, but the presentation of a historical self, a full presence that is in and of a particular world.' It is a artistic performance that takes being heard and included as a 'starting point' to encompass a portrayal of "an embodied, historical self that constructs and is constructed by a matrix of social and political processes . . . wedded to experience and history" (173).

Another undocumented American interviewee in the audience commented on the painting in the following way:

> I could see myself in the painting. I know it wasn't me but it could have been me sitting in the golden cage; it could have been any of us. The image kinda said it all about how we feel and how we live. The fact that you are always on guard even when you go to the mall, tense wondering if you are going to be stopped, you sometimes think you

> have a label on saying you have no documents and everyone can see it. You just want to be invisible. Yet you want to be here, to contribute, to participate, we want to be a citizen. . . . It makes you feel that you want to keep going. . . . .that we can enrich this country.

Denzin (1999) contends that "performance text is the single most powerful way for ethnography to recover yet interrogate the meaning of lived experience" (94). For the undocumented interviewees in the audience whose life narratives were performed, the performance was felt by them as a means of saying this is who we are, this is what we have gone through, this is what we share, and this is what we hope for and believe is possible.

Pifer (1999) considers, "that through performance the lives, voices, and events presented will have a life and power not possible through other forms of representation" (542). As one audience member in an email correspondence following the performance commented:

> . . . I like to think I understand. However, a performance like this proves me wrong. Engaging more senses in the message pulled me closer, brought me to a deeper place of compassion and appreciation for the struggles you've documented . . . I appreciate, from my own studies, how power intimidates. But I don't think I got it, or felt it so authentically, until I saw that dance. . . . Listening to the poet read with her own voice, turning the words into poetry by calling on her own personal experience, brought the depth of emotion to the surface. . . .

The kinesthetic energy of the performance provided the data with a life-like dimension, elevating those experiences and voices contained within the research, which otherwise may have remained textually subjugated. The interweaving and (re)presentation of the life history data into a performance engendered a sensuous, emotional and evocative range of meanings for audience members. Eisner (2001) speaks of the way in which the arts "communicate the way something feels, that is, its emotional character . . . it shows it and showing it makes empathy possible" (136). The performance brought the data to sensuous life, imbuing the data with a moving emotional dimension.

In terms of audience impact and the performance's ability to question and challenge taken-for-granted assumptions about social relations of power and open up political spaces for debate and critical reflection, two audience members commented:

> It made me look and think about it and say so that's where you are coming from . . . I now have more understanding. It affected me deeply and emotionally, it connected me to their stories and it made me want to support them and do something.

> I was listening and watching and thinking this could be my story, this could be my
> story, a Mexican story. In each story I saw everyone's story. I could see myself and a
> friend of mine in the audience and other friends who were not there. . . . and I
> thought we are all experiencing this and can do something positive together

In this respect these members of the audience were positioned as citizens who are seemingly touched or connected with the lived experiences of the interviewees stories via the performance and are able to see and feel their injustices, to co-join with them and others as potential agents for social change (Madison, 2005: 174). In line with Madison we do not "mean to imply that one performance can rain down a revolution, but one performance can be revolutionary in enlightening citizens to the possibilities that grate against injustice" (Madison, 2005: 174). Moreover, the impact of the performance on the audience did not end with the performance but continued to linger reflectively and critically in their minds long after the final curtain as evidenced from the continual stream of emails received even weeks later. The on-going impact and value of the performance are encapsulated in the following email sent to Ricardo. We reproduce it here in full because we believe it captures the very essence of critical arts-based research.

Dear Ricardo,

It has been almost a month since I saw *Undocumented Historias in the Desert of Dreams* and I am still thinking about it. Thank you so much for inviting me to this event.

I invited my mother to join me and the experience of this evening began even before the show. We were both moved by the photographs displayed in the waiting area as we stood in line to enter the theater. The slideshow presentation greeted us as we found our seats; I appreciated the bilingual captions. I realized how my culture had been torn away from me as my parents tried to protect their children from discrimination and racism through assimilation. They did not speak Spanish at home and I had to learn my people's language at school. The lack of welcome this country has for foreigners injures us in so many ways.

Then the performance began. I am not sure exactly what I was expecting. Each artist gave such a moving presentation of the immigrant stories. As an instructor, I was particularly struck by the notion that education feels pointless to a people who do not have legal status. That reality had never crossed my mind before, and my heart broke as I thought of all of the dreams that would be forsaken as a result of our punitive system.

At the end of the show, I was amazed at the stories these performers shared. Each of them had their own account of how being undocumented had touched their lives. It shattered the stereotypes of what an undocumented immigrant looks like, of what an undocumented immigrant can become in this country.

Here is the most amazing result of your event. The sharing of stories continued even after the show. My mother shared a story she heard many years ago, about her father immigrating to the United States in the early 1920s. He came on a train through the Southwest and was told, along with the rest of the Mexicans, to exit the train and walk around the small town of Tucson since the sheriff of the town didn't like Mexicans and always checked trains to ensure none were aboard. And then a friend Susan who was with me spoke of her grandfather. She shared his struggle in Louisiana, of speaking French, and the discrimination her family endured.

I feel close to Susan; we work together, and over the years have connected through tears, prayer, and family. But I have never identified with her in this way—I have never thought about the collective history we have, with ancestors sharing similar trials as foreigners trying to make a home in this land.

I cannot thank you enough for this event, for making it happen and for inviting me to share it with you. I was delighted to see so many people, and so diverse an audience, surrounding me that night. The profound experience I had was surely shared by many. You should be proud of the impact of this event on our community.

Thank you,

As the researchers who embarked on this project we believe the performance through a critical evocation of passion and compassion, was able artistically, sensuously and politically to interrogate and portray the experiences of undocumented Americans of Mexican origin. Furthermore, after their participation in the project, artists themselves corroborated Octavio Paz's assertion that art is "a destiny in which we discover ourselves." Choreographer-dancer Yvonne Montoya was inspired by her experience with Undocumented *Historias* to create a not-for-profit critical-performance dance company entitled "*Safos* Dance Theatre," where she continues to perform for social justice causes. In Yvonne's own words, Undocumented *Historias* "was the foundation for this company." Marisol Badilla finished her Master's degree and decided to teach at the local community college, where she now teaches a Mexican-American Studies course.

New community connections were also developed. The event drew artists and activists—people who can continue to communicate and enrich this method of conscientization—who were curious about this way of expression in the community. For example, photographer Michael Hyatt and sculptor Deborah McCullough, who are also immigrant rights activists, attended and expressed their support. Additionally, after watching the performance, a directive of Inside/Out, a local organization that promotes poetry and writing among female teenagers at the county's juvenile detention center, invited Ricardo to give a presentation about the Undocumented *Historias* project.

In positioning critical arts-based research in education as a genre within the qualitative paradigm, we are acknowledging the methodological possibilities afforded by the approach: to engage with the emotional, sensual and kinesthetic complexity of everyday lived experiences; to challenge dominant cultural norms, beliefs and values; and to uncover, recover and portray research to audiences in new ways. In so doing, we contend, critical arts-based research is able to politically move subjects, performers, audience and researchers into new cultural spaces of understanding, resistance, and hope.

Annotated Glossary

The terms Mexican, Mexican-American, Hispanic, Chicano/a, and Latino/a are utilized in this study when the consulted sources specifically refer to such terms. However, research data are not always accurate in regard to identifying specific groups, and presumptions are often made that Mexicans, Chicanos/as, Latinos/as, Cubans, Puerto Ricans, etc. are all one group. Hispanics do share many cultural characteristics but also differ in important ways. Ultimately, all of these terms are cultural and ethnic, not racial, and throughout history have had different meanings and connotations (Meier and Ribera, 1993).

Acculturation and Assimilation

Acculturation was first described as a cultural phenomenon by anthropologists (Redfield, Linton and Herskovits, 1936). Thus, the root word of acculturation is the term *culture*, which has been defined as "the master concept and dominant cause of almost everything in human life" (Barrett, 2002: 48). There is no scholarly agreement on a single definition, but, at a simple level, culture can be understood as the learned and shared behaviors of a people that are passed on from generation to generation (*Ibid.*). Acculturation has been defined as the accommodation or adjustment by members of one culture to a different culture (Szapocznik, Scopetta, Kurtines, and Arnalde, 1978). Therefore, acculturation is the cultural change that results from contact between autonomous cultural groups. It can be inferred that adaptation to the cultural norms of a society is generally a prerequisite for successful progress within its socio-economic structure, including the schooling process.

In the literature, the terms *acculturation* and *assimilation* are used interchangeably (Hurtado, 1997). However, Teske and Nelson (1974) have argued that they are, in fact, two different processes. From their perspective, the process of assimilation (see table below) is interconnected to the model of internal colonialism, where cultural adaptation is the result of the economic structures created by the U.S. capitalist system and by the labor and power relations that engender such a mode of production (Almaguer, 1974). In this thesis, the term acculturation is similar to Teske and Nelson's, implying *adaptation* or cultural change without renunciation to values or reference groups. However, since the process may also involve acculturation of values, any level of acculturation could easily involve a degree of assimilation. According to Kornblum (1994), assimilation is the process of absorbing one cultural group into a dominant community and the only way for culturally distinct groups to acquire equal statuses in the social groups and institutions of the "host civilization" (123).

Comparison of the salient characteristics of acculturation and assimilation

Acculturation	Assimilation
1. A dynamic process	1. A dynamic process
2. May be treated as either an individual or a group process	2. May be treated as either an individual or a group process
3. Involves direct contact	3. Involves direct contact
4. Two-way: It may occur in both directions	4. Unidirectional
5. Does not require change in values, though values may be acculturated	5. Change in values required
6. Reference group change not required	6. Reference group change required
7. Internal change not required	7. Internal change required
8. Out-group acceptance not required	8. Out-group acceptance required

Source: Teske and Nelson (1974).

Anglo-American

The *American Heritage Dictionary* defines the term as: "An American, especially an inhabitant of the United States, whose language and ancestry are English." *Webster's New Collegiate Dictionary* (1979) does not privilege U.S. inhabitants over Canadians and defines the term as: "A North American whose native language is English and whose culture is of English origin" (44). Huntington (2004a, 2004b) has defined the United States identity as "Anglo-Protestant" with a Creed of liberty and democracy. He argues that the Anglo-Protestant culture is not compatible with Hispanic culture and sees the ideologies of multiculturalism and diversity, as well as immigration from Mexico, as threats to "American identity" (*Ibid.*). From this perspective, popular among nativist groups, the Anglo-American nation and culture should be assimilated by all Americans; immigrants should adhere to Anglo-Protestant values, maintain their European cultural heritage, speak English, and commit to the principles of the Creed (see 2004b: 20). Interestingly, Charles Taylor (quoted by Rivera, 2006) has argued that democracy (the Anglo-Protestant Creed according to Huntington) "is *inclusive* because it is founded on the representation of a common people—the *demos*—but, paradoxically, this is also the reason that democracy leans toward exclusion" (14). Others also have identified an "Anglo-American nation" as a distinct racial community belonging to the Caucasian group (Josiah Nott quoted by Lind, 1996: 30). According to Lind (1996), most of the elite who founded the country were opposed to immigration of non-Anglo-Saxons to the U.S. The first Naturalization Act passed by Congress in 1790 only allowed citizenship to "free white persons" (*Ibid.*). The shortened term "Anglo" has been commonly utilized by CRT scholars and other U.S. researchers and writers of racial issues (see for example Bender and Ruiz, 1974; Kent-Monning, 2002; Rivera, 2006; and Wong, 2006). It is the exclusionary notion of Anglo-Protestant-Americanism that these researchers criticize and this study rejects.

Castification

An institutionalized form of exploitation of one group by another. The group that is the victim of castification is effectively reduced to a lower caste status that cannot enjoy the same rights and obligations possessed by the dominant group (Trueba, 1993).

Chicano/Chicana

Most commonly understood, the term refers to people of Mexican origin born in the United States. Chicanos strongly identify themselves with Mexican traditions and with the pre-Columbian cultures of Mexico and largely reject U.S. mainstream values. The term Chicano apparently derives from *Mexicano*. It originated in the first decades of the 19th century in the south of the U.S. as a derogatory term used by landowners to refer to their Mexican workers (Sotomayor, 1983). During the Civil Rights movement, the term acquired a new political connotation. It became increasingly popular on U.S. college campuses during the late 1960s, when many students adopted it as a sign of ethnic pride and political defiance (*Black Issues*, 2004). Today, many Americans of Mexican descent utilize the words *Chicana* or *Chicano* as a unique identity claim and some even object to being addressed either as "Mexican" or "American." They see themselves as a colonized community and are generally more politicized than other citizens of Mexican ancestry. Therefore, self-defining Chicanos represent a socio-cultural and political movement, but their consciousness does not necessarily reflect the views of most people of Mexican origin. In fact, precisely because the term refers to a socio-cultural experience in the U.S., and it implies a political stance, even people born in Mexico can define themselves as "Chicano" (Valencia, 2002).

Duncan-Andrade (2005) points out that the term Chicano has at least two distinct meanings: it can refer to a person's political identity or to their socio-ethnic background. "The flexibility of the term allows it to take on different meanings for different people, giving it the strength of diversity, much like the varied group of people finding themselves united under it (*Ibid.*: 578). Finally, it is important to point out that strong class and race prejudices exist between Mexicans born in Mexico and Mexicans born in the United States. In Mexico's classist society, the term Chicano may allude to a person of low origins and poor education who lives or has lived in the U.S. Thus, some Mexicans and self-defined Mexican-Americans find it offensive to be addressed as Chicano.

Conscientization

In Freirean pedagogy, this term refers to the promotion of ". . . reflection and action upon the world in order to transform it" (Freire, 1970: 33). Paulo Freire's work aimed at empowering the oppressed and awakening their critical consciousness or awareness about the fundamental sociopolitical conditions shaping their lives. Through this pedagogy, the intellectual transformation of the learner can lead to action toward political and social transformation. Conscientization must be developed through a "dialogical process" that produces generative themes that ultimately may incite reflective action (*Ibid.*). According to Freirean followers, this dialogical education has the potential to transform those who are objects into subjects capable of changing history and the world. Thus, conscientization also means "learning to perceive social, economic, and political contradictions, and to take action against the oppressive elements of reality" (*Ibid.*: 19).

Hegemony and Racial Hegemony

From a sociologic, neo-Marxist perspective, hegemony represents the power of the dominant capitalist classes to obtain the consent of the working class to its own exploitation (Arena, 2003). Gold (2004) argues that inequalities in the United States are reproduced through a system of racial hegemony that tolerates certain advances by racialized people and, "at the same time, produces outcomes that are not so different from long-standing patterns of inequality" (963). The struggle for hegemony is a dynamic, ongoing process that involves a combination of practices (some of them repressive) in the ideological, economic, and political dimensions (Arena, 2003). Within these dimensions, and in the specific contexts of corporations, states, and markets, the dominant classes develop different forms of control depending on race and gender (Ibid.). From the educational perspective, Jay (2003) argues that the hidden curriculum of hegemony allows educational institutions to support multicultural programs, while simultaneously restricting the transformative potential of multicultural education. From her perspective, multicultural education has been appropriated as a "hegemonic device" that perpetuates the position of power of the dominant groups in society.

Hispanic

The official definition of Hispanic in the United States encompasses those citizens or residents who either speak Spanish as a native language or have some ancestor who did, even if these individuals speak only English (Fox, 1996). They trace their origin to four major geographical areas: Spain, Central America/Mexico, South America, and the Caribbean basin (Cuba, Dominican Republic, and Puerto Rico). The use of the noun "Hispanic" can only emphasize the common denominator of language, since the individuals do not have a common biological descent. According to the Census Bureau, Hispanics can be of any race (Martin and Gerber, 2005), and they can also be of any religion and any citizenship status. In reality, all of them don't even share the same mother tongue (some only speak English). Additionally, there are Filipinos, Mayans, Quechuas, and so forth whose ancestors may never have mastered Spanish but who had Spanish surnames imposed on them by their conquerors. These minorities are often given, and sometimes willingly take up, the label "Hispanic" (Fox, 1996). This phenomenon also occurs with many indigenous peoples from Mexico (Tarahumaras, Tarascos, Zapotecs, etc.) who are labeled "Mexican" or "Mexican-American." These Amerindians, because of racism and discrimination, often have disavowed their origins even before they immigrated to the United States (Castellanos Guerrero, 2001; de Leff, 2002).

Internal Colonialism

Barrera (1979: 194) defines this concept as "a relationship of domination and subordination which are defined along ethnic and/or racial lines when the relationship is established or maintained to serve the interests of all or part of the dominant group." Internal colonialism theory emphasizes that just as institutional discrimination can be widespread with or without the intention of individuals, governments create, legitimize, and maintain subordination of the oppressed classes (Martínez, 1999). De Genova (2005) argues that the Mexican labor immigration system is a kind of "imported colonialism" that has produced an agricultural proletariat within the national space but excluded from the national polity.

Internalized Oppression

Occurs when the oppressed/colonized individual legitimizes the dominant group's view of him/her as an inferior "other" and, "consequently, will lead to a process of inferiorized personas reproducing their own oppression (Mullaly, 1997: 151).

Latino

Broadly the term in the United States refers to "a person of Latin-American ancestry in general" (Samora and Vandel-Simon, 1993). The term Latino, and "Latin," as is commonly used in the U.S. is also utilized as a synonym of "Hispanic." However, such connotation is inaccurate and can easily create confusion outside of the United States. Accurately speaking, the adjective "Latino," or Latin, relates to the peoples who speak the Romance languages that evolved from Latin in countries as diverse as Italy, France, Spain, and Portugal. Hence, Latinos are really any of the peoples who trace their origins to those countries. As utilized in the U.S., however, the term generally excludes Hispanics from Europe or Latinos from other European nations. Nevertheless, such connotation is so widely used that the U.S. Census Bureau accepts the identifiers "Latino" and "Hispanic" as synonymous (U.S. Census, 2011).

Mexican

When this term refers to people living in the United States, it mostly refers to documented or undocumented people born in Mexico who are now permanent or temporary residents. Some Native Americans born in Mexico, who are legally Mexican citizens but now live in the United States, willingly assume the labels "Mexican" and "Mexican-American." Many of them are proud of their ancestral origin and, although they do not reject the Mexican culture (most of them speak Spanish and share religious, musical, culinary, and other Mexican traditions), they identify themselves more with Chicanos than with Mexicans. They argue that the myth of racial democracy in Mexico is easily shattered by the fact that Mexicans on the lighter end of the color-race spectrum hold profound prejudices against those toward the darker end (NACLA, 1992). See also "Chicano/Chicana" and "Hispanic."

In the most ample sense of the concept, Mexicans are the result of the fusion of European, mostly Spanish, and Amerindian cultures. Although the ethnic categories are questionable, according to the CIA *World Fact Book* (CIA, 2010), more than 60% of Mexicans are *Mestizo*, (a mix of Amerindian-Spanish), while the Amerindian and predominantly Amerindian populations are nearly 30%. Only 9% of Mexicans are Caucasian and 1% belong to a multitude of ethnic backgrounds. Mexico's population is 112 million, with a net migration rate of –3.24 migrant(s)/1,000 population (*Ibid.*: 2011 est.). The great majority of this large emigration flow goes to the United States.

Mexican-American(s)

The quick definition of Mexican-American is "an American of Mexican descent" (Samora and Vandel-Simon, 1993). Mexican-Americans, however, are not a monolithic population. They are the largest Hispanic sub-minority in the U.S., the members of which are themselves very diverse in social, economic, and cultural experiences. Many Mexican-Americans are assimilated within the dominant society, and they do not necessarily exalt their Mexican ancestry. Mexican-American is a term "used by many scholars and activists as a more descriptive but less political term. It is also a term that has been more commonly used by segments of the community" (Nieto, 1996, 24). Thus, the use of the term "Mexican-American" in this book provides an inclusive category that refers to all peoples of Mexican ancestry. It provides consistency within the existing academic discussion, but it is deliberately written with a hyphen as a symbolic act explained in Chapter I.

Many people of Mexican ancestry living in the United States are the descendants of people who were in these lands long before they became the United States of America. Others are the offspring of more recent immigrants who have come from the most impoverished rural areas in Mexico. Some of them come from destitute urban areas, expelled from their homes by the economic failures of the Mexican economic paradigm. Yet, the most recent settlers increasingly come from more educated sectors and include professionals and technicians from different fields. The complexity of this population is not only a result of their different socio-economic, historical and geographic origins but is also due to the different realities in which they live, whether as fully assimilated citizens or as members of a cultural minority that resists change. Some of them identify themselves simply as Mexican. Others think of themselves as Mexican-Americans, and yet another group specifically wants to be addressed as "Chicanos." We not negate any of these terms as valid identifiers, although the designation "Mexican-American" has been utilized as inclusive of all these designations in this study.

Mexican-American/Chicano/Latino/Hispanic Culture

These identifiers have been used as synonyms and as mutually exclusive terms for Americans of Mexican descent, depending on different sociological, cultural, and political perspectives. Nevertheless, it has been argued that, irrespective of name designations and self-identification, Mexican-Americans/Chicanos(as)/Latinos(as)/Hispanics have important cultural characteristics in common. In a study about the adaptation of Mexicans in the United States, Hurtado, Gurin, and Peng (1994) found that "Mexican descendants have consistently shown a strong commitment to family, especially extended kin" (136), as well as cultural loyalty and positive attitudes toward maintenance of Spanish. More broadly, but consistent with these findings, Velázquez (2004) has classified Hispanic values into four groups. Since cultures constantly evolve and such characteristics may be more prevalent in less assimilated populations, no cultural generalization will apply to everyone, but some of these traits appeared repeatedly in the interviews conducted by Castro-Salazar. With this in mind, Velázquez's classification may serve as a possible tool for analysis of cultural patterns, trends, attitudes, and behaviors:

1. **Loyalty and identification with family, community, and ethnic group:**

a) They use Spanish when among Hispanics.
b) Students see achievement as "for the family."
c) Cooperation is valued over individual achievement or competitive achievement.

2. **Personalization of interpersonal relationships:**
a) Sensitivity to the feelings of others.
b) Expectation that another person be aware of my feelings.
   (i.e., I shouldn't need to ask for help)
c) Extended family concept. Two or more generations in same household.
d) Friends can be part of the extended family.
   (i.e., *padrinos* and *madrinas* or godfathers and godmothers)

3. **Well-defined status in family and community:**
a) Everybody is expected to know his/her role and responsibility.
b) Age and gender determine the role. The older the person, the more respect expected.
c) Learning social roles and behaviors is as important as academic education (i.e., a "bien educado" or well-educated person is not the one with the most schooling but the one who knows best how to behave in social occasions).
d) Parents teach by modeling behavior, modeling a preferred teaching style.

4. **Identification with Catholic ideology (even when not Catholic):**
a) Emphasis on respect for the conventional way of doing things.
b) Disrespect and rebelliousness are considered sinful (or disrespectful).

Racialization

It is the process by which racial formation emerges. Such a process is dynamic and multidimensional, and it can involve coercive social practices, a foundation for class formation, an ideological pretext for economic domination and nation building, among others (Winant, 1994). In turn, the corresponding social practices are institutionalized, "racial meanings are attributed, and racial identities assigned" (*Ibid.*: 23).

Racism(s)

Racism has been defined in multiple contexts and with many adjectives: class racism (Nearman, 2002), defensive racism (Steele, 2004), environmental racism (Checker, 2005), ethnoracism (Aranda and Rebollo-Gil, 2004), historiographic racism (Goggin, 1984), passive racism (Marx, 2006), reverse racism (Derman-Sparks, Brunson-Phillips, and Hilliard, 1997; O'Sullivan, 1995;

Steele, 2004), welfare racism (Neubeck, 2001), and others. In this study, racism refers to "practices which restrict the chances of success of individuals from a particular racial or ethnic group, and which are based on, or legitimized by, some form of belief that this racial or ethnic group is inherently morally, culturally, or intellectually inferior" (Peter Foster cited by Gillborn, 1995: 57 and 1998: 43). This traditional concept of racism involves an element of discriminatory action and the superiority-inferiority dichotomy but excludes institutionalized racism. Thus, as Gillborn (1995, 1998) points out, 'unintentional' or institutional racism also must be taken into account when defining the concept. Through institutionalized racism, people and organizations carry out biased practices that are not intended to be racist but are discriminatory in their effects (Gillborn, 1998). Darder (1991) defines institutional racism as "a form of racial discrimination that is woven into the fabric of the power relations, social arrangements and practices through which collective actions result in the use of race as a criterion to determine who is rewarded in society" (41).

From a CRT approach, race and racism can be incorporated in all stages of the research process (Solórzano and Yosso, 2002). Furthermore, CRT challenges traditional definitions and discourses on race, gender, and class arguing that these three elements actually converge to shape the experiences of the oppressed (*Ibid.*). In the specific case of people of Mexican origin, researchers have referred to anti-Mexican racism (De Genova, 2005; Fuentes, 2004; Mariscal, 2005; Pulido, 2007; Rojas, 2001) and the anti-immigrant racism (De Genova, 2005) directed against Mexicans. In his doctoral dissertation, Rojas (2001) argues that between 1910 and the 1930s, when hundreds of thousands of Mexicans entered the U.S., they found themselves in a situation of "super-inferiority." Mexican racism clashed with U.S. racism against Mexicans, who were inferiorized beneath Jews and Asians, alongside African-Americans in the U.S. racial hierarchy. In other words, Mexicans in the U.S. became more inferior than those they had learned to regard as inferior (Rojas, 2001: 16). It could be argued that, similarly in our day, as the U.S. is experiencing a great flow of Mexican immigrants, they are being "super-inferiorized" by new forms of anti-Mexican racism.

Another definition of racism that concerns this study is internalized racism, where the person internalizes negative stereotypes of his/her own racial group and self-devalues (Cokley, 2002; Kich, 1992). Such negative stereotypes can become a vicious circle that fuels the marginalized status of the racial group and, consequently, reinforces the stereotypes (Cokley, 2002). Similarly, Freire (1970) and García (2004) and Mullaly (1997) argue that the oppressed can internalize the conscience and dominant values of the oppressors and come to despise their own race (see also definition of "internalized oppression" in this glossary). From a CRT perspective, narratives and stories like the ones revealed by this research help the oppressed to create a shared memory and history (what is counter-history today may be official history tomorrow) (Villenas and Deyhle, 1999). Equally important, community memory and history help to repel the internalization of the colonizer's mentality and the self-blame produced by racist structures (*Idem*). Finally, as our counter-history shows, the concept of "crisis racism" (Goldberg, 2002) can be utilized to explicate the anti-immigrant movement referred to in this study. Crisis racism can be explained as "a common disposition to ascribe social threat to an outside, whether an internalized exterior, the alien within, or the stranger without" (*Ibid.*: 247). Scholars and politicians like Huntington (2004a, 2004b) and Buchanan (2002) incarnate this type of racism and openly speak about the "Mexican threat."

References

Acuña, R. (2003). *Occupied America: A History of Chicanos* (5th ed). New York: Pearson Longman.

Aguirre Jr., A. (2004, March). "Profiling Mexican American Identity: Issues and Concern." *American Behavioral Scientist, 47(7)*: 928–42.

Alaniz, M. L., R. S. Cartmill, and R. N. Parker. (1998). "Immigrants and Violence: The Importance of Neighborhood Context." *Hispanic Journal of Behavioral Sciences, 20(2)*: 155–74.

Alba R., J. Logan, A. Lutz, and B. Stults. (2002). "Only English by the Third Generation? Loss and Preservation of the Mother Tongue among the Grandchildren of Contemporary Immigrants." *Demography, 39(3)*: 467–84.

Alberta, M. G., J. Castellanos, A. G. Lopez, and R. Rosales. (2005). "An Examination of Academic Nonpersistance Decisions of Latino Undergraduates." *Hispanic Journal of Behavioral Science, 27(2)*: 202–23.

Alcoff, L., and E. Mendieta. (2003). *Identities: Race, Class, Gender and Nationality.* Malden, MA: Blackwell Publishing, Ltd.

Allen, J. P. (2006). "How Successful Are Recent Immigrants to the United States and Their Children?" *Yearbook of the Association of Pacific Coast Geographers, 68*: 9–32.

Almaguer, T. (1974). "Historical Notes on Chicano Oppression: The Dialectics of Racial and Class Domination in North America." *Aztlán, 5(1–2)*: 27–56.

Alonso, A. M. (2004). "Conforming Disconformity: 'Mestizaje,' Hybridity, and the Aesthetics of Mexican Nationalism." *Cultural Anthropology, 19(4)*: 459–90.

Alva, S. A., and A. M. Padilla. (1995). "Academic Invulnerability among Mexican Americans: A Conceptual Framework." *The Journal of Educational Issues of Language Minority Students, 15 (Winter)*: 27–47.

Alvarez-McHatton, P., C. P. Zalaquett, and A. Cranson-Gingras. (2006). "Achieving Success: Perceptions of Students from Migrant Farmwork Families." *American Secondary Education, 34(2)*: 25–39.

Aman, C. L. (2005). *Responding to Demographic Change: A Case Study of Schooling and Community in Rural Nebraska* (unpublished doctoral dissertation). The Pennsylvania State University, University Park, PA.

American Civil Liberties Union (ACLU). (2010). *Frequently Asked Questions: Update on Legal Challenges to Arizona's Racial Profiling Law (SB 1070).* ACLU: New York. Retrieved from http://www.aclu.org/immigrants-rights-racial-justice/frequently-asked-questions-update-legal-challenges-arizonas-racial- On January 2, 2011.

American Graduate School of International Management (Thunderbird). (2003). *Economic & Community Development Report Summary.* Glendale, AZ: Thunderbird.

Amster, R. (2010, December 29). "Arizona Bans Ethnic Studies and, Along with It, Reason and Justice." *Huffington Post.* Retrieved from http://www.huffingtonpost.com/randall-amster/arizona-bans-ethnic-studi_b_802318.html on Decembrer 31, 2010.

Andersen, M.L. and Hill Collins, P. (2007). "Why Race, Class, and Gender Still Matter." In Andersen, M.L. and Hill Collins, P. (Eds.). *Race, Class, & Gender. An Anthology (Sixth Edition)* (pp. 1–16). Belmont, CA: Thomson Wadsworth.

Andrade, J. (1998). *A Historical Survey of Mexican Immigration to the United States and an Oral History of the Mexican Settlement in Chicago, 1920–1990* (unpublished doctoral dissertation). Northern Illinois University, DeKalb, IL.

Aranda, E. M., and G. Rebollo-Gil. (2004). "Ethnoracism and the 'Sandwiched' Minorities." *The American Behavioral Scientist, 47(7):* 910–27.

Arce, C. H., E. Murguia, and W. Frisbie. (1987). "Phenotype and Life Chances among Chicanos." *Hispanic Journal of Behavioral Sciences, 9(1):* 19–32.

Archibold, R. C. (2010, July 28). "Judge Blocks Arizona's Immigration Law." *The New York Times.* Retrieved from http://www.nytimes.com/2010/07/29/us/29arizona.html on December 8, 2010.

——. (2006, November 10). "Democratic Victory Raises Spirits of Those Favoring Citizenship for Illegal Aliens." *The New York Times,* p. A27.

Arena, J. (2003). "Race and Hegemony." *American Behavioral Scientist, 47(3):* 352–80.

Arizona Board of Regents. (2000). "Historical Context of the Bisbee Deportation." In *The Bisbee Deportation of 1917. A University of Arizona Web Exhibit.* UA Special Collections. Retrieved from http://www.library.arizona.edu/exhibits/bisbee on September 7, 2006.

Arizona Chapter of the American Mining Congress. (1917?). "Deportations from Bisbee and a Resume of Other Troubles in Arizona." In *The Bisbee Deportation of 1917. A University of Arizona Web Exhibit.* UA Special Collections. Retrieved from http://www.library.arizona.edu/exhibits/bisbee on September 7, 2006.

Arizona Department of Health Services. (2004). *Arizona Health Status and Vital Statistics 2004 Report.* Phoenix: Arizona Department of Health Services, Division of Public Health Services. Retrieved from http://www.azdhs.gov/diro/reports/index.htm on July 28, 2007.

"Arizona Graduation Speech Criticizing Immigration Laws Elicits Boos, Jeers." (2010, May 24). *Huffington Post.* Retrieved from http://www.huffingtonpost.com/2010/05/24/arizona-graduation-speech_n_586946.html on July 17, 2011.

Arizona Independent Media Center. (2005, December 2). *Record Year in an Escalating Crisis.* Arizona Independent Media Center. Retrieved from http://arizona.indymedia.org/archives/archive_by_id.php?id=246 on December 22, 2005.

Arizona Public Defender Association. (2007). "R-07-0003: Comment Regarding Jul 3, 2007 Order Amending Rules 4.2, 7.2, 7.4, 2.7, and 31.6 of the Rules of Criminal Procedure." *Arizona Supreme Court Rules Forum.* Retrieved from http://www.supreme.state.az.us/rules/ on October 27, 2007.

Armijo, L. E. (2001). "Mixed Blessing: Expectations about Foreign Capital Flows and Democracy in Emerging Markets." In L. E. Armijo (Ed.), *Financial Globalization and Democracy in Emerging Markets (International Political Economy)* (pp. 309–336). New York: Palgrave.

Arredondo, G. F., A. Hurtado, N. Klahn, and O. Najera-Ramirez (Eds.). (2003). "Introduction: Chicana Feminism at the Crossroads: Disruptions in Dialogue." In *Chicana Feminisms: A Critical Reader (Post-Contemporary Interventions)* (pp. 1–18). Durham, NC: Duke University Press.

Associated Press. (2006, April 10). "Officials: Radio Host's Call to Kill Border Crossers Dangerous." www.KVOA.com. Tucson, AZ: WorldNow and KVOA. Retrieved from http://kvoa.com/Global/story.asp?S=4744652&nav=HMO6 on July 14, 2007.

——. (2005, July 20). "Hispanic Kids Less Likely to Be Insured, Vaccinated." *Arizona Daily Star.* Retrieved from http://www.azbilingualed.org/News%202005/hispanic_kids_less_likely_to_be.htm on February 26, 2009.

Aycock, W. (1980). "Editor's Column." *The Journal of the Society for the Study of the Multi-Ethnic Literature of the United States (MELUS), 7(1):* 1–2.

Bach, R. L. (1978). "Mexican Immigration and the American State." *International Migration Review* (Special Issue: *Illegal Mexican Immigrants to the United States), 12(4):* 536–58.

Bacon, D. (2004a). "The Political Economy of Immigration Reform." *Multinational Monitor, 25(11):* 9–13.

——. (2004b). *The Children of NAFTA: Labor Wars on the U.S./Mexico Border.* Berkeley, CA: University of California Press.

Bagley, C. (2009). "The Ethnographer as *Impresario-Joker* in the (Re)presentation of Educational Research as Performance Art: Toward a Performance Ethic." *Ethnography and Education, 4(3):* 283–300.

Bagley, C., and R. Castro-Salazar. (2011). "Critical Arts-Based Research in Education: Performing Undocumented *Historias.*" *British Educational Research Journal:* 1–22.

Bagnato, K. (2005). "Undocumented Immigrants and College." *Diverse Issues in Higher Education, 22(16):* 25.

Bailey, T., and V. Smith Morest. (2006). *Defending the Community College Equity Agenda.* Baltimore, MD: The Johns Hopkins University Press.

Baker, R. (1996). "Sociological Field Research with Junior High School Teachers: The Discounting of Mexican American Students." *The Journal of Educational Issues of Language Minority Students, 18:* 49–66.

Bales, K. (1999). *Disposable People: New Slavery in the Global Economy.* Berkeley: University of California Press.

Balfanz, R., J. M. Bridgeland, L. A. Moore, and J. H. Fox. (2010). *Building a Grad Nation. Progress and Challenge in Ending the High School Dropout Epidemic* (report). Produced by Civic Enterprises, Everyone Graduates Center at Johns Hopkins University, and America's Promise Alliance.

Bandhauer, C. A. (2001). *A Global Trend in Racism: The Late-20th-Century Anti-Immigrant Movement in Southern California* (unpublished doctoral dissertation). Binghamton, NY: State University of New York.

Barclay, E. (2005, September). "Mexican Migrant Communities May Be on Verge of HIV/AIDS Epidemic." Population Reference Bureau. Retrieved from http://www.prb.org/Articles/2005/MexicanMigrantCommunitiesMayBeonVergeofHIVAIDSEpidemic.aspx on August 20, 2006.

Barkin, D. (1997). "The Effects of Globalization on the Prospects for Sustainable Development in Mexico." Prepared for the International Flows and the Environment Project (World Resources Institute). Mexico City: Universidad Autónoma Metropolitana, Unidad Xochimilco. Retrieved from http://pdf.wri.org/iffe_barkin.pdf on June 23, 2007.

Barlett, D. L., J. B. Steele, L. Karmatz, and J. Levinstein. (2004, Sep. 20). "Who Left the Door Open?" *Time*, 51–66.

Barndt, J. R. (2007). *Understanding and Dismantling Racism: The Twenty-First Century Challenge to White America*. Minneapolis, MN: Fortress Press.

Barone, T., and E. Eisner. (2006). "Arts-Based Educational Research." In J. Green, G. Camilli, and P. Elmore (Eds.), *Complementary Methods in Research in Education*. Mahwah, NJ: Lawrence Erlbaum.

——. (1979). *Race and Class in the Southwest: A Theory of Racial Inequality*. South Bend, IN: University of Notre Dame.

Barrera, M. (1979). *Race and class in the Southwest: A theory of racial inequality*. Notre Dame: University of Notre Dame Press.

Barrett, S. R. (2002). *Culture Meets Power*. Westport, CT: Praeger Publishers.

Bartlett, B. (2006, May 11). "The Illegal Immigrant Taxpayer." *The Wall Street Journal* (eastern ed., p. A10). New York: Dow Jones & Company, Inc.

Battle, J., and R. Cuellar. (2006). "Obstacles to Overcome: Mexican-American Pre-Service Teachers Share Their Insights." *National Forum of Multicultural Issues Journal 3(2)*. Retrieved from http://www.nationalforum.com/Electronic%20Journal%20Volumes/Battle,%20Jennifer %20Obstacles%20to%20Overcome%20Mexican%20American%20PreService%20Teache rs%20Share%20Their%20Thoughts.pdf on August 1, 2006.

Baum, S., J. Ma, and K. Payea. (2010). *Education Pays 2010. The Benefits of Higher Education for Individuals and Society*. New York, NY: College Board Advocacy & Policy Center. Retrieved from http://trends.collegeboard.org/downloads/Education_Pays_2010.pdf on February 23, 2011.

BBC News. (2006, March 13). "UK Troop Numbers to Fall by 800." Retrieved from http://news.bbc.co.uk/1/hi/uk/4801624.stm on March 9, 2007.

Bean, F. D., M. Tienda, and National Committee for Research on the 1980 Census. (1987). *The Hispanic Population of the United States*. New York: Russell Sage Foundation

Bell, L. A. (2003). "Telling Tales: What Stories Can Teach Us about Racism." *Race, Ethnicity and Education, 6(1)*: 3–28.

Bender, P. S., and R. A. Ruiz. (1974). "Race and Class as Differential Determinants of Underachievement and Underaspiration among Mexican-Americans and Anglos." *Journal of Educational Research, 68(2)*: 51–55.

Bendersky, J. W. (1995). "The Disappearance of Blonds: Immigration, Race and the Reemergence of 'Thinking White'." *Telos, 104* (Summer): 135–57.

Benson, L. (2007, June 18). "Importing Teachers Misses Point." *Deseret Morning News*. Salt Lake City, UT: The Deseret News Publishing Co.

Bergman, M. (2006, March 21). "Growth of Hispanic-Owned Businesses Triples the National Average." *U.S. Census Bureau News*. Washington, D.C.: U.S. Department of Commerce. Retrieved from http://www.census.gov/Press-Release/www/releases/archives/business _ownership on November 28, 2009.

——. (2004, March 18). "Census Bureau Projects Tripling of Hispanic and Asian Populations in 50 Years, Non-Hispanic Whites May Drop to Half of Total Population." *U.S. Census Bureau News.* Washington, D.C.: U.S. Department of Commerce. Retrieved from http://www.census.gov/Press-Release/www/releases/archives/population/001720.html on December 26, 2006.

Berlinger, D. C., and B. J. Biddle. (1995). *The Manufactured Crisis: Myths, Fraud, and the Attack on America's Public Schools.* Reading, MA: Addison-Wesley.

Bernard, W. S. (1998). "Immigration: History of U.S. Policy." In D. Jacobson (Ed.), *The Immigration Reader: America in a Multidisciplinary Perspective* (pp. 48–71). Malden, MA: Blackwell Publishers.

Bernstein, R. (2006, December 22). "Louisiana Loses Population, Arizona Edges Nevada as Fastest-Growing State." *U.S. Census Bureau News.* Washington, D.C.: U.S. Department of Commerce. Retrieved from http://www.census.gov/Press-Release/www/releases/archives/population/007910.html on December 26, 2006.

Bhattacharyya, G., J. Gabriel, and S. Small. (2002). *Race and Power: Global Racism in the Twenty-First Century.* London: Routledge.

Billeaud, J. (2007, January 24). "Immigrant Students in Arizona Brace for Higher Tuition." *North Country Times (Associated Press).* Phoenix, AZ. Retrieved from http://www.nctimes.com/articles/2007/01/25//news/state/15_54_091_24_07.txt on January 2, 2008.

Black Issues in Higher Education. (2004). "University of New Mexico Changing Name of Chicano Program." *Black Issues in Higher Education, 21(Nov. 18):* 20.

Blanton, C. K. (2003). "From Intellectual Deficiency to Cultural Deficiency: Mexican Americans, Testing, and Public School Policy in the American Southwest, 1920–1940." *Pacific Historical Review, 72(1):* 39–62.

——. (2000). "'They Cannot Master Abstractions, but They Can Often Be Made Efficient Workers': Race and Class in the Intelligence Testing of Mexican Americans and African Americans in Texas During the 1920s." *Social Science Quarterly, 81(4):* 1014–26.

Blauner, R. (1972). *Racial Oppression in America.* New York: Harper and Row.

Bohon, S. A., H. Macpherson, and J. H. Atiles. (2005). "Educational Barriers for New Latinos in Georgia." *Journal of Latinos & Education, 4(1):* 43–58.

Bonnand, S. (1997). "Overview." *The Bisbee Deportation of 1917. A University of Arizona Web Exhibit.* UA Special Collections. Retrieved from http://www.library.arizona.edu/exhibits/bisbee on September 8, 2006.

Bowden, C. (1998). *Juarez: The Laboratory of Our Future.* New York: Aperture.

Bowers, C. A. (1983). "Linguistic Roots of Cultural Invasion in Paulo Freire's Pedagogy." *Teachers College Record, 84(4):* 939–43.

Brading, D. A. (1991). *The First America: The Spanish Monarchy, Creole Patriots, and the Liberal State, 1492–1867.* Cambridge, UK: Cambridge University Press.

Brandolini, A., and T. M. Smeeding. (2006). *Inequality: International Evidence.* Prepared for Banca d'Italia, Economic Research Department, Syracuse University & Luxemburg Income Study. Retrieved from http://www-cpr.maxwell.syr.edu/faculty/smeeding/pdf/Palgrave_v4.pdf on November 10, 2006.

Buchanan, P. J. (2006). *State of Emergency: The Third World Invasion and Conquest of America.* New York: Thomas Dunne Books.

——. (2002). *The Death of the West: How Dying Populations and Immigrant Invasions Imperil Our Country and Civilization.* New York: Thomas Dunne Books.

Bukowczyk, J. (2008). *A History of Polish Americans.* Piscataway, NJ: Transaction Publishers.

Bustamante, J. (1976). "Structural and Ideological Conditions of the Mexican Undocumented Immigration to the United States." *The American Behavioral Scientist, 19(3):* 364–76.

Byrkit, J. W. (1972). *Life and Labor in Arizona, 1901–1921: with Particular Reference to the Deportations of 1917.* Ann Arbor, MI: Claremont Graduate School Dissertation.

Cabrera, N. L., and A. M. Padilla. (2004). "Entering and Succeeding in the 'Culture of College': The Story of Two Mexican Heritage Students." *Hispanic Journal of Behavioral Sciences, 26(2):* 152–70.

Cacho, L. M. (2000). "'The People of California Are Suffering': The Ideology of White Injury in Discourses of Immigration." *Cultural Values, 4(4):* 389–418.

Cahill, C. (2004). "Defying Gravity? Raising Consciousness Through Collective Research." *Children's Geographies, 2(2):* 273–86.

Cahnmann-Taylor, M. (2008). "Arts-Based Research: Histories and New Directions." In M. Cahnmann-Taylor and R. Siegesmund (Eds.), *Arts-Based Research in Education. Foundations for Practice.* New York: Routledge.

Capps, R., R. M. Castaneda, A. Chaudry, and R. Santos. (2007). *Paying the Price: The Impact of Immigration Raids on America's Children.* Paper prepared for the Urban Institute. Washington, D.C.: National Council of La Raza. Retrieved from http://www.urban.org/url.cfm?ID=411566 on October 3, 2009.

Carrigan, W. D., and C. Web. (2003). "The Lynching of Persons of Mexican Origin or Descent in the United States, 1848 to 1928." *Journal of Social History, 37(2):* 411–38.

Castellanos Guerrero, A. (2001). "Notas para estudiar el racismo hacia los indios de México." *Papeles de Población, 7(28):* 165–179. México: Centro de Investigación y Estudios Avanzados de la Población de la Universidad Autónoma del Estado de México.

Castillo, L. G., C. W. Conoley, and D. F. Brossart. (2004). "Acculturation, White Marginalization, and Family Support as Predictors of Perceived Distress in Mexican American Female College Students." *Journal of Counseling Psychology, 51(2):* 151–57.

Castro-Salazar, R., and C. Bagley. (2010). "'Ni de aquí ni from There'. Navigating Between Contexts: Counter-Narratives of Undocumented Mexican Students in the United States." *Race Ethnicity and Education, 13(1):* 23–40.

CBS News. (2006, June 6). "Filling The Classroom Void. U.S. Schools Are Recruiting Foreign Teachers to Fill Shortages." *CBS Broadcasting, Inc.* Baltimore, MD. Retrieved from http://www.cbsnews.com/stories/2006/06/06/eveningnews/main1689748.shtml on July 23, 2007.

Center for American Progress. (2010, January 21). *Comprehensive Immigration Reform Helps Workers and the Economy.* Washington, D.C.: Center for American Progress. Retrieved from http://www.americanprogress.org/issues/2010/01/econimmigration_numbers.html on June 12, 2010.

Chang, G. (2000). *Disposable Domestics: Immigrant Women Workers in the Global Economy.* Cambridge, MA: South End Press.

Channing, W. E. (1837). *A Letter to the Hon. Henry Clay, on the Annexation of Texas to the United States.* Boston: James Munroe and Company.

Chávez E. (2002). *"¡Mi Raza Primero!" (My People First!): Nationalism, Identity, and Insurgency in the Chicano Movement in Los Angeles, 1966–1978.* Los Angeles: University of California Press.

Chávez, L. (2005, December 20). "Immigration: The Real World. The Quiet Assimilation of the Undocumented." *Los Angeles Times,* B15.

Checker, M. (2005). *Polluted Promises: Environmental Racism and the Search for Justice in a Southern Town.* New York: New York University Press.

Chiquiar, D., and G. H. Hanson. (2005). "International Migration, Self-Selection, and the Distribution of Wages: Evidence from Mexico and the United States." *University of Chicago Journal of Political Economy, 113(2):* 239–81.

CIA. (2010). *The World Factbook.* Retrieved from https://www.cia.gov/library/publications/the-world-factbook on October 6, 2010.

———. (2006). *The World Factbook.* Retrieved from http://www.cia.gov/cia/publications/factbook on July 18, 2006.

Clarren, R. (2003). "Fields of Poison." *Nation, 277(22):* 23–25.

Clemmer, R. O. (1995). *Roads in the Sky: The Hopi Indians in a Century of Change.* Boulder, CO: Westview Press.

Cline, Z. (2001). "Silenced Now: Living the Undivided Life." *The Hispanic Outlook in Higher Education, II(16).* University of Arizona Online Databases: ProQuest.

Cockcroft, J. D. (1986). *Outlaws in the Promised Land: Mexican Immigrant Workers and America's Future.* New York: Grove Press.

Cokley, K. O. (2002). "Testing Cross's Revised Racial Identity Model: An Examination of the Relationship Between Racial Identity and Internalized Racialism." *Journal of Counseling Psychology, 49(4):* 476–83.

Coleman, M. (2007). "A Geopolitics of Engagement: Neoliberalism, the War on Terrorism, and the Reconfiguration of US Immigration Enforcement." *Geopolitics, 12(4):* 607–34.

Collins, G. (2010, September 4). "The Ungreat Debate." *The New York Times.* Retrieved from http://query.nytimes.com/gst/fullpage.html?res=9405E5DB173EF937A3575AC0A9669D8B63 on January 19, 2011.

Community College Week. (2007). "New Law Has Immigrant Students in Arizona Bracing for Higher Tuition, Fees at Colleges." *Community College Week, 19(12):* 4–9.

Condon, S. (2011, March 18). "Arizona Lawmakers Reject 'Birthright' Immigration Bills." CBSNews.com. Retrieved from http://www.cbsnews.com/8301-503544_162-20044639-503544.html on April 4, 2011.

Cooper, J. A. (1899). "Editorial Comment." In J. Gordon Mowat, John Alexander Cooper, Newton MacTavish (Eds.), *The Canadian Magazine of Politics, Science, Art and Literature* (vol. 12). Toronto: The Ontario Publishing Co., Ltd.

Córdova, T. (2005). "Agency, Commitment, and Connection: Embracing the Roots of Chicano and Chicana Studies." *International Journal of Qualitative Studies in Education, 18(2):* 221–33.

Coser, L. (1992). "Introduction." In M. Halbwachs and L. A. Coser (Eds.), *Halbwachs/Coser: On Collective Memory* (pp. 1–34). Chicago: University of Chicago Press.

———. (1998). *Qualitative Inquiry and Research Design: Choosing among Five Traditions.* Thousand Oaks, CA: Sage Publications.

Crowley, M., D. T. Lichter, and Q. Zhenchao. (2006). "Beyond Gateway Cities: Economic Restructuring and Poverty among Mexican Immigrant Families and Children." *Family Relations, 55 (3)*: 345–60.

Cummings, J. (1981). "Age on Arrival and Immigrant Second Language Learning in Canada: A Reassessment." *Applied Linguistics, II(2)*: 132–49.

Damrosch, L. F. (2005). "War and Uncertainty." *The Yale Law Journal, 114(6)*: 1405–18.

Daniels, R. (2005). *Guarding the Golden Door: American Immigration Policy and Immigrants since 1882*. New York: Macmillan.

Darder, A. (1991). *Culture and Power in the Classroom: A Critical Foundation for Bicultural Education*. Westport, CT: Bergin and Garvey.

Davenport, P. (2010, June 25). "Jan Brewer: Most Illegal Immigrants Are Smuggling Drugs." *Huffington Post*. Retrieved from http://www.huffingtonpost.com/2010/06/25/jan-brewer-drug-smuggling_n_626258.html on October 26, 2011.

Davis, D. (2007). "Illegal Immigrants: Uncle Sam Wants You." *In These Times, 31(8)*: 32–35.

Dawson, G. F. (1880). *Republican Campaign Text Book for 1880*. Washington, D.C.: Republican Congressional Committee.

De Genova, N. (2005). *Working the Boundaries: Race, Space, and Illegality in Mexican Chicago*. Durham, NC: Duke University Press.

——. (2004). "The Legal Production of Mexican/Migrant 'Illegality'." *Latino Studies, 2(2)*: 160.

——. (1998). "Race, Space, and the Reinvention of Latin America in Mexican Chicago." *Latin American Perspectives, 25(5)*: 87–116.

DeGuzmán, M. (2007). "Mass Production of the Heartland: Cuban American Lesbian Camp in Achy Obejas's 'Wrecks'." In L. Di Iorio Sandín and R. Perez (Eds.), *Contemporary U.S. Latino/A Literary Criticism* (247–76). New York: Macmillan.

De Hoyos, R. E. (2005). *Constructing Inequality and Poverty Indexes Using Mexican ENIGH*. Paper prepared for University of Cambridge, Faculty of Economics. United Kingdom: University of Cambridge. Retrieved from http://www.econ.cam.ac.uk/phd/red29/Tools/using %20ENIGH.pdf on October 6, 2007.

De Janvry, A., and E. Sadoulet. (2001). "Adjustment Policies, Agriculture, and Rural Development in Latin America." In A. Singh and H. Tabatabai (Eds.), *Economic Crisis and Third World Agriculture* (pp. 118–46). New York: Cambridge University Press.

Del Castillo, A. R. (2002). "Illegal Status and Social Citizenship: Thoughts on Mexican Immigrants in a Postnational World." *Aztlán: A Journal of Chicano Studies, 27(2)*: 9–32.

de Leff, J. F. (2002). "Racism in Mexico: Cultural Roots and Clinical Interventions." *Family Process, 41(4)*: 619–23.

Delgado, R. (2006). "The Current Landscape of Race: Old Targets, New Opportunities." *Michigan Law Review, 104(6)*: 1269–87.

——. (2003). "Crossroads, Directions, and A New Critical Race Theory/Ethical Ambition: Living a Life of Meaning and Worth." *Texas Law Review, 82(1)*: 121–52.

Delgado, R., and J. Stefancic. (2001). *Critical Race Theory: An Introduction*. New York: New York University Press.

Delgado-Bernal, D. (1999). "Chicana/o Education from the Civil Rights Era to the Present." In J. F. Moreno (Ed.), *The Elusive Quest for Equality: 150 Years of Chicano/Chicana Education* (77–108). Cambridge, MA: Harvard Educational Review.

——. (1998). "Grassroots Leadership Reconceptualized: Chicana Oral Histories and the 1968 East Los Angeles School Blowouts." *Frontiers, 19(2)*: 113–42.

Delgado-Gaitan, C. (2001). *The Power of Community: Mobilizing for Family and Schooling*. Lanham, MD: Rowman and Littlefield Publishers, Inc.

Delgado-Gaitan, C., and H. Trueba. (1991). *Crossing Cultural Borders: Education for Immigrant Families in America*. New York: Falmer Press.

D'Emilio, J. (2000). "Cycles of Change, Questions of Strategy: The Gay and Lesbian Movement after Fifty Years." In C. A. Rimmerman, K. D. Wald, C. Wilcox (Eds.), *The Politics of Gay Rights* (The Chicago Series on Sexuality, History, and Society; pp. 31–53). Chicago: University of Chicago Press.

Dennis, R. (2003). "W. E. B. Du Bois's Concept of Double Consciousness." In J. Stone and R. Dennis (Eds.), *Race and Ethnicity: Comparative and Theoretical Approaches* (pp. 13–27). Hoboken, NJ: Blackwell Publishers.

Denzin, N. K. (1999). "Interpretive Ethnography for the Next Century." *Journal of Contemporary Ethnography 28(5)*: 510–19.

——. (2001). *Interpretive Interactionism*. Thousand Oaks, CA: Sage Publications.

——. (2003). *Performance Ethnography. Critical Pedagogy and the Politics of Culture*. Thousand Oaks, CA: Sage Publications.

Derman-Sparks, L., C. Brunson-Phillips, and A. G. Hilliard III. (1997). *Teaching/Learning Anti-Racism: A Developmental Approach*. New York: Teachers College Press.

Dervarics, C. (2006). "Congress Takes up Competing Bills on In-State Tuition for Illegal Immigrants." *Diverse Issues in Higher Education, 23(11)*: 7.

Derzipilski, K. (2004). *Arizona*. New York: Marshall Cavendish Co.

"DHS: Border, Interior, USCIS, Data." (2010). *Migration News, 17(3)*: No page no. Produced by the University of California, Davis. Retrieved from http://migration.ucdavis.edu/mn/more.php?id=3613_0_2_0 on January 4, 2011.

Dhunpath, R. (2000). "Life History Methodology: 'Narradigm' Regained." *International Journal of Qualitative Studies in Education, 13(5)*: 543–51.

Dittgen, H. (1999). "The American Debate About Immigration in the 1990s: A New Nationalism After the End of the Cold War?" *Stanford Electronic Humanities Review, 5(2)*. Retrieved from http://www.stanford.edu/group/SHR/5-2/dittgen.html on February 12, 2011.

Dixon, P. B., and M. T. Rimmer (2009). *Restriction or Legalization? Measuring the Economic Benefits of Immigration Reform*. Trade Policy Analysis no. 40. Washington, D.C.: CATO Institute.

Donato, R. (2003). "Sugar Beets, Segregation, and Schools: Mexican Americans in a Northern Colorado Community, 1920–1960." *Journal of Latinos & Education, (2)2*: 69–88.

——. (1997). *The Other Struggle for Equal Schools: Mexican Americans During the Civil Rights Era*. Albany, New York: State University of New York Press.

Donato, R., and C. de Onis. (1995). "Better Middle-Schooling for Mexican Americans." *Education Digest, 61(3)*: 53–56.

Dong, X., and Platner, J. W. (2004). "Occupational Fatalities of Hispanic Construction Workers from 1992 to 2000." *American Journal of Industrial Medicine, 45(1)*: 45–54.

Dotson-Blake, K. P. (2006). *A Praxis of Empowerment: Critically Exploring Family-School-Community Partnerships in Mexico and the United States* (unpublished doctoral dissertation). School of Education, The College of William and Mary, Williamsburg, VA.

Downes, L. (2007, October 28). What part of "illegal" don't you understand? *New York Times.* Retrieved from http://www.nytimes.com/2007/10/28/opinion/28sun4.html?_r=1 on April 4, 2010.

Drachman, E. (2006). "Access to Higher Education for Undocumented Students." *Peace Review, 18(1):* 91–100.

D'Souza, D. (1996). *The End of Racism.* New York: Free Press.

Dueñas González, R. (2000). "Acknowledgements." In R. Dueñas González (Ed.) with I. Melis (Ed.). *Language Ideologies: Critical Perspectives on the Official English Movement, Volume I: Education and the Social Implications of Official Language* (pp. xxi–xxvi). USA: National Council of Teachers of English (NCTE).

Duncan-Andrade, J. M. R. (2005). "An Examination of the Sociopolitical History of Chicanos and Its Relationship to School Performance." *Urban Education, 40(6):* 576–605.

Eckstein, L. (2006). *Re-Membering the Black Atlantic: On the Poetics and Politics of Literary Memory* (Cross/Cultures: Readings in the Post/Colonial Literatures in English, vol. 84). Amsterdam, the Netherlands: Editions Rodopi B. V.

Economist, The. (2007, July 5th). "Illegal Immigration. Nowhere to Hide." *The Economist.* Retrieved from http://www.economist.com/node/9443515 via subscription on July 26, 2007.

——. (2006, October 26). "The American Economy. Slow Road Ahead." *The Economist.* Retrieved from http://www.economist.com/node/8079134 via subscription on December 27, 2006.

——. (2001, January 25). "The Immigration Contradiction." *The Economist.* Retrieved from http://www.economist.com via subscription on June 12, 2007.

——. (2000, March 9). "Oh, say, can you see?" *The Economist.* Retrieved from http://www.economist.com/node/289744 via subscription on November 30, 2006.

Eisner, E. (2008). "Persistent Tensions in Arts-Based Research." In M. Cahnmann-Taylor and R. Siegesmund (Eds.), *Arts-Based Research in Education* (pp. 16–27). . New York, Routledge.

——. (2001). "Concerns and Aspirations for Qualitative Research in the New Millennium." *Qualitative Research 1(2):* 135–45.

Elenes, A. (2002). "Border/Transformative Pedagogies at the End of the Millennium: Chicana/o Cultural Studies and Education." In A. J. Aldama and N. H. Quiñonez (Eds.), *Decolonial Voices: Chicana and Chicano Cultural Studies in the 21st Century* (pp. 245–61). Bloomington, IN: Indiana University Press.

Ensher, E. A., and S. E. Murphy. (1997). "Effects of Race, Gender, Perceived Similarity, and Contact on Mentor Relationships." *Journal of Vocational Behavior, 50(3):* 29–42.

Eschbach, K., J. Hagan, N. Rodriguez, R. Hernandez-Leon, and S. Bailey. (1999). "Death at the Border." *International Migration Review, 33(2):* 430–54.

Espinosa, G., V. Elizondo, and J. Miranda. (2005). *Latino Religions and Civic Activism in the United States.* New York: Oxford University Press.

Espinoza-Herold, M. (2007). "Stepping Beyond *Sí Se Puede: Dichos* as a Cultural Resource in Mother–Daughter Interaction in a Latino Family." *Anthropology & Education Quarterly, 38(3):* 260–77.

——. (2003). *Issues in Latino Education: Race, School Culture, and the Politics of Academic Success.* New York: Allyn and Bacon.

Ewing, W. A. (2003). *Migrating to Recovery: The Role of Immigration in Urban Renewal* (Immigration Policy Brief). Washington, D.C.: The American Immigration Law Foundation.

Ewing, W. A., and B. Johnson. (2003, October). *Immigrant Success or Stagnation?: Confronting the Claim of Latino Non-Advancement.* Washington, D.C.: American Immigration Law Foundation. Retrieved from http://www.ailf.org/ipc in January 2008.

Excelencia in Education. (2004). *Arizona's Human Capital: Latino Students and Their Families.* Washington, D.C.: Excelencia in Education. Retrieved from http://www.edexcelencia.org/pdf/AZ-ACHE-FINAL.pdf on December 3, 2007.

Fairlie, R. W. (2006). *Kauffman Index of Entrepreneurial Activity: National Report 1996–2005.* Kansas City: Ewing Marion Kauffman Foundation.

Federal Bureau of Investigation. (2010). *Uniform Crime Report. Hate Crime Statistics, 2009.* Washington, D.C.: U.S. Department of Justice. Retrieved from http://www2.fbi.gov/ucr/hc2009/documents/incidentsandoffenses.pdf on April 29, 2011.

——. (2007). *Hate Crime Statistics 2006.* Washington, D.C.: U.S. Department of Justice, Criminal Justice Information Services. Retrieved from http://www.fbi.gov/ucr/hc2006/index.html on November 30, 2007.

Feldblum, M. (2000). "Managing Membership: New Trends in Citizenship and Nationality Policy." In D. B. Klusmeyer and T. A. Aleinikoff (Eds.), *From Migrants to Citizens: Membership in a Changing World* (pp. 475–99). Washington, D.C.: Carnegie Endowment for International Peace.

Fendrich, J. M. (1983). "Race and Ethnic Relations: The Elite Policy Response in Capitalist Societies." *The American Behavioral Scientist, 26(6):* 757–72.

Fernandez, R. E. and G. G. Gonzalez. (2003). *A Century of Chicano History: Empire, Nations and Migration.* New York: Routledge.

Fina, A. D. (2000). "Orientation in Immigrant Narratives: The Role of Ethnicity in the Identification of Characters." *Discourse Studies, 2(2):* 131–57.

Finch, B. K., B. Kolody, and W. A. Vega. (2000). "Perceived Discrimination and Depression among Mexican-Origin Adults in California." *Journal of Health & Social Behavior, 41(3):* 295–313.

Fine, M., R. Jaffe-Walter, P. Pedraza, V. Futch, B. Stoudt. (2007). "Swimming: On Oxygen, Resistance, and Possibility for Immigrant Youth under Siege." *Anthropology & Education Quarterly, 38(1):* 76–96.

Flores, L. A. (2003). "Constructing Rhetorical Borders: Peons, Illegal Aliens, and Competing Narratives of Immigration." *Critical Studies in Media Communication, 20(4):* 362–87.

Flores, L. Y., and E. M. Obasi. (2005). "Mentor's Influence on Mexican American Students' Career and Educational Development." *Journal of Multicultural Counseling & Development, 33(3):* 146–64.

Flores, W. V., and R. Benmayor. (1997). "Constructing Cultural Citizenship." In W. V. Flores and R. Benmayor (Eds.), *Latino Cultural Citizenship* (pp. 1–26). Boston: Beacon Press.

Flores-Crespo, P. (2007). "Ethnicity, Identity and Educational Achievement in Mexico." *International Journal of Educational Development, 27(3):* 331–39.

Fong, R. (Ed.). (2004). *Culturally Competent Practice with Immigrant and Refugee Children and Families*. New York: Guilford Press.

Forbes, J. D. (1964). *The Indian in America's Past*. Englewood Cliffs, NJ: Prentice-Hall.

Ford, D. Y. (2005). "Recruiting and Retaining Gifted Students from Diverse Ethnic, Cultural, and Language Groups." In J. A. Banks and C. A. McGee Banks (Eds.), *Multicultural Education: Issues and Perspectives* (5th ed., pp. 379–98). Hoboken, NJ: John Wiley and Sons, Inc.

Fordham, F., and J. Ogbu. (1986). "Black Students' School Success: Coping with the Burden of Acting White." *Urban Review, 18(3)*: 176–206.

Fox, G. (1996). *Hispanic Nation*. Tucson: University of Arizona Press.

Francaviglia, R., and D. W. Richmond (Eds). (2000). *Dueling Eagles: Reinterpreting the U.S.–Mexican War, 1846–1848*. Fort Worth: Texas Christian University Press.

Freire, P. (1997). *Mentoring the Mentor: A Critical Dialogue with Paulo Freire*. New York: Peter Lang.

——. (1996). *Letters to Cristina. Reflections on My Life and Work*. New York: Routledge.

——. (1970). *Pedagogy of the Oppressed* (trans. M. Bergman Ramos). New York: Continuum.

Friedman, J. (1992). "The Past in the Future: History and the Politics of Identity." *American Anthropologist, 94(4)*: 837–59.

Fry, R. (2002). *Latinos in Higher Education: Many Enroll, Too Few Graduate*. A Pew Hispanic Center Report. Washington, D.C.: Pew Hispanic Center. Retrieved from http://pewhispanic.org/files/reports/11.pdf on March 28, 2010.

Fuentes, C. (2004). "Huntington and the Mask of Racism." *NPQ: New Perspectives Quarterly, 21(2)*: 77–81.

Gabusi, J. (2005). Vice Chancellor for Government and External Relations at Pima Community College District in Tucson, Arizona. Personal conversation, February 1, 2005.

Galindo, R., C. Medina, and X. Chávez. (2005). "Dual Sources of Influence on Latino Political Identity: Mexico's Dual Nationality Policy and the Dream Act." *Texas Hispanic Journal of Law & Policy, 11(1)*: 74–98.

Gándara, P. C. (1995). *Over the Ivy Walls: The Educational Mobility of Low-Income Chicanos*. Albany, NY: State University of New York Press.

Gans, J. (2007). *The Economic Impact of Immigrants in Arizona*. Report commissioned by the Thomas R. Brown Foundations. Tucson: Udall Center for Studies in Public Policy at The University of Arizona.

——. (2006). *A Primer on U.S. Immigration in a Global Economy*. Immigration Policy Program at the Udall Center for Studies in Public Policy. Tucson: Udall Center for Studies in Public Policy, The University of Arizona.

García, E. E. (1999). "Chicanos/as in the United States: Language, Bilingual Education, and Achievement." In J. F. Moreno (Ed.), *The Elusive Quest for Equality* (pp. 141–68). Cambridge, MA: Harvard Educational Review.

García, J. L. A. (2004). "Three Sites for Racism: Social Structures, Valuings, and Vice." In M. P. Levine and T. Pataki (Eds.), *Racism in Mind* (pp. 35–55). Ithaca, NY: Cornell University Press.

García, M. T. (1995). *Memories of Chicano History: The Life and Narrative of Bert Corona*. Berkeley, CA: University of California Press.

Garza, E., P. Reyes, and E. T. Trueba. (2004). *Resiliency and Success: Migrant Children in the United States*. Boulder, CO: Paradigm Publishers.

Gawronski, D. (2010). *An Introduction to Arizona History and Government* (10th ed.). New York: Learning Solutions.

Gecas, V. (1973). "Self-Conceptions of Migrant and Settled Mexican Americans." *Social Science Quarterly (Southwestern Social Sciences Association), 54(3)*: 579–95.

Gibson, M. A. (2003, July). "Improving Graduation Outcomes for Migrant Students." *ERIC Digest*. Charleston, WV: ERIC Clearinghouse on Rural Education and Small Schools. Retrieved from http://www.ericdigests.org/2004-1/outcomes.htm on May 18, 2008.

———. (1998). "Promoting Academic Success among Immigrant Students: Is Acculturation the Issue?" *Educational Policy, 12(6)*: 615–33.

Gibson, M. A., and L. F. Bejínez. (2002). "Dropout Prevention: How Migrant Education Supports Mexican Youth." *Journal of Latinos and Education, 1(3)*: 155–75.

Gibson, M. A., and J. Ogbu. (1991). *Minority Status and Schooling: A Comparative Study of Immigrants and Involuntary Minorities*. New York: Garland.

Giddings, J. R. (1853). *Speeches in Congress (1841–1852)*. Cambridge, MA: J. P. Jewett and Company.

Gillborn, D. (2006). "Critical Race Theory and Education: Racism and Anti-Racism in Educational Theory and Praxis." *Discourse: Studies in the Cultural Politics of Education, 27(1)*: 11–32.

———. (2005). "Education Policy as an Act of White Supremacy: Whiteness, Critical Race Theory and Education Reform." *Journal of Education Policy, 20(4)*: 485–505.

———. (1998). "Racism and the politics of qualitative research: learning from controversy and critique." In P. Connolly and B. Troyna (Eds.), *Researching Racism in Education*. Buckingham, PA: Open University Press.

———. (1995). *Racism and Antiracism in Real Schools: Theory, Policy, Practice*. Philadelphia, PA: Open University Press.

Gillborn, D., and H. S. Mirza. (2000). *Educational Inequality. Mapping Race, Class and Gender: A Synthesis of Research Evidence*. London: Office for Standards in Education. Retrieved from http://www.ofsted.gov.uk on October 14, 2006.

Gilory, P. (2000). *Beyond Race: Imagining Political Culture Beyond the Color Line*. Cambridge, MA: Belknap Press.

Glaser, B. G., and A. L. Strauss. (1967). *The Discovery of Grounded Theory: Strategies for Qualitative Research*. New York: Aldine.

Glick, J. E., and M. J. White. (2004). "Post-Secondary School Participation of Immigrant and Native Youth: The Role of Familial Resources and Educational Expectations." *Social Science Research 33(2)*: 272–99.

Goggin, J. A. (1984). *Carter G. Woodson and the Movement to Promote Black History* (unpublished doctoral dissertation). University of Rochester, Rochester, New York.

Gold, S. (2004). "From Jim Crow to Racial Hegemony: Evolving Explanations of Racial Hierarchy." *Ethnic & Racial Studies, 27(6)*: 951–68.

Goldberg, D. T. (2002). *The Racial State*. Oxford, UK: Blackwell Publishers.

Gonzales, M. G. (2000). *Mexicanos: A History of Mexicans in the United States*. Bloomington: Indiana University Press.

González de Bustamante, C. (2010, June 3). "Public Needs to Know Fact from Fiction about Undocumented Migrants." *The Arizona Daily Star.* Retrieved from http://azstarnet.com/news/opinion/article_368f7d45-450d-5942-901c-04295f426542.html on July 11, 2011.

Gonzáles, N. A., L. E. Dumka, J. Deardorff, S. J. Carter, and A. McCray. (2004). "Preventing Poor Mental Health and School Dropout of Mexican American Adolescents Following the Transition to Junior High School." *Journal of Adolescent Research, 19(1):* 113–31.Gonzalez, G. G. (2001). "The Mexican Problem: Empire, Public Policy, and the Education of Mexican Immigrants, 1880-1930." *Aztlán, 26(2):* 199-207.

——. (1990). *Chicano Education in the Era of Segregation.* Cranbury, NJ: Associated University Presses.

González, J. (2006). *Life Along the Border: A Landmark Tejana Thesis.* College Station: Texas A&M University Press.

Gonzalez, M. L., A. H. Macias, and J. V. Tinajero. (1998). *Educating Latino Students.* Lancaster, MI: Technomic Publishing.

González, N. (2001). *I Am My Language: Discourse of Women and Children in the Borderlands.* Tucson: The University of Arizona Press.

Gorman, A. (2006, Apr 17). "Here Illegally, but Choosing to Pay Taxes, Some Undocumented Workers Hope That by Establishing a Record of Their Time in the United States, It Will Be Easier to Gain Citizenship Later." *Los Angeles Times,* B1.

Grant, E. (2005). *Cumulative Advantage: A New Look at the Effect of Family Social Class on Children's Educational Achievement and the Black-White Achievement Gap* (unpublished doctoral dissertation). Palo Alto, California: Stanford University.

Grant, U. S. (1995/1885). *Personal Memoirs of U. S. Grant.* Mineola, NY: Courier Dover Publications.

Grogger, J., and S. J. Trejo. (2002). *Falling Behind or Moving Up? The Intergenerational Progress of Mexican Americans* (A Report of the Public Policy Institute of California). San Francisco, CA: Public Policy Institute of California. Retrieved from http://www.ppic.org/content/pubs/report/R_502JGR.pdf on may 4, 2009.

Groody, G. D. (2000). *Corazón y Conversión: The Dynamics of Mexican Immigration, Christian Spirituality and Human Transformation* (unpublished doctoral dissertation). Graduate Theological Union, Berkeley, California.

Grzywacz, J. G., S. A. Quandt, T. A. Arcury, and A. Marín. (2005). "The Work-Family Challenge and Mental Health." *Community, Work & Family, 8(3):* 271-79.

Gutiérrez, D. G. (2004). *The Columbia History of Latinos in the United States since 1960.* New York: Columbia University Press

——. (1999). "Migration, Emergent Ethnicity, and the 'Third Space': The Shifting Politics of Nationalism in Greater Mexico." *Journal of American History, 86(2):* 481-517.

Guzman, R. (1969). *Mexican-American Casualties in Vietnam.* Santa Cruz, CA: Merrill College.

Hall, T., and Sutton, A. (2002). *Visa Tracking* (policy brief). New York: The Century Foundation. Retrieved from http://www.tcf.org/Publications/HomelandSecurity/visatracking.pdf on August 12, 2006.

Haney-López, I. F. (2003). *Racism on Trial: The Chicano Fight for Justice.* Boston, MA: President and Fellows of Harvard College.

——. (2001). "Protest, Repression, and Race: Legal Violence and the Chicano Movement." *University of Pennsylvania Law Review, 150(1):* 205-44.

Hanson, G. H. (2005). *Why Does Immigration Divide America?: Public Finance And Political Opposition to Open Borders*. Washington, D.C.: Institute for International Economics.

Harrison, R. A. (1994). *Mexicans in Western Motion Pictures: A Historical Study on Racism, 1894–1952* (unpublished doctoral dissertation). California State University, Fresno.

Hatch, J. A., and R. Wisniewski. (2003). "Life History and Narrative: Questions, Issues, and Exemplary Works." In J. A. Hatch and R. Wisniewski (Eds.), *Life History and Narrative* (Qualitative Studies Series, vol. 1, pp. 113-36). Great Britain: Burgess Science Press.

Hayes-Bautista, D. (1997). *The Health Status of Latinos in California*. Woodlands Hills, CA: The California Endowment & California Health Care Foundation.Heater, D. (1999). *What Is Citizenship?* Cambridge, UK: Polity Press.

Hebel, S. (2007a). "Arizona's Colleges Are in the Crosshairs of Efforts to Curb Illegal Immigration." *The Chronicle of Higher Education, 54(10)*: A15.

——. (2007b). "The Graduation Gap." *The Chronicle of Higher Education, 53(29)*: A20.

Hedges, C. (2010, November 13). "Chris Hedges: The Death of the Liberal Class." Interviewed by Laura Flanders. GRITtv.org Retrieved from http://www.grittv.org/2010/11/13/chris-hedges-the-death-of-the-liberal-class on February 2, 2011.

Hernandez, C. (1995). *LULAC: The History of a Grass Roots Organization and Its Influence on Educational Policies, 1929–1983* (unpublished doctoral dissertation). Loyola University.

Hernández, S. (2001). "The Legacy of the Treaty of Guadalupe Hidalgo on Tejanos' Land." *Journal of Popular Culture, 35(2)*: 101–09.

Hil, R. (2005). "Life Lottery." *New Internationalist, 378(May)*: 8.

Hill, S. (2006). "Purity and Danger on the U.S–Mexico Border, 1991-1994." *South Atlantic Quarterly, 105(4)*: 777–99.

Hill, T. (2011, March 21). "Teacher's Letter to Sen. Russell Pearce." *The Arizona Republic*. Retrieved from http://www.azcentral.com/community/glendale/articles/2011/03/21/20110321arizona-teacher-letter-to-russell-pearce.html on April 5, 2011.

Hing, B. O. (2006). *Deporting Our Souls: Values, Morality, and Immigration Policy*. Cambridge, New York: Cambridge University Press.

Hinojosa-Ojeda, R. (2010). *Raising the Floor for American Workers. The Economic Benefits of Comprehensive Immigration Reform*. A report of the Immigration Policy Center and the Center for American Progress. Washington, D.C.: Immigration Policy Center and Center for American Progress.

——. (2003, October). *Transnational Migration, Remittances and Development in North America: Globalization Lessons from the Oaxa California Transnational Village/Community Modeling Project*. Paper presented at the Conference on Remittances as a Development Tool in Mexico, Mexico City (October). Sponsored by Multilateral Investment Fund (MIF) of the Inter-American Development Bank (IDB).

——. (2001, August 29). *Comprehensive Migration Policy Reform in North America: The Key to Sustainable and Equitable Economic Integration*. A publication of the North American Integration and Development Center, University of California, School of Policy and Social Research. Los Angeles, CA: North American Integration and Development Center, University of California.

Hiott, A., J. G. Grzywacz, T. A. Arcury, and S. A. Quandt. (2006). "Gender Differences in Anxiety and Depression among Immigrant Latinos." *Families, Systems & Health: The Journal of Collaborative Family Health Care, 24(2)*: 137–46.

Hirsch, J. (2005, December 5). "Picking a Battle over Shortage of Farmworkers. As Some Winter Crops May Be Left to Rot, Farm Advocates Lobby for Immigration Reform." *Los Angeles Times*, p. C1.

Hoefer, M., N. Rytina, and B. C. Baker. (2010). *Estimates of the Unauthorized Immigrant Population Residing in the United States: January 2010*. A report of the Department of Homeland Security, Office of Immigration Statistics. Washington, D.C.: DHS, Office of Immigration Statistics.

——. (2009). *Estimates of the Unauthorized Immigrant Population Residing in the United States: January 2008*. A report of the Department of Homeland Security, Office of Immigration Statistics. Washington, D.C.: DHS, Office of Immigration Statistics.

Holguín-Cuádraz, G. (2006). "Myths and the 'Politics of Exceptionality': Interpreting Chicana/o Narratives of Achievement." *Oral History Review, 33 (1)*: 83–105.

Holleran, L. K. (2003). "Mexican American Youth of the Southwest Borderlands: Perceptions of Ethnicity, Acculturation and Race." *Hispanic Journal of Behavioral Science, 25(3)*: 352–69.

Hondagneu-Sotelo, P. (1994). "Regulating the Unregulated?: Domestic Workers' Social Networks." *Social Problems, 41(1)*: 50–64.

hooks, b (1989) *Talking back: thinking feminist, thinking black*, Toronto: Between the Lines.

hooks, bell. (1994). *Outlaw Culture: Resisting Representation*. New York: Routledge.

Hovey, J. D. (2000). "Psychosocial Predictors of Acculturative Stress in Mexican Immigrants." *Journal of Psychology, 134(5)*: 490–512.

Huffstutter, P. J. (2006, May 11). "Putting a Roof over Illegal Immigrants, A State Program in Illinois Helps Migrants Get Mortgages." *Los Angeles Times*, A21.

Huntington, S. P. (2004a). "The Hispanic Challenge." *Foreign Policy 141(March/April)*: 30–45.

——. (2004b). *Who Are We? The Challenges to America's National Identity*. New York: Simon & Schuster.

Hurtado, A. (1997). "Understanding Multiple Group Identities: Inserting Women into Cultural Transformations." *Journal of Social Issues, 53(2)*: 299–328.

Hurtado, A., P. Gurin, and T. Peng. (1994). "Social Identities—A Framework for Studying the Adaptations of Immigrants and Ethnics: The Adaptations of Mexicans in the United States." *Social Problems, 41(1)*: 129–151.

Iglesias, N. (2003). "Border Representations. Border Cinema and Independent Video." In M. Dear (Ed.), *Postborder City: Cultural Spaces of Bajalta California* (pp. 183–213). New York: Routledge.

Immigration Policy Center. (2011, April 18). "Unauthorized Immigrants Pay Taxes, Too. Estimates of the State and Local Taxes Paid by Unauthorized Immigrant Households" [online article]. Washington, D.C.: American Immigration Council. Retrieved from http://immigrationpolicy.org/just-facts/unauthorized-immigrants-pay-taxes-too on April 20, 2011.

——. (2010, June 22). "Arizona's Punishment Doesn't Fit the Crime: Studies Show Decrease in Arizona Crime Rates over Time." A fact sheet of the Immigration Policy Center. Washington, D.C.: American Immigration Council.

impreMedia. (2011). "Latino Voters Concerned About Costs of Higher Education Support Variety of Non-Partisan Solutions." impreMedia.com press release. Retrieved from http://www.impremedia.com/press/pr20110818_impremedia_latino_decisions_political.php on August 20, 2011.

Institute of International Education. (2010). "Open Doors 2010 Fast Facts." From the *Open Doors Report on International Education Exchange.* Retrieved from http://www.iie.org/Research-and-Publications/Research-Projects/~/media/Files/Corporate/Open-Doors/Fast-Facts/Fast%20Facts%202010.ashx on October 22, 2011.

Instituto Nacional de Estadística Geografía e Informática (INEGI). (2006a). *Encuesta Nacional de Ingreso Gasto de los Hogares 2000–2005.* México. Retrieved from http://www.inegi.gob.mx/ on November 8, 2006.

———. (2006b). "Number of Maquiladoras and Employment" [online article]. Retrieved from http://www.twinplantnews.com/Maquila%20Scoreboard.htm on September 4, 2007.

Ireland, S. (2001). "Translating Immigrant Identities in Mounsi's *Territoire d' outré-ville.*" In S. Ireland and P. J. Proulx (Eds.), *Immigrant Narratives in Contemporary France* (Contributions to the Study of World Literature, pp. 69–82). Westport, CT: Greenwood Publishing Group.

Jacobo, J. R. (2004). *Los Braceros: Memories of Bracero Workers, 1942–1964.* San Diego, CA: Southern Border Press.

Jay, M. (2003). "Critical Race Theory, Multicultural Education, and the Hidden Curriculum of Hegemony." *Multicultural Perspectives, 5(4)*: 3–9.

Jennings, J. F. (1987). "The Sputnik of the Eighties." *Phi Delta Kappan, (69)2*: 104–09.

Jiménez, M. (2009). *Humanitarian Crisis: Migrant Deaths at the U.S.-Mexico Border.* Report prepared by the American Civil Liberties Union–San Diego and Mexico's National Commission of Human Rights. San Diego and Mexico City. Retrieved from http://www.aclu.org/files/pdfs/immigrants/humanitariancrisisreport.pdf on December 20, 2010.

Johnson, K. R. (2004). *Hernandez v. Texas: Legacies of Justice and Injustice* (UC–Davis Law, Legal Studies Research Paper No. 19). Paper presented at *Hernandez v. Texas* at Fifty Conference, University of Houston Law Center (November 18–19).

———. (2003). *The "Huddled Masses" Myth: Immigration and Civil Rights.* Philadelphia: Temple University Press.

Johnston, P. (2001). "The Emergence of Transnational Citizenship among Mexican Immigrants in California." In T. A. Aleinikoff and D. B. Klusmeyer (Eds.), *Citizenship Today: Global Perspectives and Practices* (pp. 253–77). New York: International Migration Publications from the Carnegie Endowment for International Peace.

Joppke, C. (1999). *Immigration and the Nation-State. The United States, Germany, and Great Britain.* New York: Oxford University Press.

Jordan, M. (2010, April 30). "Arizona Grades Teachers on Fluency." *The Wall Street Journal.* Retrieved from http://online.wsj.com/article/SB10001424052748703572504575 2138832764275 28.html on April 2, 2011.

———. (2006, October 11). "U.S. Banks Woo Migrants, Legal or Otherwise." *The Wall Street Journal (Eastern Edition)*, p. B1.

Kao, G., and J. S. Thompson. (2003). "Racial and Ethnic Stratification in Educational Achievement and Attainment." *Annual Review of Sociology, 29*: 417–43.

Kaplan, A. (2004). "Violent Belongings and the Question of Empire Today. Presidential Address to the American Studies Association." *American Quarterly, 56(1)*: 1–18.

Katrandjian, O. (2011, June 19). "John McCain's Illegal Immigrants Started Arizona Wildfires Disputed by Forest Service." *ABC World News*. Retrieved from http://abcnews.go.com/US /john-mccain-claims-illegal-immigrants-started-arizona-wildfires/story?id=13879568 on August 31, 2011.

Kaufka Walts, J. (2010). "Letter to Senators Richard J. Durbin and Mark S. Kirk." The Center for the Human Rights of Children, Loyola University Chicago. Retrieved from :http://www.luc.edu/chrc/pdfs/DREAM_letterhead.pdf on May 24 2011.

Kay-Oliphant, E. J. (2005). "Considering Race in American Immigration Jurisprudence." *Emory Law Journal, 54(1)*: 681–719.

Kelley, D. R. (2006). *Frontiers of History: Historical Inquiry in the Twentieth Century*. New Haven, CT: Yale University Press.

Kennedy, R. (2002). *Psychoanalysis, History and Subjectivity*. New York: Brunner-Routledge.

Kent-Monning, L. (2002). "The Border Versus Ivan Santos." *Qualitative Studies in Education, 15(1)*: 85–97.

Kern, S. (2003). *The Culture of Time and Space, 1880–1918* (2nd ed). Cambridge, MA: Harvard University Press.

Kich, G. K. (1992). "The Developmental Process of Asserting a Biracial, Bicultural Identity." In M. P. P. Root (Ed.), *Racially Mixed People in America* (pp. 304–17). Newbury Park, CA: Sage Publications.

Kiefer, M., and R. Ruelas. (2011, April 13). "Neighbor Found Guilty in Man's Shooting Death. *Tucson Citizen*. Retrieved from http://tucsoncitizen.com/arizona-news/2011/04/13/ neighbor-found-guilty-in-mans-shooting-death on April 15, 2011.

King, T. (1993). *Green Grass, Running Water*. New York: Bantam Books.

Kittrie, O. F. (2006). "Federalism, Deportation, and Crime Victims Afraid to Call the Police." *Iowa Law Review, 91*: 1449–1508.

Klusmeyer, D. B., and T. A. Aleinikoff (Eds.). (2000). *From Migrants to Citizens: Membership in a Changing World*. New York: Carnegie Endowment for International Peace.

Konradi, A., and M. Schmidt. (2004). *Reading Between The Lines: Toward an Understanding of Current Social Problems* (3rd ed.). New York: McGraw-Hill.

Kornblum, W. (1994). *Sociology in a Changing World* (3rd ed.). Fort Worth, TX: Harcourt Brace College Publishers.

Kotkin, J. (2010). *The Next Hundred Million: America in 2050*. New York: Penguin Press.

Kronholz, J. (2006, September 6). "Immigration Stalemate. Congress's Failure to Resolve Issue Feeds Ire of Activists on Both Sides." *The Wall Street Journal*. Retrieved from http://online.wsj.com/public/article/SB1157503144249545843G3Mt9JBmvFo3sBfeaPxv dBsV7M_20070906.html on January 15, 2008.

Ladson-Billings, G. J. (1999). "Preparing Teachers for Diverse Student Populations. A Critical Race Theory Perspective." *Review of Research in Education, 24*: 211–47.

——. (1998). "Just What Is Critical Race Theory and What's It Doing in a Nice Field Like Education?" *International Journal of Qualitative Studies in Education, 11(1)*: 7–24.

Lamon, W. H. (1895). *Recollections of Abraham Lincoln, 1847–1865*. Chicago: A.C. McClurg and Company.

Landau, S. (2006). "Latino Mercenaries for Bush. (Features)." *Canadian Dimension, 40(2)*: 44–47.

Lane, K. (2002). "Hispanics Enroll in College at High Rates, but Many Fail to Graduate." *Black Issues in Higher Education 19(16)*: 9.

Leavy, P. (2009). "Social Research and the Creative Arts. An Introduction." In P. Leavy (Ed.), *Method Meets Art. Arts-Based Research Practice* (1–24). New York: Guilford.

Ledesma, A. (2002). "Narratives of Undocumented Mexican Immigrants as Chicana/o Acts of Intellectual and Political Responsibility." In A. J. Aldama and N. H. Quiñonez (Eds.), *Decolonial Voices: Chicana and Chicano Cultural Studies in the 21st Century* (pp. 330-54). Bloomington, IN: Indiana University Press.

Lee, M. K. (1983). "Multiculturalism: Educational Perspectives for the 1980s." *Education, 103(4)*: 405-09.

Lee, S. (1996). "Poverty and Violence." *Social Theory & Practice, 22(1)*: 67-82.

Levi, D. E. (1991). "C. L. R. James: A Radical West Indian Vision of American Studies." *American Quarterly, 43(3)*: 486-501.

Lewis, G. B. (1988). "Progress Toward Racial and Sexual Equality in the Federal Civil Service?" *Public Administration Review, 48(3)*: 700-07.

Lichter, D. T., Q. Zhenchao, and M. L. Crowley. (2005). "Child Poverty among Racial Minorities and Immigrants: Explaining Trends and Differentials." *Social Science Quarterly Supplement, 86(1)*: 1037-59.

——. (1988). "Racial Differences in Underemployment in American Cities." *The American Journal of Sociology, 93(4)*: 771-92.

Lincoln, Abraham. (1848, January 12). *Speech on Declaration of War on Mexico.* Washington, D.C.: United States House of Representatives. Retrieved from http://www.lincolnbicentennial.gov on March 7, 2011.

Lincoln, Y., and N. Denzin (2003). "The Revolution of Representation." In Y. S. Lincoln and N. Denzin (Eds.), *Turning Points in Qualitative Research: Tying Knots in a Handkerchief* (17–20). Walnut Creek, CA: AltaMira Press.

Lind, M. (1996). *The Next American Nation: The New Nationalism and the Fourth American Revolution.* New York: Free Press.

Lindauer, O. (1996). "The Archeology of Americanization: Assimilation and Changing Identity of Phoenix Indian School Pupils." *Cultural Resource Management, 9*: 37-41.

London, H. I., and F. A. Rodgers. (1975). *Social Science Theory: Structure and Application.* New York: New York University Press.

López, D. E., and R. D. Stanton-Salazar. (2001). "Mexican-Americans: A Second Generation at Risk." In R. G. Rumbaut and A. Portes (Eds.), *Ethnicities: Children of Immigrants in America* (pp. 57-90). Berkeley: University of California Press.

López, I. H. (2004). *Racism on Trial: The Chicano Fight for Justice.* Boston: Belknap Press of Harvard University Press.

Lopez, M. H., R. Morin, and P. Taylor. (2010). *Illegal Immigration Backlash Worries, Divides Latinos.* A Pew Hispanic Center report. Washington, D.C.: Pew Hispanic Center. Retrieved from http://pewhispanic.org/reports/report.php?ReportID=128 on September 11, 2009.

Love, B. J. (2004). "Brown Plus 50 Counter-Story Telling: A Critical Race Theory of the 'Majoritarian Achievement Gap' Story." *Equity & Excellence in Education, 37(3)*: 227-46.

Lowell, B. L., and R. Suro. (2002). *The Improving Educational Profile of Latino Immigrants*. A Pew Hispanic Center report. Washington, D.C.: Pew Hispanic Center. Retrieved from http://pewhispanic.org /reports/report.php?ReportID=14 on January 24, 2007.

Lowell, B. L., J. Teachman, and Z. Jing. (1995). "Unintended Consequences of Immigration Reform: Discrimination and Hispanic Employment." *Demography, 32(4)*: 617–28.

Lucas, J. R., and G. L. Stone. (1994). "Acculturation and Competition among Mexican-Americans: A Reconceptualization." *Hispanic Journal of Behavioral Sciences, 16(2)*: 129–42.

Lucero, H. R. (2004). *Plessy to Brown: Education of Mexican Americans in Arizona Public Schools During the Era of Segregation* (unpublished doctoral dissertation). The University of Arizona, Tucson.

Luna, D. (2004). *When "Inclusion" Means Exclusion: The Educational Experiences of First- and Second-Generation Mexican Immigrant Females and Their Parents' Reflections*. Paper presented at the American Educational Research Association 2004 Annual Meeting. San Diego, CA (April 16).

Lunsford, A. A. (1999). "Toward a Mestiza Rhetoric: Gloria Anzaldúa on Composition and Postcoloniality." In G. A. Olson and L. Worsham (Eds.), *Race, Rhetoric, and the Postcolonial* (pp. 43–80). Albany: State University of New York Press.

Macedo, D., and P. Gounari. (2006). "Globalization and the Unleashing of New Racism: An Introduction." In D. Macedo and P. Gounari (Eds.), *The Globalization of Racism* (Series in Critical Narrative, pp. 3–35). Boulder, CO: Paradigm Publishers.

Macedo, D. (2000). "The Colonialism of the English Only Movement." *Educational Researcher, 29(3)*: 15–24.

Madison, D. S. (2005). *Critical Ethnography. Methods, Ethics and Performance*. Thousand Oaks, CA: Sage Publications.

Malanczuk, P., and M. B. Akehurst. (1997). *Akehurst's Modern Introduction to International Law* (7th rev. ed.). New York: Routledge.

Malkin, M. (2002). *Invasion: How America Still Welcomes Terrorists, Criminals, and Other Foreign Menaces to Our Shores*. Washington, D.C.: Regnery Publishing.

Mariscal, J. (2005). "Homeland Security, Militarism, and the Future of Latinos and Latinas in the United States." *Radical History Review, 93(Fall)*: 39–52.

Markovitz, J. (2004). *Legacies of Lynching: Racial Violence and Memory*. Minneapolis: University of Minnesota Press.

Marshall, C., and G. B. Rossman. (2006). *Designing Qualitative Research*. Thousand Oaks, CA: Sage Publications.

Marshall, T. H. (1998). "Citizenship and Social Class." In G. Shafir (Ed.), *The Citizenship Debates: A Reader* (93–112). Minneapolis: University of Minnesota Press.

Martin, E., and E. Gerber. (2005). "Results of Recent Methodological Research on the Hispanic Origin and Race Questions" (research report). Washington, D.C.: U.S. Bureau of the Census Statistical Research Division. Retrieved from http://www.census.gov/srd/papers/pdf/rsm2005-04.pdf on November 25, 2006.

Martinez, T. A. (1999). "Storytelling as Oppositional Culture: Race, Class, and Gender in the Borderlands." *Race, Gender & Class, 6(3)*: 33–51.

Marx, S. (2006). *Revealing the Invisible: Confronting Passive Racism in Teacher Education*. New York: Routledge.

Massey, D. S. (2005). "Five Myths about Immigration: Common Misconceptions Underlying U.S. Border-Enforcement Policy." *Immigration Policy in Focus, 4(6)*: 1–11.

Massey, D. S., J. Durand, and N. J. Malone. (2004). *Beyond Smoke and Mirrors: Mexican Immigration in an Era of Economic Integration.* New York: Russell Sage Foundation.

Massey, D. S., and K.E. Espinosa. (1997). "What's Driving Mexico-U.S. Migration? A Theoretical, Empirical, and Policy Analysis." *American Journal of Sociology, 102(4)*: 939–99.

Matsuda, M. J., C. R. Lawrence, R. Delgado, and K. W. Crenshaw. (1993). *Words That Wound: Critical Race Theory, Assaultive Speech, and the First Amendment.* Boulder, CO: Westview.

McCollum, P. (1998, March 15). "Parental Involvement in Bilingual Education." *NABE News,* pp. 41–42.

McGlynn, A. P. (1999, March 26). "Improving the Future for Hispanic Americans." *Hispanic Outlook,* pp. 23–25

McGuire, S., and K. Martin. (2007). "Fractured Migrant Families: Paradoxes of Hope and Devastation." *Family & Community Health. Immigrant/Migrant Health Issues. 30(3)*: 178–88.

McKenna, T. (1988). "'Immigrants in Our Own Land': A Chicano Literature Review and Pedagogical Assessment." *ADE Bulletin, 91(winter)*: 30–38. Retrieved at http://www.mla.org/ade/bulletin on July 19, 2006.

McKenzie, P. (2004). *The Mexican Texans.* San Antonio: University of Texas Institute of Texan Cultures.

McKinley Jr., J. C. (2005, March 22). "Mexican Pride and Death in U.S. Service." *New York Times,* A6.

McWhirter, E. H., D. M. Torres, S. Salgado, and M. Valdez. (2007). "Perceived Barriers and Postsecondary Plans in Mexican American and White Adolescents." *Journal of Career Assessment, 15(1)*: 119–38. Thousand Oaks, CA: Sage Publications.

Meed, D. V. (2002). *The Mexican War 1846–1848.* Oxford, UK: Osprey Publishing.

Meeks, E. V. (2007). *Border Citizens: The Making of Indians, Mexicans, and Anglos in Arizona.* Austin: University of Texas Press.

Meier, M. S., and M. Gutierrez. (2000). *Encyclopedia of the Mexican American Civil Rights Movement.* Westport, CT: Greenwood Press.

Meier, M. S., and F. Ribera. (1993). *Mexican Americans and American Mexicans: From Conquistadors to Chicanos.* New York: Hill and Wang.

Melcher, Mary. (1999). "'This Is Not Right': Rural Arizona Women Challenge Segregation and Ethnic Division." *Frontiers: A Journal of Women Studies, 20(2)*: 190–215.

Menchaca, M. (1993). "Chicano Indianism: A Historical Account of Racial Repression in the United States." *American Ethnologist, 20(3)*: 583–603.

Méndez-Negrete, J., L. P. Saldaña, and A. Vega. (2006). "Can a Culturally Informed After-School Curriculum Make a Difference in Teen Pregnancy Prevention? Preliminary Evidence in the Case of San Antonio's Escuelitas." *Families in Society, 87(1)*: 95–104.

Merriam, S. B., J. Johnson-Bailey, M. Y. Lee, Y. Kee, G. Ntseane, and M. Muhamad. (2001). "Power and Positionality: Negotiating Insider/Outsider Status Within and Across Cultures." *International Journal of Lifelong Education, 20(5)*: 405–16.

Meyer, M. C., and W. H. Beezley (Eds.). (2000). *The Oxford History of Mexico.* New York: Oxford University Press.

Michelson, M. R. (2001). "The Effect of National Mood on Mexican American Political Opinion." *Hispanic Journal of Behavioral Sciences, 23(1):* 57-70.

Migration Information Source. (2005, December 1). "Top 10 Migration Issues of 2005." (Issue 7: Extreme Measures: What Migrants Are Willing to Do to Get in and What Governments Will Do to Stop Them). A publication of the Migration Policy Institute. Retrieved from http://www.migrationinformation.org/Feature/display.cfm?id=356 on December 22, 2005.

Miller, T. (2010). "Arizona, the Anti-Immigrant Laboratory." NACLA Report. New York: North American Congress on Latin America (NACLA). Retrieved from https://nacla.org/node/6681 on March 1, 2011.

Mills, C. W. (2003). *From Class to Race. Essays in White Marxism and Black Radicalism.* Lanham, MD: Rowman & Littlefield Publishers, Inc.

Misztal, B. A. (2003). *Theories of Social Remembering.* Philadelphia, PA: Open University Press.

Mize Jr., R. L. (2006). "Mexican Contract Workers and the U.S. Capitalist Agricultural Labor Process: The Formative Era, 1942-1964." *Rural Sociology, 71(1):* 85-108.

Mohanty, S. A., S. Woolhandler, D. U. Himmelstein, S. Pati, O. Carrasquillo, and D. H. Bor. (2005). "Health Care Expenditures of Immigrants in the United States: A Nationally Representative Analysis." *American Journal of Public Health, 95:* 8: 1431-38.

Molineu, H. (1990). *U.S. Policy Toward Latin America: From Regionalism to Globalism* (2nd ed.). Boulder, CO: Westview Press.

Money, J. (1999). *Fences and Neighbors: The Political Geography of Immigration Control.* Ithaca, NY: Cornell University Press.

Monroe, R. D. (2000). "Congress and the Mexican War, 1844-1849." Abraham Lincoln Historical Digitization Project, Northern Illinois University Libraries. Retrieved from http://lincoln.lib.niu.edu/biography4.html on July 14, 2005.

Montoya, A. G. (2006). *Successful Latino Students: A Study of Five Mexican American Families* (unpublished doctoral dissertation). Arizona State University, Phoenix.

Moody, K. (2007). "Harvest of Empire." *Against the Current, 22(1):* 10-14.

Morales, E. (2002). *Living in Spanglish: The Search for Latino Identity in America.* New York: St. Martin's Press.

Morawetz, N. (2006). *The Invisible Border: Restrictions on Short-Term Travel for Noncitizens* (New York University Public Law and Legal Theory Working Paper No. 37). New York: New York University School of Law. Retrieved from http://lsr.nellco.org/cgi/viewcontent.cgi?article=1036&context=nyu/plltwp on June 12, 2007.

Moreno, J. F. (1999). *The Elusive Quest for Equality: 150 Years of Chicano/Chicana Education.* Cambridge, MA: Harvard Educational Review.

Morgan Quitno Press. (2006). *Education State Rankings 2006-2007.* Washington, D.C.: Morgan Quitno Press. Retrieved from http://www.morganquitno.com/edrank.htm on March 19, 2011.

Morris, S. D., and J. Passé-Smith. (2001). "What a Difference a Crisis Makes: NAFTA, Mexico, and the United States." *Latin American Perspectives, 118(28-3):* 124-49.

Mowry, S. (1859). "Arizona and Sonora." *Journal of the American Geographical and Statistical Society* (March): 66-75.

Mullaly, B. (1997). *Structural Social Work: Ideology, Theory, and Practice* (2nd ed.). Toronto, Canada: Oxford University Press.

Murguia, E., and E. E. Telles. (1996). "Phenotype and Schooling among Mexican-Americans." *Sociology of Education, 69(4):* 276–89.

NACLA (North American Congress on Latin America). (1992). "Myth of Racial Democracy in Latin America and the Caribbean: An Interpretation." *NACLA Report on the Americas, 25(4):* 40–45.

National Center for Public Policy and Higher Education. (2006). *Measuring Up: 2006. The National Report Card on Higher Education.* San Jose, CA: National Center for Public Policy and Higher Education. Retrieved from http://measuringup.highereducation.org on December 5, 2007.

National Geographic. (2010). *National Geographic Style Manual.* Washington, D.C.: National Geographic Society. Retrieved from http://stylemanual.ngs.org on December 13, 2010

Nearman, C. M. (2002). *No Class Multiculturalism: Contradictions and Evasions in Education* (unpublished doctoral dissertation). Greensboro: The University of North Carolina at Greensboro.

Nebeker, K. C. (1998). "Critical Race Theory: A White Graduate Student's Struggle with the Growing Area of Scholarship." *International Journal of Qualitative Studies in Education, 11(1):* 25–41.

Neubeck, K. (2001). *Welfare Racism: Playing the Race Card Against America's Poor.* New York: Routledge.

New York Times, The. (2011, October 20). "It's What They Asked for." Editorial. *The New York Times,* p. A28

Nieto, S. (1996). *Affirming Diversity* (2nd ed.). White Plains, NY: Longman.

Nostrand, R. L. (1975). "Mexican Americans Circa 1850." *Annals of the Association of American Geographers, 65(3):* 378–90.

Nugent, D. (1993, April 29). "Inventando las Fronteras. Inventing the Borderlands." *Notes on the Conference: Mythologizing the Border: Visions and Images.* Tucson: University of Arizona.

Obama, B. H. (2007). Barack Obama: Remarks to the National Council of La Raza in Miami (July 22). *The American Presidency Project,* Document Archive. Retrieved from http://www.presidency.ucsb.edu/ws/index.php?pid=77009#ixzz1ct1EfKbJ on August 29, 2011.

Office of the Deputy Assistant Secretary of Defense for Military Manpower and Personnel Policy. (1997). *Hispanics in America's Defense.* Washington, D.C.: DIANE Publishing Company.

Office of the High Commissioner for Human Rights. (2010, May 10). "Arizona: UN experts warn against "'a disturbing legal pattern hostile to ethnic minorities and immigrants'." *United Nations Human Rights.* News and Events. Retrieved from http://www.ohchr.org/en/NewsEvents/Pages/DisplayNews.aspx?NewsID=10035&LangI D=E on September 4, 2011.

Ogbu, J. (1986). "The Consequences of the American Caste System." In U. Neisser (Ed.), *The School Achievement of Minority Children: New Perspectives* (19–56). Hillsdale, NJ: Erlbaum.

O'Neill, M and Bagley, C (1998) Renewed Methodologies for Social Research: Inter-textual representation and praxis as ethnomimesis. Paper presented at the British Sociological Association Conference, University of Edinburgh, April.

O'Neill, M., P. Breatnach, C. Bagley, D. Bourne, and T. Judge. (2002). "Methodologies for Social Research: Ethno-Mimesis as Performative Praxis." *The Sociological Review, (50)1*: 69–88

Oppenheimer, A. (2007, November 6). "Anti-Migrant Hysteria Could Lead to Uprising." *The Arizona Daily Star.* Tucson, Arizona. Retrieved from http://www.azstarnet.com/sn/printDS/210056 on. November 11, 2007.

Orfield, G., and C. Lee. (2005). *Why Segregation Matters: Poverty and Educational Inequality.* Cambridge, MA: Harvard University, The Civil Rights Project. Retrieved from http://www.civilrightsproject.harvard.edu on September 22, 2006.

Orrenius, P., and M. Zavodny. (2005). "Self-Selection among Undocumented Immigrants from Mexico." *Journal of Development Economics, Elsevier, 78(1)*: 215–40.

Ortiz, D. L. (1996). "Male Hispanic High School Dropout Dilemma: Self-Reported Perceptions." *The Journal of Educational Issues of Language Minority Students, 18(Winter)*: 35–47.

O'Sullivan, J. (1995). "Reverse (for) Racism." *National Review, 47(5)*: 6.

Padilla, A. M. (1980). "The Role of Cultural Awareness and Ethnic Loyalty in Acculturation." In A. M. Padilla (Ed.), *Acculturation: Theory, Models and Some New Findings* (pp. 47–84). Boulder, CO: Westview Press.

Padilla, L. M. (2001). "'But You're Not a Dirty Mexican': Internalized Oppression, Latinos & Law." *Texas Hispanic Journal of Law & Policy, 7(1)*: 59–113.

Pansters, W.G. (2005) "Authenticity, hybridity, and difference: debating national identity in twentieth-century Mexico." *Focaal– European Journal of Anthropology* 45: 71–93

Paredes, A. (1995). *A Texas-Mexican Cancionero: Folksongs of the Lower Border.* Austin: University of Texas Press.

Parker, L., D. Deyhle, and S. Villenas. (1999). *Race Is . . . Race Isn't. Critical Race Theory and Qualitative Studies in Education.* Boulder, CO: Westview Press.

Parker, L., and M. Lynn. (2002). "What's Race Got to Do with IT? Critical Race Theory's Conflicts with and Connections to Qualitative Research Methodology and Epistemology." *Qualitative Inquiry, 8(1)*: 7–22.

Parker, L., and D. O. Stovall. (2004). "Actions Following Words: Critical Race Theory Connects to Critical Pedagogy." *Educational Philosophy and Theory, 36(2)*: 167–82.

Passel, J. S. (2005). *Unauthorized Migrants: Numbers and Characteristics.* A Pew Hispanic Center report. Washington, D.C.: Pew Hispanic Center. Retrieved from http://pewhispanic.org/reports/report.php?ReportID=46 on September 12, 2007.

Passel, J. S., and D. Cohn. (2011). *Unauthorized Immigrant Population: National and State Trends, 2010.* A Pew Research Center report. Washington, D.C.: Pew Research Center.

——. (2008). *U.S. Population Projections: 2005–2050.* A Pew Research Center report. Washington, D.C.: Pew Research Center. Retrieved from http://pewhispanic.org/files/reports/85.pdf on April 29, 2010.

Paz, O. (1990). *The Collected Poems of Octavio Paz, 1957–1987: Bilingual Edition* (Trans. E. Weinberger, E. Bishop, P. Blackburn, and L. Kemp.). New York: New Directions Publishing Co.

——. (1982). *Las Peras del Olmo.* Barcelona: Seix Barral.

Pearl, A. (2002). "The Big Picture: Systemic and Institutional Factors in Chicano School Failure and Success." In R. R. Valencia (Ed.), *Chicano School Failure and Success* (2nd ed., pp. 335–64). New York: RoutledgeFalmer.

Perea, J. F. (1992). *Official English Laws, Demography and Distrust: An Essay on American Languages, Cultural Pluralism, and Official English.* The University of Dayton School of Law. Retrieved from http://academic.udayton.edu/race/02rights/engonly1.htm on July 15, 2006.

Perez, L. A. (2011). Interviewed by Ricardo Castro-Salazar after the presentation: "Undocumented Students Speak About Hardships, Tenacity and Perseverance" at *Prepárate: Educating Latinos for the Future of America College Board Conference,* San Antonio, TX (March 10).

Perez, W., R. Espinoza, K. Ramos, H. Coronado, and R. Cortes. (2010). "Civic Engagement Patterns of Undocumented Mexican Students." *Journal of Hispanic Higher Education 9(3):* 245–65.

———. (2009). *Undocumented Students Pursuing the American Dream.* Sterling, VA: Stylus Publishing.

Perin, D., and K. Charron. (2006). "Lights Just Click on Every Day." In T. Bailey and V. Smith Morest, *Defending the Community College Equity Agenda* (pp. 155–94). Baltimore: The Johns Hopkins University Press.

Perreira, K. M., M. V. Chapman, and G. L. Stein. (2006). "Becoming an American Parent: Overcoming Challenges and Finding Strength in a New Immigrant Latino Community." *Journal of Family Issues, 27(10):* 1383–1414.

Pescador Osuna, J. A. (1998). "War Between Mexico and the U.S.A. and the Treaty of Guadalupe Hidalgo of 1848." *Southwestern Journal of Law and Trade in the Americas, 5(1):* 193–99.

Pew Hispanic Center. (2010). "Table 13. Hispanic Population, by State: 2008." In *Statistical Portrait of Hispanics in the United States, 2008.* Washington, D.C.: Pew Research Center. Retrieved from http://pewhispanic.org/factsheets/factsheet.php?FactsheetID=58 on March 26, 2011.

———. (2006a). "Table 10: Hispanic Population by State 2000–2005." In *A Statistical Portrait of Hispanics at Mid-Decade.* Pew Hispanic Center. Retrieved from http://pewhispanic.org/reports/middecade on November 27, 2006.

———. (2006b). *From 200 Million to 300 Million: The Numbers behind Population Growth.* Pew Hispanic Center Reports and Fact Sheets. Retrieved from http://pewhispanic.org/factsheets/factsheet.php?FactsheetID=25 on December 18, 2006.

Pifer, D. (1999). "Small Town Race." *Qualitative Inquiry, 5(4):* 541–62.

Pilkington, A. (2004). "Institutional Racism in the Academy? Comparing the Police and University in Midshire." In I. Law, D. Phillips, and L. Turney (Eds.), *Institutional Racism in Higher Education* (pp. 15–26). London: Trentham Books.

Plath, D. (1990). "Field Notes, Filed Notes, and the Conferring of Note." In R. Sanjek (Ed.), *Fieldnotes.* Ithaca, NY: Cornell University Press.

Ponce, P. A. (2002). *Pioneer Chicana and Chicano Doctorates: An Examination of Their Educational Journey and Success* (unpublished doctoral dissertation). University of California, Los Angeles.

Porter, E. (2005, April 5). "Illegal Immigrants Are Bolstering Social Security with Billions." *The New York Times,* A1.

Portes, A., and R. Rumbaut. (2001). *Legacies: The Story of the Immigrant Second Generation*. New York and Los Angeles: Russell Sage Foundation and University of California Press.

Powers, J. M. (2008). "Forgotten History: Mexican American School Segregation in Arizona from 1900–1951." *Equity & Excellence in Education (41)4*: 467–81.

Powers, M. G., and W. Seltzer. (1998). "Occupational Status and Mobility among Undocumented Immigrants by Gender." *International Migration Review, 32(1)*: 21–55.

PRA. (2002). *Defending Immigrant Rights: An Activist Resource Kit*. Somerville, MA: Political Research Associates. Retrieved from http://www.publiceye.org/ark/immigrants/CriminalIssue.html on July 6, 2009.

Pritchard, J. (2004, March 14). "AP Investigation: Mexican Worker Deaths Rise Sharply Even as Overall U.S. Job Safety Improves." The Associated Press. University of Arizona Online Databases. Lexis-Nexus Academic Universe, University of Arizona Database. Retrieved on December 5, 2006.

Provine, D., and R. Doty. (2011). "The Criminalization of Immigrants as a Racial Project." *Journal of Contemporary Criminal Justice. 27(3)*: 261–277.

Pulido, L. (2007). "A Day Without Immigrants: The Racial and Class Politics of Immigrant Exclusion." *Antipode 39 (1)*: 1–7.

Quiroga, J. (1997). "Hispanic Voices: Is the Press Listening?" In C. E. Rodríguez (Ed.), *Latin Looks: Images of Latinas and Latinos in the U.S. Media*. Boulder, CO: Westview Press.

Raleigh Yow, V. (1994). *Recording Oral History. A Practical Guide for Social Scientists*. London: Sage Publications.

Ramirez, A. Y. F. (2003). "Dismay and Disappointment: Parental Involvement of Latino Immigrant Parents." *Urban Review, 35(2)*: 93–110.

Ramírez, S. (2002). "Borders, Feminism, and Spirituality: Movements in Chicana Aesthetic Revisioning." In A. J. Aldama and N. H. Quiñonez (Eds.), *Decolonial Voices: Chicana and Chicano Cultural Studies in the 21st Century* (223–43). Bloomington, IN: Indiana University Press.

Ramos Cardoso, A. (2007). *Monitoreo de Iniciativas Anti-immigrantes en Arizona*. Presentation for Fundación México by the Mexican Consul for Media and Political Analysis, Tucson, AZ (October 27).

Raymond, R., and M. Sesnowitz. (1983). "Labor Market Discrimination against Mexican American College Graduates." *Southern Economic Journal, 49(4)*: 1122–36.

Ream, R. K. (2005). *Uprooting Children: Mobility, Social Capital, and Mexican-American Underachievement (The New Americans)*. El Paso, TX: LFB Scholarly Publishing.

Redden, E. (2006, November 16). "Racism Rears Its Head." *InsideHigherEd.com*. Retrieved from http://insidehighered.com/news/2006/11/16/racism on January 22, 2007.

Redfield, R., R. Linton, and M. J. Herskovits. (1936). "Memorandum on the Study of Acculturation." *American Anthropologist, 38(1)*: 149–52.

Reeves, J. and A. A. Caldwell. (2011, October 20). "After Alabama Immigration Law, Few Americans Taking Immigrants' Work." *The Huffington Post Business*. Retrieved from http://www.huffingtonpost.com/2011/10/21/after-alabama-immigration-law-few-americans-taking-immigrants-work_n_1023635.html on October 21, 2011.Rendón, A. B. (1996). *Chicano Manifesto*. Berkeley, CA: Ollin & Associates.

Renshon, S. A. (2005). *The 50% American: Immigration and National Identity in an Age of Terror*. Washington, D.C.: Georgetown University Press.

Reyes, P., J. D. Scribner, and A. Paredes-Scribner. (1999). *Lessons from High-Performing Hispanic Schools: Creating Learning Communities* (Critical Issues in Educational Leadership Series). New York: Teachers College Press, Columbia University.

Rhoads, R. A., V. Saenz, and R. Carducci. (2005). "Higher Education Reform as a Social Movement: The Case of Affirmative Action." *Review of Higher Education, 28(2):* 191–220.

Rivas-Rodriguez, M. (Ed.). (2005). *Mexican Americans and World War II.* Austin, TX: University of Texas Press.

Rivera, J. M. (2006). *Emergence of Mexican America: Recovering Stories of Mexican Peoplehood in U.S. Culture.* New York and London: New York University Press.

Robbins, T. (2010, October 6). "Illegal Immigrant Deaths Set Record in Arizona." *Morning Edition.* National Public Radio. Retrieved from http://www.npr.org/templates/story/story.php?storyId=130369998 on February 2, 2011.

Roberts, P. (2000). *Education, Literacy, and Humanization.* Westport, CT: Bergin and Garvey.

Robinson, W. I. (2006). "'Aqui estamos y no nos vamos!' Global Capital and Immigrant Rights." *Race & Class. 48(2):* 77–91.

Rocco, R. (2004). "Transforming Citizenship: Membership, Strategies of Containment, and the Public Sphere in Latino Communities." *Latino Studies, 2(1):* 4–25.

Rodríguez, C. E. (Ed.). (1997). *Latin Looks: Images of Latinas and Latinos in the U.S. Media.* Boulder, CO: Westview Press.

Rodríguez, N., and J. M. Hagan. (2004). "Fractured Families and Communities: Effects of Immigration Reform in Texas, Mexico, and El Salvador." *Latino Studies, 2(3):* 328–51.

Rodríguez, R. (1997). *Justice: A Question of Race.* Tempe, AZ: Bilingual Press.

Rojas, D. A. J. (2001). *The Making of Zoot Suiters in Early 1940s Mexican Los Angeles* (unpublished doctoral dissertation). University of California, Berkeley.

Romero, M. (2006). "Racial Profiling and Immigration Law Enforcement: Rounding Up of Usual Suspects in the Latino Community." *Critical Sociology, 32(2–3):* 447–73.

Romo, H. D., and T. Falbo. (1997). *Latino High School Graduation, Defying the Odds.* Austin: University of Texas Press.

Rosales, F. A. (1999). *Pobre Raza! Violence, Justice and Mobilization among Mexico Lindo Immigrants, 1900–1936.* Austin: University of Texas Press.

Ross, A. (Ed.). (1997). *No Sweat: Fashion, Free Trade, and the Rights of Garment Workers.* New York: Verso Books.

Rozental, A. (2007). "The Other Side of Immigration." *Current History, 106(697):* 89–90.

Ruiz, V. (2004). "Morena/o, blanca/o y café con leche: Racial Constructions in Chicana/o Historiography." *Mexican Studies, 20(2):* 343–59.

———. (2001). "South by Southwest: Mexican Americans and Segregated Schooling, 1900–1950." *Organization of American Historians (OAH) Magazine of History, 15 (winter).* Retrieved from http://www.oah.org/pubs/magazine/deseg/ruiz.html on October 4, 2006.

Rumbaut, R. G. (1997). "Paradoxes (and Orthodoxies) of Assimilation." *Sociological Perspectives, 40(3):* 483–511.

Rumberger, R. W., and G. M. Rodríguez. (2002). "Chicano Dropouts: An Update of Research and Policy Issues." In R. R. Valencia (Ed.), *Chicano School Failure and Success* (2nd ed., pp 114–146). New York: RoutledgeFalmer.

Ryman, A., and O. Madrid. (2004, January 17). "Hispanics Upset by Teacher's Discipline." *The Arizona Republic*. Retrieved from http://www.azbilingualed.org/AABE%20Site/ AABE–News%202004/hispanics_upset_by_teacher.htm on March 2, 2011.

Salas, E. M. (2003). *Factors That Shape Success in Mexican-American Students* (unpublished doctoral dissertation). New Mexico State University, Las Cruces.

Samora, J., and P. Vandel-Simon. (1993). *A History of the Mexican-American People* (rev. ed.). South Bend, IN: University of Notre Dame Press.

Sanders, J. Jr., and R. C. Sanders. (1998, December). "Anti-Dropout Interventions." *The Educational Digest, 64(4)*: 33–34.

San Miguel, G., and R. Valencia. (1998). "From the Treaty of Guadalupe Hidalgo to Hopwood: The Educational Plight and Struggle of Mexican Americans in the Southwest." *Harvard Educational Review, 68(3)*: 353–412.

Saramago, J. (2001). *Somos cuentos de cuentos*. Madrid, España: Grupo Santillana de Ediciones.

Sarther, D. P. (2006). *An Exploratory Study of the Experiences of Mexican American Women Attending Community College* (unpublished doctoral dissertation). DeKalb, IL: Northern Illinois University.

Schaefer, R. (2005). *Racial and Ethnic Groups* (10th ed.). Upper Saddle River, NJ: Prentice Hall.

Scharf, D. A. (2006). "For Humane Borders: Two Decades of Death and Illegal Activity in the Sonoran Desert." *Case Western Reserve Journal of International Law, 38(1)*: 141–72.

Schmidt, P. (2003). "Academe's Hispanic Future." *The Chronicle of Higher Education, 50(14)*: A8. Retrieved from http://chronicle.com/weekly/v50/i14/14a00801.htm on February 16, 2007.

Schneider, G., J. Knoedler, and C. Sackrey. (2005). *Introduction to Political Economy* (4th ed.). Boston, MA: Economic Affairs Bureau, Inc., Capital City Press.

Segal, E. A., and K. M. Kilty. (2003). "Political Promises for Welfare Reform." In K. M. Kilty and E. A. Segal (Eds.), *Rediscovering the Other America: The Continuing Crisis of Poverty and Inequality in the United States* (pp. 51–68). Philadelphia, PA: The Haworth Press.

Seidman, I. E. (2006). *Interviewing as Qualitative Research: A Guide for Researchers in Education and the Social Sciences*. New York: Teachers College Press.

Shannon, S. M. (1996). "Minority Parental Involvement. A Mexican Mother's Experience and a Teacher's Interpretation." *Education & Urban Society, 29(1)*: 71–84.

Shannon, S. M., and K. Escamilla. (1999). "Mexican Immigrants in U.S. Schools: Targets of Symbolic Violence." *Educational Policy, 13(3)*: 347–70.

Shannon, S. M., and S. L. Latimer. (1996). "Latino Parent Involvement in Schools: A Story of Struggle and Resistance." *The Journal of Educational Issues of Language Minority Students, 16(summer)*: 301–19.

Sheridan, T. E. (1995). *Arizona. A History*. Tucson and London: University of Arizona Press.

——. (1986). *Los Tucsonenses: The Mexican Community in Tucson, 1841–1941*. Tucson: University of Arizona Press.

Shields, C. M. (2004). "Dialogic Leadership for Social Justice: Overcoming Pathologies of Silence." *Educational Administration Quarterly, 40(1)*: 111–34.

Sieber, S. D. (2005). *Second-Rate Nation: From the American Dream to the American Myth*. Boulder, CO: Paradigm Publishers.

Simon, J. L. (1995). *Immigration. The Demographic and Economic Facts.* A publication of the Cato Institute and the National Immigration Forum. Retrieved from http://www.cato.org/pubs/policy_report/pr-immig.html on November 2, 2009.

Skrentny, J. D. (1996). *The Ironies of Affirmative Action: Politics, Culture, and Justice in America.* Chicago: University of Chicago Press.

Smith, J. P., and B. Edmonston (Eds). (1997). *The New Americans: Economic, Demographic, and Fiscal Effects of Immigration.* Washington, D.C.: National Research Council, National Academy of Sciences Press.

Smith, N. (2002). "New Globalism, New Urbanism: Gentrification as Global Urban Strategy." *Antipode, 34(3)*: 427–50.

Smith, P. H. (1996). "Mexico since 1946." In L. Bethell (Ed.), *The Cambridge History of Latin America* (pp. 83–159). New York: Cambridge University Press.

Smith, R. C. (2005). *Mexican New York: Transnational Lives of New Immigrants.* Berkeley, CA: University of California Press.

Solórzano, D. G., and T. J. Yosso. (2002). "Critical Race Methodology: Counter-Storytelling as an Analytical Framework for Education Research." *Qualitative Inquiry, 8(1)*: 23–54.

——. (2001). "Critical Race and LatCrit Theory and Method: Counter-Storytelling." *Qualitative Studies in Education, 14(4)*: 471–95.

——. (2000). "Toward a Critical Race Theory of Chicana and Chicano Education." In C. Tejada, C. Martínez, and Z. Leonardo (Eds.), *Charting New Terrains of Chicana(o)/Latina(o) Education* (pp. 35–65). Cresskill, NJ: Hampton Press.

Soros, G. (1998). *The Crisis of Global Capitalism: Open Society Endangered.* New York: PublicAffairs.

Sosa, A. (1993). *Thorough and Fair: Creating Routes to Success for Mexican- American Students.* Charleston, WV: Clearinghouse on Rural Education and Small Schools.

Sotomayor, F. (1983, July 25). "A Box Full of Ethnic Labels." *The Los Angeles Times.* Retrieved from http://www-new.latinosandmedia.org/jawards/works/ LAT83_008.html on July 15, 2006.

Southern Poverty Law Center (SPLC). (2011). *Ideology. Anti-Immigrant.* SPLC Intelligence File. Montgomery, AL: Southern Poverty Law Center. Retrieved from http://www.splcenter.org/get-informed/intelligence-files/ideology/anti-immigrant on February 5, 2011.

——. (2007, Spring). *Intelligence Report. The Year in Hate.* SPLC Intelligence Report. Montgomery, AL: Southern Poverty Law Center. Retrieved from http://www.splcenter.org/intel/intelreport/article.jsp?aid=762 on July 22, 2007

Sowell, T. (2004). *Affirmative Action Around the World: An Empirical Study.* Chicago: R.R. Donnelley & Sons.

——. (1984). *Civil Rights: Rhetoric or Reality.* New York: William Morrow and Company, Inc.

Spener, D. (2009). *Clandestine Crossings: Migrants and Coyotes on the Texas-Mexico Border.* Ithaca, NY: Cornell University Press.

Stacy, L. (2003). *Mexico and the United States.* Tarrytown, NY: Marshall Cavendish.

Stanton-Salazar, R. D. (1997). "A Social Capital Framework for Understanding the Socialization of Racial Minority Children and Youths." *Harvard Educational Review, 67(1)*: 1–40.

Stanton-Salazar, R. D., and S. M. Dornbusch. (1995). "Social Capital and the Reproduction of Inequality: Information Networks among Mexican-origin High School Students." *Sociology of Education, 68(2)*: 116–35.

Stavans, I. (2003). *Spanglish: The Making of a New American Language.* New York: HarperCollins Publishers Inc.

———. (2001). *The Hispanic Condition: The Power of a People.* New York: HarperCollins Publishers.

Steele, E. J. (2004). *Defensive Racism.* Sagle, ID: ProPer Press.

Stephenson, N. W. (1921). *Texas and the Mexican War: A Chronicle of the Winning of the Southwest.* New Haven, CT: Yale University Press.

———. (2001). "Segmented Assimilation." In J. Ciment (Ed.), *Encyclopedia of American Immigration,* (vol. 2, pp. 460–67). Amonk, NY: M.E. Sharpe, Inc.

Stein, R. F. (1990). "Closing the Achievement Gap of Mexican-Americans: A Question of Language, Learning Style, or Economics?" *Journal of Multilingual and Multicultural Development, 11(5)*: 405–19.

Steinberg, S. (1981). *The Ethnic Myth.* Boston, MA: Atheneum Publishers.

Stewart, D. M. (1998). "Why Hispanics Need to Take the SAT." *The Education Digest (April)*: 33–36.

St-Hilaire, A. (2002). "The Social Adaptation of Children of Mexican Immigrants: Educational Aspirations Beyond Junior High School." *Social Science Quarterly, 83(4)*: 1026–43.

Stoler, A. L. (2002). "Racial Histories and Their Regimes of Truth." In P. Essed and D. T. Goldberg (Eds.), *Race Critical Theories* (pp. 369–391). Oxford, UK: Blackwell Publishing.

Stone, S., and M. Han. (2005). "Perceived School Environments, Perceived Discrimination, and School Performance among Children of Mexican Immigrants." *Children & Youth Services Review, 27(1)*: 51–66.

Suárez-Orozco, M. M., and M. M. Páez. (2002). *Latinos: Remaking America.* Berkeley, CA: University of California Press.

Suárez-Orozco, C., I. L. G. Todorova, and J. Louie. (2002). "Making Up for Lost Time: The Experience of Separation and Reunification among Immigrant Families." *Family Process 41(4)*: 625–43.

Sullivan, M. M., and R. Rehm. (2005). "Mental Health of Undocumented Mexican Immigrants." *Advances in Nursing Science, 28(3)*: 240–51.

Sullivan, S., and N. Tuana. (Eds). (2007). *Race and Epistemologies of Ignorance.* Albany: State University of New York Press.

Sum, A., N. Fogg, and P. Harrington. (2002). *Immigrant Workers and the Great American Job Machine: The Contributions of New Foreign Immigration to National and Regional Labor Force Growth in the 1990s.* Report prepared for the National Business Roundtable: Center for Labor Market Studies, Northeastern University (August).

Suro, R., and G. Escobar. (2006). *2006 National Survey of Latinos: The Immigration Debate.* A Pew Hispanic Center report. Washington, D.C.: Pew Hispanic Center. Retrieved from http://pewhispanic.org/files/reports/68.pdf on December 31, 2006.

Szapocznik, J., M. A. Scopetta, W. Kurtines, and M. A. Arnalde. (1978). "Theory and Measurement of Acculturation." *Interamerican Journal of Psychology, 12*: 113–30.

Szelényi, K., and J. C. Chang. (2002). "Educating Immigrants: The Community College Role." *Community College Review, 30(2)*: 55–73.

Takaki, R. (2008). *A Different Mirror: A History of Multicultural America*. New York: Back Bay Books.

——. (2007b). "A Different Mirror: Studying the Past for the Sake of the Future." *A Conversation with Ronald Takaki. National Conference on Race and Ethnicity*. San Francisco, CA (June 1).

——. (1993). *A Different Mirror: A History of Multicultural America*. New York: Back Bay Books.

Tancredo, T. (2006). *In Mortal Danger: The Battle for America's Border and Security*. Nashville, TN: WND Books.

Tarkington, B. (1905). *The Beautiful Lady*. New York: McClure, Phillips & Co.

Taylor, E. (2007). "Transformative Learning: Developing a Critical World View." In J. L. Kincheloe and R.A. Horn (Eds.), *The Praeger Handbook of Education and Psychology, Volume 1* (354). Westport, CT: Praeger Publishers.

Taylor, P., R. Fry, and R. Kochhar. (2011, July 26). "Wealth Gaps Rise to Record Highs Between Whites, Blacks, Hispanics." *A Pew Research Center report*. Retrieved from http://www.pewsocialtrends.org/2011/07/26/wealth-gaps-rise-to-record-highs-between-whites-blacks-hispanics/ on July 30, 2011.

Taylor Gibbs, J., and T. Bankhead. (2001). *Preserving Privilege: California Politics, Propositions, and People of Color*. Westport, CT: Praeger Publishers.

Telles, E. E., and V. Ortiz. (2009). *Generations of Exclusion: Mexican Americans, Assimilation, and Race*. New York: Russell Sage Foundation

Teske, R. H. C., and B. H. Nelson. (1974). "Acculturation and Assimilation: A Clarification." *American Ethnologist, 1(2)*: 351–67.

Thompson, M. S., K. L. Alexander, and D. R. Entwisle. (1988). "Household Composition, Parental Expectations and School Achievement." *Social Forces, 67(2)*: 424–51.

Tienda, M., and F. Mitchell. (2006). *Multiple Origins, Uncertain Destinies: Hispanics and the American Future* (National Research Council, Division of Behavioral and Social Sciences and Education). Washington, D.C.: National Academies Press.

Tierney, W. (1993). *Building Communities of Difference: Higher Education in the Twenty-First Century*. Westport, CT: Bergin & Garvey.

Tierno, J. T. (2007). "On the Justification of Affirmative Action." *Public Affairs Quarterly, 21(3)*: 295–326.

Tinto, V. (1987). *Leaving College*. Chicago: University of Chicago Press.

Tocqueville, A., de. (2003). *Democracy in America*. New York: Random House, Inc.

Toh, S. H. (2004). *Uprooting Violence, Cultivating Peace: Education for an Engaged Spirituality*. Lecture at Griffith University (June 17). Retrieved from http://www.griffith.edu.au/ins/collections/proflects/toh04.pdf on December 8, 2006.

Toussaint-Comeau, M. (2006). "The Occupational Assimilation of Hispanic Immigrants in the U.S.: Evidence from Panel Data." *International Migration Review, 40(3)*: 508–36.

Treaty of Guadalupe Hidalgo. (1848, February 2). The Library of Congress Online Collections. Retrieved from http://www.loc.gov/rr/hispanic/ghtreaty on August 2, 2006.

Trueba, H. T. (1993). "Castification in Multicultural America." In H. Trueba, C. Rodríguez, Y. Zou, and J. Cintron (Eds.), *Healing Multicultural America: Mexican Immigrants Rise to Power in Rural California* (pp. 29–51). Washington, D. C.: Falmer.

——. (1983). "Adjustment Problems of Mexican and Mexican-American Students: An Anthropological Study." *Learning Disabilities Quarterly, 6(4)*: 393–415.

Tutu, D. (2010, April 29). "Arizona: The Wrong Answer." *The Huffington Post*. Retrieved from http://www.huffingtonpost.com/desmond-tutu/arizona—the-wrong-answ_b_557955.html on September 8, 2010.

United Nations General Assembly. (1948, December 10). *The Universal Declaration of Human Rights*. United Nations Department of Public Information. Geneva, Switzerland: UN Office of the High Commissioner for Human Rights. Retrieved from http://www.unhchr.ch/udhr on November 19, 2007.

U.S. Census Bureau (2011a). *Facts for Features. Hispanic Heritage Month 2011: Sept. 15–Oct. 15*. U.S. Census Bureau News. U.S. Department of Commerce. Retrieved from http://www.census.gov/newsroom/releases/pdf/cb11ff-18_hispanic.pdf on October 12, 2011.

——. (2011b). "State & County QuickFacts. Hisanic Origin." U.S. Census Bureau. Retrieved from http://quickfacts.census.gov/qfd/meta/long_RHI725206.htmon October 14, 2011.

——. (2010a, March 18). *Facts for Features. Cinco de Mayo*. News release. U.S. Department of Commerce. Retrieved from http://www.census.gov/newsroom/releases/pdf/cb10-ff08.pdf on April 17, 2011.

——. (2010b). *Facts for Features. Hispanic Heritage Month 2010: Sept. 15–Oct. 15*. News release. Census Bureau's Public Information Office. Retrieved from http://www.census.gov/newsroom/releases/archives/facts_for_features_special_editions/cb10-ff17.html on January 15, 2011.

——. (2009). *Facts for Features. Hispanic Heritage Month, Sept. 15–Oct 15, 2009*. U.S. Census Bureau News. U.S. Department of Commerce. Retrieved from http://www.census.gov/newsroom/releases/pdf/cb09-ff17.pdf on December 26, 2009.

——. (2007, February). *The American Community. Hispanics: 2004*. American Community Survey report, U.S. Census Bureau. Retrieved from http://www.census.gov/prod/2007pubs/acs-03.pdf on July 22, 2007.

U.S. Census Bureau and U.S. Bureau of Economic Analysis. (2010). *U.S. International Trade in Goods and Services July 2010*. Trade report. Washington, D.C.: U.S. Department of Commerce. Retrieved from http://www.census.gov/foreign-trade/data on March 1, 2011.

U.S. Department of Education. (2007). *Status and Trends in the Education of Racial and Ethnic Minorities*. Washington, D.C.: Institute of Education Sciences (IES), National Center for Education Statistics. Retrieved from http://nces.ed.gov/pubs2007/minoritytrends/index.asp on September 17, 2007.

Valdez, L. (1972). "Introduction: 'La Plebe'." In L. Valdez and S. Steiner (Eds.), *Aztan: An Anthology of Mexican American Literature*. New York: Knopf.

Valencia, R. R. (2008). *Chicano Students and the Courts: The Mexican American Legal Struggle for Educational Equality*. New York and London: New York University Press.

——. (2005). "The Mexican American Struggle for Equal Educational Opportunity in *Mendez v. Westminster*: Helping to Pave the Way for *Brown v. Board of Education*." *Teachers College Record, 107(3)*: 389–423.

——. (Ed.). (2002). *Chicano School Failure and Success* (2nd ed.). New York: RoutledgeFalmer.

——. (1991). *Chicano School Failure and Success: Research and Policy Agendas for the 1990s*. London: Falmer Press.

Valencia, R. R., and M. S. Black. (2002). "'Mexican Americans Don't Value Education!' On the Basis of the Myth, Mythmaking, and Debunking." *Journal of Latinos and Education, 1(2)*: 81–103.

Valencia, R. R., and D. Solorzano. (1997). "Contemporary Deficit Thinking." In R. R. Valencia (Ed.), *The Evolution of Deficit Thinking: Educational Thought and Practice* (pp. 160–210). Albany: State University of New York Press.

Valenzuela, A. (1999). *Subtractive Schooling: U.S.-Mexican Youth and the Politics of Caring*. Albany, NY: State University of New York Press.

Van Hook, J., and K. S. Balistreri. (2002). "Diversity and Change in the Institutional Context of Immigrant Adaptation: California Schools 1985–2000."

Varsanyi, M. W. (2006). "Interrogating 'urban citizenship' vis-à-vis undocumented migration." *Citizenship Studies 10(2)*: 229–249.

Vázquez, J. Z. (2000). "Los Primeros Tropiezos." In Colegio de México. *Historia General de México. Versión 2000* (pp. 525–82). México, D.F.: Colegio de México. *Demography, 39(4)*: 639–54.

Velázquez, L. C. (2004). "Some Facts about Hispanics and Education in the USA." In O. Ebert and W. Hawk (Eds.), *ESL Start-up Kit*. Retrieved from http://cls.coe.utk.edu/lpm/esltoolkit/default.html#toc on July 20, 2007.

Vélez-Ibáñez, C. G. (2004). "Regions of Refuge in the United States: Issues, Problems, and Concerns for the Future of Mexican-Origin Populations in the United States." *Human Organization, 63(1)*: 1–20.

———. (1996). *Border Visions: Mexican Cultures of the Southwest United States*. Tucson: The University of Arizona Press.

Veranes, M., and A. Navarro. (2005, June 1). "Anti-Immigrant Legislation in Arizona Leads to Calls for a State Boycott." *CIPAmericas.org*. Silver City, NM: Americas Program, International Relations Center. Retrieved from http://americas.irc-online.org/articles/2005/0506prop200.html on July 17, 2005.

Vertovec, S. (2004). *Trends and Impacts of Migrant Transnationalism* (University of Oxford Center on Migration, Policy and Society Working Paper No. 3). Paper presented at the Social Science Research Council / International Migration Review Conference on 'Conceptual and Methodological Developments in the Study of International Migration,' Princeton University, New Jersey (May 23–25, 2003).

Villalpando, O. (2004). "Practical Considerations of Critical Race Theory and Latino Critical Theory for Latino College Students." *New Directions for Student Services, 105(spring)*: 41–50.

———. (2003). "Self-Segregation or Self-Preservation? A Critical Race Theory and Latina/o Critical Theory Analysis of a Study of Chicana/o College Students." *Qualitative Studies in Education, 16(5)*: 619–46.

Villenas, S., and D. Deyhle. (1999). "Critical Race Theory and Ethnographies Challenging the Stereotypes: Latino Families, Schooling, Resilience and Resistance." *Curriculum Inquiry, 29(4)*: 413–45.

Wagner, D. (2010, June 4). "Altered Mural Fuels Racial Debate in Prescott." *USA Today*. Retrieved from http://www.usatoday.com/news/nation/2010-06-04-altered-mural-arizona-race-debate_N.htm on February 26, 2011.

Wall Street Journal, Editorial. (2006, June 20). "Immigration Consensus." *The Wall Street Journal* (eastern ed.), A20.

——. (2005, May 4). "Immigration Reality Check." *The Wall Street Journal* (eastern ed.), A18.

Warf, B. (2006). "Demographic Transition." In B. Warf (Ed.), *Encyclopedia of Human Geography* (pp. 92–94). Thousand Oaks, CA: Sage Reference.

Warren, J. R. (1996). "Educational-Origin Inequality among White and Mexican-origin Adolescents in the American Southwest." *Sociology of Education, 69(April)*: 142–58.

Washington Post. (1996, November 2). "As Peso Slips, Mexicans Fear a Repeat of 1994's Economic Crisis." *Washington Post,* A19. Mexico City: The Washington Post Foreign Service.

Watson, F. (1977). "Still on Strike! Recollections of a Bisbee Deportee." *Journal of Arizona History, 18(summer)*: 171–84. Retrieved from http://www.library.arizona.edu/exhibits/bisbee/docs/jahwats.html on September 4, 2006.

Weaver, C. N. (2005). "The Changing Image of Hispanic Americans." *Hispanic Journal of Behavioral Sciences, 27(3)*: 337–54

——. (2000). "Work Attitudes of Mexican Americans." *Hispanic Journal of Behavioral Sciences, 22(3)*: 275–95.

Webster's New Colligiate Dictionary. (1979). Springfield, MA: G. & C. Merriam Company.

Weider History Group. (2006). "Always an Immigrant Nation." *American History, 41(4)*: 19.

Weiler, K. (2003). "Paulo Freire: On Hope." *Radical Teacher, 67(Spring)*: 32–35.

Weinberg, M. (1977). *A Chance to Learn.* London: Cambridge University Press.

Weiner, L. (2006). "Challenging Deficit Thinking." *Educational Leadership, 64(1)*: 42–45.

White, M. J., and J. E. Glick. (2000). "Generation Status, Social Capital, and the Routes out of High School." *Sociological Forum, 15(4)*: 671–92.

Wilmot, F. (2006). "Inside the Data Center." *IN Context, 7(2)*: 5.

Wilson, E. J. (2004). *Diversity and U.S. Foreign Policy: A Reader.* New York, London: Routledge, Taylor and Francis Group.

Wilson, T. D. (2000). "Anti-Immigrant Sentiment and the Problem of Reproduction/Maintenance in Mexican Immigration to the United States." *Critique of Anthropology, 20(2)*: 191–213.

Winant, H. (1994). *Racial Conditions: Politics, Theory, Comparisons.* Minneapolis: University of Minnesota Press.

Witt, H. (2007, September 25). "School Discipline Tougher on African Americans." *Chicago Tribune Web Edition.* Retrieved from http://www.chicagotribune.com/news/nationworld/chi-070924discipline,1,6597576.story?ctrack=1&cset=true on September 29, 2007.

Wittgenstein, L. (1969). *On Certainty.* New York: Harper & Row Publishers.

Wolcott, H. (1999). *Ethnography: A Way of Seeing.* Oxford: AltaMira Press.

Wong, J. (2006). *Democracy's Promise: Immigrants and American Civic Institutions* (The Politics of Race and Ethnicity). Ann Arbor: The University of Michigan Press.

Wright, W. E. (2005). "English Language Learners Left Behind in Arizona: The Nullification of Accommodations in the Intersection of Federal and State Policies." *Bilingual Research Journal, 29(1)*: 1–29.

Yamamoto, E. K. (1997). "Critical Race Praxis: Race Theory and Political Lawyering Practice in Post-Civil Rights America." *Michigan Law Review, 95(4)*: 821–900.

Yoshikawa, H., E. B. Godfrey, and A. C. Rivera. (2008). "Access to Institutional Resources as a Measure of Social Exclusion: Relations with Family Process and Cognitive Development in the Context of Immigration." In H. Yoshikawa and N. Way (Eds.), *New Directions for Child and Adolescent Development, Number 121. Special Idssue: Beyond the Family: Contexts of Immigrant Children's Development* (pp. 63–86). Wiley Periodicals, Inc.

Yosso, T. J. (2006). *Critical Race Counterstories along the Chicana/Chicano Educational Pipeline* (The Teaching/Learning Social Justice). New York: Routledge, Taylor and Francis Group.

———. (2002). "Critical Race Media Literacy: Challenging Deficit Discourse about Chicanas/os." *Journal of Popular Film & Television, 30(1)*: 52–62.

Zavodny, M. (2000). "The Effects of Official English Laws on Limited-English-Proficient Workers." *Journal of Labor Economics, 18(3)*: 427–52.

Zehr, M. A. (2006a). "Appeals Court Rejects Orders For English-Learners in Arizona." *Education Week, 26(1)*: 33.

———. (2006b). "Arizona Gets Ultimatum on Aid for English-Learners." *Education Week, 25(16)*: 13.

———. (2002). "Oregon School District Reaches out to New Arrivals from Mexico." *Education Week, 21(28)*: 16–22.

Studies in the Postmodern Theory of Education

General Editor
Shirley R. Steinberg

Counterpoints publishes the most compelling and imaginative books being written in education today. Grounded on the theoretical advances in criticalism, feminism, and postmodernism in the last two decades of the twentieth century, Counterpoints engages the meaning of these innovations in various forms of educational expression. Committed to the proposition that theoretical literature should be accessible to a variety of audiences, the series insists that its authors avoid esoteric and jargonistic languages that transform educational scholarship into an elite discourse for the initiated. Scholarly work matters only to the degree it affects consciousness and practice at multiple sites. Counterpoints' editorial policy is based on these principles and the ability of scholars to break new ground, to open new conversations, to go where educators have never gone before.

For additional information about this series or for the submission of manuscripts, please contact:

Shirley R. Steinberg
c/o Peter Lang Publishing, Inc.
29 Broadway, 18th floor
New York, New York 10006

To order other books in this series, please contact our Customer Service Department:

(800) 770-LANG (within the U.S.)
(212) 647-7706 (outside the U.S.)
(212) 647-7707 FAX

Or browse online by series:
www.peterlang.com